Religion, Discourse, and Society

This book focuses on the utility and application of discourse theory and discourse analysis in the sociological study of religious change. It presents an outline of what a "discursive sociology of religion" looks like and brings scholarly attention to the role of language and discourse as a significant component in contemporary processes of religious change. Marcus Moberg addresses the concept of discourse and its main meta-theoretical underpinnings and discusses the relationship between discourse and "religion" in light of previous research. The chapters explore key notions such as secularism and public religion as well as the ideational and discursive impact of individualism and market society on the contemporary Western religious field. In addition to providing scholars with a thorough understanding and appreciation of the analytic utility of discourse theory and analysis in the sociological study of religious change, the book offers a cohesive and systematized framework for actual empirical analysis.

Marcus Moberg is a Professor in the Study of Religions at Åbo Akademi University, Finland.

Routledge Studies in Religion

Jewish Approaches to Hinduism
A History of Ideas from Judah Ha-Levi to Jacob Sapir
(12th–19th centuries)
Richard G. Marks

Spiritual, Religious, and Faith-Based Practices in Chronicity
An Exploration of Mental Wellness in Global Context
Edited by Andrew R. Hatala and Kerstin Roger

An Anthropology of the Qur'an
Ahmed Achrati

**Contrasts in Religion, Community, and Structure at
Three Homeless Shelters**
Changing Lives
Ines W. Jindra, Michael Jindra and Sarah DeGenero

Enhancement Fit for Humanity
Perspectives on Emerging Technologies
Michael Baggot

Catholic Peacebuilding and Mining
Integral Peace, Development, and Ecology
Edited by Caesar A. Montevecchio and Gerard F. Powers

Religion, Discourse, and Society
Towards a Discursive Sociology of Religion
Marcus Moberg

For more information about this series, please visit: https://www.routledge.com/religion/series/SE0669

Religion, Discourse, and Society
Towards a Discursive Sociology of Religion

Marcus Moberg

LONDON AND NEW YORK

First published 2022
by Routledge
2 Park Square, Milton Park, Abingdon, Oxon OX14 4RN

and by Routledge
605 Third Avenue, New York, NY 10158

Routledge is an imprint of the Taylor & Francis Group, an informa business

© 2022 Marcus Moberg

The right of Marcus Moberg to be identified as author of this work
has been asserted in accordance with sections 77 and 78 of the
Copyright, Designs and Patents Act 1988.

All rights reserved. No part of this book may be reprinted or
reproduced or utilised in any form or by any electronic, mechanical,
or other means, now known or hereafter invented, including
photocopying and recording, or in any information storage or
retrieval system, without permission in writing from the publishers.

Trademark notice: Product or corporate names may be trademarks
or registered trademarks, and are used only for identification and
explanation without intent to infringe.

British Library Cataloguing-in-Publication Data
A catalogue record for this book is available from the British Library

Library of Congress Cataloging-in-Publication Data
A catalog record has been requested for this book

ISBN: 9780367435752 (hbk)
ISBN: 9781032193632 (pbk)
ISBN: 9780367435837 (ebk)

DOI: 10.4324/9780367435837

Typeset in Sabon
by codeMantra

Contents

Preface		vii
1	Introduction	1
2	Discourse theory and analysis	8
3	A three-level discursive approach to "religion" and related categories	34
4	The "secular" and the "post-secular"	65
5	Religion, the individual, and individualism	113
6	Religion in market society	157
	Bibliography	213
	Index	233

Preface

This book has been in the making for quite a long time. Its primary aim can be described as simply as this: to explicate and illustrate the value of discourse theoretical and analytical perspectives in the sociological study of religion in a way that has not been done previously. Although the book provides a coherent analytical framework for discourse-sensitive research in the sociology of religion, it should nevertheless be thought of as a work in progress. This is because it, first and foremost, aims to inspire and provide an impetus for further discourse-sensitive research in the sub-field. Hence the subtitle "towards a discursive sociology of religion." A single book can obviously only engage with a limited set of themes. This book is, of course, no exception. To the extent that the perspectives and arguments presented in this book manage to spark further debate and become adopted, expanded on, and modified by other scholars in the sub-field, the book will fulfill its main purpose.

This book builds and expands on my previous work in the areas of discourse and religion research and the sociological study of religion. As such, it contains shorter sections of work that have already been published elsewhere. Parts previously published as "First-, Second-, and Third-Level Discourse Analytic Approaches in the Study of Religion: Moving from Meta-Theoretical Reflection to Implementation in Practice" (in *Religion* 43/1, 2013, Taylor and Francis, doi:10.1080/0048721X.2013.742742) are included in Chapters 2 and 3. Parts previously published as "The Concept of the Post-Secular and the Contemporary Nexus of Religion, Media, Popular Culture, and Consumer Culture" (co-authored with Kennet Granholm, in *Post-Secular Society*, Routledge, 2012) and "Trajectories of Post-Secular Complexity: An Introduction" (co-authored with Kennet Granholm and Peter Nynäs in *Post-Secular Society*, Routledge, 2012) are included in Chapter 4. Parts previously published as "From Socialization to Self-Socialization? Exploring the Role of Digital Media in the Religious Lives of Young Adults in Ghana, Turkey, and Peru" (co-authored with Sofia Sjö, Ben-Willie Kwaku Golo, Habibe Erdiş Gökçe, Rafael Fernández Hart, Sidney Castillo Cardenas, Francis Benyah, and Mauricio

viii *Preface*

Javier Villacrez Jó (in *Religion* 49/2, Taylor and Francis, doi:10.1080/00 48721X.2019.1584353) are included in Chapter 5. Parts previously published as *Church, Market and Media* (published 13 Jul 2017, Bloomsbury Academic, an imprint of Bloomsbury Publishing Plc.) are included in Chapters 2, 5, and 6. Parts previously published as "Religious Change in Market and Consumer Society: The Current State of the Field and New Ways Forward (co-authored with Tuomas Martikainen, in *Religion* 48/3, Taylor and Francis, doi:10.1080/0048721X.2018.1482616) are included in Chapter 6. Parts previously published as "Studying Change in Religious Organizations: A Discourse-Centered Framework" (in *Method & Theory in the Study of Religion* 32/2, Brill, doi:10.1163/15700682-12341472) are included in Chapters 2 and 6.

This book is based on research funded by the Academy of Finland (application number: 314751).

Hyppeis, Houtskär, 18 June 2021

1 Introduction

The sociological study of religion remains centrally concerned with ongoing processes of "religious change" across the liberal democratic societies of the West, and increasingly beyond. A wide range of different types of modern changes, transformations, and mutations in the religious field have been studied under this general and somewhat ambiguous rubric. These include (but are not limited to) progressive long-term institutional religious decline; the proliferation of "individualized" religious outlooks and "alternative spiritualties"; significant increases in the numbers of people who self-identify as "non-religious"; the growing public presence and visibility of religion; the increasing commodification and/or marketization of religion; and changes in the environments, spaces, and "locations" of religion following continuous developments in new media and digital communication and information technologies. While several additional developments could be added to the list, taken together, these processes clearly point to the ways in which the Western religious field has been – and been perceived to have been – in a continuing state of flux over the past five to six decades, if not for longer.

The sociological study of religion has for some time already found itself in a transitional phase, marked by the rethinking and increasing abandonment of secularization theory coupled with a growing emphasis on the need for novel perspectives and further theoretical innovation.[1] While there is wide agreement among sociologists of religion that the general character of religion and religious life and practice has undergone significant changes and transformations in the late-modern era, there is less agreement, and indeed some degree of confusion, as to how these changes should best be approached and conceptualized. But although contemporary social and sociological theory has displayed a steadily growing interest in discourse and language and developed understandings of modernity which, in various ways, "center upon language or imply an enhanced role for language in modern social life as compared to pre-modern social life," the sociological study of religion has so far rarely devoted any serious attention to the role of language and discourse as key components in processes of religious change.[2]

DOI: 10.4324/9780367435837-1

2 Introduction

"Religious change" is, of course, not adequately understood as something that occurs in isolation from changes at broader societal and cultural levels. Rather, religious change constitutes a particular type of *social* change that, like all processes of social change, includes significant ideational and discursive components. As Norman Fairclough points out, from the perspective of discourse theory, "Discourse is part of social change, and no satisfactory account of it can ignore relations between discourse and other elements of social reality."[3] This is not least because "changes in the wider social reality commonly begin as, and are 'driven by', changes in discourse which are operationalized ... in them."[4] In this perspective, "linguistic phenomena *are* social phenomena of a special sort, and social phenomena *are* (in part) linguistic phenomena."[5] This, however, is not to say that social change can be reduced to changes in discourse and discursive practice. Rather discursive and social change need to be understood in dialectical terms. While discourses are indeed expressed and articulated through the medium of language and other semiotic forms, they also become varyingly operationalized or "put into practice": enacted in particular ways of acting, communicating, and interacting; inculcated in particular "ways of being"; and tangibly materialized in the form of actual places, spaces, and social organizational structures.[6] Hence, as Lilie Chouliaraki and Fairclough point out,

> It is an important characteristic of the economic, social and cultural changes of late modernity that they exist as *discourses* as well as processes that are taking place outside discourse, and that the processes that are taking place outside discourse are substantively shaped by these discourses.[7]

Discourse and discursive practice therefore need to be viewed "as part of society, and not somehow external to it" and as "conditioned ... by other (non-linguistic) parts of society."[8]

When viewed in this light, all of the abovementioned processes of religious change have been "discourse-driven" to a considerable degree. That is to say that they have been deeply implicated in changing ways of constructing and understanding social, cultural, and "religious" reality through the medium of language and discourse. For example, the accelerating "individualization" of religion and religious life since the early 1950s is directly and dialectically related to the increasing salience of discourses on the primacy of the individual, "personal autonomy," and "personal choice" throughout Western society and culture as a whole. The "commodification" and/or "marketization" of religion is likewise closely connected to the wide proliferation and naturalization of economic, "market"-associated language and terminology throughout ever more social and cultural domains. The (supposed) growing public visibility of religion is, in turn, closely entwined with contemporary political discourses on

Introduction 3

the "secular" and scholarly discourses on the "deprivatization" of religion and the "post-secular." These examples, moreover, all point to the ways in which late-modern society has become increasingly marked by discoursal hybridity, whereby the boundaries between the language practices of different social and cultural domains (such as politics, economy, science, and religion) have become increasingly porous.[9] As broader changes in language use and discursive practice leave their imprint on the ways in which "religion" is expressed, practiced, and understood, "religious change" needs, in no small part, to be understood as consisting of changes in discursive practices on and about "religion."

Towards a discursive sociology of religion

This book outlines the contours of a discursive sociology of religion. This, first, is a sociology of religion that brings discourse theoretical and analytical perspectives into direct conversation with sociological perspectives in a transdisciplinary spirit. In particular, it views discourse analysis as providing a set of particular tools for broader "theory-driven process[es] of constructing objects of research... for research topics" which cannot be adequately analyzed through a focus on discourse alone.[10] While discourse analysis will always be theoretically informed, what it brings to the table is a particular way of theorizing "the mediation between the social and the linguistic."[11] This book does not, therefore, present a "revisionist" agenda for the sociology of religion in the sense of aiming to supplant previously established perspectives and argue that developments in the religious field can be reduced to a common core, i.e., discourse. Rather, the main purpose is to highlight and explicate how a sustained focus on the social function of discourse provides a valuable supplement and, in some cases, a crucial corrective to some of the most widely established theoretical perspectives and approaches in the sub-field. A discursive sociology of religion will therefore need to enter into a continuous, sometimes largely supportive, sometimes expressly critical, dialogue with various "non-discursive" approaches in the sub-field by bringing the perspectives and methodological tools of discourse theory and analysis to bear on the study of the construction, constitution, and social function of "religion" in modern society. In this, the approach advanced in this book aligns with previous language- and discourse-sensitive views on the discipline of sociology as a whole. For example, for Bryan S. Turner, "Sociology broadly defined consists of the study of social interaction involving the exchange of meaning, symbols, values, objects and occasionally persons. At the core of this notion of exchange is language."[12] Similarly, Zygmunt Bauman and Tim May point out that sociological thinking is "distinguished by its relationship to so-called 'common sense'"[13] or the vast amounts of "*tacit knowledge* that enables us to get on with daily life."[14] There are few social practices or phenomena "which have not been endowed with meaning before the sociologists appear" on

4 Introduction

the scene.[15] Each of the terms that sociologists use to make sense of social and cultural life – "family," "nation," "religion" – is therefore already deeply laden with "meanings given by commonsensical knowledge."[16] A discursive sociology of religion therefore pays particular attention to the central social function that language and discourse performs in shaping both popular and scholarly perceptions of the "real" and consequently approaches categories like "religion," "religious," "belief," "spirituality," and the "secular" as fundamentally discursive categories that always gain their meanings in the particular communicative, relational, and interpretive contexts in which they appear and are used.

Second, a discursive sociology of religion is also one that constantly strives to maintain a high degree of critical awareness of the multitude of ways in which scholarly theorizing itself contributes to the construction of particular "realities" about "religion," the "religious," and related social categories and phenomena. In the chapters that follow, several influential and much-debated theoretical perspectives in the sociology of religion will be subjected to critical examination from a discursive point of view. This is in order to highlight the notable extent to which our theoretical perspectives and their associated terminological repertoires supply us with particular ways of perceiving and understanding the "realities on the ground," what we understand "religion" to "be," how "religion" interacts with and entwines with other social and cultural forces and phenomena, how we set out to gather data on our chosen topics of research, what we count and/or perceive as data in the first place, how we eventually analyze and explain our findings, and so on. A discursive sociology of religion, in short, therefore invites us to view both the category of "religion" *and* its study through the prism of discourse and discursive practice. What is advocated, therefore, is an approach that strives to remain constantly self-aware of how it is itself situated within broader epistemic cultures and their associated genres of factual discourse.

In order to be able to explicate the perspective advanced in this book in sufficient depth and detail, the chapters that follow focus on a limited set of cases, and mostly (but not exclusively) on developments in the Western world. This is mainly because the theoretical perspectives that are critically engaged with in subsequent chapters have all primarily been developed in Western settings and (in most cases) also initially been intended to be applied in research on Western contexts. While this certainly reflects a long-standing and persistent Western bias in the humanities and social sciences more generally, there is no denying the fact that originally Western theorizations of the social place and function of "religion" in the modern era continue to dominate the sociological study of religion on an international level. But although subsequent chapters will primarily focus on Western contexts, the Western category of "religion" will be subjected to repeated critical scrutiny.

Structure of the book

The book consists of five main chapters, each of which plays their own respective parts in outlining, explicating, and advancing a discursive sociology of religion as envisioned in this book. While they focus on different themes, they include frequent cross-references to one another. Chapters 2 and 3 focus on theory and method and thus set the stage for subsequent chapters. Chapter 2 explicates the concept of discourse and outlines a framework for analysis particularly suited for theory-driven sociological research that incorporates elements from various perspectives, both Foucauldian and those focused more on text and social analysis. Chapter 3 provides a critical discussion of the Western category of "religion" in light of previous research focused on language and discourse in the study of religion. It devotes particular attention to previous scholarship in the so-called "critical religion" approach and the "discursive study of religion" as part of a deliberate effort to highlight the value of this scholarship for the sociological study of religion more generally, and especially for a discursive sociology of religion as outlined in this book. At the heart of this scholarship lies the nature of the category of "religion" and its relationship to, as well as differentiation from, its conceptual and theoretical "others," such as the "secular," "political," and "cultural." The chapter also presents a broader framework for analysis that serves to structure subsequent chapters and that pays equal attention to meta-theoretical issues, the ideational underpinnings of specific theoretical perspectives and approaches, and the actual analysis of discourse.

Chapters 4–6 focus on (varyingly interconnected) areas of longstanding and extensive debate in the sociological study of religion. Each chapter offers particular illustrations of the approach advanced in this book. While the focus of the book lies firmly on theoretical and methodological issues, it also makes an empirical contribution. It moreover outlines a general agenda for future discourse-focused research in relation to each main theme explored. Chapter 4 focuses on the category of the "secular," the notion of "public religion," and more recently developed perspectives on the "post-secular." It traces the historical development of these notions, explores their ideational and discursive underpinnings, and provides a critical discussion of their current employment in the sociological study of religion. Particular attention is devoted to more recently established perspectives on the "post-secular," which are subjected to more detailed critical scrutiny. In this chapter, the focus thus primarily lies on the constructive and evocative power of scholarly discourse itself.

Chapter 5 focuses on the ideational and discursive impact of individualism on the modern-day Western religious field. It traces the historical development of the Western notion of the "individual" and the establishment of an ethos of individualism throughout the Western world. This discussion

6 Introduction

highlights, in particular, how the modern era has witnessed a constant expansion in the "vocabulary of the individual" and the diffusion of this vocabulary through ever more areas of social and cultural life. From this, the chapter turns to discuss the impact of individualism on the contemporary religious field in light of previous research on the topic. Here, our focus mainly lies on how the proliferation of the concept of "spirituality" since approximately the 1960s has further contributed to the wide diffusion and naturalization of individualized discourse in the field of religion, including the ways in which it has been theorized and studied. The final part of the chapter moves on to discuss the analytical utility of Q methodology for discourse-focused empirical explorations of the increasingly individualized religious outlooks and sensibilities of contemporary populations. The utility of the method is illustrated in light of selected findings from the international research project Young Adults and Religion in a Global Perspective (2015–19) that explored the religious outlooks of young adult university students in 13 countries around the world. Here, the analyses to a greater extent also focus on the impact of individualized discourse on the religious outlooks of individuals in non-Western contexts.

Chapter 6 focuses on the ideational and discursive impact of "market society" on the contemporary religious-organizational field. It traces the historical development of the liberal conception of the "market" and explores its enduring ideational influence on contemporary social and cultural life, and especially as perpetuated by contemporary neoliberal political economy and consumer culture. This is followed by a relatively extensive critical discussion of how the "religion–market" relationship has been theorized and understood in the sociological study of religion over roughly the past three decades. Building and expanding on my own previous work, the remaining part of the chapter moves on to explore the ideational and discursive impact of neoliberal market society on the present-day discursive practices of traditional religious organizations. More specifically, this part of the chapter focuses on the increasing diffusion and naturalization of market-associated and managerial language within the context of the so-called mainline Protestant churches in the United States.

Focusing on these much-debated areas – the "secular"; the ethos of individualism; and the ideational impact of market society – entails engaging with a set of themes, concepts, and issues that have occupied a central position in the intellectual, political, and religious life of the West ever since the advent of the Enlightenment. For example, as Craig Calhoun et al. argue, the very fact that the term "secular" has become part of common parlance "signifies that we are buying into a secular/religious distinction that in some way defines not only the secular sphere itself but also the realm of the religious."[17] Following Don Slater, individualism and market economics likewise constitute motifs that recapitulate "the preoccupations and characteristic styles of thought of the modern West."[18] At the root of these motifs is "the nature of 'the social'" and how it should most appropriately

Introduction 7

be conceived and understood.[19] In engaging with these themes, we will therefore be dealing with some of the most ideationally forceful and enduringly salient discursive formations of contemporary society and culture and their impact on the modern-day Western religious field.

In engaging with these themes and scholarly debates, the book outlines a particular approach to the sociological study of religion as a whole. This is in large part an exploratory, and to some extent even experimental, endeavor. The aim is to provide a first general, thoroughly explicated, and empirically grounded blueprint for what a discursive sociology of religion would "look like," how it would be carried out in actual practice, how it would approach central theoretical and analytical concepts and terms in the sub-field, how it would assess the analytical utility and ideational underpinnings of established theoretical perspectives, and how actual analyses would be conducted. As such, this book aims to inspire rather than prescribe.

Notes

1 E.g. Linda Woodhead, "Old, New, and Emerging Paradigms in the Sociological Study of Religion," *Nordic Journal of Religion and Society* 22, no. 2 (2009): 103–21; Courtney Bender *et al.*, "Religion on the Edge: De-centering and Re-centering," in *Religion on the Edge: De-centering and Re-centering the Sociology of Religion*, ed. Courtney Bender, Wendy Cadge, Peggy Levitt, and David Smilde (Oxford: Oxford University Press, 2012).
2 Norman Fairclough, *Critical Discourse Analysis: The Critical Study of Language* (Oxon: Routledge, 2010), 168.
3 Norman Fairclough, *Language and Power*, Third edition (Oxon: Routledge, 2015), 37.
4 Ibid.
5 Ibid., 56.
6 Fairclough, *Critical Discourse*, 233.
7 Lilie Chouliaraki and Norman Fairclough, *Discourse in Late Modernity: Rethinking Critical Discourse Analysis* (Edinburgh: Edinburgh University Press, 1999), 4.
8 Fairclough, *Language and Power*, 55–6.
9 Chouliaraki and Fairclough, *Discourse in Late Modernity*, 83.
10 Fairclough, *Critical Discourse*, 5.
11 Chouliaraki and Fairclough, *Discourse in Late Modernity*, 16.
12 Bryan S. Turner, *Religion and Modern Society: Citizenship, Secularisation and the State* (Cambridge: Cambridge University Press, 2011), 194.
13 Zygmunt Bauman and Tim May, *Thinking Sociologically*, Second edition (Malden, MA: Blackwell Publishing, 2001), 5.
14 Ibid., 6.
15 Ibid.
16 Ibid.
17 Craig Calhoun, Mark Juergensmeyer, and Jonathan VanAntwerpen, "Introduction," in *Rethinking Secularism*, eds. Craig Calhoun, Mark Juergensmeyer, and Jonathan VanAntwerpen (Oxford: Oxford University Press, 2011), 5.
18 Don Slater, *Consumer Culture and Modernity* (Cambridge: Polity Press, 1993), 1.
19 Ibid., 2.

2   Discourse theory and analysis

In the early 1970s, the humanities and social sciences experienced a general shift in focus away from modernist and positivist epistemologies towards a more sustained focus on culture and meaning. Inspired in particular by 1960s post-structuralist and post-modernist critiques of modernist epistemologies and meta-narratives, this shift became known as the "cultural turn." Followed by the subsequent "linguistic" or "discursive" turn in the early 1980s, there have emerged a wide range of varyingly related approaches for studying how our language use and modes of representation fundamentally affect and shape our understandings of reality and our constructions of meaningful social worlds.[1] The centrality of language and discourse to late modern social and cultural life was already noted in the Introduction. But as Fairclough notes, simply making this observation will only take us so far. What is needed, in addition, is a "theoretical specification of the social power of language which could be operationalised as ways of showing in detail within particular social research projects how language and other forms of semiosis perform the social magic which they are credited with."[2] This, in essence, is what discourse theory and analysis aims to provide. This chapter provides a general overview of discourse theory and analysis and its meta-theoretical grounding in social constructionism. It is not the intention to provide anything by means of a comprehensive account. Rather, the aim is to outline an analytical framework particularly suited for sociological analyses that pays equal attention to the analysis of actual texts (i.e., particular instances of discourse), the social and interactional contexts in which they are produced and circulated, and the wider social and cultural contexts in which they are embedded.

Social constructionism and the relationship between "word" and "world"

The term "discourse" has become widely established throughout the humanities and social sciences and given rise to a bewildering variety of more particular understandings and approaches. This variety notwithstanding, the vast majority of discourse-theoretical and analytic perspectives

DOI: 10.4324/9780367435837-2

Discourse theory and analysis 9

nevertheless build on social constructionist meta-theory. Understood as a general meta-theoretical orientation, social constructionism is grounded in the idea, and indeed conviction, that we as people, as social and communicative beings, in various ways are constantly and continually involved in collaboratively constructing and reconstructing our own sense of ourselves and our conceptions of reality. In large part, social constructionism thus centers on the long-debated meta-epistemological predicament concerning the question on what grounds we humans can be said to be able to attain "knowledge" about the world that surrounds us separately from our own individual experiences of it.[3]

The term "social construction" was originally introduced by Peter L. Berger and Thomas Luckmann in their influential treatise in the sociology of knowledge, *The Social Construction of Reality* (1966),[4] which also paved the way for the subsequent establishment of the theme of "social construction" as a topic of scholarly inquiry.[5] Berger and Luckmann set out to reveal and explicate the principal means by which people collectively construct their social world, yet end up experiencing that very same world as non-constructed and "objective."[6] Through being born and socialized into a particular social and cultural context with already established categories and conceptual frameworks,[7] people come to experience their own constructed world as a pre-given "reality" to which they have to respond. Significant as Berger's and Luckmann's contribution has been, the meta-theoretical foundations for social constructionism nevertheless predate their agenda-setting work. Indeed, important precursors for social constructionist perspectives can be found across a wider range of disciplines in the humanities and social sciences. They are found, for example, in the early twentieth-century sociolinguistics of Ferdinand de Saussure; the symbolic interactionism of George Herbert Mead; the ethnomethodology of Harold Garfinkel; the language philosophy of Ludwig Wittgenstein; the deconstruction of Jacques Derrida; and the archaeology and genealogy of Michel Foucault. While differing in their main foci and emphases, these perspectives are all united by their radical questioning of the modernist "picture metaphor" view of language, or the view that words and language correspond to and are able to communicate pictures of the world "as it is."[8] In sharp contrast to this view, scholars like de Saussure, Wittgenstein, and Foucault, in their own respective times and ways, all emphasized how words and sentences always gain their meanings in the particular human interactional and relational contexts in which they appear and are used.[9]

Much of the groundwork was laid already in de Saussure's *Course in General Linguistics* (1916). Here, de Saussure argued that a distinction always needs to be made between "language" (*langue*) and "speech" (*parole*), that is, between "language" as the *structure* and the "speech" that occurs within the structure's framework.[10] This observation paved the way for a new understanding of language as an impersonal structure or system of relationships.[11] In this view, the meaning of each individual word and

10 *Discourse theory and analysis*

term within a particular language system can only be determined on the basis of its difference from and differentiation vis-à-vis other words and terms within that same system. From this followed a second central observation, namely, that of the arbitrary relationship between *signifier* (i.e., a particular word) and *signified* (what the word refers to, or that for which the word stands). The fundamental insight that emerges from this is that the relationship between "word" and "world" is therefore also arbitrary or, as Kenneth Gergen puts it, that "the world makes no demands as to how we talk about it."[12]

Another particularly important precursor for social constructionist perspectives is found in the language philosophy of Ludwig Wittgenstein. In what marked a notable departure from his own previous thinking, in *Philosophical Investigations* (1953) Wittgenstein abandoned the picture-metaphor view of language in favor of that of the *game*, arguing that words and terms always gain their meaning and intelligibility through the particular ways in which they are situated and used within various "language games." He illustrated his point by making a simile with the game of chess. The game of chess contains a certain set of different pieces, each of which can be moved in certain ways, at certain times, in accordance with a certain set of rules, with each single piece deriving its meaning from the game as a whole. Wittgenstein then proceeded to argue that language use is governed by similar "game-like" implicit rules on the basis of which individual words and phrases gain their intelligibility and meaning. Moreover, as all individual pieces in a game of chess gain their meaning within the particular context of the game as a whole, so language games must also be understood as being situated within broader contexts of human interaction, which Wittgenstein termed "forms of life."[13] In Wittgenstein's view, words therefore have no independent meaning in and of themselves. Rather, the meaning of words is "supported by an entire background of actions and practices."[14] As Dan Stiver points out, "This suggests to some extent that we must participate in or at least have some empathy for a particular form of life in order to understand the meaning of language particular to it."[15] Wittgenstein did not, however, elaborate on his notion of "forms of life" in any greater detail, which is why scholars have interpreted it as referring to anything from entire cultures, to particular segments of a culture, to more specific communal contexts.[16] Wittgenstein's contribution can be summarized in the following key insights: that language is a fundamentally relational phenomenon; that it makes little sense to speak of a "private" language; that language is a central form of social action; and that knowing a language equals knowing how to use it.[17] Wittgenstein's ideas were further developed by numerous scholars. One particularly notable and influential further elaboration can be found in the "speech-act theory" of John Austin, which introduced an additional emphasis on what language *does* rather than what it simply *says*.[18]

Discourse theory and analysis 11

The work of Michel Foucault has exerted an enormous overall influence on the humanities and social sciences and also played a foundational role for the development of discourse theory and analysis.[19] Indeed, in more than one sense, this is where discourse analysis "begins." Scholars tend to divide Foucault's extensive body of work into two principal phases: his early *archaeological* work, and his later *genealogical* work. To simplify, the main aim of his archaeological work (not to be confused with the discipline of archaeology but rather to be understood as a form of historiographical "excavation" of ideas) was to identify the rules by which, and the conditions under which, particular "knowledges" are constructed and established at particular points in time. For this purpose, he developed the concept of "discursive formation," which refers to "linguistic facets of 'domains of thought',"[20] or the "rules of formation" that serve to determine "which statements are accepted as meaningful and true in a particular historical epoch."[21] Foucault then used the term "discourse" to refer to those groups of statements that could be shown to be part of the same discursive formation. His key point was that discursive formations, once established, work to set the parameters for what can meaningfully be said and accepted as "true" in relation to particular objects of "knowledge" at particular points in time. One key objective of archaeological research therefore becomes to trace the origins of discursive formations and reveal their *conditions of establishment*. In his later genealogical work, Foucault shifted his focus towards the historical and dialectical relationship between knowledge and power. Without going into this body of work in any further detail, suffice to say that it introduced a new focus on the ways in which the "*social world, including its subjects and objects,* [are] *constituted in discourses.*"[22] Put another way, it underscored how "truth" needs to be viewed as something that is always created and produced in and through discourses and the structures and systems of power in which they are embedded.[23]

During the 1960s and 1970s, the relationship between language and "world" also continued to be debated throughout the fields of semiotics and literary theory. These debates, which are often coupled together under headings such as "post-structuralism" and "post-modernism/post-modern critique," played an important role in the definitive establishment of social constructionism as a recognized meta-theoretical and meta-epistemological orientation.[24] Although it is important to recognize "post-structuralism" and "post-modernism" as umbrella terms that encompass a wide range of different viewpoints and perspectives,[25] for the purposes of our present discussion it is enough to note that the post-structuralist and post-modernist questioning of modernist epistemologies and meta-narratives played an instrumental role in bringing about what is commonly referred to as a general "legitimation crisis" in the humanities and social sciences.[26] As Tim Murphy has pointed out, "although many theoretical and philosophical questions remained unanswered by this labor, its net effect was to change the way many scholars understood their own research."[27]

12 *Discourse theory and analysis*

Grounded in the understanding of the nature and social function of language and representation that emerged through the contributions and debates outlined above, social constructionism holds that communication and relationships are central to human meaning-making and that it is primarily through our language use and other modes of representation that we construct and maintain meaningful worlds. From a social constructionist perspective, language is therefore not adequately understood in terms of a "neutral information-carrying vehicle," but rather as something that always also "creates what it refers to."[28] Although social constructionist perspectives have developed in many different versions, the following set of interrelated key assumptions remains widely shared among most social constructionists. First among these is a critical stance towards received and taken-for-granted understandings of knowledge and reality.[29] Second, social constructionism holds that, as possible constructions of reality and the world are multiple, all modes of understanding need to be viewed as being intimately tied to and informed by particular historical, social, and cultural contexts. Third, social constructionism views all forms of knowledge and understanding as being fundamentally relational in character and "sustained by social processes."[30] Fourth, social constructionism maintains that "knowledge and social action go together."[31] Different constructions of the world make possible different forms of social action, which will have particular "implications for what it is permissible for different people to do, and for how they may treat others."[32]

It is important to acknowledge the implications of these key assumptions for social constructionist claims themselves.[33] Indeed, social constructionism has been repeatedly criticized for adopting an ultimately self-refuting radical relativist epistemological position that denies the existence of a material, physical reality outside language.[34] However, as Fiona Hibberd notes, in contrast to realist and post-positivist epistemology, "the constructionist's rejection of an absolute concept of truth extends to a nihilism about truth, and to a quite different account of the nature of assertion."[35] As she goes on to point out: "In many cases, the critics' charge of relativism and self-refutation against the metatheory is *ignoratio elenchi*; it assumes the legitimacy of concepts which constructionists explicitly reject."[36] It should be stressed, though, that the vast majority of constructionist scholars do not reject the existence of a material, physical reality outside language. But this should by no means be taken to suggest that the language–material/physical-reality debate can simply be left unaddressed in discourse analytic research.

Many established discourse analytical frameworks situate themselves in relation to these debates by adopting a *critical realist* approach to discourse based on what could be termed a "moderate" or "contingent" form of social constructionism. In this view, what is constructed in "the social construction of reality" is first and foremost *social* reality.[37] A critical realist perspective therefore recognizes the existence of an external reality, a "real world," outside language, "which exists irrespective of whether or how well we know and understand it,"[38] while simultaneously maintaining that discourse functions to construct *social* reality as meaningful in particular ways. Following Fairclough, such a perspective therefore distinguishes between *construal* and *construction* in the social functioning of discourse.[39] While the world can be construed (i.e., represented) through discourse in a large variety of different ways, not all construals will end up having equally strong socially constructive effects. Rather, which particular construals end up having the strongest constructive effects will be contingent upon not only power relations but also the "properties of whatever parts or aspects of the world are being constructed."[40]

These observations also pertain not least to how the sociological study of religion approaches the category of "religion" and the wide variety of ways and situations in which "religion" can be, and indeed both has been and very much continues to be, construed across particular locations and sites in society. From the perspective of a discursive sociology of religion, any construal of "religion" is therefore potentially interesting in and of itself. Having said that, it is nevertheless beyond dispute that a much more specific set of (Western) construals of "religion" have had disproportionately strong constructive effects on how the category of "religion" has come to be understood throughout large parts of the world. Indeed, as we shall continue to discuss in Chapter 3, these particular construals have become established and institutionalized to such an extent that they have come to provide the "blueprint" or general conceptual backcloth against which alternative construals of "religion," in one way or other, have to be fashioned.

The concept of discourse

As noted, the concept of discourse has been developed in a large variety of different forms and directions and given rise to a wide range of varyingly related and contrasting understandings and approaches.[41] For example, while widely established approaches such as Foucault's archaeology and genealogy, Ernesto Laclau and Chantal Mouffe's[42] post-Marxist discourse theory, and Fairclough's textually oriented "three-dimensional" critical discourse analysis share many similarities, they also display many notable differences with regard to their respective terminological apparatuses and their more specific theorizations of the concept of "discourse." But as Fairclough observes, the large variety of different understandings notwithstanding, the concept of discourse tends to be most commonly employed in either one of the three following main senses: as an element of *meaning-making* in social processes; as the *language* and types of *language use* that are associated with particular social fields and types of social practice; and as a "way of construing aspects of the world associated with a particular social perspective."[43] When it comes to the issue of definition, and given the huge abundance of already existing definitions, it is important to recognize at the outset that any new definition of discourse will almost inevitably

14 *Discourse theory and analysis*

need to be designed on the basis of already existing, previously established definitions.[44] But since the concept of discourse also needs to be designed for specific research purposes, an "all-purpose" definition is not only unattainable, but would even be undesirable. While accepting these caveats, it nevertheless remains pivotal that any study that employs the concept of "discourse" provides a reasonably specific account of its meaning within the context of that study.

As briefly discussed above, Foucault's work has been of central importance for the development of all types of discourse theory and analysis. Having said that, while some subsequently developed approaches remain more distinctively "Foucauldian" in that they retain a stronger focus on issues of power and/or the historical constitution of "truths," other approaches instead bring Foucault's key analytical concepts into conversation with additional perspectives and analytical categories derived from fields such as linguistics, the sociology of knowledge, or the philosophy of language, as integrated components of broader analytical frameworks. Examples of originally Foucauldian concepts commonly employed throughout various strands of discourse analytic research include "discursive formation," "dispositif," "subject position," and "discourse strand." Foucault's own understanding of "discourse" was, however, always fleeting and changeable. Throughout his extensive *œuvre*, he provided numerous explanations of the concept, many of which could be viewed as definitions of sorts. A more concrete explication can be found in *The Archaeology of Knowledge*, where Foucault writes that discourses should be treated

> as practices that systematically form the objects of which they speak ... discourses are composed of signs; but what they do is more than use these signs to designate things. It is this more that renders them irreducible to the language (langue) and to speech. It is this more that we must reveal and describe.[45]

As comes across clearly in this passage, Foucault was keen to emphasize that discourses should not be reduced to words and language. In his view, while discourses are indeed expressed and articulated through language, they are also embedded in social institutions, structures, established "knowledges," and their associated practices – all of which have a range of tangible effects on the character and organization of social life on the whole. Actual social realities, therefore, not only reflect but also work to *reproduce* the discourses that underpin them. Adopting this perspective makes up a first step in the formulation of an understanding of the concept of discourse that is particularly suitable for sociological analyses. As a next step, we can then proceed by adopting Stuart Hall's Foucault-inspired, but nonetheless decidedly more specific and concrete definition of discourse:

> Discourses are ways of referring to or constructing knowledge about a particular topic or practice: a cluster (or formation) of ideas, images

Discourse theory and analysis 15

and practices, which provide ways of talking about forms of knowledge and conduct associated with a particular topic, social activity or institutional site in society.[46]

In yet one further step, we can then supplement Hall's definition with the more text- and language-emphasizing definition provided by Vivien Burr:

> A discourse refers to a set of meanings, metaphors, representations, images, stories, statements and so on that in some way together produce a particular version of events. It refers to a particular picture that is painted of an event, person or class of persons, a particular way of representing it in a certain light.[47]

Through combining these definitions, we arrive at an understanding of discourse that views the relationship between the linguistic elements of discourse and actual social structures in *dialectical* terms.

In light of the above, discourses should therefore be viewed as being both *constructive* and *constitutive* of *socially meaningful* reality. Different discourses construct the social world in different ways, each providing "shortcut paths" into particular notions about good and bad, right and wrong, true and false, normal and abnormal, etc.[48] Discourses, however, are never static. Nor do they function in isolation from one another. Rather, they constantly mutate and cross-fertilize in various ways. More often than not, particular phenomena or states of affairs tend to be simultaneously surrounded by multiple, varyingly related, mutually supporting, and competing discourses.[49] Different discourses construct the world in different ways; each presenting a different account of a given phenomenon or states of affairs, each highlighting certain aspects or elements at the expense of others, and each purporting to articulate and present the "truth" about that given phenomenon or states of affairs.[50] Discourse is therefore also to be viewed as a central form of *social action*. To engage in discursive practice is to *act* in the social world. Consequently, as Titus Hjelm puts it, "A discursive approach is therefore interested not only in what is being said but in what is being *done* when something is said."[51] In this capacity, discourses are also dialectically linked to different forms of social *practice* (understood in the sense of "habitual" ways of acting that have become established in relation to certain types of social activity). Indeed, as Lilie Chouliaraki and Fairclough point out: "All practices have a "reflexive dimension: people always generate representations of what they do as part of what they do."[52] This, then, is how discourses both inform and become reproduced through people's social practices.[53] As to the implications of these observations for the sociological study of religion, more generally, they bring to our attention to the ways in which the relationship between peoples' "religious" practices and their representations of these practices need to be understood in dialectical terms and therefore also need to be studied as such. More specifically, they serve to highlight how people's "religious" practices – what people

16 *Discourse theory and analysis*

"actually do" – will always be informed and shaped by the particular ways in which these practices are discursively constructed *as* "religious." These "religious" practices will then, conversely, serve to further reinforce and reproduce the particular discourses that underpin and inform them.

In addition to the above, discourses also perform a range of other important social functions. For one thing, they play a central role in the shaping of social relationships through the particular ways in which they work to *position subjects* as both producers and addressees of discourse. Every time we engage in discursive practice we *adopt* certain subject positions in relation to what is being said and the particular version of events, persons, or states of affairs that is being constructed. As part of this, we also *ascribe* various subject positions to the person/persons who are addressed by the particular discourse/s that we engage in.[54] By the same token, we also become correspondingly positioned *by* others. Since we always base our continuous relational constructions of reality on already existing constructions and ways of understanding the world, we cannot speak from a position "outside" of discourse. Rather, we enter the realm of discourse as soon as we start to speak, write, or represent in any other way.[55] It follows from this that the range of subject positions that we can meaningfully adopt in relation to particular discourses always will be limited. As explored in detail by Foucault, in "taking up" the subject positions that particular discourses make available to us and that others ascribe to us, we also become "subjected to the regulatory power" of these discourses.[56] These are processes that we are rarely able to exercise more than partial control over. For example, provided that we are successfully *socialized* into certain subject positions, we learn to accept them, to gradually internalize them, and thus also to *reproduce* them.[57] These observations have a range of implications for how we are to understand "religion" as a social and cultural category and (perceived) "phenomenon" in the world. Various representations and discourses on "religion" serve to position subjects in particular ways (i.e., as "believers," "adherents," "heretics," "fanatics," and so on), while simultaneously making available a set of subject positions for people to adopt.

On a broader societal level, discourses are also intimately tied to the perpetuation and reproduction of *power relations* and dominant *ideologies* and *hegemonies*.[58] These issues provide the main focus for a set of particular approaches to discourse and its analysis that have become known as "critical discourse studies" or "critical discourse analysis" (CDA). CDA denotes a particular type of normative discourse analytic research that is primarily concerned with revealing how particular discourses and types of discursive practice serve to underpin, perpetuate, and sustain various forms of social inequality, marginalization, exclusion, etc. with the expressed aim of seeking out avenues to mitigate or overcome these. As such, the notion of *ideology* is central to most CDA-grounded work.[59] At its most general, the concept of ideology can be understood as "meaning in the service of power."[60] As Fairclough explains with particular reference to

Discourse theory and analysis 17

the ideological function of discourse: "interpretations and explanations can be said to be ideological if they can be shown to be ... necessary to establish and keep in place particular relations of power."[61] An equally central notion in CDA is that of *hegemony*. As principally developed in the social theory of Antonio Gramsci,[62] hegemony can be defined as "leadership as well as domination across the economic, political, cultural and ideological domains of a society."[63] Hegemony thus refers to the struggle of the dominant classes to win the *consent* of subordinate classes in order to maintain the status quo, i.e., their own power and domination, through persuasion and integration rather than coercion or force. However, as hegemony is unstable in its nature, it is never absolute and always only partially and temporarily achieved. As such, hegemony can be thought of as the "focus of constant struggle around points of greatest instability between classes and blocs" and which play out "on a broad front which includes the institutions of civil society."[64] We shall return to the notions of ideology and hegemony in Chapter 6.

Some representatives of CDA have insisted on the inherently normative character of the approach. In this view, adopting a normative stance should be viewed as a basic prerequisite for CDA to be able to fulfill its purpose, i.e., to be *critical*.[65] That, of course, is a completely reasonable demand. Such an agenda is certainly motivated by the multitude of ways in which discourse and discursive practice are continually used to underpin and sustain social injustices, inequalities, and discriminatory practices based on such things as race, ethnicity, class or socioeconomic status, gender, and religious affiliation, to name just a few. This should not, however, be taken to mean that the analytical categories and methodological tools of CDA could not equally well be utilized in research that is not guided by any expressed critical or emancipatory agenda. For example, although the framework outlined below draws extensively on that of Fairclough,[66] which constitutes one of the most widely employed frameworks in CDA, it does so without connecting the framework *as such* to any type of normative agenda. For sure, a critical stance towards all claims to "commonsense" knowledge constitutes an in-built feature of most, if not all, forms of discourse theory and their associated methods of analysis. These methods, however, can be employed in a large variety of different types of research for a wide variety of different research purposes. Although it is no simple or straightforward matter, explicitly normative approaches in the sociology of religion tend to be contested (which is not to deny the continued *implicit* presence of normative agendas in the field). The main reason for this arguably lies in the sub-discipline's aspirations (or pretentions) to "objectivity," its "methodological atheism," and fear of coming across as "choosing sides" in matters that relate to its principal object of research, i.e., "religion," the "religious," and religious communities. The intention here is by no means to disparage normative approaches in the field. Indeed, our discussion in upcoming chapters will, at times, unfold in direct connection to perspectives closely

18 *Discourse theory and analysis*

associated with critical theory. But whatever is to be regarded as critical *enough* should be left for each individual researcher to decide.

The analysis of discourse

At its most general, the analysis of discourse can be described as the analysis of *language in use*. Somewhat more specifically, in an oft-cited description by Teun van Dijk, discourse analysis consists of the "the systematic and explicit analysis of the various structures and strategies of different levels of text and talk."[67] As such, it can generally be described as a type of analysis that focuses on identifying *patterns* and *recurring elements* in a given body of data or collection of data which appear to be central to how events, persons, phenomena, or states of affairs are construed in particular ways and how, as a consequence, particular meanings are produced.[68] Typical types of data in discourse analytic research include (but are far from limited to) face-to-face interactions, different types of textual sources (e.g., official documents, media reports, legislation, political platforms), and different types of audiovisual data such as TV shows, web pages, and so on. There does not, however, exist any clearly formulated set of generally agreed upon or accepted "rules" as to how exactly researchers should go about identifying recurring patterns and key elements in any given body of data. A large number of particular discourse analytical frameworks have nevertheless been developed over the years. Many of these, however, tend to cover such an extensive breadth of themes, levels, and types of analyses as to often fall beyond the capacities of a single researcher.[69] The particular ways in which analyses are actually conducted will nevertheless always reflect the specific research purposes and aims of a given study, its main theoretical underpinnings, its disciplinary anchoring, the nature of the data analyzed, and, not least, the understanding of "discourse" that it operates with.[70] But regardless of the character of the particular framework used, the analysis of discourse needs to be understood as a fundamentally *interpretative* endeavor that always involves *active choices* on the part of individual researchers, each of which will have consequences for what will count as data in the first place and how these data will eventually be assembled, analyzed, interpreted, and explained.[71]

The framework for analysis outlined below is constructed on the basis of a selection and slight modification of a set of key terms and analytical concepts derived from Fairclough's "three-dimensional" CDA combined with several additional perspectives derived from other frameworks. Fairclough's "three-dimensional" CDA combines the analysis of text (i.e., written and spoken language in itself), practices (i.e., the production, distribution, and interpretation of texts), and socio-cultural practices (i.e., the ideational level of ideology and systems of knowledge and beliefs, or the broader societal contexts in which texts are embedded). In this approach, any particular instance of discourse "is seen as being simultaneously a piece of text, an

Discourse theory and analysis 19

instance of discursive practice, and an instance of social practice."[72] The three main dimensions of the framework can also be thought of in terms of three interrelated levels in the social functioning of discourse, each of which actualizes different forms of analysis. While a given study may direct particular focus at one of these dimensions or levels, an adequate overall analysis needs to pay some degree of attention to all three of them.[73]

While discourses are often multi-modal, combining several semiotic forms (e.g., the use of symbols, images) that work in mutually reinforcing ways, *language* remains by far the most significant semiotic form.[74] There are also important qualitative differences to be observed between spoken and written language and discourse. As Fairclough points out, writing constitutes a "spatialisation" of spoken language which transforms the moments of discourse from points in time (spoken) to positions in space (written) by allowing "communicative action to take place at a temporal and spatial distance."[75] Partly for this reason, written discourse remains the most significant form of data for discourse analysis (although by no means the only one).

Although the analysis of discourse can unfold in a range of different ways, it can usefully be thought of as unfolding on three main, closely interrelated and overlapping levels. Following Fairclough, these can be generally described as, respectively, focusing on "description," "interpretation," and "explanation." The three levels also roughly correspond to the three main dimensions of Fairclough's framework as outlined above. Textual analysis therefore makes up only one part of a three-pronged analysis, each level of which will require engaging in different types of analysis.[76]

Description

As a first main level of analysis, *description* focuses on the formal properties of texts (i.e., a particular instance of discourse as articulated in language, or converted from, e.g., recorded talk to text-form).[77] As a general rule, the formal textual properties of a particular text always need to be understood against the background of the broader context in which the text is situated.[78] Analyses on this level can be made more or less extensive and detailed, depending on the number of particular textual properties focused on. Hence, the more properties the analysis focuses on, the more extensive and complicated the analysis will consequently also become. It is therefore recommended to carefully choose and focus only on those properties that are relevant for particular research purposes or that are otherwise theoretically motivated.

Vocabulary or *lexis*. Lexical analysis principally involves looking at the use and frequency of particular "content-carrying" words, terms, metaphors, euphemisms, etc. that can be found in a text.[79] Paying attention to the employment of *metaphors* can be especially worthwhile since metaphors constitute words that are used to "stand in" for other

20 Discourse theory and analysis

words not otherwise connected to them, thereby working to construct various kinds of analogous relationships (as when the dynamics of the religious field are described through the metaphor of the "market").[80] Lexical analysis can also look at *collocation*, or the ways in which certain words may recurrently figure in close proximity to one another "in order to show how similar words accumulate to establish particular emphases or frameworks of thought."[81] Often, it is also worth paying attention to *coherence*, or the main sequential parts of which a text is built up.[82] As Donald Matheson rightly points out, "Lexical analysis is therefore at its strongest when it finds something more than choices between words, but consistent patterns which suggest preoccupations within the particular discursive context."[83]

Grammar. Textual analysis can also look at any number of grammatical features in a text, such as predominant participants and processes, the ascription of agency, and the employment of active or passive, or positive or negative, sentences. Main focal points of analysis include *modality*, or the degree of certainty or commitment that is expressed towards what is being said in a text (e.g., through the use of modal auxiliary verbs like "can"/ "cannot," "must"/ "must not," "should"/ "should not," "ought," "may").[84] They also include *nominalization*, or instances where clauses or verbs are turned into nouns, "thereby making an action into a *thing* and often into an *abstract thing*"[85] (as when what "X decided" is turned into "a decision was made"). In the words of Matheson, nominalizations "allow the writer to leave out who did the action to whom, and when or how it happened."[86] In close relation to this, looking at *transitivity* involves looking at "representation of actions in discourse," such as either the ascription of or the "masking or deletion of agency through passive sentence construction"[87] (as when what "X did" is turned into "X occurred"). Analyses of grammar also typically pay attention to instances of *recontextualization*, or the "transfer of main arguments" from one text into another text[88] (as when religious communities talk about their proselytizing efforts in terms of "marketing" and "branding").

Lastly, on a more practical note, it is also worth mentioning that many forms of discourse transcend language-barriers and, partly, also the peculiarities of different social and cultural contexts. In some cases, however, translated discourse can considerably complicate detailed lexical and grammatical analyses since the vocabulary and grammar used in an original text can become significantly altered and transformed as part of a translation process. Indeed, different languages make different constructions of the world possible, which will also affect the character that a particular discourse takes across particular linguistic contexts. However, as Chouliaraki and Fairclough point out, "Increasingly the balance between endogenous and exogenous forces shaping the development of discourse practices in a particular language is shifting towards the latter, so that commonalities of discourse practices increasingly transcend linguistic differences."[89]

Discourse theory and analysis 21

Interpretation

A second main level of analysis consists of *interpretation*, focusing on the "relationship between text and interaction – with seeing the text as the product of a process of production, and as a resource in the process of interpretation."[90] Interpretation therefore necessarily needs to unfold on the basis of an adequate understanding of the more specific context in which a particular text is produced, circulated, and interpreted. Interpretation can thus usefully begin by considering a more general set of questions such as these: In what broader social, communal, or organizational context is a particular text situated? Who produced the text, for what principal purposes, and in connection with what type of activity? Who is the text addressed to, or who make up the primary, either actual or imagined, audience for the text? In which particular ways is the text circulated and disseminated? Overall, interpretation needs to be viewed as a fundamentally reflexive process that will always be informed by the theoretical underpinnings and stated aims of a particular study. For as Chouliaraki and Fairclough point out, "Any discourse is open to no end of formal analysis, and all forms of formal analysis are theoretically informed."[91] Like analyses of lexis and grammar, interpretation can also usefully unfold in relation to, as well as be further aided by, a particular set of analytical categories.

Intertextuality. Still remaining on the level of text, paying attention to intertextuality involves looking at the particular ways in which a text draws on and makes any number of manifest connections with other texts (as when a speech on political policy mentions or includes quotations from a newspaper article). More generally, looking at intertextual relationships therefore reveals how each "individual text gets its meaning not from something else that structures it but from its intertextual references to all the other texts which precede or surround it."[92] Indeed, as Matheson points out, "Intertextual meaning will often arise directly from the text's echoing of previous texts – in aspects such as its words or structure or narrative progression or visual form."[93]

Interdiscursivity. On a somewhat more general level than that of intertextuality, it is equally worth paying attention to the interdiscursive properties of texts. This involves, principally, examining the ways in which texts "draw upon and articulate together multiple discourses, multiple genres, and multiple styles"[94] (as when changes in the organizational culture of a religious community are described through discourses derived from management literature).

Genre. Looking at genre principally involves identifying main types of situational discourse use. In discourse analytic research, a genre is most commonly understood as "a relatively stable set of conventions that is associated with, and partly enacts, a socially ratified type of activity."[95] Examples of genres include everyday conversation, various types of meetings in organizations (e.g., boardroom meetings), different types

22 *Discourse theory and analysis*

of interviews (e.g., media interviews, job interviews), and various types of socially and culturally prescribed modes of interaction (e.g., between teacher and pupil or between doctor and patient). As part of acquiring competence in a language, people develop (different degrees of) knowledge and awareness of the appropriateness of different discourse genres to different situations. Looking at genres thus draws our attention to the ways in which people normally tend to conform to the particular sets of "rules" that have come to govern language use in particular interactional or communicational settings (some analysts also use the term *register* for this).[96]

Style. Genres tend to be further associated with particular styles. Styles can be classified according to "tenor," that is, whether a particular text or activity should be considered "formal" or "informal," "official" or "casual," and so on. Styles can also be classified according to "rhetorical mode," or according to whether a text primarily should be regarded as "argumentative," "descriptive," "prescriptive," and so on.[97] It should be noted, however, that styles may also be used to denote the ways in which discourse serves to constitute various distinguishable "forms of being" or types of identities (as in the "styles" of politicians, businesspeople, or clergy).[98]

Discursive formation. As noted above, the concept of discursive formation originates in the early work of Foucault[99] and refers to the "linguistic facets of 'domains of thought'"[100] or "rules of formation" which serve to determine the possibilities "for certain statements but not others to occur at particular times, places and institutional locations."[101] Discursive formations serve to construct particular objects of knowledge in particular ways in particular social contexts at particular points in time such as, for example, the objects recognized as entities of study in various scientific disciplines or broader social categories such as "religion/religiosity," "the market," or "mental illness." In the words of Matheson, discursive formations thus consist of "the *accumulated* and *interlinked* statements about a topic, which *between them* comprise a particular way of talking and thinking that shapes how we understand the topic, and which *sets the terms* for more statements on the topic."[102] A discursive formation can thus be thought of as a relatively stable, although never static but rather constantly evolving, broader discursive frame of reference within which, and in relation to which, certain phenomena and states of affairs are represented, talked about, and understood at certain points in time. As such, the concept alerts us to the ways in which people, groups, organizations, and institutions alike typically produce and engage with particular texts and discourses with certain either explicit or implicit intentions, and how they do so in relation to the particular "interpretative principles" that have become established and "naturalized" in relation to specific institutionalized objects of knowledge and their associated practices.[103]

Discourse theory and analysis 23

The concept of discursive formation can therefore be of great help in identifying broader sets or chains of interrelated and mutually supporting discourses that have developed and solidified within particular social settings over longer periods of time. Following Foucault, in doing this, it is well worth inquiring into the conditions of possibility of particular discursive formations. It is worth considering, therefore, which particular developments that can be shown to have played a particularly central role in making the emergence and development of particular discursive formations possible in the first place. Hence, the concept of discursive formation can also help us pinpoint and trace notable discursive developments in the religious and scholarly fields alike. As an example of the former, we could consider how the wide-ranging reforms that followed in the wake of the Second Vatican Council (1962–65) served to bring about a range of significant changes to the ways in which the global Catholic Church viewed and *talked* (and *could* view and talk) about itself and its activities. As will be discussed in more detail in Chapter 3, as an example of the latter, we could consider how different sociological theoretical perspectives on the character of contemporary "religion" and "religious life" each provide us with particular languages and interpretive frameworks for conceptualizing and talking about changes and developments in the contemporary "religious field."

Order of discourse. Any analysis of discursive formations can usefully unfold with close attention to the character of wider orders of discourse. As defined by Chiapello and Fairclough,

> An order of discourse is a social structuring of semiotic difference – a particular social ordering of relationships amongst different ways of making meaning, i.e. different discourses and genres and styles. One aspect of this ordering is dominance: some ways of making meaning are dominant or mainstream in a particular order of discourse, others are marginal, or oppositional, or "alternative".[104]

Situated at the highest level of abstraction, orders of discourse therefore encapsulate the "totality of discursive practices (including discourses, genres, and styles) within an institution or society, and the relationships between them."[105] Owing to its "broadness," the concept of order of discourse is perhaps best employed as referring to the totality of discourses that operate within particular institutional or organizational domains, as will also be our approach in Chapter 6. Domains such as politics, the economy, the judiciary, or the educational system within a particular national context could hence each be viewed as being governed by their own respective orders of discourse, all of which, in turn, would comprise any number of varyingly connected discursive formations and mutually supporting or contrasting individual discourses. In this view, particular religious organizational or communal contexts could therefore also be viewed as being governed by their own respective orders of discourse.

24   *Discourse theory and analysis*

More than most other academic disciplines, the study of religion has to grapple with the peculiarities of *religious language*, i.e., the particular types of language use that are associated with those contexts that we conventionally designate as "religious." Hence, analyses at the level of interpretation may very well involve analyses of different types of religious language.

As Stiver points out, having occupied philosophers and Christian theologians for centuries, the relationship between language and "religion" has historically been "deep and pervasive"[106] throughout the Western world.[107] Prior to the development of structural linguistics in the early twentieth century, philosophers and theologians had, in their various ways, typically aimed to "segregate religious language as the language of faith from the language of reason."[108] For example, Thomas Aquinas, whose approach long provided the "standard model for understanding religious language"[109] throughout the Western world, argued that religious language is fundamentally *analogical* and that it therefore "conveys truth but not literal truth."[110] Although this understanding was somewhat altered following the new emphasis that the Reformers put on the literal meaning of the biblical text,[111] the so-called "two-language view" nevertheless continued to provide the main grounds on which "religious" language use was distinguished from other types of language use. As Ted Peters explains, in the two-language view, whereas science is seen to speak the "language of fact" and to ask questions about "penultimate reality," "religion" is instead seen to speak the "language of meaning" and to ponder questions that pertain to "ultimate reality."[112] While the two-language view remains widespread, the publication of Wittgenstein's *Philosophical Investigations* served to propel a general shift in the philosophy of religious language "from being primarily concerned with *whether* religious language refers to the *way* it refers."[113]

The social and cultural field that we conventionally refer to as the "religious" field is marked by several distinctive types of language use that we would normally not encounter in "non-religious" settings. In a Western (Judeo-Christian) understanding, "religion" tends to be strongly associated with "sacred texts" that adherents afford "special authority and power."[114] The origins and authorship of such texts tend to be shrouded in myth and legend. For example, in Judaism, the Decalogue (i.e., the Ten Commandments) is believed to have been handed down to Moses at Mount Sinai. In Islam, the Qur'an is perceived to represent the actual words of God, communicated directly to the prophet Muhammad. This is why, as John F. Sawyer points out, in many religious communities "the authority of a sacred text is closely bound up with firmly held beliefs about its origin and special nature."[115] In addition to their perceived origin and content, particular importance also tends to be attached to the language in which sacred texts are written.[116] In Islam, the Qur'an is conventionally perceived to "have been composed in an inimitable variety of Arabic in heaven."[117] In

Discourse theory and analysis 25

Judaism, Hebrew is ascribed special sacred status as the language in which God "spoke" the universe into being, that the original Torah was written in, and the language that was spoken and understood by the angels as well as by Adam and Eve in the Garden of Eden.[118] Christianity, by contrast, has instead historically been marked by a strong impulse to translate the Bible into as many languages as possible.[119]

The ways in which deities are talked about in religious language also tends to be surrounded by particular prescriptions and rules. In Judaism, for example, God's name is secret; hence, the use of the Tetragrammaton YHVH.[120] Another related characteristic of religious language is its frequent use of *performative utterances*, and especially in the form of "Words of God."[121] In Genesis, God creates the world through issuing the command "Let there be light!" In the Qur'an, God says simply "Be!" In Hindu mythology, the God Prajapati creates heaven and earth by uttering a set of syllables, with the syllable *Om* being perceived to encapsulate the essence of the Vedas and therefore to possess special sacred power.[122] Moreover, as Turner observes, since "religious communicative acts" have historically been closely linked to prevailing structures of power, "metaphors of divinity tend to be couched in the language of an absolute monarchy."[123] An example would be how the Bible refers to Jesus as the "King of Kings" (e.g., Timothy 6:15). In the mythopoetic language of Christianity, the "Word of God" also "became flesh" (John 1: 14). Hence, "God incarnate in Jesus the Christ is also the Incarnate 'Word' of God."[124]

In addition to the above, what we conventionally refer to as "religious" settings also tend to be marked by various types of special language use. Special languages are typically employed as part of practices such as prayer, liturgy, ritual, preaching, and so on.[125] Sometimes, these types of special languages can even be devoid of any clear connection to other forms of established language use. The practice of glossolalia (i.e., "speaking in tongues") provides a particularly illustrative example of this.

The above provides just a few examples of the peculiarities of religious language. In what reflects a constructionist approach, Bruce Lincoln argues that "religious" texts and language are generally distinguished by

> the claims they advance for their more-than-human origin, status, and authority. For characteristically, they connect themselves – and explicitly or in some indirect fashion – to a sphere and a knowledge of transcendent or metaphysical nature, which they purportedly mediate to mortal beings through processes such as revelation, inspiration, and unbroken primordial tradition. Such claims *condition* the way devotees regard these texts and receive their contents: indeed, that is their very raison d'être.[126]

Like other specialist languages, religious languages require special competencies that people must acquire through active learning and/or socialization

26 Discourse theory and analysis

into particular religious communicative frameworks. Religious language may, of course, include any number of intertextual and interdiscursive references to "non-religious" factors, events, states of affairs, etc. But because it tends to be strongly marked by grammatical features such as metaphor, allegory, analogy, and incantation, it nevertheless tends to work according to its own peculiar logics. For this reason, the precise meaning of "religious" texts and writings is often elusive and open to different interpretations. But as William Arnal and Russell McCutcheon point out, "the failure of a text to make sense, to clearly mean *anything*, in no way inhibits the text's functional generation of new textual practices; if anything, it enhances it."[127] Whether the claims made in religious languages are to be regarded as "true" or "false" is typically of little or no relevance. Rather, the power of religious languages resides "precisely [in] their unusual and distinctive *dissonance* from ordinary expectations or claims about the world: It is of their very nature and essence to be somewhat at odds with more ordinary types of factual discourse."[128] And so, it is precisely because of its ambiguity that religious language works to invite continuous commentary and interpretation as part of people's continuous efforts to make their own particular "sense" of it.

As briefly exemplified above, religious language provides the basis for a particular type of discourse that we can call "religious discourse." As Lincoln observes, "Discourse becomes religious not simply by virtue of its content, but also from its claims to authority and truth."[129] A "religious discourse" can therefore generally be defined as "*A discourse whose concerns transcend the human, temporal, and contingent, and that claims for itself a similarly transcendent status.*"[130] Understood in this way, religious discourse could then be further categorized according to particular genres, styles, and so on.

In addition to analyses of religious language and discourse itself, the level of interpretation is likely to also involve looking into the intertextual and interdiscursive connections that can be identified between a particular piece of religious discourse and other types of texts and discourses. For example, as will be explored in more detail in upcoming chapters, the discourse of religious communities tends to combine elements of different discourse types in new types of *hybrid* discourses that constitute mixes between religious and other types of discourse genres. Lastly, it is important to note once again that adequate analyses of religious discourse of any kind will always require a high degree of familiarity with particular religious languages and discourses and the broader social contexts in which they are embedded.

Explanation

In contrast to the levels of description and interpretation, explanation cannot unfold in relation to any ready-made categories. While all levels

Discourse theory and analysis 27

of analysis ("description" included) will always be theoretically informed, "explanation" will need to unfold in direct connection with the particular theoretical perspectives of a given study. To simplify, if the main objective of description is to account for *what* is being said and *how* it is being said, and the main objective of interpretation is to account for *whom* is saying what to *whom*, then the main objective of explanation is to account for *why* it is being said. Because theoretical perspectives (e.g., in the form of theoretical assumptions, hypotheses) will largely determine what needs to be explained in the first place, *why* something "happens" in discourse cannot be explained through an analysis of discourse alone. Having said that, all attempts towards explanation should be guided by the more fundamental insight that the relationship between discourse and social practice is dialectical in nature. As already noted, there are several ways in which discourses can become operationalized in ways that extend beyond and cannot be reduced to discourse.

Efforts towards explanation can also usefully consider a "historical variable" for the purposes identifying broader "qualitative shifts in the '*cultural dominant*'" with respect to the "nature of the discursive practices which have most salience and impact in a particular epoch."[131] The task, in other words, is to strive to identify the particular sets of discourses and discursive formations that can be shown to hold particular prominence and salience across different social and cultural domains during certain points in time. As already noted in the Introduction, since it is primarily through the medium of discourse that new "knowledges," values, and ways of conceptualizing social and cultural reality make their ways into and become internalized within the orders of discourse of social domains, institutions, and organizations, most types of social changes tend to include manifest and clearly identifiable discursive components. For example, as Chiapello and Fairclough point out, several of the most significant social changes of the post-World War II era have been directly driven by economic factors and economic ideologies.[132] As will be explored in more detail in Chapter 6, the wide dissemination and perpetuation of neoliberal political economy since the early 1980s have served to put in motion an accelerating general process of *marketization* that has now come to extend over nearly all social and cultural domains. As a central part of this process, past decades have witnessed a wide diffusion and naturalization of economistic and consumer–capitalist-associated discourse and terminology across a range of traditionally "non-economic" social and cultural domains, including education, healthcare, the non-profit organizational sector, and religion. As a consequence, long-established traditional Christian churches have increasingly reconfigured their organizational structures according to new market-associated criteria of organizational "effectivity" and "performance" while many smaller, more recently established religious communities and organizations have fully embraced practices such as marketing, advertising, and branding. To single out

28   *Discourse theory and analysis*

marketization as a forceful contemporary cultural dominant is therefore to argue that it should be regarded as among the most influential ideational and discursive forces shaping the religious field today.

As will be explored further in Chapters 5 and 6, the development of market and consumer society is closely interlinked with the rise of individualism throughout the Western world, and indeed beyond. Individualism counts among the most (perhaps *the* most) ideationally forceful and largely discourse-driven phenomena of contemporary societies that finds expression in a wide variety of different forms across the social and cultural spectrum. In its ideational and discursive dimensions, individualism centers on personal autonomy and self-determination as supreme social values, it emphasizes the primacy of the unique individual as the "basic unit of social reproduction"[133] and champions values such as individual rights and personal choice. The effects of individualism/individualization on contemporary religion, religious life, and practice have been the subject of a great deal of scholarly debate and have been studied under many different headings. To single out individualization (whether it be under that precise heading or related headings such as "subjectivization") is therefore to identify individualism as a contemporary cultural dominant that exerts a highly notable, and primarily ideational and discursive, influence on the contemporary religious field.

Depending on their respective disciplinary backgrounds and research interests, scholars might certainly (or are perhaps even likely to) single out different cultural dominants and also disagree on their significance and relative broader social and cultural impact. Whatever the case, as in scholarship generally, sufficiently convincing support has to be marshaled for each view. When approached from a discursive perspective, developments in the religious field nonetheless need to be examined in direct relation to those broader social processes, forces, and phenomena that can be persuasively shown to exert a particularly strong ideational and discursive influence *across* large parts of the social and cultural field as a whole at a particular point in history. Only in this way are we able to adequately account for the ways in which broader prevalent discourses and discursive practices work to affect the religious field, its organization, practices, sensibilities, and so on. Although the identification of cultural dominants takes place at a relatively high level of abstraction and generalization, it plays a central heuristic role in determining the macro-theoretical bases of particular research projects. For example, a stronger focus on the ideational and discursive dimensions of the cultural dominant of marketization and its impact on the contemporary religious field will require a firmer engagement with both previous and current theorizing in that area. Conversely, a focus on the cultural dominant of individualism would require a different type of broader theoretical grounding. In both cases, particular disciplinary or sub-field specific theoretical perspectives would also provide particular theory-informed frames of explanation.

Concluding remarks

The above has explicated the concept of discourse and outlined some main analytical categories to guide analysis. The aim has not been to provide anything by means of a comprehensive discussion, but rather to outline the contours of a more particular type of framework to aid empirically grounded research in the sociology of religion specifically. This framework emphasizes the dialectical relationship between discourse and social structures and practices and views social and cultural changes and transformations as partly changes in discourse and language.[134] As such, it highlights the *discourse-driven* character of all forms of social, cultural, and "religious" development and change. A discursive sociology of religion will therefore focus its attention on the ways in which changing discourses and discursive practices work to affect changes in the religious field by studying the particular ways in which "religion," the "religious," and "religious practice" come to be discursively constructed by individuals, groups, organizations, and institutions alike across various types of social situations and contexts. In terms of analysis, the framework outlined affords equal attention to the analysis of texts, the particular contexts in which texts are produced and disseminated, and the wider social and cultural contexts in which they are embedded. This framework will be also be varyingly applied in subsequent chapters.

Notes

1 For example, Titus Hjelm, "Discourse Analysis," in *The Routledge Handbook of Research Methods in the Study of Religion*, eds. Michael Stausberg and Steven Engler (London: Routledge, 2011), 136.
2 Fairclough, *Critical Discourse*, 170.
3 Kenneth Gergen, *An Invitation to Social Construction* (London: Sage, 1999), 35.
4 Peter L. Berger and Thomas Luckmann, *The Social Construction of Reality: A Treatise in the Sociology of Knowledge* (Harmondsworth: Penguin, 1966).
5 Steven Engler, "Constructionism versus What?," *Religion* 34, no. 4 (2004): 292; Jonathan Potter, *Representing Reality: Discourse, Rhetoric and Social Construction* (London: Sage, 1996), 12.
6 Vivien Burr, *Social Constructionism*, Second edition (London: Routledge, 2003), 13.
7 Ibid., 7.
8 Gergen, *An Invitation to Social Construction*, Second edition (London: Sage, 2009), 33–5; Potter, *Representing Reality*, 11–3.
9 Ibid., 33–8.
10 Dan S. Stiver, *The Philosophy of Religious Language: Sign, Symbol & Story* (Malden, MA: Blackwell Publishing, 1996), 164.
11 Ibid., 165.
12 Gergen, *An Invitation*, 17.
13 Ibid., 33–5.
14 Stiver, *The Philosophy*, 61.
15 Ibid.

30 *Discourse theory and analysis*

16 Ibid., 62.
17 Donald Matheson, *Media Discourses: Analyzing Media Texts* (Maidenhead: Open University Press, 2005), 8.
18 Stiver, *The Philosophy*, 81.
19 For an extended discussion of Foucault and discourse analysis, see Fairclough, *Discourse and Social*, 37–61.
20 Ibid., 31.
21 Marianne Jørgensen and Louise Phillips, *Discourse Analysis as Theory and Method* (London: Sage, 2002), 12.
22 Ibid., 13.
23 Ibid., 14.
24 For example, Burr, *Social Constructionism*, 11–5; Gergen, *An Invitation*, 24–6.
25 Potter, *Representing Reality*, 69; 88.
26 Burr, *Social Constructionism*, 11–15; Engler, "Constructionism," 292; Gergen, *An Invitation*, 29.
27 Tim Murphy, "Discourse," in *Guide to the Study Religion*, eds. Willi Braun and Russell T. McCutcheon (London: Cassell, 2000), 397.
28 Stephanie Taylor, "Locating and Conducting Discourse Analytic Research," in *Discourse as Data: A Guide for Analysis*, eds. Margaret Wetherell, Stephanie Taylor, and Simeon T. Yates (London: Sage, 2001), 8, emphasis added.
29 Burr, *Social Constructionism*, 3.
30 Ibid., 4.
31 Ibid., 5.
32 Ibid., 9.
33 Ibid., 5–7; Taylor, "Locating and Conducting," 11–3.
34 Engler, "Constructionism," 295–6.
35 Fiona J. Hibberd, *Unfolding Social Constructionism* (New York: Springer, 2005), 53.
36 Ibid.
37 Fairclough, *Critical Discourse*, 4.
38 Ibid.
39 Ibid., 5.
40 Ibid.
41 See for example, Ruth Wodak, "What CDA Is About – A Summary of Its History, Important Concepts and Its Developments," in *Methods of Critical Discourse Analysis*, Second edition, eds. Ruth Wodak and Michael Meyer (London: Sage, 2008).
42 Ernesto Laclau and Chantal Mouffe, *Hegemony and Socialist Strategy: Towards a Radical Democratic Politics* (London: Verso, 1985).
43 Fairclough, *Critical Discourse*, 230.
44 Martin Reisigl and Ruth Wodak, "The Discourse-Historical Approach," in *Methods of Critical Discourse Analysis*, Second edition, eds. Ruth Wodak and Michael Meyer (London: Sage, 2008), 89.
45 Michel Foucault, *The Archaeology of Knowledge* (London: Routledge, 2002 [1969]), 55.
46 Stuart Hall, "Introduction," in *Representation: Cultural Representations and Signifying Practices*, ed. Stuart Hall (London: Sage, 1997), 4.
47 Burr, *Social Constructionism*, 64.
48 Jean Carabine, "Unmarried Motherhood 1830–1990: A Genealogical Analysis," in *Discourse as Data: A Guide for Analysis*, eds. Margaret Wetherell, Stephanie Taylor, and Simeon J. Yates (London: Sage, 2001), 269.
49 Burr, *Social Constructionism*, 65.
50 Ibid.

Discourse theory and analysis 31

51 Titus Hjelm, "Mapping the Discursive Study of Religion", *Journal of the American Academy of Religion* 88, no. 4 (2020): 1005.
52 Chouliaraki and Fairclough, *Discourse in Late Modernity*, 22.
53 Ibid.
54 Fairclough, *Discourse and Social*, 43.
55 Burr, *Social Constructionism*, 91.
56 Chris Barker and Dariusz Galasinski, cited in Matheson, *Media Discourses*, 61.
57 Fairclough, *Language and Power*, 122.
58 Fairclough, *Discourse and Social*, 3–4.
59 For an extended discussion of the critical dimensions of CDA, see Fairclough, *Critical Discourse*, 7–11; 231.
60 John Thompson, *Studies in the Theory of Ideology* (Cambridge: Polity Press, 1984).
61 Fairclough, *Critical Discourse*, 9.
62 Antonio Gramsci, *Selections from the Prison Notebooks* (London: Lawrence & Wishart, 1971).
63 Fairclough, *Critical Discourse*, 61.
64 Ibid., 61–2.
65 See for example, ibid., 10–1.
66 Ibid.
67 Theun van Dijk, cited in Ruth Wodak, "Introduction: Discourse Studies – Important Concepts and Terms," in *Qualitative Discourse Analysis in the Social Sciences*, eds. Ruth Wodak and Michal Krzyżanowski (Hampshire: Palgrave Macmillan, 2008), 3.
68 For example, Taylor, "Locating and Conducting," 6.
69 Cf. Marcus Moberg, "First-, Second-, and Third-Level Discourse Analytic Approaches in the Study of Religion: Moving from Meta-Theoretical Reflection to Implementation in Practice," *Religion* 43, no. 1 (2013): 12; Pete Thomas, "Ideology and the Discourse of Strategic Management: A Critical Research Framework," *Electronic Journal of Radical Organisation Theory* 4, no. 1 (1998): [11].
70 For example, Taylor, "Locating and Conducting," 28–9; Margaret Wetherell, "Debates in Discourse Research," in *Discourse Theory and Practice*, eds. Margaret Wetherell, Stephanie Taylor, and Simeon J. Yates (London: Sage, 2001a), 380; Reisigl and Wodak, "The Discourse-Historical," 89.
71 Taylor, "Locating and Conducting," 39.
72 Fairclough, *Discourse and Social*, 4.
73 Fairclough, *Critical Discourse*, 59.
74 For example, Fairclough, *Language and Power*, 8; 60.
75 Chouliaraki and Fairclough, *Discourse in Late Modernity*, 42.
76 Ibid., 58.
77 For a more detailed framework of analysis, see Fairclough, *Language and Power*, 129–30.
78 Ibid.
79 Ibid., 180.
80 Ibid.
81 Matheson, *Media Discourses*, 177.
82 Fairclough, *Language and Power*, 102.
83 Matheson, *Media Discourses*, 22.
84 Ibid., 142.
85 Ibid., 57, emphasis added.
86 Ibid., 180.
87 Titus Hjelm, "Theory and Method in Critical Discursive Study of Religion: An Outline," in *Making Religion: Theory and Practice in the Discursive*

32 *Discourse theory and analysis*

Study of Religion, eds. Kocku von Stuckrad and Frans Wijsen (Leiden: Brill, 2016), 25.
88 Wodak, "Introduction," 3.
89 Chouliaraki and Fairclough, *Discourse in Late Modernity*, 80.
90 Fairclough, *Language and Power*, 58.
91 Chouliaraki and Fairclough, *Discourse in Late Modernity*, 7.
92 Matheson, *Media Discourses*, 9.
93 Ibid., 47.
94 Fairclough, *Critical Discourse*, 7.
95 Fairclough, *Discourse and Social*, 126.
96 Matheson, *Media Discourses*, 178; 181.
97 Ibid., 127.
98 Eve Chiapello and Norman Fairclough, "Understanding the New Management Ideology: A Transdisciplinary Contribution from Critical Discourse Analysis and New Sociology of Capitalism," *Discourse & Society* 13, no. 2 (2002): 193–4.
99 Foucault, *The Archeology*.
100 Fairclough, *Discourse and Social*, 31.
101 Ibid., 40.
102 Matheson, *Media Discourses*, 178, emphases added.
103 Ibid., 84.
104 Chiapello and Fairclough, "Understanding the New," 194.
105 Fairclough, *Discourse and Social*, 43.
106 Stiver, *The Philosophy*, 6.
107 Ibid.; see also Thomas Kohnen, "Religious Discourse," in *Historical Pragmatics*, eds. Andreas H. Jucker and Irma Taavitsainen (Berlin: de Gruyter, 2010), 523.
108 Stiver, *The Philosophy*, 12.
109 Ibid., 23.
110 Ibid., 15.
111 Ibid., 34.
112 Ted Peters, "Protestantism and the Sciences," in *The Blackwell Companion to Protestantism*, eds. Alister E. McGrath and Darren C. Marks (Oxford: Blackwell, 2004), 315.
113 Stiver, *The Philosophy*, 59.
114 Turner, *Religion and Modern Society*, 194.
115 John F. Sawyer, "Sacred Texts and Translations: Introduction," in *Concise Encyclopedia of Language and Religion*, eds. John F. Sawyer and J. M. Y. Simpson (Oxford: Elsevier, 2001), 99.
116 Ibid.
117 John F. Sawyer, "Language in the Context of Particular Religions: Introduction," in *Concise Encyclopedia of Language and Religion*, eds. John F. Sawyer and J. M. Y. Simpson (Oxford: Elsevier, 2001), 3.
118 John F. Sawyer, "Beliefs about Language: Introduction," *Concise Encyclopedia of Language and Religion*, eds. John F. Sawyer and J. M. Y. Simpson (Oxford: Elsevier, 2001), 285.
119 Sawyer, "Language in the Context," 3.
120 Turner, *Religion and Modern*, 198.
121 P. Collins, "Performative Utterances," in *Concise Encyclopedia of Language and Religion*, eds. John F. Sawyer and J. M. Y. Simpson (Oxford: Elsevier, 2001), 237.
122 Sawyer, "Beliefs about Language," 285.
123 Turner, *Religion and Modern Society*, 199.

Discourse theory and analysis 33

124 J. Martin Soskice, "Christian Views on Language," *Concise Encyclopedia of Language and Religion*, eds. John F. Sawyer and J. M. Y. Simpson (Oxford: Elsevier, 2001), 291.

125 John F. Sawyer, "Special Language Uses: Introduction," in *Concise Encyclopedia of Language and Religion*, eds. John F. Sawyer and J. M. Y. Simpson (Oxford: Elsevier, 2001), 237.

126 Bruce Lincoln, *Gods and Demons, Priests and Scholars: Critical Explorations in the History of Religions* (Chicago, IL: Chicago University Press, 2012), 2; for a somewhat similar but much more ambiguous view of "religious discourse," see Dominique Maingueneau, "Religious Discourse and its Modules," in *Discourse Research and Religion: Disciplinary Use and Interdisciplinary Dialogues*, eds. Jay Johnston and Kocku von Stuckrad (Berlin: De Gruyter, 2021).

127 William E. Arnal and Russell T. McCutcheon, *The Sacred is the Profane: The Political Nature of Religion* (Oxford: Oxford University Press, 2013), 148.

128 Ibid., 152.

129 Bruce Lincoln, *Holy Terrors: Thinking about Religion after September 11* (Chicago, IL: University of Chicago Press, 2003), 5.

130 Ibid.

131 Fairclough, *Discourse and Social*, 138, emphasis added.

132 Chiapello and Fairclough, "Understanding the New."

133 Matthew Adams, *Self and Social Change* (London: Sage, 2007), 7.

134 Chouliaraki and Fairclough, *Discourse in Late Modernity*, 4.

3 A three-level discursive approach to "religion" and related categories

This chapter discusses the relationship between discourse and "religion" in light of previous language- and discourse-sensitive research in the study of religion. Our discussion will largely take the form of a critical appraisal of previous notable contributions in the so-called "critical-religion" approach and the "discursive study of religion." Since the key perspectives of this scholarship are of central importance to the academic study of religion as a whole, they are consequentially also of great relevance for the sociological study of religion. These perspectives pertain, in particular, to the indeterminate and contested character of the category of "religion," its arbitrary relationship to its supposed "referent," its relationship to related categories such as the "secular," and its limitations as an analytical category. For this reason, as in the Introduction, whenever we refer to the category of "religion" as such, the word will appear in quotation marks so as to constantly remind us of its inherently constructed character.

The introduction of discourse analytical or more broadly "discursive," perspectives in the study of religion is fairly recent. In 2013, I argued that the work that had been produced on discourse and religion up to that time could be divided into three main categories, situated at different points along a continuum, ranging from purely meta-theoretical work, to work that contextualizes meta-theoretical reflection in relation to theorizing within particular sub-fields in the study of religion, to work that employs discourse analysis as a method in empirical research.[1] These main categories, I argued, could be conceptualized in terms of first-, second-, and third-level types of work. Although recent years have witnessed a considerable expansion in religion and discourse research, the great majority of all the more recent contributions can nevertheless be subsumed under these three categories. These categories should be understood in a dual sense, as simultaneously referring both to main *types of work* and main *levels of analysis*. On the one hand, this categorization therefore serves the more general heuristic purpose of providing us with a bird's eye view of the field of religion and discourse research as a whole by differentiating between main types of work, which are largely determined on the basis of the types of analyses that they engage in. Conversely, the categorization therefore also serves to

DOI: 10.4324/9780367435837-3

Three-level discursive approach 35

delineate main levels of analysis, each of which tends to be associated with particular types of work in field.

In terms of *type of work*, the three levels can be thought of as being situated on a vertical scale, with first-level work that engages in the highest degrees of abstraction and meta-theoretical reflection on top, followed by more contextualized sub-field-specific second-level work in the middle, followed by third-level work at the lower, hands-on end of concrete empirical analyses. In terms of *levels of analysis*, first-level analyses primarily engage with key categories and terms in the study of religion (e.g., the categories of "religion," the "secular," "belief"). Second-level analyses inquire into the inherent presumptions and classificatory schemes of particular types of sub-field-specific theorizing (e.g., "secularization," the "post-secular," "religious subjectivization"). Third-level analyses focus on actual instances of discourse and apply discourse analysis as a method (on for example data such as interviews, official documents, newspaper articles, social media, or, for that matter, scholarly discourse itself). The three levels should thus be understood in terms of closely intersecting, overlapping, and *complementary* levels of analysis. While it is perfectly possible (and indeed completely permissible) to engage in first-level meta-theoretical reflection and analysis without much reference to either sub-field-specific theorizing or analyses of actual instances of discourse (apart, that is, from scholarly discourse itself), this becomes more difficult when it comes to second-level analyses, and nearly impossible when it comes to third-level work. First-level meta-theoretical reflection and analysis should thus *inform* (and usefully also precede) analyses on the other two levels. But in an empirically oriented discipline such as the sociology of religion, meta-theoretical reflection will only ever take us so far. For this reason, the primary purpose of both first- and second-level work is to provide third-level analyses with solid foundations on which to build. This is because scholars who engage in third-level analyses need to do so on the basis of an adequate, critical, and reflexive understanding of the key concepts and categories that they employ. For example, a study that aims to analyze actual portrayals or construals of "religion" in the news media (third-level) will first need to engage with the category of "religion" as such, how it is most adequately understood, and the particular ways in which it can be employed as part of actual empirical research (first-level). The study then also (almost necessarily) needs to align with one or several sub-field-specific theoretical frameworks, for example, on mediatization or republicization on the "contemporary media environment"-side, or secularization, public religion, or the post-secular on the "current state of the religious field"-side (second-level). As part of this, the study will need to critically and reflexively engage with the particular sets of concepts and presumptions that are associated with the respective sub-field-specific theoretical perspectives that it aligns with. In all this, the key objective is to maintain a high degree of *critical awareness* of the multitude of ways in which our concepts, categories, and classificatory schemes work

36 *Three-level discursive approach*

to fundamentally shape how we identify our objects of research, how we approach and study them, how we perceive "realities on the ground," what we count as "data" and how we set out to gather them, and, not least, how we assemble, analyze, interpret, and explain them.

First-level work and analysis: "religion," discourse, and meta-theoretical reflection

First-level approaches come in many different forms. In terms of *type of work*, this category includes various types of critical studies that inquire into the historical development and epistemological underpinnings of the discipline of the study of religion itself and the nature of its terminological and conceptual apparatus. While previous contributions of this type have engaged with and utilized discourse theory and analysis to varying extents, the large majority of them have not been explicitly framed as "discursive" studies. In terms of *level of analysis*, analyses on this level primarily inquire into the nature of the category of "religion" itself and its relationship to, and differentiation from, other concepts and categories such as the "secular," "culture," or "politics." As such, the "data" for analyses at this level mainly consist of scholarly discourse itself. Overall, following Brad Stoddard and Craig Martin, one could say that the modern period has witnessed the emergence and wide establishment of several, by now deeply socially and culturally ingrained, "clichés" about "religion." The task of first-level reflection is essentially to dispel these clichés by tracing their respective historical developments, critically examining their conditions of establishment, and reveal their continued effect on how the category of "religion" (along with several associated categories and terms) most commonly tends to be approached and understood.[2] Such examinations will inevitably also connect to questions of power since particular clichés "allow people who use the cliché to frame all 'religion' as they perceive it."[3]

Critical religion

As noted, first-level work is particularly focused on critically inquiring into the nature of the category of "religion" itself. The mid-1970s witnessed the start of a critical debate on the inherently problematic nature of the Western category of "religion" that continues to this day. These debates have given rise to a particular body of scholarship that has become known as the "critical-religion" approach. In *Map is not Territory* (1978) Jonathan Z. Smith, who was a particularly central and prolific progenitor of these debates, argued that "Religion is an inextricably human phenomenon" and that it is only from the "post-Kantian ... humane, post-Enlightenment perspective that the academic interpretation of religion becomes possible."[4] In his influential and widely read *Imagining Religion* (1982) he then went

Three-level discursive approach 37

on to famously proclaim that *"there is no data for religion,"* that "Religion is solely the creation of scholars' study," and that acute awareness and self-consciousness of one's use of categories, concepts, and classifications, should comprise a scholar's "primary expertise" and "foremost object of study."[5] For Smith, the study of religion is therefore, first and foremost, the study of the *category* of "religion."

A somewhat more recent example of influential first-level work of this kind can be found in McCutcheon's *Manufacturing Religion,*[6] which explores the historical development, diffusion, and enduring influence of the *sui generis* understanding of religion, or the notion that "religion" constitutes a "transhistorical essence" that is irreducible to sociological, psychological, political, economic, or any other determinative factors that are supposedly "external" to it, and hence that it is something that can only be adequately studied on the basis of its "own" peculiar premises. Having shown the postulates of the *sui generis* approach to be both untestable, unprovable, and thus untenable, McCutcheon arrives at the conclusion that the category of "religion" only retains its usefulness

> in first-order, descriptive research *but not* at the level of second-order interpretive or explanatory analysis ... [since] the category of religion is itself part of the problem to be analyzed and *is not itself* a tool in its own analysis.[7]

This insight has serious implications not only for how the category of "religion" becomes defined, but also for how we come to understand the very act and practice of *defining*. It invites us to accept Thomas Lawson's and Robert McCauley's more rudimentary insight that "definitions are only as good as the theories that inspire them."[8] Even though the *sui generis* approach to religion, especially as developed and articulated by its most prominent representative, Mircea Eliade, has been the subject of a great deal of controversy and debate in the study of religion, it still continues to reappear in new forms and incarnations, which is why first-level work of this type has found it necessary to continue to counter and critique it.

Significant as critical debates on the *sui generis* approach have been, the heuristic value, explanatory power, and analytical utility of the category of "religion" – or lack thereof – remains a contested issue. As Murphy observes with specific reference to the employment of discourse theory in the study of religion, the central challenge is to find some way to "retain a critical stance towards the object level of discourse (i.e., the 'data' of religion) on the one hand, while remaining reflexively self-critical about the meta-level of discourse (the *study* of the 'data' of religion) on the other hand."[9] A similar point is made by Steven Engler when he underscores the importance of our distinguishing between two "levels of construction" or "theory-ladenness" with regard to the category or label of "religion": "facts described as religious, and data theorised as religious."[10]

38 Three-level discursive approach

A more distinctive and original contribution to these debates is provided in Tomoko Masuzawa's *The Invention of World Religions*,[11] which traces the historical development and diffusion of the notion of "world religions" that continues to dominate much lay discourse on "religion," the "religion"-related legislation of states, the "religion"-related discourse of supra-national institutions such as the United Nations, and school and university curricula alike.[12] Through a detailed genealogical examination of influential publication projects such the *Sacred Books of the East* (edited by Max Müller between 1897 and 1910), the impact of events such as the first World's Parliament of Religions held in Chicago in 1893, and the influence of a range of private actors and associations, Masuzawa traces the development and gradual establishment of a "pluralist discourse" that orders the global "religious field" into a set of clearly delineated "world religions." Echoing McCutcheon's critique of the *sui generis* approach, she highlights how this pluralist discourse "spiritualizes what are material practices and turns them into expressions of something timeless and supra-historical, which is to say, it depoliticizes them."[13] As her exploration also makes clear, the subsequent adoption of the Western concept of "world religions" throughout many parts of the world was never simply "a matter of international trade in concepts" but rather a process "that took place in the context of colonialism, or under the forceful impact of the European epistemic field."[14]

The historical constitution and perpetuation of the Western category of religion as an integral component of Western colonialist projects has been the main focus of a certain sub-category of first-level studies. Focusing on different regions, historical periods, and socio-cultural contexts, some of the most influential among these include David Chidester's *Savage Systems*[15] and *Empire of Religion*[16] and Talal Asad's *Genealogies of Religion*[17] and *Formations of the Secular*.[18] Of particular note here is Asad's introduction of a new emphasis on the *co-constitution* of "religion" and its "Other," namely, the "secular."[19] Rather than defining the "secular" in merely negative terms (i.e., as simply denoting the "absence" of "religion"), Asad argues that the relation between "religion" and the "secular" needs to be understood in dialectical terms. The "secular," therefore, needs to be understood as possessing its own ideological content so that what we imagine "religion" to be will be directly connected to what we imagine the "secular" to be and vice versa. As we will continue to discuss in Chapter 4, these observations are of key relevance to the sociological study of religion, which continues to occupy itself with the theme of secularization and the character and position of "religion" in "secular" societies.

Another closely related influential type of first-level meta-theoretical work can be found in the production of Timothy Fitzgerald. As laid out in volumes such as *The Ideology of Religious Studies*,[20] *Discourse on Civility and Barbarity*,[21] and *Religion and Politics in International Relations*,[22] Fitzgerald has devoted particular attention to the ways in which the

Three-level discursive approach 39

"construction of modern discourses on generic religion has been made possible and conceivable by the parallel construction of a number of overlapping discourses on nonreligious/secular science, politics, the nation state, economics, law, and education."[23] He notes that, while "any attempt to describe or analyse a culture or a period of history without recourse to it [religion] would be deficient, strange, and perhaps even unthinkable,"[24] it is nevertheless of crucial importance that scholars of religion recognize that "Religion as a distinct and substantive reality in the world or as a universal and autonomous domain of human experience and action is a myth, or a rhetorical discursive formation"[25] – a peculiar product of Western modernity that was also originally peculiar to that Western modernity. Studying "religion" in contemporary times therefore involves inquiring into "the history of a modern idea" and viewing the category of "religion" as "a system of classification."[26] Of all of the first-level perspectives discussed here, Fitzgerald's has arguably been the most uncompromising and "radical" in that he has, at times, advocated the complete abandonment of "religion" as a scholarly category.

Lincoln's first-level work stands out from the contributions discussed so far in its explicit engagement with discourse theory. In his well-known "Theses on Method" Lincoln approaches both "religion" and its study (in the form of the history of religions) as two separate "discourses." Of "religion" he writes that it is "that discourse whose defining characteristic is its desire to speak of things eternal and transcendent with an authority equally transcendent and eternal."[27] The sub-discipline of the history of religions, in its turn, is described as

> a discourse that resists and reverses the orientation of that discourse with which it concerns itself [i.e. "religion"]. To practice history of religions in a fashion consistent with the discipline's claim of title is to insist on discussing the temporal, contextual, situated, interested, human, and material dimensions of those discourses, practices, communities, and institutions that characteristically represent themselves as eternal, transcendent, spiritual, and divine.[28]

Lincoln further expands on these arguments in *Holy Terrors*,[29] where he lays out an explicitly discursive framework for the study of religion. On the basis of his view of "religious discourse" as already discussed in Chapter 2, Lincoln proceeds to argue that what we call "religion" can be understood as *"a set of practices whose goal is to produce a proper world and/or proper human subjects, as defined by a religious discourse to which these practices are connected."*[30] There are no such things as "inherently religious" practices, however. Rather, practices "may acquire a religious character when connected to a religious discourse that constitutes them as such."[31] A "religious community" can therefore, in turn, be understood as the type of *"community whose members construct their identity with*

40 Three-level discursive approach

reference to a religious discourse and its attendant practices"[32] while a "religious institution" can be understood as *"An institution that regulates religious discourse, practices, and community, reproducing them over time and modifying them as necessary, while asserting their eternal validity and transcendent value."*[33]

In their respective ways, the contributions discussed above all point to the ways in which the academic study of religion has historically aimed to assert itself and its credibility "through the generation of 'commonplaces'" about its principal object of inquiry, i.e., "religion."[34] As part of this, the discipline has generated its own legitimizing rhetoric and discourse, the wider ideational effects and pitfalls of which it becomes the task of critical disciplinary histories to reveal.[35]

Most of the key observations and perspectives discussed above come together in Arnal's and McCutheon's more recent *The Sacred is the Profane.*[36] Their central concern is to critically examine the principal ways in which a "highly effective *interiorization*, and thus a *dehistoricization* and a *depoliticization* of the social" continues to take place "in much recent work on the category of 'religion.'"[37] Such a critical examination is, not least, motivated by how "the folk and scholarly category 'religion' can be understood as part of a wider discourse on the modern, universal subject."[38] When it comes to the definition of "religion," following decades of debate, Arnal and McCutcheon argue that we need to come to terms with the fact that "the concept of religion is a sufficiently artificial or *synthetic* construct such that its very creation is itself an implicit theorization of cultural realities."[39] Our inquiries should therefore move beyond the quagmire of what religion "as such" "is" towards a more sustained focus on what religion means or "is" to *who*, in which social and cultural contexts, for what particular purposes, and with what particular consequences. What needs to be theorized, therefore, is *"why* some humans (hardly all) use 'religion' to name aspects of their social world, thereby studying the various ways in which the taxon (and its wider discourse) is used and the practical effects of these uses."[40] Echoing Fitzgerald's observations above, this would require developing a study of religion that takes the form of a "theory of signification."[41] Recognizing the artificiality of the category of "religion" does not, however, automatically amount to a call for its wholesale abandonment. Rather, as Arnal and McCutcheon continue, when we recognize that *all* mental categories are artificial and arbitrary by nature, we can continue to use the concept of "religion" in a taxonomical sense "even if it fails to correspond perfectly to some real object in the world" and "as long as our intellectual creativity in doing so is kept firmly in mind."[42] The principal focus of our research should therefore be on "deconstructing the category and analyzing its function within popular discourse."[43]

In light of all of the limitations and inherent problems with the (Western) category of "religion" discussed above, some representatives of the critical religion approach (most notably Fitzgerald) have, as noted, suggested that it be abandoned as a scholarly category. That would, however, be a mistake, if only for the simple reason that it is much too late for that. From a discursive perspective, the category of "religion" does indeed need to be approached as an empty signifier that has no intrinsic meaning in and of itself. The category of "religion" should therefore not be taken to refer to some trans-human and trans-historical "essence" that "hides" behind the word "religion" and that supposedly exists independently somewhere "out there" irrespective of the particular ways in which people choose to construct it through language and discourse. Yet this is nonetheless precisely how the category of "religion" has largely come to figure in everyday discourse throughout large parts of the world.[44] As a consequence, individuals and social organizations and institutions alike have long ago become increasingly prone to perceive, treat, and respond to "religion" *as if* it had its own independent "existence." This can, for example, be seen in the ways in which particular states grant official recognition to particular "religions," or how an understanding of "religion" as a private "individual elective" has come to dominate the "religion"-related discourse of supra-national institutions such as the United Nations.[45]

Throughout the Western world and beyond, as people grow up, they are socialized into comprehending "religion" as having its own independent "existence." People learn about "religion" in school. They are also quite likely to learn about "world religions" such as Christianity, Islam, and Buddhism, and come to understand them as belonging to the same *genus*, i.e., as constituting individual manifestations of the phenomenon of "religion *as such*." Regardless of their own personal connections to "religion," people also learn to recognize particular spaces and places, such as churches, mosques, and temples as "religion"-related places that "religious" people visit in order to engage in "religious" activities or practices. People might not be able to provide elaborate explanations of what religion "is" or what it means to them; yet it has become increasingly difficult to imagine a person for whom the word "religion" is devoid of *any* meaning (which is not to say that there are no such persons). This, moreover, equally applies to people who self-identify with the position of "non-religion" – a demographic of constantly growing interest to sociologists of religion. And so, regardless of people's respective personal connections to "religion," they are increasingly likely to both view and to respond to "religion" as something that simply "exists" in society and culture independently of themselves as individuals. But, as noted, it is not only individuals that have come to comprehend "religion" in this way. Such an understanding of "religion" has also been adopted, and has thereby also been further perpetuated, by core societal institutions such as political, legal, and educational establishments throughout the world. As Peter Beyer observes, the understandings of "religion" constructed in such institutional contexts "are neither 'theological' nor 'scientific'; they are also not 'folk' or 'popular' conceptions."[46] Rather, he argues, they are perhaps most adequately described as "official" since they

42 Three-level discursive approach

are "made manifest in the legal decisions, the state constitutions, the political policies and the educational curricula of different countries around the world" and, as such, work significantly to inform and shape how the "religious domain" is socially constituted in actual practice.[47] At the same time, as numerous studies have noted, institutional and public discourse on "religion" in Western societies simultaneously tends to be marked by a high degree of "religious illiteracy."

The above observations are not novel in any sense. The wide establishment of an understanding of "religion as such" as discussed above can be viewed in light of the classic Durkheimian notion of "social fact." As Durkheim argued:

> collective ways of acting and thinking have a reality outside the individuals who, at any moment in time, conform to it. These are things which exist in their own right. The individual finds them already formed, and he cannot act as if they did not exist or were different from how they are.[48]

Echoing Berger and Luckmann, the same basic argument is also made by Lincoln when he points out how "Understanding the system of ideology that operates in one's own society is made difficult by two factors: (a) one's consciousness is itself a product of that system, and (b) the system's very success renders its operations invisible."[49] And so, following the wide diffusion and institutionalization of the *sui generis* understanding of "religion," the so-called "World Religions-paradigm," and the gradual establishment of a "global discourse on religion,"[50] people across many parts of the world have come to perceive "religion" as "real," as something that exists independently of themselves as individuals, as something that was "there" in the world before they arrived and that will remain there after they are gone.[51] And so, as the Thomas theorem teaches us, what people perceive to be "real" will become real in its consequences.[52] To the extent that the world is constructed in discourse, "religion" therefore *is* "real." It is precisely for this reason, to reconnect to Arnal's and McCutcheon's argument above, that the study of religion very much needs to continue to occupy itself with the category of "religion," but *not* in the sense of some external "reality" or "experience" to which the term supposedly refers, but rather in light of the particular ways in which the category is *construed, constructed*, and *used* in and across particular social and cultural situations and contexts, and with what social effects and consequences.

Lastly, it is worth noting that critical religion scholarship has also engaged with several additional "religion-related" concepts such as "belief" and "faith" in particular. Indeed, as Robyn Faith Walsh points out, the study of religion has been deeply implicated in the interiorization (and thus depoliticaztion) of "religion" as a matter of private, individual, and deeply held "belief" or "faith." Historically, this can be seen in Friedrich

Schleiermacher's emphasis on "religion" as a "private affair," in William James's understanding of "religion" as "belief in an unseen order" and distinction between "institutional and personal religion,"[53] in Rudolph Otto's location of "religion" in so-called *numinous* experiences of the "wholly other," in Gerardus Van der Leeuw's location of "religion" in the individual's encounter with the "sacred," in Paul Tillich's definition of "faith" as pertaining to individuals' "ultimate concern," and (to some extent) in Wilfred Cantwell Smith's dividing of "religion" into the categories of "faith" and "cumulative tradition."[54] From having been viewed as being rooted in adherence to formal creeds, obedience of ecclesiastical authorities and hierarchies, and collective ritual participation in pre-modern times, "religion" has gradually transformed into something rooted in personal "feeling," "experience," or "inner persuasion" of the mind. This modern way of conceptualizing "religion" has become encapsulated in the widely established concept of "belief." As principally popularized through the Reformation, the concept of "belief" has come to extend *beyond* what has conventionally been understood as "religion." In the words of Sean McCloud:

> Many of us have been socially habituated to assume that the thing we call religion is first and foremost about belief and – even more – that what one believes is the basis for an individual's action, whether that action is seen as *religious* or not.[55]

The notion of "belief," however, remains problematic in several respects. For one thing, following McCloud, it can "presuppose that humans hold to concepts and ideas that are all coherent and logically consistent over time," suggesting that "religion" is something that is exclusively located in thought and mind.[56] Hence the widespread notion of "religions" as "belief systems."

The wide establishment of the concept of "belief" has also played a central role in further cementing the widely held notion that people who self-identify as "religious" hold *single* religious identifications and "belongings." Indeed, this notion continues to inform state policy and regulation of religion throughout large parts of the Western world.[57] This is the perception that people cannot reasonably "belong" to several religions at the same time. By contrast, the notion that every individual should be able to freely *choose* which religion to identify with or "believe in" is widely accepted. In modern societies, religious identification or affiliation (or the lack thereof) therefore almost inevitably becomes as matter of *deliberate* personal choice or "religious preference."[58] We shall return to this theme in Chapter 5.

The view of "religion" as a private, "individual elective" and "deeply held personal belief" has long since also come to dominate the "religion"-related discourse of supra-national institutions. Examples include the discourse of offices such as the UN Special Rapporteurs on the Freedom of Religion or Belief and declarations such as the European Convention of Human Rights,

44 *Three-level discursive approach*

the Arab Charter of Human Rights, and the ASEAN Declaration on Human Rights. Declarations and charters such as these have come to be based on what Helge Årsheim refers to a as "radical individualism in the legal concept of religion."[59] As he goes on to note, "Numerous states have incorporated provisions from these instruments more or less verbatim in their domestic legal frameworks, securing a wide-reaching and profound impact on the conceptualization and scope of the freedom of religion or belief on a global scale."[60] The net-effect of these developments has been the wide establishment of "belief" and "faith" as commonsense terms."[61] For as Arnal and McCutheon point out, in what reflects a Western understanding of the secular state where religion is largely confined to the private sphere, "Religion, precisely, is constructed as in scholarship and law as that which is *not* social, *not* coercive, *is* individual, *is* belief-oriented, and so on."[62]

In addition to the above, especially in Anglophone contexts, we can also observe an increasing tendency to employ the term "faith" to *stand in* for the term "religion."[63] Initially popularized through the Reformation emphasis on *sola fides* ("faith alone") as the "single most important element of [true Protestant] Christianity,"[64] "faith" has come to be commonly perceived to emanate from "inside" the individual, whereas "religion" has come to be understood as "an outward expression of individual, private faith."[65] The key point to note is that the terms "belief" and "faith" possess no analytical utility in and of themselves and therefore must not be employed in such ways. Rather, like the category of "religion," they constitute central objects of study.[66]

The discursive study of religion

Following Kocku von Stuckrad's initial invitation to a discourse-centered study of religion in an article for *Method & Theory in the Study of Religion* in 2003,[67] the past couple of decades have witnessed the gradual emergence of a body of scholarship grounded in "explicitly discursive" approaches that has become known as the "discursive study of religion" (DSR). DSR has therefore largely developed alongside the critical-religion approach as discussed above. To date, von Stuckrad remains DSR's single most prolific contributor, which is why his work deserves both special attention and scrutiny.

Through a series of contributions that in many respects both build on and align with the types of "not-explicitly-discursive" first-level work discussed above, von Stuckrad has forged an explicitly discursive agenda for the study of religion rooted in Foucauldian perspectives and meta-theoretical concerns.[68] With a discourse-focused research agenda for the study of religion, he wrote in 2003, "it will no longer be the 'truth' of our theories and descriptions that will be of primary interest but the conditions of their establishment."[69] A fundamental premise of DSR must therefore be to approach the category of "religion" as an empty signifier that has no intrinsic meaning in and of itself. Or as von Stuckrad puts it,

Three-level discursive approach 45

"*an integrative theory of religious studies* that no longer depends on any definition of religion, should take the form of a *theory of discourse.*"[70] Approaching "religion" from a discursive perspective therefore entails developing an understanding of the category of "religion" to which discourse, communication, and representation are intrinsic. For as von Stuckrad quite rightly observes, "there simply is no escaping the fact that the only thing that scholars of religion have as a basis for scrutiny is visible and *expressed* religion, i.e., religious propositions that are communicated in sentences, signs, and symbolic action."[71] As he is also careful to point out, this most certainly needs to apply to academic discourses on "religion" as well. For in the end, he notes, "there is no way of escaping the relativistic stance that leads to methodological dilemmas. But discursive study of religion provides an instrument for *coping* with it."[72]

In later work, von Stuckrad describes DSR as providing a "research perspective rather than a single method to study religion."[73] Echoing the arguments of the contributions discussed above, if and when we accept and adopt a discursive perspective, he writes, "It is no longer necessary – in fact, it would be counterproductive – to apply a generic definition of religion … As contributions to a discourse on religion, these definitions are *objects* of discursive analysis rather than its *tools.*"[74] Consequently, just like categories such as "science" or "the economy," the category of "religion" should be approached as "*the societal organization of knowledge about religion.*"[75] While von Stuckrad's arguments consistently reflect a Foucauldian approach and understanding of discourse, these are all solid and agreeable observations from a discourse analytic perspective focused on text and social analysis, as outlined in Chapter 2. Having said that, von Stuckrad's work has also been marked by a stubborn insistence on the supposed superiority of Foucauldian-historical perspectives on discourse as opposed to those more commonly adopted in text-focused approaches. This can, for example, be seen in the types of definitions he has offered for the concept of "discourse" itself. In his early work, he defined "discourse" as that which "conceptualizes representations of social positions that are negotiated among groups in a complex process of identity formation and demarcation" and hence as an "ideal type used to make visible continuities, adaptations, and transfers of meanings and positions in a setting of changing power relations."[76] Now, as I have commented previously, although this can be seen as a neat way of describing what discourse "does" from a Foucauldian perspective, it does not provide much in terms of an actual definition of "discourse" per se.[77] von Stuckrad has nevertheless continued to refine his understanding of the concept of discourse, and especially as part of his efforts to develop distinctively *historical* perspectives in DSR. In *The Scientification of Religion* he provides the following more detailed definition:

> Discourses are communicative structures that organize knowledge in a given community; they establish, stabilize, and legitimize systems

meaning and provide collectively shared orders of knowledge in an institutionalized social ensemble. Statements, utterances, and opinions about a specific topic, systematically organized and repeatedly observable, form a discourse.[78]

Although generally compatible with the more firmly language- and text-oriented definitions of discourse of Burr and Hall as cited in Chapter 2, this definition still remains primarily reflective of Foucauldian concerns, as can be seen, for example, in its foregrounding of the importance of *orders of knowledge*. On this basis, von Stuckrad then proceeds to explain that the main objective of a historical *analysis* of discourse is to address

the relationship among communicational practices and the (re)production of systems of meaning, or orders of knowledge, the social agents that are involved, the rules, resources, and material conditions that underlie these processes, as well as their impact on social collectives.[79]

The objective is therefore also to trace *"the development of discourses in changing sociopolitical and historical settings, this providing means to reconstruct the genealogy of discourse."*[80] Whereas von Stuckrad's definition of the concept of discourse, cited above, is reasonably clear, his explication of the analysis of discourse remains highly abstract and imprecise. And so, whereas he provides a reasonably clear outline of what a Foucauldian-historical approach and analysis would concentrate on or be "about," he provides little by means of explanation as to *how* such analyses should be carried out in actual practice. In light of this, it also becomes difficult to know what to make of it when he simultaneously also underscores the importance that "contributions to a discourse must be 'repeatedly observable'" as a "relevant detail" in his definition of discourse.[81] What is lacking, again, is a clearer explanation of exactly *how* discourses become "observable." Considering that von Stuckrad himself expressly posits that the "notion of discourse" itself "is of particular value if we are to establish a self-reflexive" and "serious referential framework for a (self-)critical study of religion,"[82] one would perhaps expect to find a more concrete explication of that very notion in his own work.

In addition to the above, von Stuckrad's advancement of a Foucauldian perspective has, at times, assumed an almost polemical tone. For example, in *The Scientification of Religion* he laments that "most contributions [in DSR] still base themselves on linguistic and textual analyses of discourse."[83] But as is also noted by Hjelm, the situation is rather the reverse, with most previous contributions having been grounded in Foucauldian rather than textual perspectives.[84] From the perspective advanced in this book, DSR would no doubt benefit from *more* textual studies and the development of more cohesive text-oriented analytical frameworks. Indeed,

Three-level discursive approach 47

this is precisely what this book aims to provide, albeit with a special eye towards the sociological study of religion. Although von Stuckrad is correct in pointing out that "We can understand the working of discursive structures only if we know their genealogy and formation," this, by and of itself, does not privilege historical over text-oriented approaches. As noted in Chapter 2, textual analyses can usefully include a historical variable and also pay attention to the ways in which discourses may become varyingly operationalized and tangibly materialized. The same also applies to von Stuckrad's admonition that the analysis of discourse should not be "limited to textual sources" (while the vast majority of his own sources are indeed textual).[85] For, as should be clear from our discussion of the concept of discourse and its analysis in Chapter 2, the analysis of text (i.e., lexis and grammar) only makes up one particular level of analysis in textual approaches. von Stuckrad's comments therefore not only reveal a weak appreciation of textual approaches but, it appears, a limited understanding of them as well. Foucauldian-historical and textual approaches are best conceived of as *complementary* approaches that make possible different types of analyses. But as the framework outlined in Chapter 2 demonstrates, it is equally possible to combine key elements of both. Having said that, it is nevertheless primarily through the analysis of texts (i.e., actual, concrete instances of discourse) that discourses become empirically observable and concretely analyzable in ways that remain accessible and open to scholarly scrutiny and alternative interpretations.

In addition to von Stuckrad's valuable and agenda-setting work, DSR has also come to encompass a much wider range of first-level work, although it is not possible to account for every individual contribution here. One particularly notable example is found in Adrian Hermann's work on the historical constitution of a "global discourse of religion."[86] As Hermann notes, and as also noted above, the Western understanding of "religion" has typically emphasized "plurality, as the distinction of one 'religion' from another, and differentiation, as the distinction of 'religion' from other social domains."[87] As part of these endeavors, the study of religion has historically also aimed to identify "equivalents" for Western concepts and conceptualizations of "religion" across various non-Western cultural contexts. Such attempts, however, have frequently become "caught up in a tautological paradox, first having to define a specific understanding of 'religion', and then searching for equivalents in ancient European or non-Western languages and cultures and subsequently claiming their existence (or non-existence)."[88] In order to be able to move beyond these difficulties, Hermann suggests that,

> instead of seeing the global spread of 'Western' understandings of 'religion' as a problem, the global establishment of equivalents of 'religion' in non-Western languages has to be understood as the *condition of possibility* for the emergence of a 'global discourse of religion.'[89]

48   Three-level discursive approach

Searches for "equivalents of religion" in non-Western languages therefore need to be reoriented "towards a historical investigation of the generation of such equivalents through processes of *translingual practice.*"[90]

As originally developed by Lydia Liu,[91] the concept of translingual practice focuses on "the production of equivalence in the context of historical processes of translation."[92] In order to avoid getting bogged down in ultimately unresolvable questions about the commensurability or incommensurability of different cultures and languages, or the existence or non-existence of trans-historical and trans-discursive connections in the "religious" field, the translingual-practice approach, Liu argues, redirects our focus at "the occurrences of historical contact, interaction, translation, and travel of words and ideas between languages."[93] In this approach, translatability

> refers to the historical making of hypothetical equivalence between languages ... [which] tend to be makeshift inventions in the beginning and become more or less fixed through repeated use or come to be supplanted by the preferred hypothetical equivalences of a later generation.[94]

Translation, therefore, does not occur "between equivalents; rather one creates tropes of equivalence in the middle zone of translation between the host and guest languages."[95] Rather than being a "neutral" endeavor, however, the process of translation constitutes a central site of ideological and political tension and struggle "until new meanings emerge in the host language itself."[96] These observations pertain directly to how we are to approach and understand the accelerating contemporary circulation, transmission, and "glocalization" of "religious" discourses and ideas. But they also pertain to the particular ways and manner in which the category of "religion" as such has become constructed throughout different parts of the world.

The construction of "religion," both historical and contemporary, in China provides a case in point. The Chinese term *zongjiao* gradually developed into a Chinese equivalent to "religion" as a result of "a variety of cross-cultural translations and processes of cultural adaptation between China, Japan, and the West" that unfolded throughout the nineteenth and early twentieth centuries.[97] Following its adoption by the Chinese state, *zongjiao* eventually came to replace the previously more widely used but more ambiguous term *jiao* and increasingly started to be used to designate a "separate" and "independent" sphere of culture and society. In what is further reflective of a strong Western influence, as part of this process, *zongjiao* also became more firmly differentiated from the term *mixin* ("superstition"). The *zongjiao/mixin* distinction subsequently developed into a central element in the construction of the category of "Chinese religion," thereby also serving as the principal basis for the Chinese state's initial official recognition of the five "religions" of Catholicism, Protestantism, Islam, Buddhism, and Daoism in the early twentieth century. The present-day Chinese religious landscape remains firmly regulated by the state. While atheism remains the official ideology of the Communist Party of China (CPC), the state still publicly recognizes and accepts the operation of the just mentioned five "religions."[98] Past decades have also witnessed a more general reappreciation and revitalization of traditional "native" Confucianism, and especially for the purposes of harnessing its capacity to inform and underpin a particular version of state-sponsored Chinese patriotism and nationalism.[99] As the example of "Chinese religion" illustrates, the "export" and "import" of Western understandings of "religion" into non-Western contexts have often resulted in the creation and institutionalization of new types of amalgamations between Western and non-Western concepts.

Several scholars have also constructed broader categorizations or typologies of major approaches and perspectives in DSR similar to the one provided here.[100] These are included in the first-level category since, as with the one provided here, they are at least partly concerned with constructing particular versions of DSR as a whole, what it "is," what it can or should be, and so on. Indeed, as Hjelm rightly points out, the construction of typologies and mappings of a field are "not an innocent exercise. It is also a practice of boundary-making and (de)legitimation."[101] Among the typologies offered to date, Hjelm's own "three-dimensional model" is of particular note. He describes it as being mainly designed to aid researchers in positioning their own respective approaches within what has developed into an increasingly diverse and fragmented field. With each dimension encompassing a spectrum or axis of perspectives, Hjelm's first "world in discourse – discourse in the world" dimension centers on *ontology* and differentiates between perspectives that put a stronger emphasis on the constitutive and reality-constructing power *of* discourse on the one hand ("world in discourse"), and perspectives that instead emphasize the "real-world" contextual determination of discourse on the other hand ("discourse in the world"). Analogous to the categorization provided here, Hjelm's second "metatheoretical-empirical" dimension focuses on *abstraction* and differentiates between perspectives oriented towards meta-theoretical reflection on the one hand ("meta-theoretical"), and more empirical analysis-oriented perspectives on the other hand ("empirical"). The defining feature of the third "analytical-critical" dimension is *power*. As Hjelm explains, "'analytical' on this axis refers to approaches that do not consider power a relevant component of analysis," whereas critical approaches aim to "show how 'language use contribute[s] to one-sided constructions of things or events that serve the interests of particular social groups.'"[102]

If we were to situate the approach of this book within Hjelm's three-dimensional model, it would lean more towards the "discourse in the world" end of the spectrum in the first dimension, be situated somewhere close to the middle of the meta-theoretical–empirical divide of the second dimension, and align more firmly with the "analytical" side in the third

50 *Three-level discursive approach*

dimension. The last principally because the issue, as I see it, is not *whether* approaches on the "analytical" end of Hjelm's "analytical–critical" axis would deem power a "relevant" category of analysis or not, but rather *how* relevant as opposed to other relevant categories of analysis in each individual case. This discussion, of course, also raises the question as to whether this book should be viewed as constituting a contribution to DSR. To the extent that the label is taken to refer to research that consciously and systematically employs discourse-theoretical and methodological perspectives for the purposes of inquiring into the constructed nature of the category of "religion" and analyzing the multitude of ways in which "religion" and "the religious" are continuously constructed across different social and cultural institutional fields (scholarship included), the answer to that question is yes. But to the extent that the label is taken to refer to some parochial understanding of DSR or perhaps even some particular understanding of "discourse," the answer has to be no.

Since the ambition of DSR has never been to develop any distinctively "new" theorizations of the concept of discourse as such, but rather to explicate the implications of already existing theorizations for the study of religion and its various sub-disciplines specifically, it perhaps comes as no surprise that DSR, too, has been highly uneven when it comes to the specificity, consistency, and rigor by which individual studies have engaged with the concept of "discourse."[103] A firmer engagement with the concept of "discourse" should nevertheless be expected from work that explicitly describes itself as "discursive." Future work in the field could also usefully elaborate further on a set of issues that pertain to the employment of discourse theory and analysis in the study of religion specifically. Pertinent questions to that effect would include: Which *particular* theorizations of the concept of discourse would appear to be particularly applicable in the study of religion and why? How do different understandings of the concept of discourse affect the ways in which "religion" is viewed as a discursively constructed category? How do various theorizations of discourse relate to or connect with other theoretical perspectives on the nature of religious language? Engaging with questions such as these would no doubt enhance the ability of first-level work to provide solid bases for second- and third-level work.

The sociology of religion

Although explicitly discursive perspectives have so far only been adopted by a handful of scholars in the sociological study of religion,[104] the sub-discipline has not been completely devoid of constructionist and more generally language-focused contributions. For example, following the wide establishment of social constructionist and discourse analytic approaches throughout the humanities and social sciences more generally, they have

Three-level discursive approach 51

also become fairly widely employed among sociologists of religion. One notable example is found in James Beckford's *Social Theory and Religion*, which argues for the adoption of a "moderate" social constructionist approach as a general lens through which "to analyse the processes whereby the meaning of the category of religion is, in various situations, intuited, asserted, doubted, challenged, rejected, substituted, re-cast, and so on."[105] Mirroring the main arguments of the first-level contributions discussed above, Beckford is also careful to point out that "religion" "does not 'do' anything by itself" and that it has no agency of "its own."[106] As a further reflection of our discussion above of how the category of "religion" has come to be understood to possess its own independent "existence" and "reality" throughout contemporary society and culture on the whole, he also makes the important observation that "The sedimented meanings associated with religion in the course of social life constitute authoritative guides not only to usage of the term but also to social action" and that the "category of 'religion' is an abstraction from, or distillation of, these meanings and actions."[107] Hence, he concludes, "social scientific analysis cannot safely go beyond the investigation of the uses to which notions of religion are put in social life."[108] However, in spite of his constructionist approach, Beckford hardly ever mentions, let alone provides any discussion of, the concept of discourse. Nor does he provide any account of exactly *how* "sedimented meanings associated with religion" or "notions of religion ... in social life" are to be empirically identified and analyzed. But with this no small exception, Beckford's approach is otherwise fully compatible with a discursive sociology of religion as envisioned here.

Another notable example of work in the sociology of religion that foregrounds the constitutive and constructive function of language is found in Peter Beyer's *Religion in Global Society*.[109] Grounding his argument in the systems theory of Niklas Luhmann – which itself conceives of the social world as constituted through communication – Beyer starts with the assumption that "to the degree that religion is a social phenomenon, it will construct itself as communication and not as something else like experience or consciousness, let alone mystical insight."[110] To make this argument, moreover, is not to provide a definition for "religion," but merely to "set the parameters of observation in which the conceptualization of religion will take place."[111] This is because "what counts as specifically religious communication will depend on its thematization as something called religion, usually in implicit or explicit contrast to communication that is not religion."[112] Although grounded in a particular understanding of communication, Beyer's argument closely connects to Hermann's argument on the emergence of a "global discourse on religion" as discussed above. To simplify, "religion" emerges as a global "social fact" through the establishment of a global system of communication on "religion" and the "religious." When investigating the various ways in which "religion" becomes constructed and understood

52 Three-level discursive approach

in different social and cultural contexts, sociologists of religion should therefore consider the degrees to which such constructions and understandings align with, as well as become affected by, already established systems of communication on "religion" and the "religious." The crucial point, however, is that "religion" will remain a meaningful category for people as long as communication about "religion" continues. The particular versions of "religion" that are constructed through such communication systems should therefore be our primary concern, although we always also need to consider how these systems of communication have evolved over time.

A final example of first-level work in the sociology of religion can be found in the work of Hjelm. While his work has often traversed the lines of all three levels, he has also outlined what he terms a "critical sociology of religion" in which discourse theory occupies a central position.[113] Basically, Hjelm argues for the establishment of a sociological study of religion that recognizes the work that discourse performs in the creation of "hegemonic understandings of 'religion' in everyday (mediated) social interaction" on the one hand, and that also a provides "a framework through which to analyse the discursive construction, reproduction and transformation of inequality in the field of religion" on the other hand.[114] While the former has already been discussed in ample detail, the latter is unique to Hjelm's approach and efforts towards establishing CDA in the study of religion more generally. Grounded in Marxist perspectives on the inextricable connection between political-economic power and structural inequality, Hjelm envisions a sociology of religion that would pay closer attention to the ways in which prevailing ideologies and relations of power work to significantly shape the ways in which certain understandings of "religion" are constructed as more "legitimate" than others. Although this is a simplification of Hjelm's argument, for present purposes, suffice it to say that it draws our attention to the principal *reasons* why certain conceptions of "religion" come to dominate how "proper religion" is conceived and understood in particular social and cultural contexts as opposed to others.

The critical appraisal of previous first-level work (both not explicitly and explicitly discursive) provided above illustrates the breadth and scope of the contributions already made. More importantly, it also serves to draw our attention to a set of ongoing and partly unresolved debates on issues of fundamental importance for the discipline of the study of religion as a whole. Although the individual contributions surveyed above differ somewhat in their respective main focuses and emphases, and although they might not be in perfect agreement with one another, they all share a set of core premises and insights with which any discursive sociology of religion needs to concur. A discursive sociology of religion therefore needs to remain acutely aware of the historical constitution of the Western category of "religion," its serious limitations as an analytical category, and its dialectical relationship to categories such as the "secular." Such an awareness should, more generally, inform all individual research endeavors in the sub-field.

Three-level discursive approach 53

Second-level work and analysis: discourse and scholarly theorizing within particular sub-fields in the study of religion

In contrast to first-level work and analyses, second-level work and analyses unfold in relation to specific sub-fields in the study of religion. In terms of *type of work*, this category includes studies that utilize discursive or more broadly constructionist perspectives for the purposes of highlighting the character of sub-field-specific scholarly theorizing, its tacit assumptions, and problematic aspects and flaws. In terms of *type of analysis*, second-level approaches take a step further from pure meta-theoretical reflection and aim to provide more contextualized accounts of the application of discursive perspectives in the context of sub-field-specific explorations. As such, as in first-level work and analysis, the "data" for second-level work mainly comprise scholarly discourse itself. Second-level approaches are thus interested in critically examining the broader discursive underpinnings of particular theoretical perspectives in various sub-fields in the study of religion in light of questions such as the following: When did a particular theoretical perspective in a given sub-field in the study of religion initially emerge and what other discourses were prevalent at the time? In which ways did/ does the perspective align with broader prevalent discursive formations? What was the perspective originally intended to explain or sensitize scholars to? What were the more specific scholarly institutional and disciplinary contexts within which the perspective initially developed, evolved, and crystalized? Has the application of the perspective expanded beyond its original disciplinary context and, if so, in which particular ways and directions? Second-level work and analysis therefore constitutes a crucial "way station" between first-level meta-theoretical reflection and third-level analyses. The precise boundary between first and second level work can, however, at times be rather fleeting. For example, to the extent that first-level work critically engages with the employment or theorization of categories such as "religion," the "secular," or "belief" within particular sub-fields in the study of religion, they could be said to engage in second-level reflection as well. But compared to the wide proliferation of different types of first-level work, thus far, second-level explorations have nonetheless been remarkably scarce.

One example of second-level work can be found in James Spickard's work on main narratives in sociological macro-level theorizing on the current and future societal significance and location of "religion."[115] When surveying sociological macro-level theorizing from around the 1980s up to the first years of the 2000s, Spickard argues that one can discern and identify at least six competing narratives on the future fate of "religion" in the modern world: (1) secularization, (2) the rise of religious fundamentalism, (3) religious reorganization, (4) religious individualization, (5) rational choice and religious markets, and (6) religion and globalization.

54 Three-level discursive approach

Although Spickard himself does not conduct any actual analyses of discourse he nevertheless proposes that the three-dimensional CDA of Fairclough could provide a useful basis to conduct actual analyses of scholarly discourse on the current and future fate of religion in the modern world. Such an analysis would, first, need to examine the structure and rhetorical appeal of such scholarly discourse(s). Second, it would then proceed by looking closely at the specific contexts in which such discourse is produced, circulated, and consumed. And, third, it would connect such discourse(s) to broader discourses prevalent within the wider academic community, as well as within wider society and culture on the whole, at a particular point in history.

Take, for example, the discourse on secularization. The sociological study of religion has increasingly come to recognize how the notion of secularization initially emerged as part of a broader set of post-enlightenment hegemonic discourses on rationality, reason, and scientific progress – all of which had an in-built markedly "secular" bias (as did the entire discipline of sociology itself).[116] Indeed, when the discourse on secularization is properly historicized, it becomes difficult to maintain that the secularization paradigm ever constituted an "objective" or "impartial" explanation of the future fate of religion in the Western world.[117] Rather than simply having provided unbiased explanations of "objective" and readily "observable" realities, the more specific secularization theories that emanated from the broader discursive formation on secularization always served to partly also create the very same "realities" that they purported to simply describe and explain. According to Grace Davie "a crucial part of the evolution" of the discipline of the sociology of religion itself lies "in its capacity to discern the implications of these beginnings for the formation of sociological thinking and to escape from them when necessary."[118] But the crumbling of the hegemony of the types of post-enlightenment discourses that long served to underpin the very idea of secularization has not only necessitated a range of considerable revisions to the general notion of secularization but also propelled the emergence and establishment of a range of alternative perspectives – a range of competing discourses – on the present-day and future societal significance and location of "religion." Building on Spickard's argument, the main point to note from a second-level perspective is therefore that each and every one of these alternative discourses will, to a lesser or greater extent, *also* serve to create the new "realities" that they each, in their turn, purport to describe or explain. As alternative sociological discourses on "deprivatization," "desecularization," "resacralization," "subjectivization," and the "post-secular" become more firmly established within the sociological study of religion on the whole, so do individual scholars also become ever more willing, inclined, and perhaps even expected to, more actively tap into and support one or more of these particular discourses. And it is worth noting that supporting one discourse often entails – and indeed sometimes requires – challenging another. Although

Three-level discursive approach 55

sociologists of religion have become both increasingly aware of and willing to openly debate issues of this kind, they rarely seem prepared to come full circle when it comes to openly and expressly recognizing how new ways of conceptualizing or reconceptualizing sociological theorizing or the supposed "reality on the ground" will always contribute to the production of new "realities" to be observed and analyzed.

As new discourses on the makeup or character of the present-day "religious" field gain more traction, soon enough, new research projects will be set up on the basis on these new discourses, the results of which will then be presented at academic conferences as well as in research articles and books. The new perspectives thus generated and communicated are likely to spur on at least some degree of wider debate and be met with either more or less enthusiasm or criticism. In the usual trajectory (that normally spans several years or more), a particular new discourse will first be "introduced," then "criticized," then "critically appraised," then "rethought," reframed," or "reconsidered," and then finally "revisited" (or in some cases even declared "dead," as one US scholar did with respect to secularization theory). The academic publishing industry and conference circuit will be deeply implicated in each and every step along this way. If a new scholarly discourse manages to pass through this process, it will have become established to such an extent that it can no longer simply be ignored, irrespective of any amount of lingering criticism against it. At this point, this new discourse will have become part of a wider scholarly discursive formation on what can *meaningfully be said* about the character of "religion" and "religious" life in the contemporary world. The central question is: to what extent should new discourses be seen to emanate from observations of actual changes "on the ground," and to what extent should they be seen to participate in the very production of these supposed changes? There is, of course, no definitive answer to this question. Trying to answer it would, however, be beside the point. The point is that we need to remain constantly aware of how our discourses and discursive practices work to shape our conceptions of the "real." A discursive sociology of religion therefore needs to keep at least one of its critical and investigate eyes focused firmly on *itself*.

Particular sociological macro-level discourses on the present-day and future societal significance and location of religion aim to provide scholars with broad interpretative frameworks to formulate research agendas and interpret various types of data within. It may therefore be especially pressing to critically examine and assess the tacit assumptions of such theorizing for the simple reason that it tends to have particularly significant spill-over effects across many other sub-fields in the study of religion. Indeed, it is highly likely that any given study that focuses on some given specific aspect or facet of contemporary religious life at some point, in some way or other, will need to ground its arguments in one or several theoretical discourses on the place of religion in the contemporary world. Second-level reflection

56 *Three-level discursive approach*

therefore alerts us to how choosing which theoretical discourse or set of discourses to ground a particular study in is no neutral endeavor.

The above discussion can also be directly related to Mitsutoshi Horii's critical second-level assessment of how sociologists of religion have responded to critical religion scholarship and its implications for how the category of "religion" needs to be approached and understood.[119] While some sociologists of religion have brushed off these implications (and sometimes failed to even recognize them at all), others have been decidedly more accommodating. But, argues Horii, even those sociologists of religion who take these implications to heart nevertheless tend to continue to employ the category of "religion" as a generic term as soon as their discussion of the constructed character of the category of "religion" has been concluded. In this, Horii points to a common enough phenomenon: a widespread failure to differentiate consistently between "religion" as a descriptive and as an analytical category.

Another related example of second-level work of this type is Martin's *Capitalizing Religion*,[120] which focuses on critiquing previous scholarship on "spirituality" for its (alleged) uncritical acceptance of prevalent contemporary discourses on individual religion. To some extent, Martin's study straddles the boundary between first- and second-level work and analysis. It is included in the second-level category here because of its strong engagement with a certain type of scholarly discourse itself. In particular, Martin faults previous scholarship on individualized or "subjectivized" spirituality for its failure to recognize the many ways in which prevalent discourses on "spirituality" serve to "naturalize the emic vocabularies and discourses of capitalism" and its *homo oeconomicus* view of the individual.[121] At issue, then, is how culturally salient capitalism-supporting discourses on the virtues of personal choice, autonomy, and constant self-enhancement have increasingly become cloaked in a language of "spirituality." By uncritically adopting these *emic* discourses and integrating them as part of *etic* scholarly vocabulary on contemporary spirituality, Martin argues, scholars of religion have (perhaps largely inadvertently as a result of their inattentiveness) contributed to their further naturalization and indeed reification. We will revisit Martin's arguments in Chapter 5.

As illustrated through these examples, in contrast to first-level work, second-level work that reflects on the character and merits of different types of sub-field-specific theorizing also highlights how theoretical debates have practical consequences. Among other things, they serve to highlight how sub-field-specific theorizing works to affect and shape how particular pieces of research come to be designed and set up in the first place, in what light the data gathered for them come to be interpreted, how these pieces of research themselves are eventually situated in relation to other research on similar topics and so on. More second-level assessments of the type discussed above would be highly welcome since they would not only provide further material for meta-theoretical reflection but also surely provoke

Three-level discursive approach 57

further much-needed contextualized discussion on the actual application and implementation of key terms and categories across different sub-fields in the study of religion. The main point to note is that *multiple* second-level approaches are needed for the development of adequately grounded third-level approaches.

Third-level work and analysis: applying discourse analysis as method

In contrast to both first- and second-level work and analyses, the third-level category comprises studies that, in some form or other, utilize discourse analysis as a method in the analyses of various types of empirical data. This category of studies has expanded considerably in recent years, probably at least partly as a consequence of the constantly growing interest in discursive perspectives among scholars of religion more generally. But it also needs to be noted that previous studies in this category have differed hugely with regards to how they have carried out their analyses in actual practice. While some have been conducted on the basis of clearly explicated understandings of the concept of discourse and unfolded in close connection with previously established discourse analytical frameworks, others have been decidedly more *ad hoc* in nearly every respect. Since the types of analyses performed at this level have already been accounted for in Chapter 2, we shall only focus on some general points here.

We can start by noting that third-level approaches have now come to be employed in research on a range of different topics. Examples include, but are far from limited to, Noel Heather's theologically grounded examination of manifestations of power in religious (mainly Christian) language;[122] Kennet Granholm's study of the discursive components of contemporary esoteric magic;[123] Robin Wooffitt's study of the language of mediums and psychics;[124] Teemu Taira's work on how "religion" can take on the function of a "discursive technique" and become variously employed by different parties and stakeholders in cases when social tensions and conflicts arise over what may pass as "religion" or "religious" in a given social context;[125] Frans Wijsen's studies of discourse on Muslim extremism in Tanzania and Indonesia[126] and Dutch public and political discourse on Islam;[127] Årsheim's study of discursive constructions of "religion" in the work of UN Special Rapporteurs on the Freedom of Religion or Belief;[128] Hjelm's studies of the construction of the notion of "folk church" in the context of Finnish church–state relations[129] and the construction of the category of "religion" in the context of Finnish parliamentary debates on religious equality and freedom;[130] and my own previous studies of the increasingly marketized discourse of contemporary religious organizations (also the topic of Chapter 6).[131] Third-level work has thus been conducted on a wide range of different topics and types of data. In large part, previous work in this category has focused on questions such as the following: What is, and

58 Three-level discursive approach

what can meaningfully be said about "religion" in a particular social context and by whom? What "normally" counts as "religion" in such contexts and who gets to decide? Who is talking about "religion" in a particular social context in the first place and what are they saying? Whose voices on "religion" appear to be the most authoritative and whose appear to be more alternative or marginal?

As noted in Chapter 2, when discourse analysis is applied as a method in the study of religion, it most often tends to be employed in combination with other disciplinary and theoretical perspectives. In other words, a study that utilizes discourse analysis as a method will typically do so in light of a range of other sub-field-specific theoretical perspectives and these will, in most cases, play a central role in determining the main aim and focus of a study, what counts as data in the first place, and how those data are analyzed and interpreted. Given the theory-driven nature of discourse analysis more generally, one therefore needs to remain aware of the importance of second-level reflection and to recognize how the adoption of any sub-field-specific theoretical perspectives will serve to determine the aim of a given study and its choice of data in important ways. It should also be noted that identifying objects of research (i.e., specific empirical instances of discourse) and engaging in actual discourse analysis obviously needs to be done on the basis of an adequate and clearly explicated understanding of the concept of discourse itself. Equally important, third-level studies also need to be based on adequate and sufficiently critical understandings of key terms and categories, which is why they need to engage first-level meta-theoretical reflection as well. The main objective, again, is to maintain *reflexive awareness* of one's own embeddedness in particular scholarly disciplinary contexts and their associated epistemic cultures and types of established factual discourse.[132] Third-level work therefore, at least to some degree, needs engage in *both* first- and second-level reflection and analysis.

In addition to the above, third-level work also needs to grapple with the concrete challenges and realities of empirical research. After all, this type of work explores the actual ways in which for example the category of "religion" or the "secular" is constructed across different social and cultural contexts by living persons. In addition to analyzing already available types of data such as official documents or newspaper articles, third-level work also actively participates in generating new types of data by utilizing methods such as interviews. What people say in interviews, however, will never simply reflect their "inner states" in straightforward ways. Rather, interview situations (a particular genre of discourse) need to be recognized as particular types of interactional contexts that often encourage and actualize certain types of discourse use and discursive practices. Interview situations, therefore, do not produce "naturally occurring" discourse. When interviewing people affiliated (and who expressly affiliate themselves) with some particular religious group or type of religiosity, researchers also need to acquaint themselves thoroughly with the particular types of religious-language use, discursive practices, and discursive complexes prevalent within that particular religious context.

More generally, as discussed in more detail in Chapter 2, discourse analysis can be described in terms of an approach that, so to speak, aims to play with "open cards" and to keep the entire research process as transparent as possible. When new bodies of data are generated by means of interviews, analyses will then typically unfold on the basis of the recorded and transcribed talk of informants. As Jonathan Potter points out, the process of transcription should therefore itself be understood as an important "research preliminary."[133] Although the style and detail of transcription will depend on the aims of a given study and the particular type of discourse analysis used, the actual transcription process should be regarded as part of the analysis itself rather than some separate stage that precedes it.[134] It is also important to keep in mind that a verbatim transcription of an interview will always itself constitute a certain kind of construction that will never reflect recorded talk in straightforward ways.[135] Nonetheless, as Potter points out: "If we have a transcribed record of discourse, rather than a set of formulations in note form, it places the reader of the research in a much stronger position to evaluate the claims and interpretations."[136]

It is also worth noting that interview data sometimes can end up having a strong impact on broader scholarly debates. For example, when Robert Bellah and colleagues interviewed the nurse Sheila Larson in the early 1980s and she described her own "personal religion" as "Sheilaism," this quickly developed into a leitmotif of contemporaneous debates on individualized religion.[137] Although this was most probably not Bellah et al.'s intention, had Sheila not been interviewed, her particular brand of "personal religion" would obviously not have become the subject of a broader scholarly debate that transformed the most emic of terms into an etic category. It is worth stressing, therefore, that scholars need to remain constantly aware of the active role that they themselves play in their own generation of new ethnographic data and the multifaceted relationship that will always inevitably exist between researcher and "researched." Data gathered by means of in-depth interviews, which are then transcribed, assembled, analyzed, and eventually interpreted and explained, should therefore be regarded as something that researchers and informants, to a very significant degree, have constructed together.

Lastly, third-level work often engages in several types of analyses that extend beyond analyses of discourse alone. Apart from analyses of discourse in text, such work may, for example, also direct particular attention to specific instances of the operationalization of discourses. Such analyses can obviously unfold in relation to any number of more specific cases. For example, a study might explore the ways in which certain discourses become tangibly materialized in certain types of organizational structures, how certain discourses find expression in the organization of particular spaces, or how certain discourses become inculcated and enacted as part of certain identities and ways of being.

Concluding remarks

This chapter has provided a general overview of the field of religion and discourse research. The categorization of the field into first-, second-, and third-level types or work and analyses is primarily made for heuristic purposes. As noted, these categories should not be understood in terms of watertight containers that can be neatly differentiated from one another. Quite the contrary, they should be understood as closely interrelated and frequently overlapping *complementary* categories. Indeed, there are many examples of studies that transcend the lines between all three of them. That, moreover, is precisely what a discursive sociology of religion would need to do. Third-level work that employs discourse analysis as a method in actual empirical research needs to be based on an adequate understanding of the key terms and concepts that it operates with (first-level) *as well as* the character and tacit assumptions of the particular sub-field-specific theoretical perspectives and conceptual frameworks that it engages with (second-level). This holistic approach will be illustrated in the thematic chapters that follow. Our exploration of each theme will start by meta-theoretical reflection on key categories, terms, and concepts, followed by critical assessments of the character of sociological theorizing within these particular areas, followed by empirical analyses of actual instances of discourse, scholarly discourse included.

Notes

1 Moberg, "First-, Second- and Third."
2 Brad Stoddard and Craig Martin, "Introduction," in *Stereotyping Religion: Critiquing Clichés*, eds. Brad Stoddard and Craig Martin (London: Bloomsbury Academic, 2017), 3–4.
3 Ibid., 4.
4 Jonathan Z. Smith, *Map Is Not Territory: Studies in the History of Religions* (Leiden: Brill, 1978), 290.
5 Jonathan Z. Smith, *Imagining Religion: From Babylon to Jonestown* (Chicago, IL: The University of Chicago Press, 1982), xi.
6 Russell T. McCutcheon, *Manufacturing Religion: The Discourse on Sui Generis Religion and the Politics of Nostalgia* (Oxford: Oxford University Press, 1997).
7 Ibid., 129.
8 Thomas E. Lawson and Robert N. McCauley, cited in McCutcheon, *Manufacturing Religion*, 205.
9 Murphy, "Discourse," 405.
10 Engler, "Constructionism," 299.
11 Tomoko Masuzawa, *The Invention of World Religions: On How European Universalism Was Preserved in the Language of Pluralism* (Chicago, IL: Chicago University Press, 2005).
12 On the impact of the "world-religions paradigm" on university religious studies curricula, see Teemu Taira, "Making Space for Discursive Study in Religious Studies," *Religion* 43, no. 1 (2013): 27–46.
13 Masuzawa, *The Invention*, 20.
14 Ibid., 282.

Three-level discursive approach 61

15 David Chidester, *Savage Systems: Colonialism and Comparative Religion in Southern Africa* (Charlottesville: University of Virginia Press, 1996).
16 David Chidester, *Empire of Religion: Imperialism and Comparative Religion* (Chicago, IL: University of Chicago Press, 2014).
17 Talal Asad, *Genealogies of Religion: Discipline and Reasons of Power in Christianity and Islam* (Baltimore, MD: The Johns Hopkins University Press, 1993).
18 Talal Asad, *Formations of the Secular: Christianity, Islam, Modernity* (Redwood City, CA: Stanford University Press, 2003).
19 Ibid., 22.
20 Timothy Fitzgerald, *The Ideology of Religious Studies* (Oxford: Oxford University Press, 2000).
21 Timothy Fitzgerald, *Discourse on Civility and Barbarity: A Critical Theory of Religion and Related Categories* (Oxford: Oxford University Press, 2007).
22 Timothy Fitzgerald, *Religion and Politics in International Relations: The Modern Myth* (London: Continuum, 2011).
23 Fitzgerald, *Discourse on Civility*, 7.
24 Ibid., 5.
25 Ibid., 9–10.
26 Fitzgerald, *Religion and Politics*, 3.
27 Lincoln, *Gods and Demons*, 1.
28 Ibid.
29 Lincoln, *Holy Terrors*.
30 Ibid., 6.
31 Ibid.
32 Ibid.
33 Ibid., 7.
34 James M.M. Good and Richard H. Roberts, "Introduction: Persuasive Discourse In and Between Disciplines in the Human Sciences," in *The Recovery of Rhetoric: Persuasive Discourse and Disciplinarity in the Human Sciences* (Charlottesville: University Press of Virginia, 1993), 1.
35 Cf. Michael Cahn, "The Rhetoric of Rhetoric: Six Tropes of Disciplinary Self-Constitution," in *The Recovery of Rhetoric: Persuasive Discourse and Disciplinarity in the Human Sciences* (Charlottesville: University Press of Virginia, 1993).
36 Arnal and McCutcheon, *The Sacred*.
37 Ibid., 14–15.
38 Ibid., 15.
39 Ibid., 18.
40 Ibid., 96.
41 Ibid., 97.
42 Ibid., 27.
43 Ibid., 28.
44 Cf. Teemu Taira, "Discourse on 'Religion' in Organizing Social Practices: Theoretical and Practical Considerations," in *Making Religion: Theory and Practice in the Discursive Study of Religion*, eds. Kocku von Stuckrad and Frans Wijsen (Leiden: Brill, 2016), 125.
45 Helge Årsheim, "Whose Religion, What Freedom? Discursive Constructions of Religion in the Work of UN Special Rapporteurs on the Freedom of Religion or Belief," in *Making Religion: Theory and Practice in the Discursive Study of Religion*, eds. Kocku von Stuckrad and Frans Wijsen (Leiden: Brill, 2016), 296.
46 Peter Beyer, *Religions in Global Society* (Oxon: Routledge, 2006), 6.

62 *Three-level discursive approach*

47 Ibid.
48 Émile Durkheim, cited in Manuel A. Vásquez, "Grappling with the Legacy of Modernity: Implications for the Sociology of Religion," in *Religion on the Edge: De-centering and Re-centering the Sociology of Religion*, eds. Courtney Bender, Wendy Cadge, Peggy Levitt, and David Smilde (Oxford: Oxford University Press, 2012), 24.
49 Lincoln, *Gods and Demons*, 2.
50 Adrian Hermann, "Distinctions of Religion: The Search for Equivalents of 'Religion' and the Challenge of Theorizing a 'Global Discourse of Religion'," in *Making Religion: Theory and Practice in the Discursive Study of Religion*, eds. Frans Wijsen and Kocku von Stuckrad (Leiden: Brill, 2016).
51 Cf. Fitzgerald, *Religion and Politics*, 2.
52 William Isaac Thomas and Dorothy Swaine Thomas, *The Child in America: Behavior Problems and Programs* (New York: Knopf, 1928).
53 Robyn Faith Walsh, "Religion Is a Private Matter," in *Stereotyping Religion: Critiquing Clichés*, eds. Brad Stoddard and Craig Martin (London: Bloomsbury Academic, 2017), 78.
54 James Dennis LoRusso, "Everyone Has a Faith," in *Stereotyping Religion: Critiquing Clichés*, eds. Brad Stoddard and Craig Martin (London: Bloomsbury Academic, 2017), 136–9.
55 Sean McCloud, "Religions Are Belief Systems," in *Stereotyping Religion: Critiquing Clichés*, eds. Brad Stoddard and Craig Martin (London: Bloomsbury Academic, 2017), 11–2.
56 Ibid., 14–5.
57 Steven W. Ramey, "Religions Are Mutually Exclusive," in *Stereotyping Religion: Critiquing Clichés*, eds. Brad Stoddard and Craig Martin (London: Bloomsbury Academic, 2017), 90; 94–5.
58 Peter Beyer, "Religion and Global Civil Society" in *Religion in Global Civil Society*, eds. Mark Juergensmeyer (Oxford: Oxford University Press, 2006), 15.
59 Årsheim, "Whose Religion," 296; see also Hans G. Kippenberg, "Dynamics of the Human Rights Discourse on Freedom of Religion – Observed from the Religious Studies Angle, in *Discourse Research and Religion: Disciplinary Use and Interdisciplinary Dialogues*, eds. Jay Johnston and Kocku von Stuckrad (Berlin: De Gruyter, 2021).
60 Ibid.
61 LoRusso, "Everyone Has a Faith," 133.
62 Arnal and McCutcheon, *The Sacred*, 28.
63 LoRusso, "Everyone Has a Faith," 133.
64 Ibid., 136.
65 Ibid., 134.
66 Arnal and McCutcheon, *The Sacred*, 13.
67 Kocku von Stuckrad, "Discursive Study of Religion: From States of the Mind to Communication and Action," *Method & Theory in the Study of Religion* 15, no. 3 (2003): 255–71.
68 For example, Kocku von Stuckrad, "Reflections on the Limits of Reflection: An Invitation to the Discursive Study of Religion," *Method & Theory in the Study of Religion* 22, no. 2–3 (2010); *Locations of Knowledge in Medieval and Early Modern Europe: Esoteric Discourse and Western Identities* (Leiden: Brill, 2010); "Discursive Study of Religion: Approaches, Definitions, Implications," *Method & Theory in the Study of Religion* 25, no 1 (2013); "Secular Religion: A Discourse-historical Approach to Religion in Contemporary Western Europe," *Journal of Contemporary Religion* 28, no. 1 (2013).
69 von Stuckrad, "Discursive Study of Religion: From States," 258.
70 Ibid., 263.

Three-level discursive approach 63

71 Ibid.
72 Ibid., 268.
73 Kocku von Stuckrad, *The Scientification of Religion: An Historical Study Discursive Change, 1800—2000* (Boston, MA: de Gruyter, 2015), 3.
74 Ibid., 13.
75 Ibid.,14.
76 von Stuckrad, "Discursive Study of Religion: From States," 266.
77 Moberg, "First-, Second-, and Third" 15.
78 von Stuckrad, *The Scientification*, 11.
79 Ibid.
80 Ibid.
81 Ibid., 16.
82 Ibid., 2.
83 Ibid.
84 Hjelm, "Mapping the Discursive," 1009.
85 von Stuckrad, *The Scientification*, 17.
86 Hermann, "Distinctions of Religion."
87 Ibid., 110.
88 Ibid., 101.
89 Ibid., 103.
90 Ibid.
91 Lydia H. Liu, *Translingual Practice: Literature, National Culture, and Translated Modernity; China, 1900–1937* (Stanford, CA: Stanford University Press, 1995).
92 Hermann, "Distinctions of Religion," 104.
93 Liu, *Translingual Practice*, 105.
94 Ibid.
95 Ibid.
96 Ibid.
97 Hermann, "Distinctions of Religion," 112.
98 L. Luke Chao and Fengang Yang, "Measuring Religiosity in a Religiously Diverse Society: The China Case," *Social Science Research* 74 (2018): 188.
99 Fengang Yang, "The Red, Black, and Gray Markets of Religion in China," *The Sociological Quarterly* 47, no. 1 (2006): 101; Anna Xiao Dong Sun, *Confucianism as a World Religion: Contested Histories and Contemporary Realities* (Princeton, NJ and Oxford: Princeton University Press, 2013), 172.
100 For example, Moberg, "First-, Second-, and Third;" Taira, "Making Space;" Hjelm, "Discourse Analysis."
101 Hjelm, "Mapping the Discursive," 1009.
102 Ibid., 1017.
103 Cf. ibid., 1006.
104 For example, Titus Hjelm, "One Volk, One Church? A Critique of the "Folk Church" Ideology in Finland," *Journal of Church and State* 62, no. 2 (2019); "National Piety: Religious Equality, Freedom of Religion and National Identity in Finnish Political Discourse," *Religion* 44, no. 1 (2014); "Religion, Discourse and Power: A Contribution Towards a Critical Sociology of Religion," *Critical Sociology* 40, no. 6 (2013); Moberg, *Church, Market*; Christopher R. Cotter, *The Critical Study of Non-Religion: Discourse, Identification and Locality* (London: Bloomsbury Academic, 2020).
105 James A. Beckford, *Social Theory & Religion* (Cambridge: Cambridge University Press, 2003), 3.
106 Ibid., 4.
107 Ibid.
108 Ibid., 17–8.
109 Peter Beyer, *Religions in Global Society* (Oxon: Routledge, 2006).

64 Three-level discursive approach

110 Ibid., 10.
111 Ibid.
112 Ibid.
113 Hjelm, "Religion, Discourse and Power."
114 Ibid., 856.
115 James V. Spickard, "Narrative versus Theory in the Sociology of Religion: Five Stories of Religion's Place in the Late Modern World," in *Therorising Religion: Classical and Contemporary Debates*, eds. James A. Beckford and John Walliss (Hampshire: Ashgate, 2006); "What Is Happening to Religion? Six Sociological Narratives," *Nordic Journal of Religion and Society* 19, no. 1 (2006).
116 Grace Davie, "Resacralization," in *The New Blackwell Companion to the Sociology of Religion*, ed. Bryan S. Turner (Chichester: Blackwell, 2010), 163.
117 For example, Philip S. Gorski, "Historicizing the Secularization Debate: An Agenda for Research," in *Handbook of the Sociology of Religion*, ed. Michele Dillon (Cambridge: Cambridge University Press, 2003); Judith Fox, "Secularization," in *The Routledge Companion to the Study of Religion*, ed. John R. Hinnells (Oxon: Routledge, 2005).
118 Davie, "Resacralization," 162–3.
119 Mitsutoshi Horii, "Critical Reflections on the Category of 'Religion' in Contemporary Sociological Discourse," *Nordic Journal of Religion and Society* 28, no. 1 (2015).
120 Craig Martin, *Capitalizing Religion: Ideology and the Opiate of the Bourgeoisie* (London: Bloomsbury Academic, 2014).
121 Ibid., 5.
122 Noel Heather, *Religious Language and Critical Discourse Analysis: Ideology and Identity in Christian Discourse Today* (Oxford: Peter Lang, 2000).
123 Kennet Granholm, *Dark Enlightenment: The Historical, Sociological, and Discursive Contexts of Contemporary Esoteric Magic* (Leiden: Brill, 2014).
124 Robin Wooffitt, *The Language of Mediums and Psychics: The Social Organization of Everyday Miracles* (Aldershot: Ashgate, 2006).
125 Teemu Taira, "Religion as a Discursive Technique: The Politics of Classifying Wicca," *Journal of Contemporary Religion* 25, no. 3 (2010).
126 Frans Wijsen, "'There Are Radical Muslims and Normal Muslims': An Analysis of the Discourse on Islamic Extremism," *Religion* 43, no. 1 (2013).
127 Frans Wijsen, "Indonesian Muslim or World Citizen? Religious Identity in the Dutch Integration Discourse," in *Making Religion: Theory and Practice in the Discursive Study of Religions*, eds. Fans Wijsen and Kocku von Stuckrad (Leiden: Brill, 2016).
128 Årsheim, "Whose Religion."
129 Titus Hjelm, "One *Volk*, One Church?"
130 Titus Hjelm, "National Piety."
131 For example, Moberg, *Church, Market*; Marcus Moberg, "Christian Churches' Responses to Marketization: Comparing Institutional and Non-denominational Discourse," in *Routledge International Handbook of Religion in Global Society*, eds. Jayeel Serrano Cornelio, François Gauthier, Tuomas Martikainen, and Linda Woodhead (Oxon: Routledge, 2020).
132 cf. Burr, *Social Constructionism*, 151.
133 Potter, *Representing Reality*, 85.
134 Taylor, "Locating and Conducting," 35.
135 Ibid. 35–8.
136 Potter, *Representing Reality*, 105–6.
137 Robert N. Bellah, Richard Madsen, William S. Sullivan, Ann Swidler, and Steven M. Tipton, *Habits of the Heart: Individualism and Commitment in American Life* (Berkeley: University of California Press, 2008 [1985]), 220–1.

4 The "secular" and the "post-secular"

This chapter focuses on the discursive dimensions of some of the most influential and enduring concepts in the sociological study of religion: the "secular," "secularity," "secularism," "secularization," "public religion," and the "post-secular." As such, it provides a more contextualized continuation of our discussion in the previous chapter. As in subsequent chapters, our discussion will unfold in relation to the three-level framework outlined in the previous chapter. We thus start out by engaging in first-level reflection on the concepts of the "secular" and its corollaries, "secularity" and "secularism." This involves looking into their historical formation and constitution over time. The aim is not, however, to provide anything by way of a thorough genealogical analysis, but rather to further illustrate and underline the importance of engaging in adequate first-level reflection with regard not only to the concept and category of "religion," but also with regard to other closely related concepts and categories. From this, we move to second-level reflection on the concepts of "secularization" and "public religion." In line with the principal goal of second-level reflection as outlined in the previous chapter, particular focus will be directed at the types of theorizing that these respective concepts represent, what tacit presumptions they build on, what broader discursive currents they connect with, and what their ideational impact has been on the sociological study of religion as a whole. Here, the concept of public religion will be approached as a particular constituent discourse of a broader discursive formation on secularization, albeit as one that also challenges some of its conventional core elements.

Our first- and second-level considerations pave the way for our subsequent and more detailed second-level examination of the "post-secular," which has risen to increasing prominence across the humanities and social sciences during the past couple of decades. The post-secular will be approached as an *emerging* discursive formation within the broader order of discourse on the role and place of religion in the modern world. In addition to examining its origins and core theoretical assumptions, we also subject the "post-secular" to third-level analysis through a critical examination of some recent scholarly work in the area. In doing this, the primary aim of the chapter is to illustrate more concretely the value and applicability of

DOI: 10.4324/9780367435837-4

66 *The "secular" and the "post-secular"*

discursive perspectives for the critical examination of scholarly discourse itself. In this, the chapter thereby also illustrates more generally one key aspect of a discursive sociology of religion as envisioned in this book. As in previous chapters, the word "religion" will be put within quotation marks each time that it is used to refer to "religion" more generally, or the category of "religion" as such.

First-level reflection: the "secular"

The "secular" counts among the most widely employed and debated terms in the sociological study of religion. While it has arguably always done so, following the publication of Charles Taylor's (sociologically ignorant but nonetheless much-discussed) *A Secular Age*[1] in 2007 coupled with intensifying debates on the "post-secular" since approximately the same time, the locus of much of the debate in the sociology of religion has increasingly shifted from secularization towards that of the "secular." Having long since developed into an integral part of (mainly Western) political language and public discourse, the "secular" tends to be most unanimously understood as the binary opposite of a (typically unspecified) "religion."[2] As already discussed in Chapter 3, "religion"/"the religious" and "the secular" need to be understood as dialectically related and mutually constitutive concepts and categories. For as Calhoun *et al.* argue, the vast majority of particular understandings or definitions of the "secular" involve "religion" in some way or other: "It is either the absence of it, the control over it, the equal treatment of its various forms, or its replacement by the social values common to a secular way of life."[3]

The term "secular" is itself derived from the Latin *saeculum*, meaning "century" or "age."[4] As Taylor explains, in its original Western Christian theological meaning, the "secular" formed "one term of a dyad," referring to the "ordinary time" of profane worldly life as opposed to the sacred, eternal time associated with ecclesiastical bodies and institutions.[5] As José Casanova further points out, in this original sense, "to *secularize* meant to 'make worldly,' to convert religious persons or things into secular ones"[6] (e.g., as in the transformation of an ecclesiastical institution into a secular one or the seizure/redistribution of its property for secular use). It is important to recognize, therefore, that the term "secular" first developed, and indeed for long also functioned, as a distinct "theological category of Western Christendom" that lacked any equivalents in other social, cultural, or religious contexts.[7]

It is only with the advent of Western modernity that the "secular" begins to gradually transform into an antonym of "religion" and "the religious." Beginning with the Protestant Reformation, continuing in the aftermath of the European Wars of Religion, and eventually being cemented with the Enlightenment, the construction of the modern category of the "secular" occurred concomitantly with that of the modern category of "religion" as

The "secular" and the "post-secular" 67

part of the establishment of a new type of modern "binary classification of reality."[8] As Calhoun observes, "in the era of the Reformation, the idea of religion as a category gained importance, not least in pleas for religious tolerance but also in the attempt to separate religion from politics, especially interstate politics and war."[9] When the Thirty Years' War came to an end with the Treaty of Westphalia in 1648, the establishment of the principle of *cuius regio eius religio* ("who rules, his religion") gave rise to a new configuration of confessional, relatively religiously homogeneous, and territorially bound nation-states.[10] The new nation-state regime resulted in a range of novel forms of "statisation" and "nationalization" of "religion"[11] and the submission of "religion" to "the modern political project carried and enacted by the state."[12] Apart from intensifying efforts to separate "religion" from the domain of politics, the developing administrative practices of the newly formed nation-states also introduced several additional types of social differentiations and "separations" such as, most significantly, that between the "public" and the "private."[13] Thus, as Peter van der Veer observes, "With the rise of the nation-state comes an enormous shift in what religion means."[14] Since the Westphalian settlement, the notion of "modern society" has also become largely synonymous with the societies of particular nation-states.[15] When we explore the "secular" in "modern society," we are therefore, in actuality, exploring it within the context of particular nation-states.

Efforts towards the ever-firmer institutionalization of new differentiations between "religion" and its "others" increased markedly as a result of the Enlightenment's strong emphasis on the triumph of reason over superstition and the "secular" over "religion." Importantly, as Calhoun *et al.* point out, these efforts also "required a clear notion of the 'religion' that was being contained," coupled with a "definition of the secular order that was assumed to be succeeding it."[16] At this juncture, the "secular" thus ceases to be understood merely as the "absence" of religion and gradually starts to acquire its own ideological content and substance as an *alternative* to "religion." Or, as Calhoun succinctly puts is, following the Enlightenment, "The secular is claimed by many not just as one way of organizing life, not just as useful in order to ensure peace and harmony among different religions, but as a kind of *maturation*."[17]

The historical constitution of the "secular" was also greatly influenced by the liberal philosophy of the seventeenth, eighteenth, and nineteenth centuries, as represented by thinkers such as Thomas Hobbes, John Locke, Jean-Jacques Rousseau, Adam Smith, David Ricardo, Jeremy Bentham, and John Stuart Mill, among many others. As much a philosophical as a political project, liberal thought emerged out of the Enlightenment and marked a decisive break with the ethos and philosophical underpinnings of the *ancien régime*. It represented a shift from a previous social order "regulated by traditional rights and obligations rooted in ascribed status and a cosmological order (the 'great chain of being'), to one in which social order emerges from

68 *The "secular" and the "post-secular"*

the independent actions of autonomous *individuals*"[18] (liberalism will be discussed further in Chapters 5 and 6). Liberal thought therefore had important implications for the ways in which "religion" and its relationship to politics and public life would come to be understood across Western societies. To take an example from a widely influential contemporaneous text, in "A Letter Concerning Toleration" (1689) Locke wrote that "The church itself is a thing absolutely separate and distinct from the commonwealth. The boundaries on both sides are fixed and immovable."[19] "True religion," he went on to assert, is "based on the inward persuasion of the mind."[20] The liberalist individual-emphasizing vision of the body politic was therefore no longer rooted in the concept of "God" or "creation," but in the "essence of the human" endowed with inalienable natural rights.[21] Indeed, as Asad perceptively argues, through liberalism, the

> essence of the human comes to be circumscribed by *legal* discourse: the human being is a *sovereign, self-owning agent – essentially suspicious of others – and* not merely a subject conscious of his or her own identity. It is on this basis that the secularist principle of the right to freedom of belief and expression was crafted.[22]

In liberalism we therefore see the formation of principles of government that "deal solely with a worldly disposition, an arrangement that is quite different from the medieval conception of a social body of Christian souls ... members at once of the City of God and of divinely created human society."[23]

Liberal philosophy, and especially that of Locke, would go on to exert an enormous influence on North American constitutionalism, as principally articulated in the Unites States' Declaration of Independence of 1776 and Constitution of 1787. Indeed, as Fitzgerald observes, "North American constitutionalism is arguably one of the most important institutionalisations of the modern idea of religion as essentially private and nonpolitical, in English at any rate."[24] Reflecting the liberal ideal of the sovereign individual subject, these documents framed "religion" as a voluntary "private right guaranteed by a nonreligious constitution."[25] This, though, was a "negative right" ensured by the US Constitution's dictum that "Congress shall make no law respecting an establishment of religion, or prohibiting the free exercise thereof." In this context, "religion" therefore emerges as "a realm of collective voluntary commitment rooted in (irrational, variable, and uncompelled) personal belief that the [secular] state would not partake of or constrain."[26] The ideas would also have a notable impact on the self-perceptions of religious communities. As explored in some detail by Asad, with the emergence of the modern "secular" and religiously indifferent state, the established churches also increasingly ascribed to the "religious–secular" framework, "shifting, as they did so, the weight of religion more and more onto the moods and motivations of the individual believer."[27] The modern

The "secular" and the "post-secular"   69

term "secular," however, has never had any fixed meaning.[28] It is clear, though, as Asad points out, that it is "neither continuous with the religious that supposedly preceded it ... nor a simple break from it."[29]

Secularity

Although the historical institutionalization of the "secular" occurred in close connection with the new social differentiations introduced by the Westphalian nation-statist regime. The term can nevertheless be used to refer to virtually any aspect or facet of modern social life that is not connected to "religion," or that has become somehow divorced from its (either actual or perceived) previous connections to "religion." But in addition to this, following its gradual establishment as an independent "epistemic category,"[30] the "secular" has also come to underpin various notions about a broader modern social and cultural "condition" of *secularity*. Casanova's general outline of three particular meanings of the notion of "secularity" is helpful here. The first is that of "mere secularity," or the "the phenomenological experience of living in a secular world and in a secular age, where being religious may be a normal viable option."[31] In this broader sense of the term, social life in contemporary Western societies with their (largely) religiously neutral states and secular constitutions can, for all practical purposes, adequately be described as "secular."[32] The second, narrower meaning is that of "self-sufficient and exclusive secularity," denoting "the phenomenological experience of living without religion as a normal, quasi-natural, taken-for-granted condition."[33] This, then, would refer to a situation where increasing numbers of people are "simply 'irreligious'" or otherwise just indifferent towards religion. Here, the "secular" is no longer understood as merely the absence of religion, but rather in terms of a "self-enclosed reality."[34] The third meaning of secularity is that of "secularist secularity," or "the phenomenological experience not only of being passively free but also actually of having been liberated from 'religion' as a condition for human autonomy and human flourishing."[35] The two latter meanings of "secularity," Casanova continues, both emanate from a modern "secularist stadial consciousness" that understands the triumph of the secular over religion in terms of a "process of maturation" and "progressive emancipation."[36] It is nevertheless the wide establishment of a "secularist stadial consciousness" which allows the "secular" to further mutate into *secularism*, that is, into an *ideology of the secular* that also "entails a theory of what 'religion' is or does."[37]

Casanova's arguments on the "secularist stadial consciousness" generally align with Taylor's more speculative (but nonetheless highly influential) arguments about "secularity 3" as laid out in *A Secular Age*, according to which secularity is to be understood as principally entailing a more fundamental change in the very basic *conditions* of "belief." Taylor's key point here is that the historical establishment of what he refers to as the

70   *The "secular" and the "post-secular"*

"immanent frame" (described as "the sensed context in which we develop our beliefs"[38]) changes the conditions for both "belief" and "un-belief" alike, establishing this-worldly "secular" self-enclosed reality as the "default option."[39] In developing his notion about the "secularist stadial consciousness," Casanova, like Taylor, therefore also acknowledges how the seeds for subsequent processes of secularization were already planted through internal historical changes within Latin Christendom, which would eventually become radicalized by the Protestant Reformation through its interiorization of "religion" and strong emphasis on personal "belief." Indeed, as previously analyzed by Berger, the Lutheran notion of the two kingdoms, of God and of man, actually provided the "autonomy of the secular 'world'" with a "theological legitimation."[40] These observations point to a significant, but sometimes overlooked, aspect of the historical constitution of the "secular" and its connection to the "religious" that, while it is worth noting, we shall not delve deeper into here.

Secularism

The term "secularism" was first introduced into the English language by mid-nineteenth-century free thinkers.[41] Nowadays, it is most commonly used to refer to different types of "normative-ideological state projects" and "legal-constitutional frameworks" that argue for a strict separation between religion and state, clear differentiations between religion and social institutional spheres such as politics, education, and law, and the restriction of the presence and visibility of religion in the public sphere.[42] Following Casanova, a general distinction can be made between "philosophical-historical" and "political" secularisms.[43] While the former refers to various types of theories of "religion" "grounded in some progressive stadial philosophies of history that relegate religion to a superseded stage," the latter instead refers to particular "secularist political theories that presuppose that religion is either an irrational force or a nonrational form of discourse that should be banished from the democratic public sphere."[44] As should be clear from the above, like the concept of the "secular," any definition of "secularism" will always and inevitably be constructed in relation to some kind of definition or understanding of "religion."[45] In its stronger *laicist* forms (as is, for example, espoused by the current French Fifth Republic), the objective of secularism is essentially to "emancipate all secular spheres from ecclesiastical control."[46] More liberal versions of secularism instead tend to be more focused on confining religion to the private sphere while curbing the presence and visibility of explicitly "religious" arguments in the public sphere.[47] In both cases, however, a clear boundary is drawn between the "religious" and the "secular" and the immanent secular world is imbued "with a quasi-transcendent meaning as the place of human flourishing."[48] From the perspective of a discursive sociology of religion, as well as more generally, the central question becomes exactly *how* and *where* particular

The "secular" and the "post-secular"   71

boundaries between the "religious" and the "secular" are drawn, for what reasons, by whom, and with what particular consequences.[49]

First-level conclusions

As should be clear from the above, the "secular" will always become imbued with particular meanings depending on the particular social, political, and philosophical contexts in which it is being used.[50] It is worth emphasizing the word *used* here. For regardless of the more particular uses to which the concept may be put, to define or designate something as "secular" will always constitute an act of social classification, a particular ordering of the social that will be based on a particular understanding of "religion," however vague or parochial that understanding may be. As such, classifying something as "secular" will also entail ascribing a particular type of social status and place to "religion."

To reiterate some of the points already made in Chapter 3, contemporary individuals and social institutions alike tend to both perceive and respond to "religion" as something "real," as part of (perceived) *sui generis* social reality. Throughout much of the Western world and beyond, "religion" remains a recurring topic of political and public debate. Both national and international news media regularly report on a variety of "religion"-related issues. "Religion" constitutes an increasingly salient theme across various forms of mass-mediated popular culture such as film, television series, computer games, and so on. Many religious communities maintain highly visible public profiles, and religious personas such as Pope Francis and the 14th Dalai Lama count among the most widely known figures on earth. Through these and other means, "religion" attains a degree of general societal visibility and perceived social reality that can scarcely be altogether ignored. The primary task of a discursive sociology of religion, again, is to inquire into the particular ways in which such perceptions become formed, established, and reproduced through discourse and other modes of representation. The same should equally apply to the concepts of the "secular" and "secularism," both of which have also become part of common parlance. Having said that, it is nevertheless worth considering the extent and variety of situations in which discourse on the "secular" and/or "secularism" is most likely to surface and become actualized.

To reconnect to Casanova's arguments on the condition of "secularity" above, there are ample empirical grounds for presuming that "Self-sufficient and exclusive secularity," or "the phenomenological experience of living without religion as a normal, quasi-natural, taken-for-granted condition," has become increasingly widespread, at least among Western European populations.[51] In such a setting, the "secular" and "secularism" would presumably mainly take the form of a largely unspecified general ideological backdrop against which the organization of modern social and public life

72 The "secular" and the "post-secular"

is generally understood. But in addition to this, there are also increasingly ample grounds for arguing that "secularist secularity," or the "phenomenological experience not only of being passively free but also actually of having been liberated from 'religion' as a condition for human autonomy and human flourishing" has also become embraced by significant portions of Western European populations, including by particular states.[52] In this type of setting, the "secular" and "secularism" would presumably acquire much more specific meanings and take the form of a fully conscious and active stance *vis-à-vis* the "proper" place and role of "religion" in society and public life. But even in these types of contexts, we should not expect the "secular" and/or "secularism" to figure in everyday public discourse to nearly the same extent as "religion" does.

Various types of discourse on or about "religion" can (and do) unfold across a wide range of (both private and public) contexts without any particular reference to either the "secular" or "secularism." Discourse on the "secular" and/or "secularism," by contrast, will almost inevitably have to unfold in some form of connection to "religion," either explicitly or implicitly. In comparison to discourse on "religion," discourse on the "secular" and/or "secularism" therefore tends to surface and become actualized in particular types of contexts and situations, and especially when "secular society" or "secular values" are perceived (or are *made* to be perceived) to come under some form of threat or even attack. In such cases, what may otherwise constitute rather un-thought about, latent, or vague notions of the "secular" and "secularism" can become "activated" and mobilized as part of efforts to counter the perceived threat of "religious intrusions" on established "secular" ways of life. In these types of situations, moreover, "religion" typically tends to become represented as *intolerant* (e.g., towards liberal values and scientific principles), *oppressive* (e.g., against certain groups of people such as women or members of the LGBTQ community), and as *encroaching* on people's individual liberties (e.g., by prohibiting women's right to an abortion) – all of which are incompatible with the core values and individual freedoms that secular liberal democracy is supposed to safeguard and uphold.[53]

The longstanding debates that continue to rage on the public visibility and presence of Islam across much of Europe provide particularly illustrative examples of this. Fueled in particular by the rise of anti-immigration right-wing populist politics, Islam and Muslim immigration have been propelled to the forefront of public and political debate in several European countries and often been framed as posing a threat to European (secular) "ways of life." Not only has such discourse become increasingly prevalent; it has since long also become operationalized in the form of a variety of political initiatives and legislative efforts. For example, in 2009 Switzerland prohibited the construction of new minarets following a widely publicized national referendum on the issue. In 2011, France enacted a law that prohibited the wearing of full-length Islamic veils such as niqābs and burqas

The "secular" and the "post-secular"   73

in public spaces. In 2018, The Danish parliament passed a law banning all face-covering garments in public, thereby also effectively prohibiting full-length veils. In 2021, following another referendum on that same issue, some very similar restrictions were also adopted in Switzerland. Past decades have also witnessed several "Islam"-related disputes over the liberal secular republican value of freedom of speech, starting with the Rushdie affair as long ago as 1989, continuing with the Danish Muhammad cartoon controversy in 2005, and then further exacerbated by the violent attack against the offices of the satirical magazine *Charlie Hebdo* in Paris in 2015.

These are but a few examples of situations where the concepts of the "secular" and "secularism" are likely to become variously employed and operationalized by politicians, representatives of social institutions, journalists, and others. As highlighted by Asad, these types of situations can be highly revealing of the ways in which Western European secularist discourse tends to build on particular notions of Europe as a *civilization* deeply marked by the historical experience of the Roman Empire, Western Christendom (Catholicism and Protestantism), the Wars of Religion, the Enlightenment, the "Age of Discovery," and the industrial revolution.[54] In the more recent European imagination, these historical moments, argues Asad, generally "reflect a history whose unconfused purpose is to separate Europe from alien *times* ('communism,' 'Islam') as well as from alien *places* ('Islamdom,' 'Russia')."[55] These, then, are issues worth taking into account when exploring discourse on the "secular" and "secularism" in Western European contexts. We need to recognize, therefore, that "the secular" and/or "secularism" are rarely discussed simply for their own sake, but rather tend to surface and become actualized in certain types of contexts and situations. The above discussion is therefore also meant to give us a clearer idea of the particular types of locations and situations where we should expect the "secular" to become visible in and through discourse and discursive practice.

Second-level reflection: "secularization," "public religion," and the "post-secular"

The concept of the "secular" stands in a dialectical relationship to the notion of secularization, which has been at the very center of broader sociological debates on the fate and future of religion in the modern world for over a century. To simplify, whereas the "secular" can be used to refer to virtually anything that is not connected to "religion," secularization refers to the extended historical social and cultural *process* whereby social institutions, activities, or practices that were *previously* connected to or associated with "religion" become gradually *divorced* or *detached* from these connections and associations and thereby become "secular." Secularization therefore, at its most general, denotes the process whereby the "secular," so to speak, "comes to be."

74 *The "secular" and the "post-secular"*

Secularization

Any exploration of the "secular" necessarily needs to engage with the notion of secularization in some form or other. Indeed, as Casanova observed already in 1994, the concept of secularization

> is so intrinsically interwoven with all the theories of the modern world and with the self-understanding of modernity that one cannot simply discard the theory of secularization without putting into question the entire web, including much of the self-understanding of the social sciences.[56]

The discursive dimensions of Casanova's observations are worth noting here. From the perspective advanced in this book, the "entire web" to which he refers should be seen as largely a web of discourse. In this view, to question the theory of secularization will therefore entail questioning (at least some of) the principal discourses that underpin it, including some of those that it might share with other deeply engrained theoretical presumptions in the social sciences more broadly. But secularization will then also have to be critiqued *through* discourse. Put another way, any more far-reaching critique of the theory of secularization will require the development of an alternative discourse to that of secularization. As will be illustrated in more detail below, while past decades have indeed seen the development and increasingly firm establishment of several alternative discourses on modern-time processes of religious change, the key analytical vocabulary of secularization theory has nevertheless proved difficult to jettison and remains still very much in play. Considering the degree of contestation that has long since come to mark debates on secularization, it has become nigh-on impossible to provide an account of secularization that would be to every scholar's satisfaction. No such attempt will be made here either. Rather, as enormous amounts of scholarly effort have already been spent on the topic of secularization, we shall not dwell on it long here and just concentrate on providing a general account of some of the main strands of theorizing in the area.

Since the foundational sociological work of Émile Durkheim and Max Weber, sociological debates on secularization have mainly concentrated on the overarching impact of processes of modernization on the present-day and future societal position and significance of "religion" (mainly in the form institutional Christianity) throughout the modern (primarily Western) world. As noted in Chapter 3, from its earliest stages of development, secularization theory was always strongly informed by contemporaneous discourses on rationality, reason, and scientific progress. As such, it was also marked by an at least tacit expectation that "religion" in all of its forms would gradually (and indeed inevitably) lose its social significance in a modern social and cultural environment increasingly marked by the "secularist stadial consciousness" referred to by Casanova (see above).[57]

The "secular" and the "post-secular" 75

Viewed as a particular type of outcome of broader processes of modernization, in its "classical" articulations, secularization theory has consequently offered a rather dismal account of the fate and future of religion in the modern world, and most typically in the form of a "running narrative" of gradual but progressive decline.[58]

Much of the current and still ongoing debate on secularization harks back to the 1960s. The latter part of the decade witnessed the publication of several foundational works that, to a large extent, served to carve out some (but not all) of the main fault-lines of the subsequent debate. These included Bryan Wilson's *Religion in Secular Society*[59] published in 1966 and Berger's *The Sacred Canopy*[60] published in 1967, both of which (while being very different in terms of theoretical grounding) advanced understandings of secularization as a progressive and irreversible process. They also, however, included Luckmann's *The Invisible Religion*[61] published in 1967 and David Martin's *The Religious and the Secular*[62] published 1969, both of which questioned the "linear" view of secularization and instead, each in its own way, argued for an understanding of secularization as religious "transformation" rather than simply decline.

While the progressive-decline view has become increasingly questioned, it remains central to the secularization theory of Steve Bruce. Basing his argument on an understanding of secularization as a paradigm consisting of a "cluster of testable explanations," Bruce views it in terms of a cyclical but essentially irreversible process of religious decline.[63] Some of the most widely debated among these "explanations" (some of which also underpin more specific secularization "theses") include, but are not limited to, the *functional differentiation* of modern societies (the relegation and confinement of "religion" to its own societal sphere); accelerating *societalization* (a shift in the locus of social life from the local village community to that of the urban, "wider society"); the *rationalization of social functions* (the "dis-enchantment" of the world); increasing *pluralism* (the rise of religious voluntarism and relativism); and the *compartmentalization* and *privatization* of religious life (the transformation of religion into a private, individual elective). In Bruce's view, the combined effects of these empirically observable and researchable processes can be shown to have greatly reduced the capacity of "religion" to remain a central and consequential part of modern social and cultural life, and especially on the macro-level of societies on the whole and the meso-level of societal institutions.

Another strand of theorizing principally focuses on identifying and comparing *secularizing tendencies* across different historical and social and cultural contexts. Such a view can be found in the secularization theory of Martin, who, while also adopting a view of secularization as a cyclical process, argues instead that it should not be viewed as "a once-for-all unilateral process," but rather be thought of "in terms of successive Christianizations followed or accompanied by recoils."[64] Martin singles out contemporary evangelical Christianity and Pentecostalism, which have both

76 The "secular" and the "post-secular"

spread on an international scale and come to run "alongside modernity in a mutually supportive manner," as the latest and most notable exemplars of such (re-)"Christianizations."[65] From this vantage point, the key question becomes whether to treat these types of religious "resurgences" as "creative restatements" of more deeply engrained "religious currents" or, more pessimistically, as "responses to secularization."[66]

In yet another strand of related theorizing, processes of secularization are viewed in light of the particular ways in which broader processes of modernization were actualized and experienced across particular wider historical, social, and cultural contexts. Often grounded in perspectives on "multiple modernities,"[67] such explorations have in large part centered on the issue of "American/European exceptionalism," or the question whether secularization should be understood in terms of a distinctively European experience or not.[68] In historical perspective, one major point of focus has been on how the Enlightenment was received and how it interacted with religious and social and cultural life on the two respective sides of the modernizing Atlantic. Scholars have, for example, emphasized how the American Enlightenment, in contrast to the European one, was never anti-clerical and always decidedly more focused on the "politics of liberty,"[69] embracing a "freedom *to* believe" rather than a "freedom *from* belief."[70] Also, whereas European religious experience remains deeply marked by the historical presence of majority state churches, or religious "monopolies," the decidedly more diverse religious landscape of the United States has instead always been organized along denominational and congregational lines. As enshrined in the so-called "establishment" and "free exercise" clauses of the First Amendment to the United States Constitution, the United States has never had a state church, and indeed always had a very different kind of state compared to how the state has been organized and understood in Europe.[71] This also provides the explanation for a range of other notable differences in religion–society relations between these two regions such as can clearly be seen, for example, in the place that "religion" occupies in the domains of education and welfare provision.[72]

In what generally aligns with this strand of theorizing, Casanova has more recently argued that the modern "secularist stadial consciousness" that has become increasingly widely established and institutionalized in Europe since the Enlightenment should be regarded as "a crucial factor in the widespread secularization that has accompanied the modernization of Western European societies."[73] We can see this, he argues, in the ways in which "Europeans tend to experience their own secularization, that is, the widespread decline of religious beliefs and practices among their midst as a natural consequence of their modernization."[74] This, he further contends, provides an important part of the explanation for European societies' apparent difficulties in "accommodating religious diversity, and particularly in incorporating immigrant religions."[75] It is therefore "the presence or absence of this secularist historical stadial consciousness ... [that] explains

The "secular" and the "post-secular" 77

when and where processes of modernization are accompanied by radical secularization."[76] Put another way, in contrast to the United States, Western European modernity, argues Casanova, has typically been experienced as antithetical to "religion." The presence or absence of a "secularist stadial consciousness" has therefore also had significant bearings on how the concepts of the "secular" and "secularism" have become historically constituted, understood, and employed in these respective broader social and cultural contexts.

The main strands of theorizing outlined above serve to illustrate some principal and enduring fault-lines in the longstanding debate on secularization. More generally, following Hugh McLeod, a general distinction can be made "between those who use this concept [secularization] to explain religious change, and those who use it merely to describe religious change."[77] In both cases, and especially the former, methods and data remain issues of pivotal concern. That is, by what kinds of methods and indicators, and on the basis what types and/or volumes of data (e.g., historical, quantitative, qualitative) can various hypotheses on secularization be adequately and confidently measured, tested, and substantiated? Other disagreements in the debate on secularization have been largely discursive in character and primarily emanated from differing understandings and employments of key terms and concepts such as those of "religion" and "secularization" themselves. Indeed, already in 1997 Sharon Hanson noted that participants in the secularization debate typically talked at "cross purposes."[78] As she pointed out:

> Critics who adhere to one definition of secularisation critically evaluate theorists who hold to another definition, without appreciating the definitional differences or the parallel problematic that a particular secularisation theory will have been constructed with a particular definition of religion in mind.[79]

Although the situation with regards to conceptual clarity and coherence has indeed been slowly improving, Hanson's observations to some extent still ring true. While the above provides only a very general account of some main strands of theorizing in the area, the debate on secularization is likely to continue for the foreseeable future. At the time of writing (2021), the debate has reached something of a standstill. While the vast majority of sociologists of religion appear to hold the view that secularization theory is in need of thoroughgoing revision and rethinking, no alternative has yet emerged to take its place.

Public religion

Since the early 1990s, the supposed global "resurgence" of religion has developed into a major topic of debate across several disciplines in the

78 *The "secular" and the "post-secular"*

humanities and social sciences, including, not least, the sociology of religion. This supposed resurgence is commonly dated back to the 1970s, a decade that witnessed both the rise of the Religious Right in the United States and the Islamic Revolution in Iran.[80] The perception of a religious resurgence was then further reinforced through the restoration and public reappearance of national churches throughout the former Soviet Union and Eastern Bloc from the early 1990s onward. In more recent times still, the increasing politicization of religion (especially as it relates to Islam) following the 2001 September 11 attacks, the Arab Spring, the Syrian Civil War, and the rise of ISIS have all served to further strengthen the sense that religion is re-entering the public arena on a worldwide scale.

The publication of Casanova's *Public Religions in the Modern World* in 1994, along with its development and elaboration of the notion of "public religion," played a central role in setting the stage for these debates.[81] Although Casanova's thinking has evolved considerably since then, he initially developed his notion of "public religion" as part of his broader critique of dominant versions of the secularization thesis. Rather than understanding secularization as a unitary process, Casanova argued instead that the thesis was built on at least three separate, but not necessarily aggregate, claims about the effects of processes of modernization on religion and religious life in the modern era. First, earlier versions of the secularization thesis had typically framed secularization as an inevitable outcome of the functional *differentiation* of modern societies, whereby religion had become confined to its own societal sphere and thereby lost much of its previous influence over other societal domains such as education, the justice system, and politics. Second, secularization had also been taken to involve a general decline in overall degrees of *individual* religiosity. And, third, it had been taken to entail a general *privatization* of religion and religious life, according to which religion had withdrawn from the public sphere and instead developed into a primarily private affair.

In his assessment of the theoretical and empirical bases for these three respective claims, Casanova concluded that it was only the differentiation thesis that could be said to enjoy broader validity, whereas declining degrees of individual religiosity and the privatization of religion both needed to be considered highly varied and context-dependent processes.[82] In light of a set of notable examples (primarily from the late 1970s and 1980s) from different national, social, cultural, and religious contexts Casanova then proceeded to argue that religious actors were evidently not content with remaining confined to their own respective differentiated spheres. The continuing public engagement on the part of religious communities and actors, he argued, took three principal forms: (1) in relation to religious communities' engagements in public debates on fundamental social rights and liberties; (2) in their public scrutiny of unjust social and political-economic policies; and (3) in their efforts to serve as bulwarks against the influence of state authorities on traditional lifeworlds.[83] Hence, rather than

The "secular" and the "post-secular" 79

suggesting any type of general "privatization" of religion, such instances, argued Casanova, were rather indicative of a *deprivatization* of religion, whereby "religion abandons its assigned place in the private sphere and enters the undifferentiated public sphere of civil society."[84] This view thus closely connects with the liberal political-theoretical ideal of a "civil society" supporting social vitality, pluralism, and democracy that occupies an independent "middle-ground" between the private sphere and that of the state and the economy.[85] And so, Casanova's went on to contend that "only those religions that cease being 'state-oriented' and become 'society-oriented' institutions are capable of entering or re-entering the public sphere of civil society."[86] In this, he largely based his notion of "public religion" on the same premises as the subsequently developed Habermasian notion of the "post-secular," which we return to in more detail below.

The "civil society" ideal on which Casanova based his argument is not without its problems. For one thing, it is not all that easily squared with actual social and political realities. For as Beckford rightly points out, states not only can, but often also do, interfere in civil society in a range of both direct and indirect ways.[87] The most obvious way is through various types of legislation and states' and governments' stated policies towards religious groups and communities. In reality, while societies will always differ with regards to the composition of their religious fields and their degrees of religious diversity, the maneuvering space of religious communities will therefore always be determined and constrained by constitutions and legal frameworks.[88] But in addition to legislation and official policy, the ways in which particular states respond to religion-related issues can also be informed by any range of additional "less formal and more subtle understandings, conventions and practices," which "allow some religious groups to function as the 'normal', taken for granted point of reference when secular agencies require information and advice about religious matters."[89]

These observations point to the composition and character of "civil society" and the "public sphere" as something always and already *determined* by powerful and dominant interests. As argued by Asad, in a critical perspective, the "public sphere" is not "simply a forum for rational debate but an *exclusionary* space."[90] This is because "The enjoyment of free speech presupposes not merely the physical ability to speak but to be *heard*."[91] As he continues, "The public sphere is not an empty space for carrying out debates. It is constituted by the sensibilities – memories and aspirations, fears and hopes – of speakers and listeners."[92] Public spheres, therefore, need to be understood as being governed by their own particular discourse norms, genres, and acceptable ways of interaction to which new entrants, including "religious" ones, are generally expected to conform. These norms and rules, moreover, are also highly likely to reflect the interests and values of prevailing structures of power, including their possible association to "secular" and "secularist" values and ideologies.

80 The "secular" and the "post-secular"

The notion of "public religion" has served to inspire countless explorations of the public visibility and presence of "religion" and "religious actors" across various national, social, and cultural contexts. The notion, however, remains marred by a range of ambiguities and unresolved questions relating to its precise meaning, conditions of establishment, empirical basis, and possible application. For example, when it comes to the most basic claims of the public religion and deprivatization thesis, Beckford has questioned the usefulness of viewing the rise of "public religion" and "religious privatization" as mutually exclusive processes or phenomena.[93] Taking Britain and the Nordic countries as examples of where the historical churches to a very large extent have remained deeply embedded in the structures of state, politics, and civil society alike, he also cautions against overstating the extent of "religion's" supposed withdrawal from the public sphere in the first place.[94] On a related note, when it comes to the notion of the "public sphere" itself, it has become increasingly widely acknowledged that it needs to be understood in the plural, i.e., in terms of a configuration of multiple public spheres.[95] Public spheres, moreover, consist of *publics*, which largely become constituted by and through the *media*. This also applies to cases where the "the public" is used in the singular (i.e., as referring to the entire population or body politic of a particular society). As Stephen Coleman and Karen Ross point out, "Naming and framing the public are central activities of contemporary, mediatized democracies in which the public can only meet itself through representation."[96] "The public," therefore, "is *invoked* through processes of mediation that are dominated by political, institutional, economic, and cultural forces."[97] As a consequence, "publics" are, in an important sense, always *invented* since, before a "public" can be "addressed," it first has to be "imagined:" "Never meeting in one place or speaking with one voice, the public is unable to represent itself. It is doomed to be represented."[98] As Coleman and Ross continue:

> Imagining the public is further complicated by the ambivalence of its role as both actor and stage. As social actor, the public comprises the people who make up society – although ... not necessarily all the people all the time. As stage, the public refers to a zone of social openness and transparency, as opposed to privacy and exclusion.[99]

This brings us to a set of additional ambiguities surrounding the terms "public" and "religion" in the "public religion" configuration. Scholars have, for example, debated what should count as "truly religious" types of activities and communications on the part of "religious actors" in strongly functionally differentiated societies. For example, in one type of argument that builds on a particular interpretation of the differentiation thesis, Jens Köhrsen[100] posits that, when religious actors move outside their own differentiated sphere and start engaging and communicating within other differentiated spheres, they thereby also become required to abide by the rules

The "secular" and the "post-secular"   81

and communicative conventions of these other spheres. Although their activities and communications within these other spheres might still remain inspired and motivated by "religious" concerns, beliefs, or values, their activities and communications will nonetheless *in and of themselves* cease to be centered on the "purely religious."[101] While this perspective remains problematic, owing to its essentialist understanding of "religion" and presumption about some form of "purely religious" type of communication, it has nevertheless provided an impetus for further specifications regarding the precise meaning of the terms "public" and "religion" in the "public religion" configuration. For example, as Mia Lövheim and Marta Axner point out, when considering the presence of "religious voices" in an expanded and increasingly mediated public sphere, it is useful to make a general "distinction between religion as the particular content or substance of an act of *communicating* religion in the public sphere and religion as a *qualifier of the actor* performing the communication."[102] While this still leaves us with the difficulty of deciding what types of "substance" or "content" should qualify as "religious," it nevertheless draws our attention to the centrality of the "religious actor" in these contexts.

According to Monica Toft *et al.*, a "religious actor" can be defined as "any individual, group, or organization that espouses religious beliefs and that articulates a reasonably consistent and coherent message about the relationship of religion to politics."[103] In this broad understanding, religious actors can be divided into a set of major categories, including *individual* actors (e.g., elected politicians who claim to be guided by religious values or convictions or internationally and locally recognized individual religious leaders) and *institutional* and *organizational* actors (e.g., religious organizations and communities themselves, religious political parties, various types of religious interest- or lobbying groups).[104] But as Jeffrey Haynes and Anja Hennig caution, there is no reason to automatically assume that "religious actors" can always be easily differentiated from "non-religious actors" when it comes to the particular means and strategies that they employ in order to realize their goals and objectives.[105] But, more generally, when considering the presence of religious actors in Western secular "public spheres," it is always important to recognize that the "public" and "political" spheres are not synonymous entities.[106]

Regardless of the more precise ways in which we choose to understand the "religious actor," it remains of pivotal importance to always keep in mind that "religion" does not act by and of itself. Nor does "religion" become "publicly visible" by and of itself. Rather, "it" does so through the conscious actions, activities, and discursive practices of various types of social actors, some of which might be more readily described as "religious" as opposed to others. As discussed above, the same applies to the concept of the "secular." The "religious" and the "secular" both need to be understood as concepts and categories that various types of actors discursively construct and operationalize in particular social contexts and with

82 *The "secular" and the "post-secular"*

particular intentions and purposes. But although "religious actors" come in many different shapes and forms, as noted, *states* (themselves particular types of both "secular" and "religious" actors) might work to actively restrict the maneuvering space of different religious actors for any number of reasons. On the flipside, the legitimacy of a state *itself* may also be tied to its continuing support of a particular (usually institutional) religious actor.[107] More commonly, certain religious actors may be directly funded or subsidized by states and governments, or occupy otherwise privileged positions *vis-à-vis* the political sphere in a particular societal context, as largely remains the case with the historical Christian churches throughout much of Europe.[108]

As should be clear from the above, rather than speculating about the supposed "resurgence" of religion "as such," the discourse of various types of "religious actors" should be at the center of our analyses. This is not least since the action and agency of various types of "religious actors" largely takes place and becomes realized through discourse and discursive practice.

Secularization and public religion in discursive perspective

From the viewpoint of a discursive sociology of religion, in terms of second-level reflection, secularization can usefully be understood as a particular (although admittedly broad and inclusive) *discursive formation* that occupies a prominent position within the broader *order of discourse* on religious change in the modern (Western) world. This is to say that secularization (broadly understood) provides a relatively stable, although never static, frame of reference and repertoire of key terms and concepts in relation to which, and through which, changes and transformations in the modern-day religious field have long been, and to a large extent continue to be, conceptualized and understood. This frame of reference, moreover, sets the parameters for what can *meaningfully be said* about that particular topic. As such, it also provides the stage for future statements on the topic. *New* ways of conceptualizing religious change within, in relation to, or in contrast to this discursive formation will therefore need to retain some kind of connection to its already established terminological and conceptual repertoire. As noted, such efforts have been steadily intensifying over a longer period of time already and also resulted in the development of several alternative discourses that have significantly both challenged and transformed the discursive formation on secularization. But the concept of secularization itself, including much of its associated core vocabulary, very much still remains in play.

On a higher level of abstraction, we could say that the currently most prominent constituent discourses of the broader discursive formation on secularization coalesce into broader clusters of mutually supporting discourses. In one clearly identifiable cluster, secularization takes the form of a "deintensification theory." This view generally holds that, although

The "secular" and the "post-secular" 83

"religion" will remain in modern society, it will eventually do so "only in a deintensified, weak and insubstantial form."[109] In another identifiable cluster of discourses, secularization instead takes the form of a "co-existence theory." In this view, institutional or so-called "churched" forms of religion are likely to continue to decline while others will increasingly adapt to modern society, which will continue to display both secularizing and "desecularizing" tendencies.[110] The public religion discourse largely falls within the latter. Whereas these clusters of discourses are largely in agreement on the *causes* of secularization, they differ notably with respect to their views on their supposed long-term *effects* on the modern-day religious field. For example, the "co-existence" view questions the claim that processes of secularization on the meso-level of societal institutions will necessarily also serve to bring about a decline in individual religiosity or a "secularization of the mind."[111] Notwithstanding these differences, however, both of these clusters of discourses accept the general *notion* of secularization and largely share the same terminological and conceptual repertoire (even when some aspects of secularization theory is critiqued).

When it comes to the particular discourse of public religion we have seen that it generally accepts the differentiation thesis, but rejects strong versions of the privatization thesis. While we can certainly debate the extent to which "religion" ever withdrew from the public sphere of most modern societies in the first place, it is hard to dispute the fact that "religion" has indeed become increasingly publicly visible on a worldwide scale during past decades, and especially following the 2001 September 11 attacks and the resulting "war on terror" and increasing "securitization of religion." This growing visibility, moreover, is in no small part attributable to the rapid development and proliferation of digital communications during the past two to three decades.[112] Therefore, as Casanova observes, although "We are not 'religious' again," we have certainly "become obsessed with religion as a question, particularly as a public issue."[113] The public religion discourse is therefore likely to remain an influential one for the foreseeable future. It also remains central to the concept of the "post-secular," which we will return to below.

As part of this discussion it is also worth noting that the broader order of discourse on religious change in the modern world also includes other prominent discursive formations that altogether reject the notion of secularization. An example of this is found in the discursive formation on the so-called "theory of religious economy," which has been at loggerheads with the discursive formation on secularization for several decades. Indeed, as will be discussed further in Chapter 6, during the 1990s and early 2000s, the sociological study of religion witnessed a drawn-out, but ultimately inconclusive, hegemonic struggle between these two discursive formations.

The "post-secular" can arguably be viewed as an *emerging* discursive formation on religious change in the modern world, and especially as it relates to Western Europe. While the notion of the post-secular itself remains

84 *The "secular" and the "post-secular"*

intimately connected to the discursive formation on secularization and the discourse of public religion, it also significantly alters the premises of the entire debate through its strong reliance on a particular set of social-philosophical ideas. In this, it also represents a more general turn from the empirical and analytical towards the normative, speculative, and even prescriptive. Our task in the remaining part of the chapter will be to critically examine the emerging discursive formation on the post-secular, the conditions of its establishment, its primary content and character, and its ideational impact on the sociological study of religion as a whole.

The post-secular

The concept of the "post-secular" has appeared in many different guises and types of scholarly writing (e.g., social philosophy, social theory, theology, sociology, geography, and more). Thus far, wider debates on the post-secular have been predominantly social–philosophical and social–theoretical in character and mainly been concerned with ideologically challenging received understandings of the "secular" and secularist principles of governance. Following Michele Dillon, these debates could therefore be described as having been most centrally concerned with reframing "the ongoing tensions between religious cultures and civic political life."[114] In what follows we continue to engage in second-level reflection on the concept of the post-secular, and with particular attention to the type of more general "imaginary" that it works to construct. While the term "post-secular" as such can be traced back to the 1960s,[115] by far the most influential version of the concept developed so far can be found in the more recent social–philosophical writing of Jürgen Habermas.[116]

In Habermas's writing, the term "post-secular" primarily refers to a general shift in "public consciousness" regarding "religion" and "religion"-related issues throughout "the affluent societies of Europe or countries such as Canada, Australia and New Zealand, where people's religious ties have steadily or rather quite dramatically lapsed in the post-World War II period."[117] As he explains (with reference to Casanova):

> Today, public consciousness in Europe can be described in terms of a "post-secular society" to the extent that at present it still has to "adjust itself to the continued existence of religious communities in an increasingly secularized environment." The revised reading of the secularization hypothesis relates less to its substance and more to the predictions concerning the future role of "religion." The description of modern societies as "postsecular" refers to a change in *consciousness*.[118]

This emphasis on a change in *consciousness* is an important one. For as Habermas is careful to point out, "in terms of *sociological indicators* ... the religious behaviour and convictions" of European populations "have

The "secular" and the "post-secular"   85

by no means changed to such an extent as to justify labelling these societies 'post-secular.'"[119] Habermas does not therefore regard the concept to be applicable to the United States, where religion in general (and Christianity in particular) retains considerable social and cultural significance. This change in "consciousness," Habermas continues, has been brought about by the following three "stimuli" in particular: (1) the increasing coupling of religion with global conflicts, which "undermines the secularistic belief in the *foreseeable disappearance* of religion and robs the secular understanding of the world of any triumphal zest"; (2) the more recent proliferation of religious voices and discourses on different national levels in connection with value-laden civil and political issues and controversies; and (3) following increasing immigration, particularly by people "from countries with traditional cultural backgrounds" (which appears to imply Muslim immigration in particular).[120]

In order for us to be able to adequately grasp this new situation, argues Habermas, both traditional secularist ideologies and monolithic theories of secularization prophesying the gradual, but ultimately inevitable, submission of "religion" to "secular" ideologies and values will have to be thoroughly re-evaluated and revised.[121] From the perspective of the sociology of religion, however, these are hardly original observations, nor were they at the time they were originally made in the mid-2000s. With regards to its "sociological" dimension, Habermas's concept of the post-secular really just reiterates the "deprivatization" thesis, as discussed above. Like much previous work in the "public religion" mold, it is therefore primarily based on the (far from uncontested) claim that Western societies are experiencing an increasing blurring of previously more clearly marked and differentiated "secular" and "religious" spheres. But as Casanova observes, Habermas quite evidently does not use the term post-secular to denote a situation where both individuals and entire societies would be "undergoing processes of religious revival, which would reverse previous secular trends."[122] Indeed, as Habermas himself emphasizes, there is little empirical evidence to suggest that. Rather, argues Casanova, it seems clear that, for Habermas, the "postsecular would [primarily] imply reflexively abandoning or at least questioning the modern secularist stadial consciousness which relegates 'religion' to a more primitive, more traditional, now surpassed stage of human and societal development."[123] The post-secular would then first and foremost refer to the need of a more thoroughgoing "correction of the secularistic self-misunderstanding."[124] Habermas's own subsequent clarifications also corroborate this view. For example, in one text from 2010 he wrote that

> The philosophically enlightened self-understanding of modernity stands in a peculiar dialectical relationship to the theological self-understanding of the major world religions, which intrude into this modernity as the most awkward element from its past.[125]

86 The "secular" and the "post-secular"

The highly problematic notion of "the theological self-understanding of the major world religions" aside, Habermas is quite clearly using the term post-secular to refer to a situation where it has become increasingly difficult to cling on to an understanding of modern societies as progressively "secular" societies where "religion" is no longer expected to occupy a visible role. In line with this general observation, in another text from 2013, he further clarifies that he uses

> the expression 'postsecular' as a sociological description of a shift in consciousness in largely secularized or 'unchurched' societies that by now have come to terms with the continued existence of religious communities, and with the influence of religious voices both in the national public sphere and on the global political stage.[126]

This largely reiterates his own previous position, although we might certainly question the degrees to which modern societies may be said to have "come to terms" with the continued presence and public visibility of religious communities and voices. Moreover, as Hans Joas comments, in Habermas's vision, "It is not the secular state that is being overcome, but merely a secularist self-understanding [*Selbstverständnis*]. And again, we might ask to whom such a self-image is in fact applied."[127] What is clear, though, is that only thoroughly *secularized* societies can become post-secular. If we were to extend the meaning of the post-secular as articulated by Habermas and apply it to entire *societies* – which is what Habermas himself to some extent does and which is also what a sizeable portion of all individual contributors to the post-secular debate routinely do – then it also seems rather clear that contemporary Western societies are not *yet* to be considered post-secular in a "sociological" sense. Rather, they might *become* so, and this is where the normative dimension of his concept of the post-secular comes into play.

The normative dimension of the concept signals a notable shift in Habermas's own thinking with regards to the possibility of religious voices and ideologies contributing to rational civil public debate in modern liberal constitutional democracies.[128] His thoughts on the matter, however, need to be understood in close relation to his broader social–philosophical thinking, both earlier and more recent.[129] The focus here has primarily been on social justice and the importance of the "public sphere" when considering the preconditions for a viable rational, inclusive, and participatory democracy.[130] In very compressed form, Habermas argues that in order for a rational and properly inclusive democracy to be achieved in highly religiously and ideologically diverse societies, both "secular" and "religious" individuals and groups need to fully recognize the right of each other to participate in and contribute to wider civic and political life. In order for them to be able to do so adequately, Habermas contends, both need to engage in mutual "complementary learning processes," whereby they will reflexively strive

The "secular" and the "post-secular"   87

to understand, respect, and accommodate the positions and arguments of one another. Ultimately, however, Habermas nevertheless clings on to what could perfectly well be called a "secularist" position when he adds that "in a constitutional state, all norms that can be legally implemented must be formulated and *publicly justified* in a language that all the citizens understand."[131] As he goes on to explain:

> The constitutional state must not only act neutrally towards worldviews but it must also rest on normative foundations which can be justified neutrally towards worldviews – and that means in postmetaphysical terms. The religious communities cannot turn a deaf ear to this normative requirement.[132]

The term "postmetaphysical" was developed by Habermas prior to his work on the post-secular. As described by Warren S. Goldstein, in its substantial sense, it refers to "agnostic positions, which distinguish 'between belief and knowledge' without giving validity to any particular religion but, at the same time, not denying their content."[133] The notion of the "postmetaphysical" therefore ties in with Habermas's broader contention that "religious semantics" and the ethical values embedded in "religion" (understood in his own particular sense) might possess the capability to become generalized into universal and commonly held norms.[134] This, then, is where the possible continued contribution of "religion" to public life essentially lies, in Habermas's view. In more practical terms, this means that the constitutional state becomes required to adopt a post-metaphysical stance and not exclude religious voices from public debate *a priori*. Religious communities must, for their part, correspondingly "open themselves" to the "normatively grounded expectation" that they renounce "political force and religious indoctrination as means of imposing religious truths."[135] If this were to happen, Habermas continues, it would amount to a "momentous step" that would involve "religious consciousness becoming reflexive when confronted with the necessity of relating its articles of faith to competing systems of belief and to the scientific monopoly on the production of factual knowledge."[136] The secular state should then strive to meet religious communities halfway and carefully consider "the question of whether it is imposing asymmetrical obligations on its religious citizens" by forcing them to articulate their values and concerns in a non-religious idiom.[137]

Following Eduardo Mendieta, in its normative dimension, the post-secular therefore comes to denote primarily

> a form of democratic enlightenment, one in which citizens' faith commitments are respected and regarded as contributions to the ethical pluralism of the community, which in turn is seen as a resource not only of dignity but of moral insight for the entire political community.[138]

88 The "secular" and the "post-secular"

The expectation that religious communities should become "reflexive," however, not only reflects Habermas' highly intellectualized understanding of religion; it also effectively excludes religious communities that are considered to use "political force and religious indoctrination as means of imposing religious truths"[139] from the very category of "religion" as such. As Michael Leezenberg points out, there is therefore clearly a sense in which those types of religious communities that for some reason are not prepared to conform to the "normatively grounded expectations" of the public sphere "cannot embody or express legitimate religious claims almost as a matter of definition."[140]

When the sociological and normative dimensions of Habermas's notion of the post-secular are both taken into account and are viewed as integral components of the same equation, it becomes rather clear that the post-secular, if applied to entire societies, largely refers to a possible *future* state of affairs. But this, it appears, is *provided that* constitutional democratic states actually rethink their secularist principles and adopt "postmetaphysical" stances; that they actually lend more room to "religious" arguments in the public sphere; and that "secular" and "religious" individuals and groups actually engage in the types of "complementary learning processes" envisioned. As such, grounded as it is in Habermas's previous thinking on "communicative action," the post-secular emerges as a fundamentally discursive and discourse-driven phenomenon.

Habermas's notion of the post-secular may be reasonably clear and easy to grasp, but it also contains a range of highly problematic aspects, most of which follow from his overly intellectualized and rationalized view of religion. For example, the "religion" that people have supposedly become more "conscious" of is repeatedly talked about in highly generalizing and essentializing terms. As Turner observes, this type of discourse on "religion" is reflective of a broader trend, whereby philosophers raise "major issues concerning the place of religion in apparently secular societies" while displaying "little engagement with the comparative empirical data that are generated by anthropologists and sociologists."[141] The resulting understanding of "religion" is therefore one that tends to be exclusively based on the formal theologies of Christianity, Judaism, and Islam.[142] In reality, of course, these three "religions" "all come in both liberal and conservative, 'open' and 'closed' forms."[143] Moreover, when examining wider public debates surrounding some contested issue in a given social context that involves both "religious" and "secular" parties, it is not always clear what constitutes a "religious" idea or argument as opposed to a "secular" one.[144] For, as Dillon points out, "Religious ideas, similar to nonreligious ideas, develop in, and out of, particular historical, social, cultural, political, and institutional contexts, and hence they are not as pure as some might like to presume."[145]

Habermas's discourse on the post-secular could generally be described in terms of a *hybrid* discourse that constitutes a mixture of several scholarly discourse types (e.g., socio-political, social-philosophical, political

The "secular" and the "post-secular" 89

theoretical, ethical, sociological, theological, and more). While it draws on several sociological discourses (e.g., "secularization," "public religion," "deprivatization"), its primary purpose is normative. The principal aim is not to describe or explain social phenomena, but to provide a normative, and largely social-philosophical, argument for what needs to, indeed *should*, come to pass if a properly inclusive democracy (as defined in Habermas's own particular way) is to be achieved. This, as we have seen, includes the adoption of a particular type of understanding of the very category of "religion" as well (some of the problematic aspects of which were also noted above). Habermas's discourse can thus also be described as a fragmented one, a discourse that strives to combine and reconcile a broader range of disciplinary perspectives and their associated key concepts and analytical categories. But while his ideas about the post-secular are certainly not without their problems from a sociological point of view, he should nevertheless be commended for having remained careful in his arguments and projections (as in his emphasis on a supposed change in people's *consciousness* of religion-related matters rather than a "resurgence of religion" as such). Whatever view one takes on the merits of Habermas's arguments, the basic meaning of the term post-secular emerges quite clearly from his writing. Or so it would seem. In what attests to its influence, individual contributors to the post-secular debate rarely fail to mention Habermas, and the broader literature on the post-secular also includes several excellent discussions and summations of his ideas on the subject. At the same time, however, the broader literature on the post-secular is also replete with all kinds of dubious, both inaccurate and sometimes directly misrepresentative, claims about what Habermas has purportedly argued about the post-secular. This has no doubt served to further muddle the concept's relation to a range of other key concepts and made the preservation of at least some degree of conceptual clarity increasingly difficult. For example, as will be illustrated through a few concrete examples below, the post-secular has long ago mutated into that of "post-secularity," "post-secularism," and even "post-secularization" – all of which tend to be used interchangeably to refer to the same abstruse "thing," "phenomenon," or "situation."

Second-level conclusions: the empirical basis of the post-secular

To say that there has emerged a multitude of different understandings of the post-secular and what it can be taken to mean or refer to would be an understatement. Rather than providing us with any type of more clearly defined research agenda, the post-secular has instead increasingly taken the form of a broad imaginary whose visions about a "resurgence of religion" and the supposed waning of the "secular" are typically simply assumed rather than actually investigated. As Beckford reminds us, "High-level abstractions operate like compressed narratives and, as such, can be rewritten

90 *The "secular" and the "post-secular"*

or reinterpreted to accommodate facts or ideas that might appear to be inconvenient."[146] Indeed, as different understandings of the post-secular have continued to proliferate, the concept as such has become less and less amenable to empirical grounding. Having said that, in the form articulated by Habermas (and indeed by some others), the notion of the post-secular could nevertheless quite easily be broken down into a set of empirically testable hypotheses.

For example, when it comes to the more "sociological" claims of Habermas's concept of the post-secular, we could devise numerous ways of empirically inquiring into whether there has indeed occurred a shift in "consciousness" with regard to people's perceptions about the continued (perhaps growing) role and visibility of "religion" in contemporary Western societies. We could also devise ways of inquiring into whether states and/or government agencies and bureaucracies are indeed becoming more attentive to the inclusion of religious voices in the public sphere. In addition, following Kim Knott, we could surely investigate the extent to which "religion has re-entered the public domain," as well as the particular ways in which "it" might have "had to adapt in order to do so."[147] If merely as a hypothesis, we could then perhaps also try to investigate to what extent the post-secular could be taken to "signify a new kind of religion that is informed and changed by its historical experience of exclusion and changing relationship with the modern nation-state and the condition of the secular,"[148] although this would still leave us with the question of what this "religion" supposedly consists of and how it should be defined and by whom.

As noted, in Habermas's version of the concept, the post-secular emerges as a fundamentally discursive and discourse-driven (alleged) phenomenon since it is first and foremost through discourse – whether in the form of state policy, the arguments of religious communities, or the dialogue between "religious" and "secular" parties – that the post-secular is supposed to become both actualized and realized. Hence, we should expect the post-secular to become visible and empirically researchable on the level of discourse and discursive practice. Actual public debates on religion-related issues would therefore constitute one obvious arena for such discourse-focused empirical investigations of the post-secular. As Knott argues, such an investigation could, for instance, focus on the "language of opposition" that often marks public debates involving "religious" and "secular" voices and stakeholders.[149] Such explorations could therefore also usefully be pursued with a close eye towards the roles that the news and current-affairs media continue to occupy *vis-à-vis* the religious field: as producers of various kinds of religion-related content, as gatekeepers and facilitators of public debate on religion-related issues, and sometimes as catalysts or even instigators of religion-related controversies. This is not least because the "The idea of a secular public sphere has ... [for long] played a major role in guiding journalism" throughout much of the Western world.[150] Explorations of this kind have, however, been remarkably scarce.

The "secular" and the "post-secular" 91

A notable exception is provided by Mia Lövheim's study of whether signs of the kinds of "complementary learning processes" envisioned by Habermas can actually be empirically observed in recent Swedish media discourse on religion-related matters. On the basis of an analysis of a larger body of broadsheet-newspaper editorials, Lövheim reaches the conclusion "that among the editorials that discuss religion as a main topic, a secularist position towards religion dominates."[151] She also, however, finds evidence of an emerging, although still fragmented, "alternative discourse" that appears to be more in line with Habermas's requirement of "complementary learning processes," and that encourages "secular" citizens to "encounter religious citizens as modern contemporaries and to see religious values as contributions to the common good in society."[152] But this alternative discourse, she notes, is *also* clearly "framed by an ideal of a homogeneous society, defined according to an imagined understanding of norms and values that hold Swedish society together" and which religious actors are, consequently, expected to conform to.[153] While Lövheim's study thus found some degree of evidence for the emergence of a more accommodating media discourse towards "religion" and the inclusion of religious voices in public civil debate, it also revealed the enduring prevalence of deeply engrained "secularist" positions. In order to substantiate various claims about the post-secular, similar types of explorations would need to be conducted in relation to the present day discourses and discursive practices of politics, state bureaucracies, and not least religious communities themselves. For to the extent, if any, that the post-secular is experienced as some kind of "reality" (or "consciousness"), we should expect this to first become visible in and through discourse and discursive practice.

Third-level analysis: the emerging discursive formation on the post-secular

In this final part of the chapter, we move on to consider the character of the emerging discursive formation on the post-secular, the main types of individual discourses that it has come to encompass, and the various ways in which key terms and concepts such as the "secular," "secularity," "secularism," "secularization," and "religion" tend to be employed. To call the post-secular an "emerging" discursive formation is to say that it has entered its "formative" stage and started to occupy an increasingly visible position within the broader order of discourse on religious change in the modern world. It is also to say, however, that it still displays a low degree of conceptual and terminological unity and coherence. As discussed in more detail in Chapter 2, a discursive formation is a relatively stable, but nevertheless constantly evolving, constellation of discourses that together provide a broader frame of reference in light of which, in relation to which, and through which a particular topic, phenomenon, or state of affairs is generally talked about and understood. Discursive formations therefore play a central role in determining what can meaningfully be said about a given

92 *The "secular" and the "post-secular"*

topic, phenomenon, or state of affairs at a given point in time. As such, discursive formations also carry their own knowledge claims and truth effects. Not only do they serve to frame, condition, and set the parameters for how particular topics, phenomena, or states of affairs are talked about and understood; they also play a central role in the construction of what counts as "knowledge" and "truth" about these topics, phenomena, or states of affairs. It is of central importance, therefore, to recognize that the "truths" and "knowledges" that particular discursive formations work to construct often end up having social and political ramifications that extend far beyond the realm of academia and scholarly theorizing. This is because, once established, discursive formations also tend to become varyingly operationalized and materialized in institutional structures and practices.

As also noted in Chapter 2, in order to gain a deeper understanding of a particular discursive formation we need to consider its conditions of possibility and development over time. Although the term "post-secular" as such has been around for quite some time already, the beginnings of the currently emerging discursive formation on the post-secular can be traced to back to Habermas's initial writings on the topic in the mid-2000s and the lively cross-disciplinary debate that they almost immediately sparked. As already noted, Habermas's more "sociological" ideas about the post-secular – general and unspecific as they are – are heavily indebted to Casanova's deprivatization thesis and notion of "public religion." Although there are several additional elements to the story, it is also worth noting that these debates on the post-secular emerge at a time marked by some particular types of, partly contrasting, scholarly developments: the wide establishment of the "public religion" discourse coupled with increasing talk about the supposed "return" or "resurgence" of "religion"; growing interest in religious pluralism in "superdiverse" societal settings; the wide normalization of highly critical views on secularization theory; growing scholarly interest in the "secular" (especially following the publication of Taylor's *A Secular Age* in 2007); and the rise of "non-religion" as a major new research topic. The broader context from which the post-secular emanated could thus be described as one that was simultaneously marked by a growing emphasis on the "secular" and the "non-religious" on the one hand, and the "return" and increasing public visibility of "religion" in "secular" societies on the other hand. In this broader context, the post-secular mostly took on the role as a particular type of heir to, and further elaboration of, the public religion discourse.

When considering the post-secular we are therefore dealing with a very young discursive formation that still remains in its formative phase. It is also a highly diverse one that has become enthusiastically adopted by scholars across a wide range of disciplines throughout the humanities and social sciences in a relatively short amount of time. But not only does the post-secular still lack sufficient empirical grounding; debates on the post-secular also remain marked by a stubborn refusal and unwillingness to engage in proper, reflexive, and sufficiently self-critical deliberation on the employment and application of key terms, concepts, and categories.

The "secular" and the "post-secular"   93

While the post-secular debate represents a more fundamental recentering of the debate on the future societal significance of "religion" in modern "secular" society, it continues to operate with ambiguous, and sometimes both misguided and misguiding, understandings of all of the concepts discussed previously in this chapter: "the secular," "secularity," "secularism," "secularization," and "public religion." In this, it contrasts sharply with the vision of a discursive sociology of religion as presented in this book. As the post-secular imaginary continues to proliferate, its (sometimes striking) lack of "discursive awareness" must therefore not be left unaddressed but rather be subjected to close and critical scrutiny.

As briefly outlined above, one could easily come up with all kinds of ways of empirically exploring various claims about the post-secular. Apart from only a few notable exceptions, this is not what the vast majority of all contributions to the post-secular debate have been interested in doing, however. Rather, following nearly two decades of debate, it still remains entirely premature to talk about "examples" or "instances" of the post-secular (or "post-secularity" or "post-secularism" for that matter). Before reaching that stage, there still needs to be considerably more clarity not only with regard to the boundaries of the concept as such, but also with regard to exactly in relation to which types or kinds of phenomena "signs" or "characteristics" of the post-secular might be empirically observed and investigated. More clarity therefore also needs to be reached with regards to methods and data. *Where* can "signs" of the post-secular be found and *how* (i.e., by which methods) can they be subjected to empirical analyses? Again, as a fundamentally discursive (alleged) phenomenon, we should expect the post-secular to become at least somehow visible in and through the discourse and discursive practices of state bureaucracies, politics, the media, religious communities, etc. Also, to the extent that the post-secular is taken to involve a *change* in people's general "consciousness" about "religion"-related matters, we should expect that "change" to be reflected too in changing discursive practices. But, unfortunately, apart from just a few notable exceptions such as that of Lövheim's study briefly discussed above, the debate has persistently been moving in the opposite direction as the term post-secular has acquired ever more and variegated meanings and continued to be predominantly used in ways divorced from any empirical grounding.

The increasing fragmentation of the post-secular debate is aptly illustrated by Beckford's survey and categorization of main understandings and approaches to the concept. More generally, he argues that

> The meanings of the postsecular are so varied and, in some cases, incompatible with each other that it would make little sense to try to assess whether any particular country or region of the world had actually entered a postsecular age.[154]

He then further divides the existing literature on the post-secular into six main groups, all but the last of which could be thought of in terms of

94 The "secular" and the "post-secular"

constituent individual discourses of a broader emerging discursive formation on the post-secular. The first "Secularization Deniers and Doubters" group comprises contributions that argue for the wholesale abandonment of the secularization thesis and hence "adopt a position termed 'postsecular.'"[155] The second "Building on the Secular" group is made up of work that takes the post-secular as primarily referring to a *scholarly position* that is characterized by a reflective and critical stance towards generalized and simplistic applications of various secularization theses, assumptions about the "secular" character of modern societies, and the associated expectation that "religion" will remain confined to its own societal sphere.[156] This understanding, which also connects to the Habermasian view as discussed above, has found relatively broad acceptance among scholars across several disciplines. The third "Reenchantment of Culture" group refers to a particular, smaller, and quite distinctive body of scholarship that "revolves around the idea that creative and artistic sensibilities are moving away from secular themes to explore a realm of enchantment and magic."[157] The fourth "Public Resurgence of Religion" group consists of contributions that argue that "Some of the most powerful implications of 'postsecularity' are said to occur in the spheres of politics and public policy" and that religion is now "returning" to the public sphere.[158] Such arguments are frequently coupled with arguments like those of the second "Building on the Secular" group. Empirical support for these types of claims could usefully be sought in changing discourses and discursive practices across (for example) politics, public-policy formation, and media. The fifth "Politics, Philosophy, and Theology" group essentially equals the Habermasian normative argument, which also tends to incorporate arguments from both the second and fourth groups. Here too, possible empirical grounding could usefully be sought in changing discourse and discursive practice across different social and cultural domains. In this highly influential (but frequently misunderstood) view, secularization and the post-secular are not, however, understood as mutually exclusive terms. The final, sixth "A Plague on All Your Houses" group refers to a variety of critical and dismissive views of the concept of the post-secular as such.[159]

As can readily be seen from the above, the post-secular has acquired a wide range of different, both varyingly relating and contrasting, meanings. Beckford is surely right in observing that this variety is at least partly attributable to "the unusually wide range of intellectual disciplines and fields with an interest in it."[160] Even so, as he goes on to point out, "the orientation of many writings about the postsecular" is "normative and speculative";[161] but what is more serious, "concern with empirical evidence and analysis is relatively underdeveloped. And curiosity about the processes whereby the basic terms of 'religion,' 'secular,' and 'postsecular' are negotiated in social life tends to be low."[162] Beckford's own conclusion reads as follows:

> The concept of "postsecular" trades on simplistic notions of the secular. It has a shortsighted view of history. It refuses to examine the legal

The "secular" and the "post-secular" 95

and political forces at work in regulating what counts as "religion" in public life. There is therefore a danger that talking about the postsecular will be like waving a magic wand over all the intricacies, contradictions, and problems of what counts as religion to reduce them to a single, bland category.[163]

As noted earlier in this chapter, previous disagreements and quarrels in the wider longstanding debate on religious change in the modern world have frequently been discursive in character and typically revolved around differing and contrasting understandings and uses of particular key terms, concepts, and categories.[164] By contrast, the post-secular debate, perhaps partly as a result of its fragmented character, maintains little, if any, conceptual hygiene. Internal critique with regard to the employment of key terms and concepts is also very rare. That is, apart from critical surveys such as that of Beckford's, individual contributors rarely critically examine or scrutinize each other's usages and employments of key terms and concepts such as "the secular," "secularism," "secularity," or "religion." Part of the explanation for this surely lies in the fact that the post-secular debate has come to encompass such a broad palette of different discourse types and repertoires so as to make disagreements over key terms and concepts practically pointless. Put another way, in a situation where so many different things can *already* be said and claimed about the post-secular, and where the post-secular can *already* be talked about in such a large variety of different "senses," disagreements on key terms and concepts such as "the secular" or "secularism" in effect cease to really matter. This is not a particularly good recipe for long-term durability, though. But in spite of its fragmented character, the post-secular imaginary has continued to spread and proliferate throughout the humanities and social sciences. As noted in Chapter 3, when new discourses on the place and role of "religion" (or the "secular") in modern society gain more traction and visibility throughout academia, they also become increasingly difficult to ignore and, so to speak, acquire a life of their own. "Talk," to put it simply, has a tendency to generate more "talk." This is clearly the case with the concept of the post-secular, which has now come to transcend so many disciplinary borders. In relation to this, Beckford makes an important point when he writes that the "breadth [and] ... range of disciplines" that have become occupied with the post-secular "may help to create the impression that there must indeed be something at the center of so many different discussions."[165]

As noted in Chapter 2, an adequate analysis of discourse and discursive practice should pay attention to the most significant contexts in which particular discourses are produced, circulated, and interpreted. The academic community, not surprisingly, constitutes the primary site for the production, circulation, and consumption of discourses on the post-secular, with academics simultaneously functioning as their primary producers, addressees, participants, and audiences. We have already seen how discourses on

96 The "secular" and the "post-secular"

the post-secular are marked by high degrees of intertextuality and inter-discursivity, typically mixing several scholarly discourse types (e.g., philosophical, theological, sociological). By now, a large number of academic conferences have included "post-secular" in their titles, several edited volumes have been devoted to the subject, and large amounts of journal articles have explored or touched upon the topic in one way or the other.[166] The year 2019 also witnessed the publication of the *Routledge Handbook of Postsecularity* – the single most extensive volume devoted to the topic thus far. In the following we shall consider this particular volume in more detail and thus submit the notion of the post-secular to actual third-level analysis. Our data will therefore consist of previous scholarly work on the topic as contained in this particular volume. The aim is not, however, to provide any detailed analyses in this regard, but rather to more generally illustrate the application of discursive perspectives in critical analyses of scholarly discourse itself.

The *Routledge Handbook* includes altogether 35 chapters, which, apart from the Introduction and Afterword, are organized in sections titled "Philosophical meditations," "Theological perspectives," "Theory, space, social relations," and "Political and social engagement." Note that the volume includes no section on "sociological perspectives" or the like. Instead, it includes an entire section on "theological perspectives," which is particularly noteworthy considering the longstanding "division of labor" between theology and the study of religion and the fact that "theological perspectives" often constitute *data* for scholars of religion.

Handbooks are particular types of publications. Most commonly, they are comprised of "state-of-the-art" types of chapters that are frequently used for instruction and teaching purposes. As such, they constitute highly significant vehicles for the wider dissemination, perpetuation, and firmer establishment of particular scholarly discourses. The main objective of the *Routledge Handbook*, Justin Beaumont and Klaus Eder state, "is to deliver the much needed theoretical and conceptual clarity and coherence across disciplines."[167] But while the volume does indeed contain several solid chapters, it clearly falls short in this regard. Rather than providing any further "conceptual clarity and coherence," the volume is more adequately described as a further testament to the conceptual confusion and incoherence that has come to mark debates on the post-secular more generally. The introduction is itself quite illustrative of this. For example, without much further discussion or clarification, Beaumont and Eder write of "post-secular*ity*" as that "generic term covering 'the postsecular', 'postsecularism', and 'postsecular society' together."[168] Having duly noted that there is little agreement as to the precise meaning of the term, they go on to state that "at its most general level, postsecularity might refer to the persistence, reformulation, or resurgence of religion in the public sphere."[169] Note the use of the word "might" here. To rephrase, "post-secularity," then, *might*

The "secular" and the "post-secular" 97

be taken to refer to the supposed enduring presence of, the changing character of, or the increasing visibility of "religion" in the public sphere, or perhaps none or all of these at once. The key word here, though, is "public," which the authors also leave undefined. Its vagueness aside, the concept of post-secularity as outlined here therefore clearly presumes the factuality of what would need to be empirically investigated and substantiated in the first place.

As to the supposed "empirical basis to the thesis of postsecular*ism*" (i.e., no longer "postsecularity"), Beaumont and Eder go on assert the following: "The simple version is that religion returns to the public sphere of secular society and that the project of secularism, based on the rule of law and on a universalist and rationalist ideology, continues to wane."[170] While we never get to read about the "complicated version," suffice it to say that the concept of (now) post-secularism comes to rest completely on the good old, highly contested, but ultimately empirically researchable and testable, claim that "religion" is now "re-entering" the public sphere. We are not, however, provided with any clarification whatsoever as to what this "religion" supposedly "is" or how it should be understood. The Introduction, therefore, simply takes the term "religion" for granted and thereby participates in the further perpetuation of a simplistic "commonsense" and reified Western (Judeo-Christian-type) understanding of "religion" as discussed in Chapter 3. In this, the introduction is also further reflective of a much broader trend in the literature on the post-secular as already identified by Beckford: a repeated failure and unwillingness to properly and reflexively engage with the category of "religion" itself. "Religion" nevertheless remains one of those key concepts and categories that would be in need of perhaps most further clarification in debates on the post-secular.

In addition to the above, at times, Beaumont's and Eder's account itself displays characteristics of a "religious discourse" as discussed in Chapter 2. Consider, for example, this statement: "Critical inquiries into postsecularity unsettle both debates on the postsecular as well as the secular and the complementarities between these two discourses. The outworking of this disturbance tends towards transcendence, philosophical monism, and pantheism."[171] Whatever this is supposed to mean, it generally reflects the increasing openness towards religious/theological discourse types that has come to characterize debates on the post-secular more generally. Indeed, as we will continue to explore in more detail below, the emerging discursive formation on the post-secular can well be described as one where the mixing of scholarly and religious/theological discourse types is not only commonplace, but sometimes even directly celebrated and encouraged. In terms of lexis, debates on the post-secular are therefore characterized by uses of words and terminology that one would not normally come across in social-scientific or sociological

98 The "secular" and the "post-secular"

discourse. Indeed, some proponents of the post-secular imaginary might even argue that such mixings of discourse types allow us to move beyond the confines of established and received "secularist" languages (at other points in the Introduction to the *Routledge Handbook*, Beaumont and Eder also come close to arguing this). But recall here our previous discussion on the difference between scholarly and folk concepts and discourse types in Chapter 3. Unreflective mixings or "dialogues" between religious and scholarly discourse types can easily work to considerably blur the boundaries and to confuse the qualitative differences between the two. As a consequence, folk or religious/theological *emic* concepts may inadvertently (or, worse, knowingly) end up being used as scholarly *etic* concepts. Put another way, through their uncritical integration into scholarly discourse, religious/theological concepts may end up assuming the role of tools in their own analysis.

In the following we shall take a closer look at some of the most salient types of conceptual confusions and conflations in the post-secular debate in light of a few concrete examples all taken from separate chapters contained in the *Routledge Handbook*. The aim is partly to provide a more general illustration of the types of discourses that we can find in the post-secular debate, and partly also to highlight the degree of confusion that can be found regarding the employment of certain key terms and concepts not just within the pages of a single volume, but within the confines of individual chapters as well.

Concept–reality confusion

As with all and any theoretical concepts, when considering the post-secular it is of the utmost importance not to confuse concept with reality. But as Beckford rightly observes, "the literature on the postsecular is shot through with uncertainty about the question of whether it refers to a concept or a reality."[172] Indeed, debates on the post-secular are replete with arguments that simply take for granted that contemporary modern societies *are* indeed post-secular. This has not, however, gone unnoticed by critically minded contributors to the post-secular debate. For example, as Herbert De Vriese and Guido Vansheewijck warn us, "disregard for this [concept-reality] distinction threatens to reinforce exactly those questionable ideas and presuppositions of classical secularization theory which are credulously assumed to have been overcome."[173] There is little awareness, therefore, of the constructed nature of the concept of the "post-secular" as such. To illustrate, consider the following passage:

> This chapter explores radical orthodoxy's (RO) genealogy of the secular, its description of the contemporary postsecular situation, and the task it has set itself in renewing Christian socialism in a postliberal form.[174]

The "secular" and the "post-secular" 99

This first example provides a general illustration of concept–reality confusion in that the author readily refers to "the contemporary postsecular *situation*." The chapter seeks to account for the notion of the post-secular that emerges from the work of radical orthodox theologians such as John Milbank and Graham Ward. The focus lies not, however, on how radical orthodox theologians *construct* a particular vision of the postsecular, but rather on how their work *describes* a supposedly already *existing* "postsecular situation." Let us consider another similar example:

> A distinguishing feature of this postsecular age is the polarization of these two tendencies. Religion is acquiring a new significance, both as an instrument for political struggle and also as the path of a new spiritual unification of the world.[175]

Here, the post-secular is referred to as an "age," thereby suggesting something much more fundamental than simply a "situation," such as in the previously quoted passage. Here, then, the presumption seems to be that we have not only already entered such an "age," but also learned to identify its "distinguishing features." This passage is also further illustrative of the typically quite unreserved mixing of scholarly and religious/theological discourses types referred to just above. In this case, apart from "an instrument in political struggle," the author asserts, the post-secular offers a path towards a "new spiritual unification of the world," whatever that could possibly mean.

Our third example is different in that it does not include any elements of a religious/theological discourse. It also provides a somewhat rare example of the application of the concept of the post-secular in a non-Western context.

> The manifestations and consequences of public religions in the postsecular condition are contingent and indefinite. In both China and Singapore, the visibilities of religions in public cultures are overseen, managed, and approved by the state, but postsecularity means very different things in the two societies—China is postsecular in the sense that the state has orchestrated and closely controlled the transition from overwhelming secularism to the revival of religions in public cultures, with the purpose of harnessing the benefits brought by faiths and religious cultures.[176]

In this excerpt, the authors speak of "the postsecular *condition*," yet end up arguing that "postsecularity *means* very different things" in China and Singapore respectively. But while "meanings" vary, the "condition" presumably remains the same. China, they also argue, "*is* postsecular" in a certain sense. That is an odd "sense," though, considering that China's "harnessing of the benefits brought by faiths and religious cultures" applies

100 *The "secular" and the "post-secular"*

only to those "religious cultures" that fulfill the requirements of "patriotic organizations" as defined by the Chinese state.[177]

The above provides just a very general illustration of the concept–reality confusion and discursive mixing that characterizes much work on the post-secular. It is also worth noting that the language in all of the passages quoted above expresses little doubt as to the supposed "reality" of their post-secular visions. Rather, we read about "*the* contemporary postsecular situation," "*this* postsecular age," and "*the* postsecular condition."

"Secular"–"secularism"–"secularity"–"secularization" conflation

Work on the post-secular is also marked by a high degree of conceptual confusion and conflation with regards to the concepts of the "secular," "secularism," "secularity," and "secularization." As should be clear from our discussion above, while these are all closely interrelated concepts, they should by no means be equated or conflated with one another. Yet such conflations abound in the literature on the post-secular.

The term "post-secular" itself suggests that something that was once "secular" is no longer so, no longer as evidently so, or no longer automatically and uncritically viewed as such. Many sociologists of religion find the last alternative at least to some extent agreeable. "Post-secularism," by contrast, suggests a situation where secularist ideologies have increasingly lost ground and viability. This might or might not be the case, varying from one particular societal context to another, but in light of our discussion above, it seems clear that secularist policies have by no means been abandoned to such an extent as to justify applying this concept to modern societies more generally. "Post-secularity," in its turn, suggests some kind of more general shift from one broader societal and cultural condition to another. In this case, that would presumably be a shift from a previous condition marked by a "secularist stadial consciousness" as identified by Casanova to one that has somehow moved "past" or "beyond" that. There is little empirical evidence to suggest this, however. These, then, are (at least some of) the implications of the prefix "post" in each case. And it is of particular importance to recognize that each and every theoretical "post-" of this type will always need to be construed and constructed on the basis of some particular understanding of what supposedly *preceded* it. Different versions of the *post*-secular, in other words, will inevitably need to be constructed on the basis of particular understandings of the "secular" and the processes of secularization that made things so. Hence the term "post-secularization," the origins of which are unclear. The term might very well have come about as a result of the emergence of "post-secularism" and "post-secularity" and the increasing confusion surrounding their relation to and differentiation from one another. The term "post-secularization", in any case, suggests that processes of secularization have "stopped" or that we have transitioned into

The "secular" and the "post-secular"   101

an era where secularization no longer occurs. There is no clear evidence for this either, although the debate certainly continues. Alternatively, and more sensibly, the term "post-secularization" might refer to a situation where scholars have increasingly abandoned or "moved beyond" secularization theory, or at least become increasingly critical towards it.

In the end, speculations about what these respective concepts might or might not refer to or be taken to mean in each individual case are quite futile. This is because large numbers of scholars routinely continue to use all of them without explaining what they take them to mean (or *not* to mean, for that matter). What is more, these terms are frequently used alongside each other in seemingly interchangeable ways. As a result, we end up in situations where we are unsure not only about the meaning and application of single concepts, but the meaning of several concepts in different combinations all at once. As a first general example, consider the following passage:

> We challenge the "historical shift" vision of postsecularism, not by advancing another grand history, but rather through a series of smaller stories, which highlight ways in which religious minorities have experienced the postsecular.[178]

Here, the authors start out by talking about "postsecularism" and then end up talking about the "postsecular" in the very same sentence. The difference, if any, between these two concepts is never made clear, nor is their relation to one another. This can nevertheless be regarded a quite innocuous example and the authors also stick to a sociological/social-theoretical type of discourse. Our second example is somewhat more complicated:

> This chapter aims to unpack the question of the sort of religiosity for which postsecularity reflects a resurgence. Most sociological literature portrays postsecularity as a quality of an age or a culture. Here, I study postsecularity additionally as a quality of people's religiosity, while going on to explore its relationship with boundary marking. Furthermore, I aim to apply quantitative analysis to postsecularism and to compile a set of questions identifying postsecular attitudes...[179]

This argument is illustrative of all three types of main confusions and conflations discussed in this section. For example, the author argues that postsecularity is "reflective" of a particular "sort of religiosity." The concept, therefore, is used as a description of a supposed empirical reality. There is also some evident concept–reality confusion in that the author unproblematically frames "postsecularity as a *quality* of an age or a culture" (although this is hardly how "most" sociological literature portrays the post-secular). With regards to conceptual conflation, within the space of just four sentences, the author manages to first talk about "postsecularity,"

102 *The "secular" and the "post-secular"*

then switch to "postsecularism," and then finally to "postsecular." Again, the distinction, if any, between these terms is never clarified, although the author at one point appears to suggest that he employs "postsecularism" as a sub-category of "postsecularity." But throughout the chapter, these three concepts continue to appear alongside each other in ways similar to that of the passage above. This, then, provides an apt example of a highly confusing employment of these concepts that forces (the conceptually attentive) reader to constantly ponder the relation of each to each, the relation of each to the other two, and the relation between all three of them – and this on each and every occasion that they appear together in some constellation throughout the text.

The above, again, provides just a few illustrations of the types of conceptual conflations we frequently encounter in work on the post-secular. On a more general level, such conflations serve to significantly obscure what is supposedly actually talked about. More specifically, they also serve to obscure the precise capacity (e.g., descriptive? analytical? evocative?) in which these concepts are being used. But perhaps most concerning of all, these recurring conflations might give scholars the impression that clear distinctions between these concepts do not need to be upheld.

"Religion" and/in the "post-secular"

As already discussed, debates on the post-secular have so far displayed a striking unwillingness to engage properly and reflexively with the category of "religion." It should therefore come as no surprise that much work on the post-secular tends to reflect "commonsense" and reified *sui generis*-type understandings of "religion." This is to say that much work on the post-secular tends to talk about "religion" in highly unspecified, generalized, and frequently essentializing ways. But since the (Western) category of the "secular" needs to be understood as standing in a dialectical and co-constitutive relation to the (Western) category of "religion," this most certainly needs to apply to the "secular" in the "post-secular" as well. We need to ask, therefore, what kind of "religion" is implied by talk about the "post-secular" (along with corollary terms such as "post-secularism" and "post-secularity"). But with the exception of a handful of critical commentators, this question is rarely asked in work on the post-secular. Rather, while contributors to the post-secular debate quite frequently engage in elaborate examinations and discussions of the concept or category of the "secular," they only very rarely display any substantial interest in the concept or category of "religion," and all too frequently none whatsoever. The post-secular debate, in short, remains one-sidedly focused on the "secular" and "secularism" while it effectively ignores the "religion" that it simultaneously alleges is now reasserting itself. Indeed, among altogether 35 contributions, only one single chapter in the *Routledge Handbook* expressly engages in a proper, reflexive, and informed (albeit brief) critical discussion

The *"secular"* and the *"post-secular"*   103

on the category of "religion."[180] What we see instead is a fair number of commentators arguing for (or rather presuming) the existence or emergence of some kind of "post-secular religion" or "religiosity." Consider the following example:

> I use the locution postsecular in a twofold sense: one, in the West, secularization refers to the historical Enlightenment whereby the vanishing point of modernity is envisioned to yield a full rationalization of religious claims. Return of the religious after the process of rationalization of religious claims (their translation without a remainder into one of the cultural spheres of modernity, i.e., sciences, law, and aesthetics) would give birth to postsecular religiosity.[181]

In a highly jargon-laden style, this author argues for the "birth" of a "post-secular religiosity" that appears to largely tie in with the "reflexive religion" envisioned by Habermas, as briefly discussed above. In the absence of any discussion of the category of "religion" or concept of "religiosity," however, one is left wondering how this new type of "religiosity" should be understood exactly, where it could be found, how it could be observed and researched, and so on. This passage also provides an illustration of the large variety of "senses" in which the post-secular tends to be employed. Our second example takes us to quite another place:

> "Radicalized postsecularism" questions Habermas' position and declares we have never been secular. Radical postsecularism is rooted in Rudolf Otto's claim that is presented in his seminal work, *The Idea of the Holy*: an inquiry into the non-rational factor in the idea of the divine and its relation to the rational (1917, 1958), which defines an essence of religious experience as a relationship with the numinous—"the Absolute Other" … From this perspective, "radicalized post-secularism" focuses on a void between stabilized elements of human existence and "the Absolute Unknown".[182]

Here, in his argument for "radicalized postsecularism," the author goes "all-in" on the *sui generis* discourse on religion, relying on the arguments of one of its most prominent earlier representatives (Rudolf Otto). In this, the author, in effect, actually sidesteps the entire debate on the "secular," "secularization," and the "post-secular" by positing that society never has been, and presumably never will be, "secular" because of humanity's inherent "religious impulse." He also devises his own particular form of "post-secularism" – "*radicalized* postsecularism" – described as being focused on "a void between stabilized elements of human existence and 'the Absolute Unknown'." Whatever this could possibly mean, it is certainly further reflective of the intermingling of scholarly and religious/theological-discourse types.

104 *The "secular" and the "post-secular"*

Our last example comes from the discipline of geography:

> Differently from exclusivist and inclusivist confessionalism, pluralism rejects the intrinsic superiority of any religion towards the others. It assumes that different religions are united by a substantial agreement on the subject matter, an ineffable living reality they all speculate on and approach towards ... since the cultivation of postsecular religiosity transcends official sacred places, the scope of planning must exceed the provision of places of worship.[183]

This author posits that all "religion" is united by its focus on the same "ineffable living reality." "Postsecular religiosity," in turn, is described as something that is currently being "cultivated," or that can be "cultivated." That "cultivation," moreover, "transcends official sacred places." "Postsecular religiosity" also seems to have a particular relationship to "pluralism," understood as some kind of philosophical stance towards "confessionalism." Presumably, then, "postsecular religiosity" also transcends the borders of particular religious communities or even particular "religions" (to the extent that such a statement is sensible in the first place). This, then, provides yet another example of the mixing of scholarly and religious/theological-discourse types. The end result is a highly muddled account that certainly obscures more that it explains.

The passages discussed above all provide concrete illustrations of particular types of unreflexive employments of the category and concept of "religion" in work on the post-secular. These shortcomings are more broadly reflective of the enduring salience of the *sui generis* approach to "religion" as discussed in more detail in Chapter 3 in the sense that "religion" – or more specifically "religiosity" in the above cases – is framed as something so commonsensical that it presumably needs no further explanation. But the meaning and explanatory value of a term like "postsecular religiosity" will obviously be directly dependent on the particular way in which both "postsecular" and "religiosity" are understood in that "postsecular religiosity" configuration.

Third-level conclusions

As illustrated above, the post-secular debate is marked by a general unwillingness to properly engage with the category of "religion," a tendency to confuse concept and reality, and a propensity to conflate closely related, but quite distinct, key terms and concepts. To be clear, these criticisms do not apply to all work on the post-secular. But considering how common and recurring these shortcomings are, debates on the post-secular can nevertheless generally be described as being marked by low degrees of discursive (self-) awareness. In this, the post-secular debate is generally marked by precisely those tendencies that a discursive sociology of religion as envisioned here

The "secular" and the "post-secular"   105

should work to counter. In addition to this, the concept also lacks sufficient empirical grounding. While these shortcomings have all been highlighted by critically minded commentators in the past, this has not had much of an effect on the broader post-secular debate, which continues to develop in a more speculative rather that empirical direction.

Our discussion above has provided a general description of the type of vocabulary and language use that has come to govern large parts of the emerging discursive formation on the post-secular. We have also briefly considered the most significant sites and contexts in which discourses on the post-secular are produced, circulated, and interpreted. We are now left with the task of trying to provide an (at least partial and tentative) explanation for *why* the post-secular imaginary has engendered such widespread and enthusiastic support among scholars across numerous different disciplines. On a more general level, the post-secular as discussed in this chapter can be viewed in light of the distinction between construal and construction with regards to the social functioning of discourse that was made in Chapter 2. Arguably, the post-secular debate has, thus far, in large part been based on certain types of construals (i.e., largely unsubstantiated claims and suppositions) of the present-day place and role of "religion" in what are (still) commonly regarded as thoroughly "secular" societies. But recall here that the concept, in many of its versions, also includes an expressed normative dimension. In these versions, the post-secular is therefore not simply about what "is," but also about what "ought to be." This, perhaps, provides part of the explanation for its wide appeal (coupled, of course, with the fact that the concept was picked up by Habermas, one of the world's most famous and influential public intellectuals).

It is certainly true that large numbers of scholars of religion, and perhaps especially sociologists of religion, used to share an expectation that "religion" would continue to decline and eventually lose its significance in highly modernized societies. Scholars have now increasingly started to see things differently. Whether reflective of these changes or not, it would not be an exaggeration to say that scholars of religion (as well as other scholars with an interest in "religion" such as perhaps theologians in particular) generally have a tendency to see and identify the "presence" of "religion" across different social and cultural contexts rather than the "absence" of it. We see this general tendency at play throughout large parts of the post-secular debate as well in the way that commentators often continue to argue for the "return" of religion (or even the emergence of "post-secular religion/religiosity") without grounding these claims in much, if any, actual empirical research or evidence. In this, they have a propensity to confuse what they expect to see (perhaps even what they would *like* to see) with what actually "is" (in the sense "can be empirically shown to be"). Provided that there is any truth to this (admittedly speculative) observation, then that would certainly provide additional parts of the explanation for the post-secular's wide appeal. This, however, in no way detracts from the fact

106 *The "secular" and the "post-secular"*

that debates on the post-secular generally remain marked by high degrees of conceptual ambiguity. Now, perhaps we should just give scholars who employ key terms like the "secular," "secularism," and "secularization" in ambiguous, fleeting, and confusing ways a "pass"? That, however, is not the kind of "courtesy" or "tolerance" that scholars normally extend to their peers, and nor should it be. Rather, we should always work to enhance our discursive awareness and call for improvements in that regard wherever we see a need for them.

Concluding remarks

Considering the character of the emerging discursive formation on the post-secular as critically discussed in this chapter, a key question becomes to what extent post-secular construals might have had any notable constructive effects within the wider order of discourse on the place and role of religion in modern society. Put another way, have post-secular construals (i.e., of the "resurgence of religion," the "waning of the secular") gained such wide acceptance that they have ceased to be understood as mere construals, but rather started to become viewed as "commonsense" *descriptions* of the way "things are?" One clear sign of this would be if and when growing numbers of scholars start to employ the term "post-secular" itself in a largely descriptive sense (for example, "in this post-secular world," "the post-secular condition," or "in a post-secular situation") in much the same way as the terms "secular" and "secularization" continue to be commonly employed (for example, "secular society" or "as a result of decades of secularization"). A further sign would be if and when the post-secular transforms into an analytical term and starts to be used to *explain* social, cultural, and "religious" developments and phenomena (for example, "X happens because society is post-secular" or "As an effect of the post-secular situation, X has...").

Sociologists of religion should remain attentive to these (partly still potential) developments. As discourses on the post-secular continue to proliferate, so too will individual sociologists of religion become increasingly compelled to address the "post-secular" in one way or another regardless of their own particular views on the topic. Indeed, sociologists of religion who are not proponents of the post-secular already tend to allude to it in various ways, although perhaps mostly to signal that they recognize what has indeed become an increasingly recognized concept. "Recognized," that is, as a concept that occupies an increasingly prominent position throughout a wide range of different scholarly disciplines. As a final comment, to the extent that the critical discussion of the post-secular provided in this chapter is found persuasive, we might want to seriously consider Dillon's warning: "If we are unsure about the secular, it may be intellectually premature to talk about the post-secular."[184]

Notes

1 Charles Taylor, *A Secular Age* (Cambridge, MA: The Belknap Press of Harvard University Press: 2007).
2 Calhoun, Juergensmeyer, and VanAntwerpen, "Introduction," 8.
3 Ibid., 5.
4 Charles Taylor, "Western Secularity," in *Rethinking Secularism*, eds. Craig Calhoun, Mark Juergensmeyer, and Jonathan VanAntwerpen (Oxford: Oxford University Press, 2011), 32.
5 Ibid.
6 José Casanova, "The Secular, Secularizations, Secularisms," in *Rethinking Secularism*, eds. Craig Calhoun, Mark Juergensmeyer, and Jonathan VanAntwerpen (Oxford: Oxford University Press, 2011), 56, emphasis added.
7 Ibid.
8 Ibid., 63.
9 Craig Calhoun, "Time, World, and Secularism", in *The Post-Secular in Question: Religion in Contemporary Society*, eds. Philip S. Gorski, David Kyuman Kim, John Torpey, and Jonathan VanAntwerpen (New York: New York University Press, 2012), 349.
10 Calhoun, Juergensmeyer, and VanAntwerpen, "Introduction", 7; François Gauthier, "From Nation-State to Market: The Transformations of Religion in the Global Era, as Illustrated by Islam," *Religion* 48, no. 3 (2018): 390.
11 Gauthier, "From Nation-State," 390.
12 Ibid., 393.
13 Calhoun, "Time, World," 351.
14 Peter van der Veer, cited in Gauthier, "From Nation-State," 393.
15 Cf. Asad, *Formations of the Secular*, 191.
16 Calhoun, Juergensmeyer, and VanAntwerpen, "Introduction", 7; cf. Fitzgerald, *Discourse on Civility*, 6.
17 Calhoun, "Time, World," 361.
18 Don Slater and Fran Tonkiss, *Market Society: Markets and Modern Social Theory* (Cambridge: Polity Press, 2001), 2.
19 John Locke, cited Stoddard and Martin, "Introduction," 6.
20 Locke, cited in Walsh, "Religion is a Private Matter," 75.
21 Asad, *Formations of the Secular*, 133.
22 Ibid., 135.
23 Ibid., 24.
24 Fitzgerald, *Discourse on Civility*, 45.
25 Ibid., 283, emphasis added.
26 Arnal and McCutcheon, *The Sacred*, 109.
27 Asad, cited in Walsh, "Religion is a Private Matter," 77.
28 For example, Calhoun, Juergensmeyer, and VanAntwerpen, "Introduction," 8.
29 Asad, *Formations of the Secular*, 25.
30 Ibid., 1.
31 Casanova, "The Secular," 60.
32 José Casanova, ""Exploring the Postsecular: "Three Meanings of 'the Secular' and Their Possible Transcendence," in *Habermas and Religion*, eds. Craig Calhoun, Eduardo Mendieta, and Jonathan VanAntwerpen (Cambridge: Polity Press, 2013), 30.
33 Casanova, "The Secular," 60.
34 Casanova, "Exploring the Postsecular," 30.
35 Casanova, "The Secular," 60.
36 Ibid., 59.

108 *The "secular" and the "post-secular"*

37 Ibid., 66.
38 Taylor, *A Secular Age*, 549.
39 José Casanova, "A Secular Age: Dawn or Twilight?" in *Varieties of Secularism in a Secular Age*, eds. Michael Warner, Jonathan VanAntwerpen, and Craig Calhoun (Cambridge, MA: Harvard University Press, 2010), 266.
40 Peter Berger, *The Sacred Canopy: Elements for a Sociological Theory of Religion* (Garden City: Doubleday, 1967), 123–4.
41 Asad, *Formations of the Secular*, 23.
42 Ibid.; cf. Calhoun, Juergensmeyer, and VanAntwerpen, "Introduction," 5.
43 Casanova, "The Secular," 66–7.
44 Ibid.
45 Calhoun, Juergensmeyer, and VanAntwerpen, "Introduction," 6.
46 Casanova, ""Exploring the Postsecular," 29.
47 Craig Calhoun, "Secularism, Citizenship, and the Public Sphere," in *Rethinking Secularism*, eds. Craig Calhoun, Mark Juergensmeyer, and Jonathan VanAntwerpen (Oxford: Oxford University Press, 2011), 77.
48 Casanova, "Exploring the Postsecular," 29–30.
49 Casanova, "The Secular," 69.
50 Cf. Asad, *Formations of the Secular*.
51 Casanova, "The Secular," 60.
52 Ibid.
53 Asad, *Formations of the Secular*, 21; 186.
54 Ibid., 166.
55 Ibid., 171, emphases added.
56 José Casanova, *Public Religions in the Modern World* (Chicago, IL: University of Chicago Press, 1994), 18.
57 Casanova. "The Secular," 41.
58 David Martin, *On Secularization. Towards a Revised General Theory* (Hampshire: Ashgate, 2005), 8.
59 Bryan R. Wilson, *Religion in Secular Society: A Sociological Comment* (Oxford: Oxford University Press, 1966).
60 Berger, *The Sacred Canopy*.
61 Thomas Luckmann, *The Invisible Religion: The Problem of Religion in Modern Society* (Basingstoke: MacMillan, 1967).
62 David Martin, *The Religious and the Secular* (London: Routledge & Kegan Paul, 1969).
63 Steve Bruce, *God Is Dead: Secularization in the West* (Oxford: Blackwell Publishing, 2002), 39.
64 Martin, *On Secularization*, 3.
65 Ibid., 5.
66 Ibid., 137.
67 Shmuel N. Eisenstedt, ed., *Multiple Modernities* (Oxon: Routledge, 2002).
68 For example, Grace Davie, *Europe: The Exceptional Case: Parameters of Faith in the Modern World* (London: Darton, Longman and Todd, 2002).
69 For example, Jason S. Lantzer, *Mainline Christianity: The Past and Future of America's Majority Faiths* (New York: New York University Press, 2012), 20; Peter L. Berger, Grace Davie, and Effie Fokas, *Religious America, Secular Europe?: A Theme and Variations* (Aldershot: Ashgate, 2008), 18.
70 Grace Davie, *Religion in Britain: A Persistent Paradox* (Malden, MA: Blackwell Publishers, 2015), 22.
71 Ibid., 135.
72 Ibid., 81; 135.
73 Casanova, "Exploring the Postsecular," 32.

74 Ibid.
75 Ibid., 38.
76 Ibid., 33.
77 Hugh McLeod, *The Religious Crisis of the 1960s* (Oxford: Oxford University Press, 2007), 16.
78 Sharon Hanson, "The Secularisation Thesis: Talking at Cross Purposes," *Journal of Contemporary Religion* 12, no. 2 (1997): 159.
79 Ibid., 161.
80 Jonathan Fox, *An Introduction to Religion and Politics: Theory and Practice* (Oxon: Routledge, 2013), 24.
81 Casanova, *Public Religions*.
82 Cf. Titus Hjelm, "Understanding the New Visibility of Religion." *Journal of Religion in Europe* 7, no. 3–4 (2014): 207.
83 Casanova, *Public Religions*, 58.
84 Ibid., 64.
85 James A. Beckford, "The Return of Public Religion: A Critical Assessment of a Popular Claim," *Nordic Journal of Religion and Society* 23, no. 2 (2010): 125.
86 Ibid.
87 Ibid.
88 Beckford, *Social Theory*, 76; for an extended discussion, see Peter W. Edge, *Religion and Law: An Introduction* (Aldershot: Ashgate, 2006).
89 Beckford, *Social Theory*, 77.
90 Asad, *Formations of the Secular*, 183–4.
91 Ibid., 184.
92 Ibid., 185.
93 Beckford, "The Return," 123.
94 Hjelm, "Understanding the New," 207.
95 Stephen Coleman and Karen Ross, *The Media and the Public: "Them" and "Us" in Media Discourse* (Chichester: John Wiley & Sons Ltd., 2010), 123.
96 Ibid., 3.
97 Ibid., emphasis added.
98 Ibid., 8–9.
99 Ibid., 9.
100 Jens Köhrsen, "How Religious Is the Public Sphere? A Critical Stance on the Debate about Public Religion and Post-Secularity," *Acta Sociologica* 55, no. 3 (2012).
101 For example, Peter Beyer, "Religion in Global Civil Society," in *Religion in Global Civil Society*, ed. Mark Juergensmeyer (Oxford: Oxford University Press, 2006), 79–81.
102 Mia Lövheim and Marta Axner, "Mediatised Religion and Public Spheres: Current Approaches and New Questions," in *Religion, Media, and Social Change*, eds. Kennet Granholm, Marcus Moberg, and Sofia Sjö (New York: Routledge, 2015), 39.
103 Monica D. Toft, Daniel Philpott, and Timothy S, Shah, *God's Century: Resurgent Religion and Global Politics* (New York: W. W. Norton, 2011), 23; cf. Jeffrey Haynes and Anja Hennig, "Introduction," in *Religious Actors in the Public Sphere: Means, Objectives, and Effects*, eds. Jeffrey Haynes and Anja Hennig (Oxon: Routledge, 2011), 1.
104 For example, Caelesta Braun-Poppelaars and Marcel Hanegraaff, "Conceptualizing Religious Advocacy: Religious Interest Groups and the Process of Public Policy Making," in *Religious Actors in the Public Sphere: Means, Objectives, and Effects*, eds. Jeffrey Haynes and Anja Hennig (Oxon: Routledge, 2011).

110 The "secular" and the "post-secular"

105 Ibid., 140.
106 Ibid., 142.
107 Fox, *An Introduction*, 88.
108 For example, Braun-Poppelaars and Hanegraaff, "Conceptualizing Religious Advocacy," 142.
109 Christopher Partridge, *The Re-enchantment of the West (vol. 1): Understanding Popular Occulture* (London: Continuum, 2004), 8.
110 Ibid.
111 See for example, Karel Dobbelaere, *Secularization: An Analysis at Three Levels* (Brussels: P.I.E.- Peter Lang, 2002).
112 For example, Jeffrey Haynes, "Introduction," in *Religion, Politics, and Institutional Relations: Selected Essays*, ed. Jeffrey Haynes (Oxon: Routledge, 2011), 5–6.
113 Casanova, "Exploring the Postsecular," 44–5.
114 Michele Dillon, "Can Post-Secular Society Tolerate Religious Differences?" *Sociology of Religion* 71, no. 2 (2010): 142.
115 James A. Beckford, "Public Religions and the Postsecular: Critical Reflections," *Journal for the Scientific Study of Religion* 5, no. 1 (2012): 3.
116 Jürgen Habermas, "Religion in the Public Sphere," *European Journal of Philosophy* 14, no. 1 (2006): 1–25.
117 Jürgen Habermas, "Notes on Post-Secular Society," *New Perspectives Quarterly* 25 (Fall 2008), 17.
118 Ibid., 19–20.
119 Ibid.
120 Ibid., 20.
121 For an extended discussion of Habermas's thoughts on the "post-secular", see for example, Austin Harrington, "Habermas and the 'Post-Secular' Society," *European Journal of Social Theory* 10, no. 4 (2007): 543–560
122 Casanova, "Exploring the Postsecular," 31.
123 Ibid., 33.
124 Ibid.
125 Jürgen Habermas, "An Awareness of What Is Missing", in *An Awareness of What Is Missing: Faith and Reason in a Post-Secular Age*, ed. Jürgen Harbermas (Cambridge: Polity Press, 2010), 16.
126 Jürgen Habermas, "Reply to My Critics," in *Habermas and Religion*, eds. Craig Calhoun, Eduardo Mendieta, and Jonathan VanAntwerpen (Cambridge: Polity Press, 2013), 348.
127 Hans Joas, quoted in Hent de Vries, "Global Religion and the Postsecular Challenge," in *Habermas and Religion*, eds. Craig Calhoun, Eduardo Mendieta, and Jonathan VanAntwerpen (Cambridge: Polity Press, 2013), 227.
128 Craig Calhoun, Eduardo Mendieta, and Jonathan VanAntwerpen, "Editor's Introduction," in *Habermas and Religion*, eds. Craig Calhoun, Eduardo Mendieta, and Jonathan VanAntwerpen (Cambridge: Polity Press, 2013), 6; For an extended discussion of Habermas' treatment of religion, see Eduardo Mendieta, "Appendix: Religion in Habermas' Work," in *Habermas and Religion*, eds. Craig Calhoun, Eduardo Mendieta, and Jonathan VanAntwerpen (Cambridge: Polity Press, 2013).
129 Michele Dillon, "Jürgen Habermas and the Post-Secular Appropriation of Religion: A Sociological Critique," in *The Post-Secular in Question: Religion in Contemporary Society*, eds. Philip S. Gorski, David Kyuman Kim, John Torpey, and Jonathan VanAntwerpen (New York: New York University Press, 2012), 251.
130 Jürgen Habermas, *The Structural Transformation of the Public Sphere* (Cambridge: Polity Press, 1992 [1964]); cf. Harrington, "Habermas and the 'Post-Secular'," 547–8; Dillon, "Can Post-Secular Society," 144.

The "secular" and the "post-secular" 111

131 Habermas, "Notes on Post-Secular," 28.
132 Habermas, "An Awareness," 20–1.
133 Warren S. Goldstein, "Redemptive Criticism or the Critique of Religion," in *The Routledge Handbook to Postsecularity*, ed. Justin Beaumont (Oxon: Routledge, 2019), 65.
134 Thomas McCarthy, "The Burdens of Modernized Faith and Postmetaphysical Reason in Habermas' 'Unfinished Project of Enlightenment'," in *Habermas and Religion*, eds. Craig Calhoun, Eduardo Mendieta, and Jonathan VanAntwerpen (Cambridge: Polity Press, 2013), 249.
135 Habermas, "An Awareness," 21.
136 Ibid.
137 Ibid.
138 Eduardo Mendieta, "The Postsecular Condition and Genealogy of Postmetaphysical Thinking," in *The Routledge Handbook to Postsecularity*, ed. Justin Beaumont (Oxon: Routledge, 2019), 56.
139 Habermas, "An Awareness," 21.
140 Michiel Leezenberg, "Postsecularism, Reason, and Violence," in *The Routledge Handbook to Postsecularity*, ed. Justin Beaumont (Oxon: Routledge, 2019), 100.
141 Turner, *Religion and Modern Society*, 147.
142 Bryan S. Turner, "Religion in a Post-Secular Society," in *The New Blackwell Companion to the Sociology of Religion*, ed. Bryan S. Turner (Chichester: Blackwell, 2010), 650.
143 McLeod, *The Religious Crisis*, 245.
144 Dillon, "Can Post-Secular Society," 146.
145 Dillon, "Jürgen Habermas," 260.
146 Beckford, *Social Theory*, 70.
147 Kim Knott, "Cutting through the Postsecular City: A Spatial Interrogation," in *Exploring the Postsecular: The Religious, the Political and the Urban*, eds. Arie L. Molendijk, Justin Beaumont, and Christopher Jedan (Leiden: Brill, 2010), 34.
148 Ibid., emphasis added.
149 Ibid.
150 Johanna Sumiala, "Introduction: Mediatization in Post-Secular Society— New Perspectives in the Study of Media, Religion and Politics," *Journal of Religion in Europe* 19, no. 4 (2017): 362.
151 Mia Lövheim, "Religion, Mediatization, and 'Complementary Learning Processes' in Swedish Editorials," *Journal of Religion in Europe* 19, no. 4 (2017): 379.
152 Ibid., 380.
153 Ibid.
154 Beckford, "Public Religions," 13.
155 Ibid., 3.
156 Ibid.
157 Ibid., 6.
158 Ibid.
159 Ibid., 11.
160 Ibid., 13.
161 Ibid.
162 Ibid.
163 Ibid., 16–7.
164 For example, Fox, "Secularization," 300–1; Beckford, *Social Theory*, 68.
165 Ibid.
166 For example Arie L. Molendijk, Justin Beaumont, and Christopher Jedan, eds., *Exploring the Postsecular: The Religious, the Political and the Urban*

112 *The "secular" and the "post-secular"*

(Leiden: Brill, 2010); Peter Nynäs, Mika Lassander, and Terhi Utriainen, eds., *Post-Secular Society* (Brunswick, NJ: Transaction Publishers, 2012); Philip S. Gorski, David Kyuman Kim, John Torpey, and Jonathan VanAntwerpen, eds., *The Post-Secular in Question: Religion in Contemporary Society* (New York: New York University Press, 2012); Craig Calhoun, Eduardo Mendieta, and Jonathan VanAntwerpen, eds., *Habermas and Religion* (Cambridge: Polity Press, 2013).

167 Justin Beaumont and Klaus Eder, "Concepts, Processes, and Antagonisms of Postsecularity," in *The Routledge Handbook to Postsecularity*, ed. Justin Beaumont (Oxon: Routledge, 2019), 8.

168 Ibid., 4.

169 Ibid., 7.

170 Ibid., 15.

171 Ibid., 7.

172 Beckford, "Public Religions," 13.

173 Herbert De Vriese and Guido Vansheewijck, "The Performative Force of the Postsecular," in *The Routledge Handbook to Postsecularity*, ed. Justin Beaumont (Oxon: Routledge, 2019), 87.

174 Matt Bullimore, "Redeeming the Secular," in *The Routledge Handbook to Postsecularity*, ed. Justin Beaumont (Oxon: Routledge, 2019), 137.

175 Mikhail Epstein, "Postatheism and the Phenomenon of Minimal Religion in Russia," in *The Routledge Handbook to Postsecularity*, ed. Justin Beaumont (Oxon: Routledge, 2019), 80.

176 Lily Kong and Junxi Qian, "Dialogue with Religious Life in Asia," in *The Routledge Handbook to Postsecularity*, ed. Justin Beaumont (Oxon: Routledge, 2019), 266.

177 For example, Yang, "The Red, Black, and Gray Markets," 102.

178 Kasia Narkowicz and Richard Phillips, "After or against Secularism: Muslims in Europe," in *The Routledge Handbook to Postsecularity*, ed. Justin Beaumont (Oxon: Routledge, 2019), 350.

179 Phra Nicholas Thanissaro, "Postsecularity in Twenty Questions: A Case Study in Buddhist Teens," in *The Routledge Handbook to Postsecularity*, ed. Justin Beaumont (Oxon: Routledge, 2019), 361.

180 Umut Parmaksız, "Beyond Salvaging Solidarity," in *The Routledge Handbook to Postsecularity*, ed. Justin Beaumont (Oxon: Routledge, 2019), 285.

181 Martin Beck Matuštík, "The Difficulty of Unforgiving," in *The Routledge Handbook to Postsecularity*, ed. Justin Beaumont (Oxon: Routledge, 2019), 38.

182 Krzysztof Nawratek, "Architecture of Radicalized Postsecularism," in *The Routledge Handbook to Postsecularity*, ed. Justin Beaumont (Oxon: Routledge, 2019), 316.

183 Giuseppe Carta, "Islamophobia, Apophatic Pluralism, and Imagination," in *The Routledge Handbook to Postsecularity*, ed. Justin Beaumont (Oxon: Routledge, 2019), 332.

184 Dillon, "Jürgen Habermas," 256.

5 Religion, the individual, and individualism

This chapter explores the phenomenon of individualism and its ideational and discursive impact on the modern-day Western religious field and people's very understanding of the category of "religion." As noted in Chapter 2, individualism can well be regarded as one of the most forceful and socially consequential "cultural dominants" of both the modern and late-modern era. Its impact on the Western religious field, along with Western social and cultural life more generally, has been multifaceted and far-reaching.

As in the previous chapter, we begin by engaging in first-level reflection on the dialectically related concepts of the "individual" and "individualism" and their historical development and constitution. These concepts therefore need to be understood as standing in a particular type of relation to one another that is similar to that of the concepts of the "secular," "secularity," and "secularism" as discussed in the previous chapter. At its most general, the concept of the "individual" or the "individual self" refers to a particular and historically specific way for people to identify and define themselves as distinct from any type of group that they might be members of or otherwise be varyingly connected to or associated with.[1] The concept of "individualism," by contrast, refers to a more encompassing ideology or *ethos* that celebrates individual autonomy and self-determination as supreme social and cultural values. But, again, the two concepts are nevertheless co-constitutive and dialectically connected: the notion of individualism presupposes a particular notion of the individual and vice versa. For example, it is commonly recognized that the individual self has acquired such importance and prominence across virtually all areas of social, cultural, and political life in the West (and indeed beyond) that it has become completely justified to describe Western societies as deeply individualist societies. Part of the reason for this, though, is that the Western notion of the individual, so to speak, requires this. As we shall discuss in more detail below, in order for the individual to function as the most central and "basic unit of social reproduction," the "individual" needs to be endowed with an absolute, non-contingent character.[2] For this to be realized, what is needed, therefore, is an ideology or ethos of the "individual," i.e., that of individualism. This ethos, moreover, needs to be instilled at all levels of social

DOI: 10.4324/9780367435837-5

114 *Religion, the individual, & individualism*

and cultural life. The associated term "individualization" therefore refers to the extended historical, social, and cultural process whereby the ethos of individualism develops, spreads, and becomes increasingly established and eventually institutionalized throughout modern Western societies, and beyond. The concept of the "individual" nevertheless lies at the heart of both historical and contemporary debates on individualism. The basic point is spelled out by Stephanie Walls: "The acknowledgement that the self exists, as opposed to the collective or social self, is significant to establishing individualism as a viable social theory."[3] As she continues, "The conclusion one arrives at about individualism derives in large part from one's perception of the history of the individual, how the individual has been established and defended in life and in the literature, and how one is able to reconcile the individual and the world around him" (the Western individual has historically primarily been a "he").[4]

The Western concept of the individual has developed gradually and concomitant with a series of highly significant social and cultural transformations of the early-modern era. As we shall discuss in more detail below, the modern notion of the individual was, in more than one sense, made possible by the Protestant Reformation. It is, however, only following the Enlightenment and the development of liberal philosophy from the seventeenth century onwards that the notion of the individual subsequently comes to occupy center stage in a new type of theory of society, where it comes to be regarded as the most central and important foundation for all social life. When we are talking about the historical constitution and establishment of the Western concept of the individual and the ethos of individualism, we are first and foremost talking about the constitution and establishment of an idea and ideal. As such, the establishment of the ethos of individualism therefore needs to be regarded as a fundamentally discursive process that has given rise to a particular set of enduringly influential discursive formations on the autonomy, self-determination, and rights of the individual.

The scholarly literature on the topic of individualism is vast, spanning every discipline in the humanities and social sciences. The discussion that follows will therefore necessarily only engage with a small fraction of this literature and only focus on a more limited set of themes of particular relevance for a discursive sociology of religion as outlined in this book. From this, we proceed with second-level reflection on some of the principal ways in which previous scholarship in the study of religion has approached and theorized the impact of individualism on the character and makeup of the contemporary (principally Western) religious field. The remaining part of the chapter is devoted to third-level analysis. Here, our principal aim is to illustrate a particular method by which the impact of individualism on contemporary religious sensibilities can be explored in actual practice. This will be done in light of the extensive body of data that was gathered as part of the international research project Young Adults and Religion in a Global Perspective (YARG, 2015–19) that explored the values and (non-)religious

Religion, the individual, & individualism   115

sensibilities of young adult university students in 13 countries through-out the world. The YARG-project used a mixed-methods research design, combining surveys with a new Q methodological instrument (explained in more detail below) and in-depth thematic interviews. The data gathered also allow us to move beyond Western contexts and consider the impact of individualism on the religious sensibilities and outlooks of young adults on a cross-cultural scale.

First-level reflection: the "individual" and "individualism"

The precise origins of the ethos of individualism are difficult to ascertain, and the term has a long and somewhat complicated history. What is certain, though, is that any adequate account of the historical development of individualism needs to recognize the impact of the Protestant Reformation. In their efforts to distinguish themselves from what they regarded as the trappings and "empty ritual" of Catholicism, the Reformers were keen to emphasize the importance of "sincerely held religious belief" as the ultimate foundation for all "true" Christianity and Christian life.[5] In line with its core principles of *sola fide* ("by faith alone"), *sola scriptura* ("by Scripture alone"), and *sola gratia* ("by grace alone") the Reformation effectively strove to remove the church as intermediary authority between God and humankind, thereby freeing people from the old "all-embracing hierarchy" through the notion of the priesthood of all believers.[6] As part of this, the Reformers introduced a completely new emphasis on the biblical text (now translated into vernacular languages), as well as on the individual believer's personal relationship to and independent interpretation of that text. In so doing, they also strove to bring about a general shift in the locus of religious life from the ritual to the discursive. As Turner comments, "Lutheranism placed the sermon as the centrepiece of Christian worship in which the chapel became a lecture theatre."[7] But most significantly for the purposes of our discussion in this chapter, as Bruce points out, "Although the Protestant Reformers were far from being democrats, one major unintended consequence of their religious revolution was a profound change in the relative importance of the community and the individual."[8] As already briefly discussed in Chapter 4, the Reformation thus set in motion a general process of individualization "within religion"[9] that would eventually result in a more widespread "*radicalization* of free religious choice" and the gradual transformation of religious institutions into voluntary associations.[10]

Building on the ideas introduced and popularized through the Reformation, the modern Western notion of the "individual" subsequently emerged as a central product of the liberal thought of the seventeenth and eighteenth centuries, as also briefly discussed in the previous chapter. As noted there, liberal thought represented a decisive break with the ethos and philosophical underpinnings of the *ancien régime*, coupled with a radical new emphasis on the rights, self-determination, and autonomy of the sovereign

116 *Religion, the individual, & individualism*

individual. As Slater puts it, this is essentially how liberalism "begins" in Hobbes and Locke, "by questioning the legitimacy of social authority from the standpoint of the individual."[11] In their rejection of the old social order based on hereditary privilege and religious custom, liberal thinkers consequently emphasized the individual as the supreme "normative foundation of social life" as they crafted a new basis for social order rooted in universal and inalienable natural rights and the expressed consent of the governed through the institution of the social contract.[12] As Walls points out, on a more fundamental level, for liberal thinkers such as Hobbes, Locke, and Rousseau, individualism therefore constituted the "basic condition from which political society emerges."[13] The liberal view of the individual also aligned closely with René Descartes's contention that all individuals possess an inherent capacity for reason, and that individuals consequently can be free and autonomous "in so far as they are not defined by others (especially not by social custom or authority) but through their own reason."[14] The individual of liberal thought was therefore above all a *rational* individual whose social action and agency essentially boiled down to his/ her (although at the time, mostly *his*) rational and self-interest-oriented pursuit of individual wants and desires.[15] Thus, as Slater puts it, whereas "Enlightenment made the individual the philosophical centre of the world; liberalism made the individual its moral and political centre."[16] At this point in history, however, the concept of individualism as it is commonly understood today did not yet exist. The concept was first introduced and popularized by Alexis de Tocqueville in the early nineteenth century, and it would take until 1839 for the word "individualism" to first appear in an English dictionary.[17]

Early liberal thought played an instrumental role in laying the philosophical groundwork for individualism as a "'theory of society' in which the well-being of individuals is an always prominent, usually primary, and often the only politically relevant value."[18] It also, however, displayed a sometimes more, sometimes less pronounced tension between what Walls refers to as "positive" and "negative" individualism. Whereas negative individualism afforded precedence to individual rights and autonomy over and against any expectations of mutual social obligation and solidarity, positive individualism, by contrast, was grounded in the view that liberal individualism could only truly be realized in a society where individual freedoms went hand in hand with certain basic social obligations and where all "natural needs for security and survival are [already] met."[19] Especially as articulated in Locke's *Second Treatise on Civil Government*, originally published in 1689, the positive view came to dominate throughout the seventeenth and eighteenth centuries and also developed into a central political-philosophical tenet of the early vision of the "American experiment" as articulated in the United States' Declaration of Independence of 1776 and Constitution of 1787.[20] The ideational influence of both of these documents remains strong in the United States to this day. For

Religion, the individual, & individualism 117

example, allusions to the supposed "rights" and "freedoms" guaranteed by the Constitution have long since developed into recurring tropes of public discourse on issues ranging from abortion to gun control.[21] As Walls goes on to argue, as negative individualism gradually gained more ground and increasingly came to dominate American (and indeed, more broadly, Western) individualism, "the tendency has been to rewrite the past through the application of 'liberal affirmations'" supposedly articulated already in the Declaration and Constitution.[22]

Political, economic, and social individualism

In tracing the historical evolution of individualism in the United States, Walls makes a general distinction between political, economic, and social individualism (this distinction resembles Bellah *et al.*'s previous distinction between "civic," "utilitarian," and "expressive" individualism). Among these historical variants of individualism, political individualism is the oldest and also "the most limited in its perspective on individual activity."[23] This is essentially the individualism of the Declaration and Constitution and associated political and philosophical writings. Political individualism is therefore a distinctively positive type of individualism that emphasizes the co-dependency of all members of a society and expressly connects individual freedoms to mutual civic obligation and solidarity. The eighteenth and nineteenth centuries would then witness a gradual transition from the political individualism of thinkers such as Locke to an economic type of individualism that was mainly inspired by the political economic ideas of Adam Smith (discussed further in Chapter 6) and the "Social Darwinism" of Herbert Spencer. As Walls points out, "Both of these [latter] bodies of thought were interpreted in a way that promoted and justified a level of individual competition that was not really a part of political individualism."[24] Grounded in a negative conception of individual liberty, economic individualism argues against all kinds of state interference in the affairs of individuals, and especially as it relates to their economic activities.[25] While economic individualism retained some connections to political individualism, it was nevertheless formed on the basis of an entirely new conception of society that increasingly came to understand the organization of social life on the whole in market-economic, transactional terms. We will return to this particular theme in more detail in Chapter 6. The core values of economic individualism would then become further reinforced through the new types of social stratifications that emerged as a result of accelerating industrialization and urbanization during the eighteenth and nineteenth centuries. Contemporaneous bourgeois discourse successfully managed to cement the notion that it is "incumbent on each of us individually to find success" as the basic definition of "freedom"[26] and individual liberty. Economic individualism therefore laid the ideational foundations for a "socially accepted economic

118 *Religion, the individual, & individualism*

opportunism that carried over into the social realm."[27] As we shall continue to discuss in Chapter 6, this notion would subsequently rise to new prominence following the global spread of neoliberal ideology and political economy from the early 1980s onwards.

The gradual but increasingly wide establishment – and indeed institutionalization – of economic individualism eventually paved the way for the emergence of social individualism, which, although it derives from both political and economic individualism, nevertheless rejects both of their core premises. As explained by Walls:

> Social individualism is the application of individualistic attitudes in the realm of one's social activity. It involves rejecting interconnectedness and societal obligations; it encourages withdrawal from social and civic life; and it teaches individuals to see one another as competitive threats who will inhibit their ability to meet their own needs and wants.[28]

Although contemporary liberal democratic political discourse continues to include elements of both political and economic individualism, during roughly the past century or so, social individualism has without doubt developed into the dominant form of individualism in the West.

The onset of social individualism was noted by Durkheim already at the end of the nineteenth century. In what remains a quite original take on the matter, Durkheim approached the issue of individualism in direct connection to his broader, and more fundamental, idea that all societies "create systems of symbolic classification to make sense of the world" in the form of a general distinction between the "sacred" and the "profane."[29] In this framework, as principally laid out in *The Elementary Forms of the Religious Life* (1912), the "sacred" refers to those things, ideas, practices, phenomena, persons, etc. that members of a particular community endow with a non-contingent and non-negotiable value or character. The sacred is therefore typically circumscribed by (sometimes very elaborate) rules that stipulate how people are to engage with and treat the sacred. As Gordon Lynch phrases it, by underpinning the basic categories and values that structure communities and societies on the whole, sacred phenomena "exert a profound moral claim" over people's lives.[30] This is why, in Durkheim's view, the community *itself* becomes the epitome of the sacred.[31] Communal constructions of the sacred are further formed in dialectical contradistinction to communal constructions of the *profane*, or those classes of things, ideas, phenomena, etc. that are perceived to belong to the sphere of mundane, everyday life and that therefore lack particular "specialness." The profane thereby also accrues a transgressive charge *relative to* the strength of the sacred: the stronger the sense of the sacred, the greater the revulsion evoked by that which threatens to profane or violate it. As outlined by Durkheim, the sacred is thus not be understood in terms of an ontologically fixed category. Nor does the sacred–profane distinction refer to any type of

Religion, the individual, & individualism 119

distinction between "good" and "evil." Rather, depending from one communal context or another, virtually anything can be constructed as sacred. And so, while the sacred has indeed traditionally been closely tied to religious frameworks and typically been imbricated with religious discourses, it extends well beyond these. "Religion" should therefore not be regarded as the "source" of the sacred, while the "profane" should not be confused or conflated with the category of the "secular."[32]

At different points throughout key works such as *The Division of Labor in Society*[33] (1893) and *Elementary Forms*, as well as the essay "Individualism and the Intellectuals" (1898), Durkheim argues that, whereas "traditional" society is underpinned by "the idea it has of itself" as a *collective*,[34] modern society instead becomes morally consolidated through what he refers to as the "cult of the individual" (*culte de la personne*). The precise meaning of this concept, however, remains somewhat unclear. At one point, he refers to it as "individualist faith," at another point as the "religion of humanity," and at yet another point as the "religion of the individual."[35] In trying to make sense of the "religion" that Durkheim appears to have had in mind, Michael Stausberg argues that it should be viewed as being grounded in a more fundamental notion about the sacredness of humanity itself.[36] The sacredness and "cult" of the individual therefore first of all needs to the understood as a product of modern society, as something that arises in a modern social context marked by the establishment of democracy, self-governance, and an increasing emphasis on social egalitarianism. As William Paden points out, in such a social and political situation, "sacredness [increasingly] becomes invested in basic freedoms, equality of opportunity, the dignity of human persons, and self-determination rather than with duties and allegiances or the protection of rank and status."[37] In this context, Durkheim also introduces the concept of "moral individualism" to refer to the general moral orientation that emerges as a result of the development of increasingly large, differentiated, and heterogeneous modern societies. Like his notion of the "cult of the individual," however, Durkheim's notion of "moral individualism" remains quite ambiguous. According to Mark Cladis, it is best understood as referring to "a cluster of dynamic beliefs and practices, symbols, and institutions that support the dignity and rights of the individual."[38] In the conclusion to *Elementary Forms*, Durkheim then also made the further argument that the sacred in modern societies primarily is expressed and communicated through language and linguistic concepts rather than collective rituals (which he argues is more characteristic of traditional societies).[39] The sacred of modern society therefore is increasingly constructed and reproduced through discourse and discursive practice.

Without going into Durkheim's ideas in any further detail, suffice it to say that they foregrounded several later strands of thought on the development of individualism and the character and dynamics of broader processes of individualization. Durkheim essentially introduced and developed the idea

120 *Religion, the individual, & individualism*

that, as societies develop, expand, and diversify, it becomes exceedingly difficult to maintain particular sets of collectively shared communal values. As a result, the value-base of modern society gradually shifts towards the "unique individual," who is accrued non-contingent, sacred status. As a central part of this process, the "sacredness of the individual" also comes to be constructed through "increasingly abstract and generalized sentiments"[40] such as "individual self-determination," "personal autonomy," and "freedom of conscience," to name just a few. This, in turn, leads to the emergence, increasing establishment, and ever-firmer institutionalization of a set of powerful discursive formations that emphasize the primacy and rights of the "individual" over and against those of any collective. As these discursive formations increasingly come to dominate the discursive practices of central social domains such as politics, law, and education, they thereby also come to set the parameters for what can meaningfully be said about not only the "individual," but about the influence of particular types of collectives over individuals as well. As a consequence, the meanings attached to terms such as "collective" and "community" (including "religious community") also undergo notable changes as these become increasingly understood as aggregates of atomized individuals.

In addition to Durkheim's influential early work, social individualism has attracted a great deal of scholarly attention and has been discussed under numerous different labels such as, for example, "expressive individualism" or "individualism of uniqueness."[41] This interest has principally been motivated by the ways in which social individualism, unlike both political and economic individualism, is premised on the idea that "an individual is unable to understand and respond to the needs of society as a whole."[42] This is not to say that individuals are inherently selfish or egoistic, but rather that they can only be assumed to be "qualified to speak to what is good for *them.*"[43] Put another way, for people who ascribe to social individualism, "society only exists in the background, while the interests of the individual (as he or she alone determines them) dominate the foreground."[44] Social individualism is therefore firmly grounded in a negative conception of liberty since, as Walls puts it, "In this model, individual freedom (and a successful democracy) requires the individual's being left alone to assume full responsibility for his or her successes and failures."[45] By extension, social individualism is thereby also intimately associated with the myth of "equal opportunity," or the idea that opportunities to achieve personal success are equally openly available to all individuals regardless of background, social class, gender, ethnicity, etc.[46] While no longer "new," this idea continues to wield enormous ideational power and remains perhaps most (in)famously encapsulated in the longstanding notion (indeed myth) of the "American Dream."

The gradual but accelerating spread of social individualism since the turn of the nineteenth century, and especially since the 1960s, has had a range of highly significant ideational and discursive effects. As we will continue

Religion, the individual, & individualism 121

to discuss below, sociologists and social theorists have typically singled out the development and wide proliferation of psychology, therapy, and counseling as having played a particularly significant role in this regard. For example, as Bellah *et al.* pointed out, "with the emergence of psychology as an academic field – and, even more important, as a form of popular discourse – in the late nineteenth and early twentieth centuries, the purely subjective grounding of expressive individualism has become complete."[47] Similarly, Jeremy Carrette and Richard King argue that:

> the psychological paradigm has become so naturalised – such a part of our everyday "common-sense" – that it has established the basic conditions for thinking about modern subjectivity itself ... Western forms of the self constantly inscribe the language of private self and private possessions and actively subvert awareness of relational and so-cial identity.[48]

The increasingly widespread "psychologization" of human experience that Carrette and King refer to needs to be understood as a fundamentally discourse-driven process that has left a deep imprint on everyday language use and significantly expanded the "vocabulary" of the individual. For example, as Gergen notes, the language that we have inherited in the West has become so deeply steeped in individualism that we now "have over 2000 terms in the English language that refer to ('make real') individual mental states."[49]

First-level conclusions

The above has provided a brief general discussion of the development and historical constitution of the concepts of the individual and individualism. A key inference from this discussion is that both of these concepts have been differently articulated and understood at various points in history. Although social individualism has no doubt come to dominate how the concept of individualism is most commonly understood in modern society, elements of both political and economic individualism nevertheless continue to figure in contemporary discourses on the individual. It is important to recognize that when tracing the historical development of these concepts we are, first and foremost, tracing the development and diffusion of a particular idea that is constructed, articulated, and disseminated in and through discourse and discursive practice. Through the influence of liberal thought in particular, the idea of the "individual" first becomes established as a primarily *political* category. But through the subsequent development of economic and social individualism, the "individual" takes on a range of additional social and cultural meanings and gradually comes to underpin a broader ethos of individualism, whereby the individual is afforded a non-contingent, "sacred" character. These developments also

122 *Religion, the individual, & individualism*

entail a considerable expansion in the "vocabulary" of the individual and the gradual extension, naturalization, and eventually institutionalization of this vocabulary throughout ever more social and cultural domains. The crucial and most basic point to note, therefore, is that the modern Western notion of the "individual" both emerges through and is sustained by discourses that construct people as "individuals." In order to properly understand the ideational and discursive impact of the ethos of individualism on the religious sensibilities and outlooks of modern populations, we therefore need to arrive at an adequate understanding of the principal ways in which these discourses are maintained and reproduced, as well as of the ways in which they entwine and interact with other prevalent contemporaneous discourses and discursive formations.

Second-level reflection: individualism, identity, and religion in "post-traditional" society

Scholarly debates on individualism and individualization started to intensify from the mid-1950s onwards, especially following the publication of David Riesman *et al.*'s widely read *The Lonely Crowd* in 1950.[50] As will be discussed on more detail in Chapter 6, the spread and definitive establishment of consumer culture and consumerism during this time also further contributed to perpetuation of the ethos of individualism in Western capitalist societies. The late 1970s and early 1980s then saw the publication of several additional and highly influential works on the topic, including Richard Sennett's *The Fall of Public Man*,[51] Christopher Lasch's *Culture of Narcissism*,[52] and Robert Bellah *et al.*'s *Habits of the Heart*.[53] To varying extents, this body of work also highlighted the discursive dimensions of individualism. For example, writing in the late 1970s, Lasch lamented the increasingly wide establishment and perpetuation of a "therapeutic culture" that had become "elevated into a program and wrapped in the rhetoric of authenticity and awareness."[54] In the early 1980s, Bellah *et al.*, in turn, argued that their large and diverse group of American interviewees shared a more fundamental "common moral vocabulary" that they referred to as the "'first language' of American individualism."[55] Although the notion of "freedom" emerged as a central trope of this "first language," Bellah *et al.* concluded that their interviewees primarily took it to mean "being left alone by others, not having other people's values, ideas, or styles of life forced upon one."[56] As they also observed, in the increasingly individualized culture of the United States, religious affiliation had also become a matter of conscious decision, a decision that "must be particularly and peculiarly one's own."[57]

The agenda-setting scholarship mentioned above was followed by another body of influential work from the late 1980s onwards, prime representatives of which include Anthony Giddens's *Modernity and Self-Identity*,[58] Scott Lash's *Reflexive Modernization*,[59] Robert Putnam's

Bowling Alone,[60] Zygmunt Bauman's *The Individualized Society,*[61] and Ulrich Beck's and Elisabeth Beck-Gernsheim's *Individualization.*[62] In contrast to the scholarship of the 1970s and early 1980s, this scholarship became particularly focused on the constitution of individual identities and "selves" in late-modern "post-traditional" society. Essentially, different approaches to the concept or notion of identity take different views on the possibilities and limits of human agency, that is, the ability of individuals to actively participate in forming their own senses of themselves in and across various social and cultural settings and contexts.[63] As Chris Weedon puts it: "In [Western] commonsense discourse, people tend to assume that they are 'knowing subjects,' that is sovereign individuals, whose lives are governed by free will, reason, knowledge, experience and, to a lesser extent, emotion."[64] An "identity" is therefore commonly viewed as stemming from a set of individual characteristics, or a "personality," through which an individual defines him/herself in *relation to* others and is then, conversely, also defined *by* others.[65] Individuals therefore not only form their identities or sense of selves on the basis of their own individual notions or perceptions about "who" or "what" they "are," but in equal measure also in relation to their respective perceptions of "who" or "what" they are *not.*[66] Identities, moreover, are never static or uniform, nor particularly stable and enduring. For example, throughout the course of our daily lives, we find ourselves in various types of situations that encourage us to take on and perform certain types of identities rather than others (for example, the identity of parent, manager, or parishioner). Our ongoing participation in the various types of discourses and discursive practices through which these categories and collective identities are constructed and reproduced results in the forming, adoption, and performance of *multiple*, although always intersecting, identities. Identities are therefore also fundamentally intersectional and deeply intertwined with numerous aspects and positionalities of social and cultural life including (but not limited to) ethnicity, gender, social class, nationality, political persuasion, religious affiliation, and so on. Like identities in general, these types of collective identities – whether they are consciously adopted, ascribed, or imposed – also rely on "active processes of identification" on the one hand, and "conscious counter-identification against institutionally and socially assigned identities, and the meanings and values that they are seen to represent" on the other hand.[67]

In addition to the above, Western understandings of identity also tend to be built around a sense of *continuity*. As "unique personalities" people understand themselves as having a history and a future. For this reason, much previous scholarship on identity and identity construction has focused on the ways and degrees to which identities are constructed and reproduced through *narrative*, i.e., through the various types of stories that people continually tell about themselves.[68] For example, in his influential and widely debated account, Giddens framed identity construction in late modernity in terms of a "reflexive project of the self." As he argued,

124 *Religion, the individual, & individualism*

maintaining a coherent identity and sense of self under conditions of late modernity requires a "capacity *to keep a particular narrative going.*"[69] This is because, in late-modern society and culture, identities are no longer simply "handed down," but rather actively adopted and achieved. People, so to speak, "have no choice but to choose" who to be.[70] Bauman similarly argues that

> 'individualization' consists of transforming human 'identity' from a 'given' into a 'task' – and charging the actors with the responsibility for performing that task and for the consequences (also the side-effects) of their performance: in other words, it consists in establishing *de jure* autonomy (although not necessarily a *de facto* one).[71]

In light of this, Bauman succinctly concludes that "Needing to *become* what one *is* is the hallmark of modern living."[72]

In what provides an important complement to most theorizing on individualism and identity formation in late modernity, Beck and Beck-Gernsheim underscore the institutionalization of individualism in modern Western societies. As they put it, "The Western type of individualized society tells us *to seek biographical solutions to systemic contradictions.*"[73] This is partly because "individualization means the disintegration of previous existing social forms" such as, for example, social class, gender roles, and family.[74] But it is partly also because modern society imposes a range of "new demands, controls and constraints" on individuals.[75] As Beck and Beck-Gernsheim explain:

> Most of the rights and entitlements to support by the welfare state are designed for individuals rather than for families. In many cases they presuppose employment (or, in the case of unemployment, willingness to work). Employment in turn implies education and both of these presuppose mobility or willingness to move. By all these requirements individuals are not so much compelled as peremptorily invited to constitute themselves as individuals.[76]

These observations further point to the ways in which thoroughly differentiated modern society no longer integrates people "as whole persons," but rather "relies on the fact that individuals are not integrated but only partly and temporarily involved as they wander between different functional worlds" such as those of, for example, education, law, healthcare, and the labor market.[77] This is why Beck and Beck-Gernsheim conclude that "One of the decisive features of individualization processes ... is that they not only permit but they also demand an active contribution by individuals."[78] It is important, again, to note the strongly discourse-driven character of these developments. The discourses whereby the ethos of individualism is sustained and reproduced in modern society are not adequately understood simply as discourses on "rights"; equally, they are also discourses on individual "responsibility" and "self-reliance." For sure, in contemporary individualist discourse, the individual is endowed with a set of "inalienable rights." But to a notable extent, that same individual is also, so to speak, expected to "live up" to the ethos that underpins these rights. This means, among other things, that the individual, rather than any type of community, is expected to take responsibility for achieving happiness, success, well-being, or the lack thereof.

The impact of individualism on the character of modern forms of religion and religious life and practice has been the subject of a great deal of interest and debate among scholars of religion.[79] This interest has principally been motivated by the particular ways and extent to which accelerating processes of individualization can be shown to have turned religious belief and practice into something chosen rather than given, adopted rather than ascribed, voluntary rather than obligatory, and subjective rather than collective. As such, the concept of individualism has figured prominently throughout several types of sociological theorizing on the character of religion and religious life in the modern world. Much of the groundwork for these debates was laid already by Luckmann in *The Invisible Religion* (1967).[80] According to Luckmann, in modern society,

> rather than religion in the churches – or similar institutional settings where 'membership' is easily identified and counted – we are surrounded by invisible religions, individual religions cobbled together by consumers who pick and choose what suits them and what will justify their personal lifestyle, given the preferences that result from their social context and personal biography.[81]

Building further on Luckmann's early work, the 1980s then witnessed the emergence of a new body of scholarship specifically focused on the proliferation of "individualized" forms of religion and religious practice. Principally developed as part of research on the changing religious sensibilities of North American populations, this scholarship also introduced an entirely new vocabulary through which to approach and make sense of new, "non-institutional" religious dispositions. For example, in *A Generation of Seekers* (1993), Wade Clarke Roof identified a significant shift in American religiosity towards a "quest-culture," underpinned by a vocabulary of "spiritual growth" and "spiritual journeys."[82] Focusing on the same "baby-boomer" demographic, in *After Heaven* (1998), Robert Wuthnow, in his turn, argued that the United States had been experiencing a general shift from a religiosity based on what he termed "dwelling" to one of "seeking" among the generation born between 1944 and 1960.[83] More broadly, this scholarship was motivated

126 *Religion, the individual, & individualism*

by the multitude of ways in which the ethos of (social) individualism had become increasingly engrained in North American social and cultural life since the 1950s. Indeed, already in 1978 a Gallup poll found 80 percent of US citizens agreeing with the view that "an individual should arrive at his or her own religious beliefs independent of any churches of synagogues."[84]

In their respective ways, scholars of "non-institutional" or "alternative" religion have almost uniformly highlighted how an increasing emphasis on personal autonomy, reflexive self-identity, and the imperative of personal choice has come to affect people's religious sensibilities and approaches to the very notion of "religion" throughout the Western world.[85] As Beckford explains,

> The notion of unconstrained choice is implicit in characterisations of individual beliefs as "pastiches," "bricolage" and "pick-and-mix" varieties. Images of "nomads," "pilgrims" and "new tribes" are deployed to capture the allegedly temporary, rootless, shifting and, above all, elective character of social relations among these individuals. "Spirituality" is thought to be a more appropriate term than "religion" as a label for their concerns with the overall meaning of things because it lacks any notion of obligation and of being permanently bound together with others.[86]

While there is nothing to add to Beckford's excellent summation, the widespread transition from "religion" to "spirituality" is worth highlighting here. This is, not least, because the scholarly story of the "individualization of religion" in the West has largely (although not exclusively) been the story of the proliferation of "spirituality." This, more specifically, has been the story of the increasing diffusion and popularity of various types of "Eastern" religious beliefs (mainly those derived from Buddhism or Hinduism), the emergence of so-called New Religious Movements, and the proliferation of a bewildering array of "alternative spiritual" teachings, ideas, and practices throughout the West, especially since the 1950s.

Individualized religion and "spirituality"

During the past three to four decades, the vocabulary and terminology through which scholars have attempted to capture and make sense of new, "non-institutional" or "alternative" forms of "religion" or "spirituality" has expanded considerably. Examples range from (but are far from limited to) terms and concepts (presumably) intended to denote or capture broader transformations, trends, and "movements" in contemporary religiosity such as "cultic milieu,"[87] "New Age religion/spirituality/movement,"[88] "alternative spirituality,"[89] "holistic spirituality,"[90] and "subjective-life

Religion, the individual, & individualism   127

spirituality,"[91] to terms and concepts intended to capture (presumably) more specific and more clearly demarcated religious spaces such as "metaphysical subculture"[92] and "stigmatized knowledge milieu."[93] There has, however, no doubt always existed quite some degree of confusion as to the precise meaning of these terms and concepts, their empirical basis, and their relation to and differentiation from one another. Indeed, already in 1997, Meredith B. McGuire noted that "we do not yet have the language or conceptual apparatus for refining our understanding of spirituality."[94] This largely still remains the case today.

As Paul Heelas, Linda Woodhead *et al.* explain:

> Most notably the term 'spirituality' is often used to express commitment to a deep truth that is to be found within what belongs to this world. And the term 'religion' is used to express commitment to a higher truth that is 'out there', lying beyond what this world has to offer, and exclusively related to specific externals (scriptures, dogmas, rituals, and so on).[95]

It is important to recognize, therefore, that "spirituality," like "individualism," is a fundamentally discursive phenomenon that is largely constituted by discourse, expressed through discourse, and circulated through the medium of discourse. More specifically, through its many conspicuous links to broader discursive formations of the individual and individualism, "spirituality" can be described as a both highly individualized and *individualizing* discourse. Indeed, the increasing prevalence of discourses on "spirituality" can well be regarded as one among the most notable discursive developments in the late-modern religious field. This is not, however, to say that discourses on "spirituality" are adequately understood as "new" or that they would be peculiar to late-modern society and culture. Rather, as explored in detail by Carrette and King, the history of "spirituality" stretches back to the latter part of the nineteenth century.[96] For example, the work of William James (the "Father of American psychology") had a profound ideational influence on the discourses on "spirituality" that gained increasing prominence in the post-World War II era. James, among other things, argued that all great "religious traditions" emanate from the "original experiences" of their founders and defined "religion" as *"the feelings, acts, and experiences of individual men in their solitude,* so far as they apprehend themselves to stand in relation to whatever they may consider the divine."[97] As Carrette and King point out, James's arguments therefore provided much of the basis "for understanding religious experience in the twentieth century, shaping 'New Age' jargon and providing the mechanisms for rethinking religion in terms of individual private experience."[98] These ideas became further cemented from the mid-1950s onwards through the work of psychologists such as Gordon Allport and

128 *Religion, the individual, & individualism*

Abraham Maslow and countercultural figures such as Aldous Huxley and Timothy Leary.[99] As argued by Carrette and King:

> With the establishment of psychology as the pre-eminent "science of the self" in the post-war period, we see an increasingly "non-religious" understanding of spirituality emerge. This changing climate within modern capitalist societies has led many traditions, including established western ones such as Christianity, to "de-mythologise," by moving away from the older cosmological and disciplinary language of the past and replacing this with the interiorised and psychologically inflected language of "spirituality."[100]

Building on the ideas and languages introduced and popularized by figures such as James, Allport, and Maslow, contemporary discourses on "spirituality" have become strongly characterized by their emphasis on personal feeling, intuition, and experience; a tendency to eclectically mix elements, languages, and vocabularies derived from various "religious" sources and "traditions"; and a general reluctance to express commitment or unconditional adherence to any one particular "religious truth," community, or "tradition."[101]

While rarely explored through the lens of discourse and discourse theory, the linguistic and semantic dimensions of "spirituality" have nevertheless been noted by numerous scholars. For example, as Heelas, Woodhead *et al.* observe, when considering, or when entering, "the holistic milieu," "one is immediately struck by the pervasive use of 'holistic language': 'harmony', 'balance', 'flow', 'integration', 'interaction', 'being at one', and 'being centred'."[102] This is a type of language that invites people to "grow," to move "beyond barriers," and to thus overcome "dis-ease."[103] To achieve this, "spiritual" people "guide,", "support," "work with," and "nurture" one another.[104] As Heelas, Woodhead *et al.* go on to observe, this type of language therefore differs notably from the traditional and long-established (Christian) religious language of the West where the experience or being a "believer" is often expressed through a language

> of unique life being 'broken', 'poured out', 'surrendered', 'sacrificed' and 'given over to God' as the full array of personal subjectivities is sacrificed in favour of a far smaller authorized repertoire that conforms to the laid-down lineaments of the faithful disciple.[105]

Indeed Heelas, Woodhead, *et al.* go so far as to argue that the language of "subjective spirituality" has by now become so widespread that "New Age, mind-body-spirit, yoga, feng shui, chi and chakra have become more common in the general culture than traditional Christian vocabulary."[106] While there is certainly truth to this claim, it is nevertheless one that would need to be explored on a firm empirical basis. For although the religious

Religion, the individual, & individualism 129

landscapes of Western societies have no doubt continued to diversify in a variety of different ways, Christianity clearly continues to provide the principal ideational and semantic backdrop against which the category of "religion" still tends to be understood across central social domains such as, for example, education, politics, and law. Having said that, it is nevertheless beyond doubt that the language of the "individual self" and "personal autonomy" has gained increasing prominence throughout the Western religious field as a whole.

The increasing prevalence of individualized language and discourse across a wider range of religious communal settings was noted already in the mid-1980s by Bellah *et al.* when they found that Americans from various walks of life displayed a marked tendency to "fall back on abstractions when talking about the most important things."[107] They also noted how, even among the more religiously conservative, there was a tendency to "revert to the popular language of therapy."[108] Indeed, as they went on to point out: "There are thousands of local churches in the United States, representing an enormous range of variation in doctrine and worship. Yet most define themselves as communities of personal support."[109] Similar observations on the proliferation of individualized discourse in traditional religious settings were also made in later scholarship, such as perhaps most notably in Philip E. Hammond's *Religion and Personal Autonomy*[110] and Robert C. Fuller's *Spiritual, but not Religious.*[111] This work has therefore pointed to a broader, ongoing transformation in the "religious semantics" of the West that has only intensified in past decades and increasingly come to affect all types of both traditional and more recently established religious communities. Indeed, the impact of individualized discourse on the contemporary discursive practices of various types of religious communities and organizations would be deserving of much further, focused study. Scholars could, for example, explore whether any notable differences can be found in the ways in which different *types* of religious communities have responded to and aligned their own discursive practices with broader prevalent individualized discourses. The individualized discourse of "seeker-sensitive" evangelical churches has already received some degree of attention in this regard. The discourse of these types of communities tends to be strongly geared towards providing for the "spiritual needs" of the individual and directly associating "faith" with successful living and personal growth and development. This is even more visible in the discursive practices of communities situated within the so-called "prosperity gospel" mold, which tend to emphasize personal social mobility and material wealth as a natural outcome of a "faithful life."[112]

Individualized religion and spirituality in discursive perspective

As is indicated in the title of Fuller's book mentioned above, one notable effect of the increasing proliferation of discourses on "individualized

130 *Religion, the individual, & individualism*

spirituality" has been the normalization of the maxim "spiritual, but not religious." As Andie R. Alexander and McCutcheon point out, this notion has become widely used "as if it names some pre-social and thus institution-free insight or feeling ... that someone just has or somehow senses."[113] As they go on to observe, "a speaker who says SBNR [spiritual, but not religious] seems to think that they're making a tradition-free, authentic claim about some interior dimension that they possess but they do so in the most tradition-bound of settings: language."[114] "Spiritual, but not religious" has therefore developed into an increasingly common (indeed almost institutionalized) discursive trope whereby people increasingly construe their own position towards what they perceive "religion" to be.

Recall, once again, the distinction that was made between construal and construction in the social functioning of discourse in Chapter 2 and our discussion on the dialectical co-constitution of the categories of "religion" and the "secular" in Chapters 3 and 4. When viewed from a discursive perspective, every distinction between "spirituality" and "religion" will inevitably entail a particular construal of not only the "spiritual," but also the "religious" from which it is distinguished. As already noted, in this particular type of construal, "religion" is typically framed as "dogmatic," "authoritative," "rigid," "conservative," "hierarchical," "patriarchal," and so forth, while "spirituality" is framed as that which emanates from the (supposedly more "authentic") "experiences," "feelings," or "intuition" of the unique individual. But as with all types of discursive practice, it is important to recognize that when people engage in these types of construals of their own position *vis-à-vis* "religion," they are doing so in direct relation to already existing and established discourses and vocabularies on the "spiritual" and "spirituality." Put another way, the language that people use to make sense of their "spiritual" dispositions will always be determined by the broader social, cultural, and discursive contexts that they occupy and find themselves varyingly embedded and positioned within. And so, to the extent that discourses and vocabularies on the "spiritual" and "spirituality" become increasingly prevalent and naturalized throughout (Western) social and cultural life as a whole, we should also expect these discourses and vocabularies to become increasingly visible in the ways in which people describe their own "spiritual" dispositions and position themselves *vis-à-vis* "religion" and the "religious." But this in no way detracts from the fact that people's construals of their "spirituality" ("but not religiosity") will always be "deeply colored and structured by the codes of expectable and understandable biographies and identities" of the particular social and cultural contexts that they find themselves in.[115] In order for such construals to gain any traction and have constructive effects, they therefore need to be recognized and confirmed by others who share in that same language and discourse, and for whom the phrase "spiritual, but not religious" forms part of what can meaningfully be said about one's "spiritual" inclinations. It is therefore important to acknowledge more generally, as François Gauthier reminds us, that "Contemporary individualism is paradoxically intensely social, as there is a constant need for forms of community, actual, or virtual, to recognise and validate these ever-constructing identities."[116]

The proliferation of discourses and vocabularies on the "spiritual" and "spirituality" as discussed above poses a range of conceptual challenges for the sociological study of religion, as well as the study of religion more broadly. Take, for example, the "spiritual, but not religious" maxim. Unlike the "religious–secular" distinction, here, we are not simply dealing with a type of discursive construal that aims to distinguish "religion" from its antonym or to mark the "absence" of "religion." Rather, we are dealing with a type of construal that, for lack of a better term, aims to *replace* "religion" with something else (i.e., "spirituality") while simultaneously also expanding on its possible meaning. Saying "spiritual, but not religious" is obviously quite different from saying, for example, "secular, not religious" (whereas saying "secular, *but not* religious" would make little sense). The difference lies in the character of the terms that are separated by "but not." Beyer captures the issue nicely when he writes that

> [S]pirituality is one of those terms which marks off the peculiarity of modern religion. Designating a variety of activity or orientation as spirituality is a way of seeking exemption from certain of the characteristics of what has come to be regarded as religion, but not others. It is a way, as it were, to 'look like a duck and quack like a duck', but avoid identification as a duck.[117]

Following the increasing prevalence of discourses on "spirituality" (including the discourse on "spiritual, but not religious") across several social and cultural domains, growing numbers of scholars have started to ask critical questions about their impact on scholarly discourse and theorizing itself. As a basic premise, just like the category of "religion," the concept of "spirituality" needs to be approached as an empty signifier that has no intrinsic meaning in and of itself. Rather than spend our energies on trying to find out what "spirituality," so to speak, "is" (a futile endeavor) our focus should be on the particular ways in which the concept of "spirituality" is being employed and used, in what situations and contexts, by whom, and with that social and cultural effects and consequences. In doing this, we also need to remain constantly aware of how currently prevalent discourses on "spirituality" tie in with several other highly ideationally influential discursive formations on the individual. Indeed, as Carrette and King rightly argue, "In trying to examine the idea of spirituality it is important to understand its 'use' rather than its 'meaning.'"[118] This, however, has rarely been the focus of previous scholarship in the area. As Carrette and King continue:

> Accepting defeat, writers normally employ a general meaning, or a working definition, which enables them to corner a fanciful market

132   *Religion, the individual, & individualism*

space drifting on the vague etymologies of the word. Out of breath, such authors usually resort to differentiating "spirituality" from "religion" – an even more complex and vague signifier – appealing to the institutional and tradition specific "baggage" that the term "spiritual" manages to avoid.[119]

We need to consider, therefore, what it means for scholars to abandon the category of "religion" and replace it with that of "spirituality." As already briefly discussed in Chapter 3, according to Martin, scholarship on individual or subjective religion has a marked tendency to simply "repeat insider's accounts" and unreflexively turn emic into etic vocabulary.[120] For, as Martin argues, when scholars position themselves in relation to the concept of "spirituality," they "tend to use the same vocabulary: organized religion vs. spirituality, communal vs. individual, social constraint vs. individual freedom, tradition vs. choice, and so on."[121] Scholars therefore need to recognize the fundamentally discursive and communal character of notions such as "self-authority," "seekership," and "spiritual, but not religious." For as Martin contends, the problem with the ethos of individualism is not that it dissolves community but that "it obscures how 'individuals' are constituted by their communities."[122] Consequently, "Social theory requires us to explain individuals rather than simply posit them as the ground of our explanations."[123] These are issues that a discursive sociology of religion as envisioned here constantly needs to remain aware of. It is important, in other words, that we do recognize particular discursive construals and constructions of the individual as precisely that, i.e., as discursive construals and constructions that do not simply reflect the "way things are" but rather actively contribute to the very constitution of "individuals."

The ideational and discursive impact of individualism on the religious outlooks and sensibilities of modern populations is also intimately related to changing modes of (religious) socialization. In a conventional understanding, the term "socialization" essentially refers to the processes whereby people are taught and gradually acquire "the social skills, social understandings, and emotional maturity needed for interaction with other individuals to fit in with the functioning of social dyads and larger groups."[124] Although the so-called "primary" and generally most enduring socialization occurs in childhood and early adolescence, socialization nonetheless needs to be understood as a process that continues throughout life and that takes different and new forms as individuals enter into new social and interactional settings.[125] The main ideas that have underpinned various theories of socialization have changed and diversified considerably over time. Current theorizing tends to put more emphasis on the agency of the subject being socialized and how socialization needs to be understood as a time- and context-dependent process that varies depending on a range of factors such as ethnicity, socioeconomic status, minority/majority position, and so forth. Current theories of socialization also make a general

Religion, the individual, & individualism   133

distinction between "narrow" and "broad" forms of socialization. According to Jeffrey Arnett and Susan Taber:

> Cultures characterized by broad socialization encourage independence, individualism, and self-expression. In contrast, cultures characterized by narrow socialization hold obedience and conformity as the highest values, and deviation from cultural expectations for behavior is condemned and punished.[126]

The "broadness" or "narrowness" of socialization will, however, vary depending on the particular aspect or dimension of socialization under consideration. As Eleanor Maccoby points out, although it is generally more likely that the importance of broad forms of socialization grows "in times of rapid cultural change," we should also recognize that "individuals can be socialized to adapt to changing social circumstances."[127] Indeed, as Walls points out, in Western societies, individualism is instilled already as part of primary socialization during adolescence. While children are

> taught and encouraged to share, to be considerate, to think of the group ... as their political socialization progresses, the emphasis in this realm focuses on the individual, what rights he or she has, how other people (especially government) might deprive him or her of these rights, and what recourse he or she has in the event that this occurs.[128]

As noted above, there is wide agreement among sociologists and social theorists that the transition from traditional to post-traditional societies in many parts of the world has resulted in a general erosion of previous moral frameworks and authority structures coupled with an increasing elevation of the individual and personal autonomy. As argued by Paul Vermeer, in such a situation it becomes more useful to regard *individuation*, understood as the "tension between the development of a unique personality on the one hand and social integration on the other," as the "core of socialization."[129] This should not, however, be taken to suggest that the basic function of socialization – i.e., the transmission of core social values and the instillation of a "minimum level of cultural-normative integration" – would not persist, but only that socialization in contemporary times needs to be understood as "an active, simultaneous process of both personality development and the acquisition of core values."[130] This, therefore, points to the multitude of ways in which people in Western societies are increasingly socialized into an already firmly institutionalized individualistic ethos.

These developments have led growing numbers of scholars to consider the possibilities and conditions of what has come to be termed "self-socialization." As outlined by Philip R. Newman and Barbara M. Newman,

> The process of self-socialization suggests that individuals draw on their own sense of agency to select the best social contexts to support their

134 *Religion, the individual, & individualism*

development, and that this process is both a product of and contributor to individual development and individualization.[131]

Self-socialization thus generally refers to types or modes of socialization that are marked by high degrees of agency on the part of the individual concerned and the absence of both clearly identifiable socialization agents and specific "socialization goals."[132] The notion of self-socialization does not, therefore, propose the disappearance of "traditional" or "conventional" modes of socialization and types of socialization agents (such as family, school, religious communities). Nor does it abandon a view of socialization as a fundamentally *social* process – i.e., as a process that always occurs in social, relational, and interactional contexts and environments. Rather, the notion of self-socialization needs to be viewed as a heuristic device that invites us to consider the role of individual agency and self-determination in social and cultural contexts where traditional modes of socialization and socialization agents remain present, but where their influence has been progressively waning, and/or where individual autonomy and self-determination has become increasingly widespread or even encouraged.

Socialization has for long also constituted a recurrent theme throughout the sociology of religion as it pertains directly to questions about how people become or stay religious, and how particular religious sensibilities and ways of "doing" religion are transmitted across generations, how these sensibilities and ways of doing religion are sustained, reproduced, regulated, and so on.[133] Religious socialization, not least, therefore also involves the learning of a particular religious language and acquiring the competencies required to independently use it. Alongside school and religious institutions, sociologists of religion have traditionally singled out the family as a key institution and agent in the religious socialization of children and youth. Indeed, the notion that early socialization by parents and extended family tends to "exert a lasting imprint on the religious belief orientations and commitments of their children"[134] has been widely validated by numerous large-scale studies.[135] Even so, the assumed importance of the family in this regard has also increasingly been brought into question.[136] This is because, in a progressively individualistic broader social and cultural environment, parents are increasingly granting their children more freedom and autonomy when it comes to religious matters. While it would be a gross exaggeration to say that the family no longer constitutes a central locus of religious socialization, it remains the case that successive generations of parents have become progressively less likely to socialize their children into any particular religious frameworks.

Again, acquiring the competencies to understand and use a particular religious language needs to be considered of key importance for successful socialization into any particular religious worldview and communal context. In spite of this, however, previous studies on religious socialization

Religion, the individual, & individualism 135

have rarely explicitly focused on the centrality of language and discourse in this regard. Yet, there is plenty of evidence to suggest that several major and ongoing processes of contemporary religious change in both the Western world and beyond (for example, institutional religious decline, the "individualization of religion," and the increasing commonality of "non-religious" outlooks) are at least partly attributable to a progressive general erosion in people's knowledge and understanding of traditional (mainly Christian) religious language. For example, the longitudinal research project The National Study of Youth and Religion carried out in the United States between 2001 and 2015 under the leadership of Christian Smith revealed that American young adults typically tended to make moral judgments without making any explicit references to any particular moral authorities, and without considering their moral judgments to be guided by any particular understandings of history, heritage, revelation, tradition, or the like.[137] Similar developments can also be discerned across large parts of Latin America, where the historically dominant Catholic Church has so far been relatively successful in containing the massive influx of Protestantism (mainly in the form of Charismatic Evangelicalism and Pentecostalism) since approximately the early 1970s. Increasingly, however, the Catholic Church finds itself in a social and cultural environment where wide support for its central tenets, values, and symbols is becoming increasingly difficult to sustain largely as a consequence of the gradual erosion and loss of meaning of the traditional language of Catholicism among younger age groups.[138]

Following the developments discussed above, scholars have also increasingly turned their attention to the present-day (digital) media environment as an increasingly central arena for religious socialization, especially among younger generations. While we can certainly question the extent to which "the media" can adequately be viewed as a socialization agent in and of itself, there is no doubt that audiences are affected by the media they consume and engage with. Compared with other key agents of religious socialization such as the family, school, and religious communities, media use also tends to be something over which individuals are often able to exercise a relatively high degree of control. While we cannot delve into the media environment's impact on contemporary modes of religious socialization in any further detail here, it is nevertheless worth highlighting the notable extent to which various types of media (in the forms of novels, magazines, television shows, films, digital culture etc.) participate in the wider circulation of all kinds of "alternative" discourses on "religion," including, not least, those on "spirituality."

Second-level conclusions

The above has offered a brief overview of the perpetuation and diffusion of individualism and individualist discourse in late modernity in light

136 *Religion, the individual, & individualism*

of previous theorizing on identity formation in late-modern, post-traditional society and the proliferation of "individualized religion" and "alternative spirituality." Although the impact of individualism on the religious sensibilities and outlooks of modern populations has received plenty of scholarly attention from the early 1980s onwards, with a few notable exceptions, this scholarship has rarely devoted much attention to the ways in which contemporary non-institutional, "individualized religion" is structured, sustained, and reproduced through discourse and discursive practice. This can, for example, be seen in the ways in which notions such as "personal autonomy," "personal choice," and "self-determination" have developed into integral parts of contemporary religious discourse more generally. It can also be seen in the wide diffusion and increasing normalization of what Heelas, Woodhead *et al.* have referred to as "holistic language" (for example, "harmony," "balance," "spiritual growth").

As the vocabulary of "spirituality" has continued to expand and diversify, we have also seen a corresponding expansion in scholarly vocabularies on "individualized religion" and "spirituality." This, however, presents a challenge that a discursive perspective helps alert us to. As discussed above, some scholars have more recently highlighted a worrying trend, whereby scholars of "alternative spirituality" have increasingly (an uncritically) started to use the concept of "spirituality" as if it were an analytical category. But, to quote McCutheon again, just like the category of "religion," the category of "spirituality" is "itself part of the problem to be analyzed and *is not itself* a tool in its own analysis."[139] The "spiritual, but not religious"-maxim must not be transformed into a scholarly etic concept. But there are already plenty of signs that this has, at least to some extent, already occurred. For example, it is not that uncommon to hear scholars of religion say that they are researching "spirituality" rather than "religion" as if these categories somehow referred to different "underlying realities" or "essences." In this, we can see the enduring influence of the *sui generis* approach to "religion," although now in the guise of "spirituality." The category of "spirituality" nevertheless needs to be approached as a category that has no meaning in and of itself. The focus of our attention should be on the particular ways in which people use that concept, what people take it to mean, in what contexts, and with what social and cultural effects. Our focus, in other words, should lie firmly on how the category of "spirituality" becomes varyingly construed and constructed through language, discourse, and other modes of semiotic representation. Indeed, this is the only "data" we have access to when it comes to "spirituality" – what people say about it, how people describe their "spiritual" outlooks, how they describe their "spiritual" practices, and so on. When it comes to the "spiritual, but not religious"-distinction, our primary focus should not lie on what is supposedly distinguished

Religion, the individual, & individualism 137

but rather on the *distinction itself*, on what people *do* and *achieve* when they make that distinction. It seems clear, therefore, that the category of "spirituality" is still in need of further and more firm theorization. Whatever form such theorization takes, though, it would no doubt benefit from engaging more directly with the perspectives of discourse theory and analysis.

Third-level analysis: exploring the impact of individualism on the religious sensibilities of contemporary individuals

In this section we move on to consider one particular way by which to investigate empirically the impact of individualism on the religious sensibilities and outlooks of contemporary individuals. It is not difficult to discern the ideational impact of the ethos of individualism on the discursive practices of the "alternative spiritual milieu" as found in associated books, magazines, webpages, and so on. Indeed, books by internationally renowned "alternative spiritual" personas such as Deepak Chopra, Eckhart Tolle, Rhonda Byrne, and Shakti Gawain have constituted prime vehicles for the wide popularization of various types of "individualistic" approaches to "religion" and "spirituality." The impact of various types of self-help, "leadership," and "management" literary genres has been equally notable. In addition, some very similar themes have also been circulated through best-selling books by more "traditional" evangelical personas such as Rick Warren, Bill Hybels, Joel Osteen, and Joyce Meyer.[140] Increasingly, the ideational impact of individualism can therefore be discerned across the religious-organizational and communal spectrum. When it comes to various types of published, either printed, audiovisual, or online materials, the data available for exploring the ideational impact of individualism on contemporary discursive practices on "religion" and "spirituality" has become virtually limitless. Researching the impact of individualism on the religious sensibilities of individuals, however, is a more difficult task. Such research has typically been conducted using methods such as surveys and/or interviews with various categories of relevant participants. But such research, of course, requires that researchers are able to find adequate numbers of relevant and willing participants in the first place. Yet, several previous studies (including some of those mentioned above) have managed to do this as well. Rather than simply following in the footsteps of previous research, what follows explicates a highly valuable, but hitherto only rarely used, method for studying people's positionings towards a broader range of contemporary themes, topics, and discourses related to "religion" and "spirituality, including discourses on "individualized religion." Our discussion will unfold in light of selected findings of the international research project Young Adults and Religion in a Global Perspective (YARG 2015–19).

138 *Religion, the individual, & individualism*

The YARG project was an international mixed-method research venture that explored the values and religious subjectivities of young adult university students (aged 18–30) in 13 different countries around the world: Canada, China, Finland, Ghana, India, Israel (three separate cases), Japan, Peru, Poland, Russia, Sweden, Turkey, and the United States. The project was located at the Department for the Study of Religions at Åbo Akademi University, Finland, and led by professor Peter Nynäs. The project focused on four thematic areas of central theoretical importance for understanding the formation of religious subjectivities and outlooks among members of the present young adult generation on an international scale: (1) contemporary modes of religious socialization; (2) the proliferation of social movements; (3) the influence of consumer culture and consumerism; (4) and the impact of the present-day digital media environment.[141] The project generated an extensive body of new data, both quantitative and qualitative, in relation to all of these areas. The choice of focusing on university students (a convenience sample) was largely motivated by reasons related to feasibility and access to participants on an international, cross-cultural scale.

The data for the project was gathered between 2016 and 2017 in all 13 locations using a systematic combination of four research instruments, both quantitative and qualitative: (1) a general survey (minimum N = 300/country, total sample N = 4,964); (2) the Schwartz Portrait Values Questionnaire (PVQ, minimum N = 300/country); (3) the Faith Q-Sort (FQS, minimum N = 45/country) – a novel instrument specifically developed for the study of contemporary religious subjectivities; and (4) semi-structured thematic interviews (minimum N = 45/country). The data gathering process consisted of two main phases: (1) the survey and PVQ; and (2) FQS and thematic interviews. In all locations other than Japan, which was only included in the survey and PVQ parts of the study, the survey results for those participants who had agreed to be contacted for further participation were used to select the most heterogeneous possible smaller sample of participants to participate in the qualitative FQS and thematic interview part of the study.

The project, as noted, generated a rich body of new data on a variety of different themes and topics. Perhaps the single most significant general finding of the project, however, was that young adults in nearly all the locations explored reported notably low overall levels of religious adherence, engagement, and practice (with the exception of the Ghanaian and the Muslim and Druze sub-samples in Israel). The YARG survey contained one item bloc on "social life" that included six items focusing on religion: on religious belonging (two items), self-assessed degrees of personal and parental family religiosity (two items), and frequency of public and private religious practice (two items). The figure below displays the mean scores for self-assessed degrees of personal religiosity (B10) and self-reported frequencies of public and private religious practice (B12, B13) for all samples included (Figure 5.1).

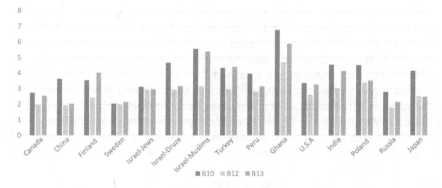

Figure 5.1 Self-assessed degree of personal religiosity and frequency of public and private religious practice.

As the figure shows, most samples revealed low overall levels of self-assessed degrees of personal religiosity and frequency of engagement in both public and private religious practice. The total sample results revealed a mean score of 3.9 for self-assessed degree of personal religiosity, and a mean of score of 4.9 for self-assessed degree of religiosity of the parental family, thereby clearly suggesting that the young adults surveyed generally viewed themselves as less religious than their parents. 27.9 percent of participants reported "never" engaging in public religious practice (e.g., participating in religious services and/or ceremonies), followed by 19.4 percent who reported doing so "less often." Regarding private religious practice (e.g., prayer and/or meditation), 32.1 percent reported "never" engaging in such practices, followed by 17.4 percent who reported doing so "less often." Regarding religious belonging, only 34.5 percent of all participants considered themselves "as belonging to one or more religious groups, communities, or traditions."

Q methodology and discourse analytic research

A representative portion of all young adults who participated in the YARG survey were invited to participate further in the qualitative part of the study. This included, most centrally, the utilization of a new Q methodological instrument: the FQS. Q methodology provides a particular foundation for the systematic study of people's viewpoints, opinions, beliefs, attitudes, and so forth on any given topic.[142] Primarily developed in the field of social psychology, the methodology is designed to explore people's subjective preferences from an internal frame of reference while at the same time utilizing the analytic procedures of quantitative analysis.[143] In a Q methodological study, people are presented with a collection of statements on a particular topic and are asked to rank-order them from their own subjective point of

140 *Religion, the individual, & individualism*

view. The statements come in the form of a set of cards called a Q-set. Together, the statements included in the set (anything from 40 up to 100) aim to capture the wider range of empirically identifiable diverging viewpoints that people might reasonably hold on the topic of interest.

The particular statements contained in a Q-set are derived from what is called a *concourse*. As Job van Exel and Gjalt de Graaf point out, "The concourse is a technical concept (not to be confused with the concept of discourse) much used in Q methodology for the collection of all the possible statements the participants can make about the subject at hand."[144] A verbal concourse may be obtained in a range of different ways, using a number of different sources, including various types of official documents; archived sources such as notes; diaries and the like; scholarly literature; research interviews; participant observation; the content of various types of mass media such as newspapers and television programs; and non-scientific literature such as novels and magazines. In the words of Steven R. Brown, in constructing and determining the concourse, the main objective is therefore to capture "the flow of communicability surrounding any topic ... [in] the ordinary conversation, commentary, and discourse of every day life."[145] This is what makes Q methodology a particularly valuable tool for discourse analytic research.

In constructing a Q methodological concourse for discourse analytical research, one would aim to bring together all of the different discourses that it is possible to identify on a particular topic at a certain point in time. But since the size of a concourse (i.e., all of the separate discourses that can be identified on a particular topic) will often exceed what is realistic to include in a particular Q-set, researchers need to construct a concourse that constitutes a representative miniature of all of the main discourses that can be identified on the topic of interest according to some structure that is determined by a particular research purpose. As van Exel and de Graaf put it: "Such a structure may *emerge* from further examination of the statements in the concourse or may be *imposed* on the concourse based on some theory."[146] Whatever structure one uses, however, it is important that the concourse one arrives at is as representative as possible of the wider range of diverging viewpoints that people might reasonably hold on the topic of interest. The concourse should, in other words, reflect both dominant and non-dominant viewpoints on the topic at hand. It is on the basis of the concourse that the individual statements included in a Q-set are then determined. As a first step, constructing the concourse therefore entails creating an overall map of the variety of different discourses, both contrasting and mutually supporting, that exist on a particular topic. As a second step, it entails converting all of these discourses into the form of statements that, taken together, communicate as many different viewpoints and positions on these respective discourses as possible. This procedure therefore closely resembles how discourse analysts would otherwise normally go about mapping the range of identifiable discourses on a particular

Religion, the individual, & individualism 141

topic. Q methodology therefore provides a particular, and indeed unique, way of empirically exploring the wider range of ways in which people position themselves *vis-à-vis* discourses on a particular topic.

Once a set of statements has been decided on and a Q-set has been created, it needs to become sorted by different categories of relevant participants. Irrespective of the particular structure and composition of the set, participants will ultimately give their own meanings to the statements by sorting them.[147] A Q-sorting situation largely resembles a research interview. Guided by the interviewer, participants are asked to rank-order the statements included in the set from their individual point of view, according to how much they either agree or disagree with them. Participants arrange the statements on a specially designed layout board that uses a quasi-normal forced distribution. The board contains columns that are each assigned a value (ranging for example from –4 to +4, or –3 to +3), with one end representing most agreement and the other end representing least agreement with any particular statement. Each column only has space for a certain number of statement cards, with relatively less space available in the columns at both the positive and negative ends. Most space is reserved for the middle section (values –1, 0, and +1), indicating little or no relevance for the participant, or being experienced as ambiguous. Because of this forced distribution design participants therefore have to place each of the statements included in the set in relation to one another. This encourages introspection, since it becomes necessary for participants to compare the statements and carefully consider their own subjective point of view in relation to each of them.[148]

Whereas each individual completed sorting of the statements will essentially be unique, through detailed factor analyses of the completed sorts using software specifically designed for the purpose, shared patterns of sortings are revealed. These patterns can be described as "socially shared viewpoints" ("factors" in the analysis) on the topic of interest among certain samples of participants. The more shared viewpoints a particular sample yields, the more divided that sample will also be regarding different viewpoints on the topic of interest. To be clear, the analysis does not therefore reveal the viewpoints of individual participants, but rather the viewpoints that certain numbers of participants share with one another. The shared viewpoints thus identified in each particular sample of participants can then be subjected to further factor analyses in order to identify socially shared and diverging viewpoints that extend across several samples of participants. These analyses therefore allow researchers to identify the wider, actual range of collectively shared understandings on the topic of interest, as well as the principal connections, commonalities, and differences that can be found between them. In this way, Q methodology provides a unique way of assessing how different categories of participants position themselves in relation to the wider range of possible viewpoints and discourses on a particular topic. As such, the methodology also allows for the empirical testing of scholarly assumptions. The methodology could therefore

142   *Religion, the individual, & individualism*

usefully be employed to investigate how different categories of people position themselves *vis-à-vis* a wider range of prevalent "religion-related" discourses, including those associated with an increasing "individualization" of religion, such as, for example, discourses on "spirituality," "spiritual, but not religious," "holistic wellbeing," and "personal choice in religious matters." Indeed, the particular Q-set employed in the YARG project provides an apt illustration of the methodology's potential in this regard.

The Faith Q-Sort

As noted, the YARG project employed a particular Q-set called the Faith Q-Sort (henceforth the instrument will be referred to as the FQS). The first version of the set was developed by the US psychologist of religion David Wulff to aid the systematic exploration of religious subjectivities, i.e., people's viewpoints, opinions, beliefs, attitudes and so forth *vis-à-vis* "religion," "spirituality," and other worldview-related topics and issues. When developing the concourse for the original version of the FQS, Wulff drew on a broad variety of sources, including theological and "insider" accounts from the world of "religions" more generally, coupled with scholarly observations from the history, sociology, and especially psychology of religion.[149] However, as he initially designed the instrument to be applied primarily in research in North American contexts, the employment of the FQS in a large cross-cultural study required some adjustments to the instrument. In cooperation with Wulff, the YARG core research team (that included the author) and its group of international partners therefore developed a revised version of the set: the FQS-b. Diverging only slightly from the original set, the new FQS covers a very broad set of themes and includes altogether 101 individual statements on a variety of "religion"-related themes, topics, ideas, and practices. Great effort was expended trying to avoid the inclusion of terms like "religion" and "spirituality" to the extent possible (the term "religion" appears once, and "spirituality" not at all), although, as Wulff comments on the original version of the instrument, "the adjectives 'religious' and 'spiritual' were considered necessary" for the statements to be comprehensible and for the set to serve its purpose.[150] These terms thus remained in the new version of the instrument as well. Other words such as "belief," along with "atheist" and "agnostic," were also avoided, although the set includes statements that, as Wulff puts it, "invite acknowledgment of these positions."[151]

The FQS was translated into 11 different languages (French, Mandarin, Finnish, Bengali, Arabic, Hebrew, Spanish, Polish, Russian, Swedish, and Turkish). As briefly discussed in Chapter 3, the translation of "religion"-related concepts and terminologies between different languages can be a challenging task. As also noted, different languages make different constructions of the world possible. In order to achieve as high a degree of

Religion, the individual, & individualism   143

coherence as possible, the translation aimed to produce equivalence of meaning rather than providing literal translations of each and every individual statement. In order to achieve this, the YARG project employed a double so-called back translation process, whereby two persons (in many cases professional translators) first translated all statements from the source language (English) to the target language, after which two additional persons independently translated the statements from the target language back to the source language (English). This procedure allowed the research team to compare and decide on the most appropriate translation for each and every individual statement. Several translation-related problems and errors could thereby also be identified and rectified before the instrument was piloted and eventually employed as part of actual, empirical research. Even so, the research team was fully aware of the fact that an elaborate procedure like this would in no way guarantee that participants would understand the statements as pertaining to the same "things." Whereas most participants across all the cultural contexts included did indeed interpret most of the statements in largely similar ways, there were also several instances where they interpreted some of the statements in light of the "religious semantics" prevalent in their own cultural contexts. Not unexpectedly, such instances were more common in the non-Western contexts of India and China in particular, as compared to the traditionally Christian contexts of, for example, Sweden, the United States, and Poland.

The statements included in the FQS can be divided into a set of main categories, each of which aims to capture a particular set of elements that are conventionally associated with "religion" (or the lack thereof). In one possible, albeit very general, categorization, the set could be described as consisting of statements on (1) views of "religion" more generally (e.g., "Views religion as the illusory creation of human fears and desires," "Rejects religious ideas that conflict with scientific and rational principles," "Is positively engaged by or interested in other people's religious traditions"); (2) personal engagement with religious organizations or communities (e.g., "Gives substantial amounts of time or money to some religious organization or worthy cause," "Is an active, contributing member of a religious or a spiritual community," "Feels closest to those who share the same faith or outlook"); (3) the perceived strength of personal beliefs or commitments (e.g., "Has frequent doubts about long-held religious convictions," "Becomes more religious or spiritual at times of crisis or need," "Seeks to intensify his or her experience of the divine or some otherworldly reality"); (4) religion and personal identity (e.g., "Being religious or spiritual is central to whom he or she is," "Takes no interest in religious or spiritual matters," "Seldom if ever doubts his or her deeply held convictions"); (5) religious practice (e.g., "Participates in religious practices chiefly to meet others' wishes or expectations," "Engages regularly in religious or spiritual practices in private," "Observes with great care prescribed religious practices and laws"); (6) thoughts on

144   *Religion, the individual, & individualism*

religious teachings and doctrines (e.g., "Thinks that the world's religious traditions point to a common truth," "Thinks that certain specific beliefs are crucial for salvation," "Considers all religious scriptures to be outdated or misguided"); and (7) experience (e.g., "Has experienced moments of intense divine, mysterious, or supernatural presence," "Feels spiritually moved and deeply sustained by music, art, or poetry," "Has used methods of attaining altered states of consciousness").[152] But in addition to these categories, the instrument also provides a way of assessing the spread and salience of a more limited set of "religion"- and "spirituality"-related discourses. For example, the FQS also includes at least eight statements that in one way or another pertain to prevalent discourses on individualized "religion" or "spirituality" as identified by previous research and as also discussed previously in this chapter. These include "Views religious faith as a never-ending quest," "Believes in some way, but does not view him or herself as religious," "Is inclined to embrace elements from various religious and spiritual traditions," "Senses a divine or universal luminous element within him- or herself," "Centers his or her life on a religious or spiritual quest," "Has moved from one group to another in search of a spiritual or ideological home," "Sees personal self-realization as a primary spiritual goal in life," and "Supports individual freedom of choice in matters of faith and morality."

The factor analyses of the completed sorts from all locations included in the YARG-project generated a total of 62 shared viewpoints (factors). These shared viewpoints do, however, need be viewed within their own respective national and cultural contexts. Most national samples generated between three and five shared viewpoints, whereas the Chinese sample generated six and the Indian sample as many as eight. The individual statements that engender most strong and widespread agreement and disagreement across the different viewpoints/factors identified in a particular sample are referred to as "consensus statements." The statement "Supports individual freedom of choice in matters of faith and morality" emerged as a consensus statement in the national samples of Canada, Peru, Russia, and the United States. And so, while these four national samples each yielded several different socially shared viewpoints, these were nevertheless all united by their strong agreement with this particular statement. For example, the Peruvian sample yielded one shared viewpoint that primarily reflects a traditional Christian "theistic" view on "religion" and "religion"-related matters (factor 2), and another one that quite evidently reflects a humanist, "non-religious" disposition (factor 1). Yet, while being otherwise notably different from one another, both of these shared viewpoints were united by their strong agreement with the statement "Supports individual freedom of choice in matters of faith and morality." In addition, this particular statement also emerged as a so-called "defining statement" in all but 39 out of a total of 62 shared viewpoints and was ranked strongly positively in every case except one, where it was ranked "neutral" (a statement is referred to as a defining statement when "a respondent's factor loading exceeds a certain limit

Religion, the individual, & individualism 145

(usually: $p < 0.01$); this is called a defining variate (or variable)"[153]). This means that not a single shared viewpoint expressed disagreement with it. This particular statement therefore received wide cross-cultural agreement among people who otherwise positioned themselves very differently in relation to a range of "religion"-related matters. These findings thus also clearly indicate how widespread the notion of being able to freely and independently choose one's religious outlook has become on a cross-cultural scale.

Thematic in-depth interviews

As noted, in the YARG project, in-depth thematic interviews (a total of 562) were conducted with all participants who participated in the FQS. This extensive body of data provides much additional depth and nuance regarding the particular ways in which participants positioned themselves in relation to the statements of the FQS. The interviews followed a pre-defined general structure and primarily focused on: (1) participants' experience of the FQS and thoughts about their own personal engagement with "religion/spirituality" or similar positions of a "non-religious" or "secular" character; (2) participants' personal history, self-understanding, and current life situation; and (3) participants' thoughts on the broader social and cultural contexts and communities that they are embedded and involved in. The local research assistants who conducted the interviews were all provided with an interview guide that they were asked to adapt to their own national and/ or local settings. As a result, with some local variations, it was possible to generate largely similar interview data from all studied contexts.

The theme that surfaced most clearly across all of the interviews was that of personal autonomy and individual choice in religious and existential matters. This was partly a result of the main focus of the interview situation as a whole and the fact that particularly large numbers of participants expressed strong agreement with the FQS statement "Supports individual freedom of choice in matters of faith and morality." We need to recognize, therefore, how the FQS partly served to "prime" participants to discuss and elaborate further on certain topics as opposed to others, and especially when it came to the particular FQS statements that they had expressed either strongest agreement or disagreement with. Below, we shall more generally illustrate how participants from different parts of the world often explained their agreement with the statement "Supports individual freedom of choice in matters of faith and morality" in ways that closely align with prevalent discourses on the primacy of the individual and personal autonomy.

For many participants, the notion of freedom of choice in religious matters emerged as a self-evident commonsensical value, as in the examples below.

> Well, I think that everyone must choose independently what he or she, what he or she -- likes more, finds more interesting, what he or she

146   *Religion, the individual, & individualism*

believes in, and there mustn't be any pressure or -- disapproval, and he or she should make a choice regardless of other people's opinion, so to say.

(Russian participant, YRUPV028)

Yeah. So this, question 100. Individual freedom of choice that, I think it's very much a starting point that you get to choose for yourself. And, I wouldn't necessarily even, even though I belong to the Lutheran parish I wouldn't necessarily baptize children. That they get to then decide it for themselves.

(Finnish participant, YFIKD150T)

Of course, the one that says "supports individual freedom," that is, as I – have – had the option [at home, among peers, and at university]... to be able to go out to find, to know, to decide what I don't know, it seems to me that after all, it has to be a personal search because – if you find it, that is – good. And if you don't find it – and you find something that satisfies you in the end you are not alone in society. You're going to find more people ... Then always there's going to be like a mattress that supports or accommodates your way of thinking or the choice you're taking against one situation or another.

(Canadian participant, YPESC030P)

Because for me how I view religion, whether or not I'm religious or not, one's relationship with God, the divine, is completely different from someone else's relationship with God, I think. And their ability to communicate with their god, whoever their god is, I think it's important because – I think being able to form your own relationship with that, and having your own perspective is extremely important. I don't know, I also think that religion and morality are so complicated that there's no way it's going to be unified. And it brings me back to one of the other ones that says something like, "all religion subscribes to the same truth" or something.

(US participant, YUSTP032)

In the first example, the participant frames individual choice as an imperative. People, in other words, "must" exercise freedom of choice in religious matters. That freedom, moreover, "must not" be restricted or curtailed in any way. As the participant says, there must be "no pressure" or "disapproval" by others in this regard as this is a fundamental freedom that everyone needs to recognize and respect. The second example is similar. Here, the participant talks about freedom of choice in religious matters as a "very much a starting point." Moreover, in a way that directly relates to our previous discussion of changing modes of religious socialization, the participant goes on to point out that he/she would "not necessarily" actively socialize his/her children into Lutheranism, but rather let them decide for themselves. The third example is somewhat different. Here, the participant more directly connects the issue of freedom of choice in religious matters to the diversity of opinion that can be seen to exist throughout society and culture more generally. As he/she says, whatever one's choices in this regard, there will always be others who share one's opinions. In the last example, the participant frames religion in general in terms of a personal relationship with whatever "god" or deity one believes in. Indeed, for this participant, people's views on religion and morality will inevitably always differ from one another. Hence, "having your own perspective is extremely important."

The importance of freedom of choice in religious matters was also highlighted by several participants who personally subscribed to more conservative religious teachings and were active members of religious communities. Such views were somewhat more commonly expressed by participants in (often non-Western) national contexts that are marked by relatively high levels of overall religious vitality.

> Um, we all believe in something so if someone at a point in time decides to go for something that is um, like not exactly what their religion is teaching, I think freedom of choice was given to everybody by God even from scratch. So if the person at some point decide no oo, am okay because in the end is not me who is going to decide is the one who gave us the freedom so if the person at some point in time says is okay to leave the belief that he or she was holding onto and then go for a different one, am okay with it. Am okay with this part.
>
> (Ghanaian participant, YGHFB115P)

> For instance, let me talk about number 100. Um, as an individual I am free to choose my own religion and faith but -- based on our society, our society is not that free. But I value individuals more than the society but I believe that I have my own individual freedom relating to this subject. That is why I support freedom for sure here. Therefore, this card describes me the best.
>
> (Turkish participant, YTRHE037P)

> My parents have been Catholics, so it was natural that they brought me up to be a Catholic. As I said before, there was a rebellion time when I was thinking about what it is for and why. After that time I consciously chose the same Catholic faith.
>
> (Polish participant, YARG101P)

In the first example, the participant talks about freedom of choice as something "God-given." As in the first set of examples above, the greatest importance is attached to having the ability to make independent choices

148 *Religion, the individual, & individualism*

in this regard. In the second example, the participant directly relates the question to broader societal and cultural expectations. According to this participant – who "values individuals more than the society" – we should all be free to make independent choices in religious matters, regardless of whether that would be generally accepted in the wider surrounding society and culture or not. But, as he/she unequivocally states, "as an individual I am free to choose my own religion and faith." The last example is illustrative of another common way in which participants often talked about their personal religious commitments, i.e., as something that they had consciously and deliberately chosen. As this participant points out, rather than having simply accepted Catholicism in his/her youth, at a later point in life, he/she "consciously chose" it.

Lastly, it is worth noting that, for some participants, freedom of choice in religious matters primarily meant the freedom to adopt a more critical stance towards received religious values and mores, as in this example:

> Although the university, well ... I wouldn't say is the greatest source of Christianity in the world but, eh, yes, partly it is ... [I]n fact, more I learnt about it, more details I discovered from it. Questioning; knowing and asking. ... one example is the Bible which now I consider should be read in a critical way, I mean like not taking it in a literal way. Ask, know, respond are frequently used instruments in the university and they are becoming an essential tool to take distance or to become more critical in relation to the received faith.
>
> (Peruvian participant, YPEMV050)

As briefly illustrated here, participants explained their agreement with the FQS statement "Supports individual freedom of choice in matters of faith and morality" in a variety of different ways. In doing so, they also typically drew on firmly established vocabularies on the importance of individual choice and self-determination, using phases such as "everyone must choose independently what he or she ... believes in" and "as an individual I am free to choose my own religion and faith." This is in no way surprising considering how widespread these notions have become on a cross-cultural scale. Indeed, prevalent discourses on the autonomy of the individual do not lend much room for other types of positions in this regard (such as *not* thinking that people should be able to exercise free choice in religious matters). The findings of the YARG project therefore contribute with further empirical support for the wide perpetuation of individualist stances towards "religion" on a cross-cultural scale.

Third-level conclusions

The above has provided a brief general explanation of Q methodology and its value for empirically oriented discourse analytic research. As highlighted above, as the method provides a unique way of exploring the salience of

Religion, the individual, & individualism 149

particular "religion"-related discourses among various categories of people, it could usefully be included in the methodological toolbox of a discursive sociology of religion. The utility of the method was further illustrated in light of the particular way that it was employed in the YARG project in the form of the FQS. Here, we focused on one key finding: the notable extent to which participants from several different locations throughout the world expressed strong agreement with the FQS statement "Supports individual freedom of choice in matters of faith and morality."

As the attentive reader will have already noticed, there is no denying that the FQS, in spite of its aim to be as encompassing as possible, largely reflects a Western (scholarly) understanding of "religion." That said, in order to be able to explore and assess people's viewpoints on a wider range of "religion"-related topics and themes, one has to start *somewhere*. Even so, considering that the FQS works so that participants are asked to rank-order 101 already formulated statements on a variety of "religion"-related issues, what one can confidently claim that the instrument actually "measures" is certainly up for debate. But, whatever conclusion one arrives at regarding that question, the instrument, at the very least, provides a unique way of assessing people's positioning towards a "global discourse on religion" as discussed in Chapter 3, as well as the extent to which that discourse has become established and naturalized throughout different parts of the world (in the case of the YARG-project, among university students specifically). Indeed, as noted above, even though some participants interpreted some of the statements included in the set in light of the established "religious semantics" of their own cultural contexts, the vast majority of all participants across all cultural contexts explored nevertheless found most of the statements perfectly intelligible. This attests to the increasing spread and establishment of a (Western) "global discourse on religion" and its associated, largely Christian-theistic, vocabulary. As further exemplified by the views of participants themselves as expressed in in-depth interviews, the findings also illustrate the extent to which individualized discourse has come to dominate and frame the ways in which people talk about and understand their religious (or non-religious) engagements. It is well worth noting that these views were expressed by young adults, who are likely to pass them on to future generations. In doing so, they will also pass on the individualized language that their views are typically couched in. This, then, provides one example of how particular types of individualized discourses on "religion" are becoming perpetuated and reproduced on a cross-cultural scale. Having said that, we also need to acknowledge that the university world constitutes a very particular type of cultural context that is intimately associated with values such as independent thought, intellectual inquiry, and informed criticism. Notwithstanding significant differences across different countries and socio-cultural contexts, university students therefore tend to inhabit a cultural world that differs considerably from that of their non-university student peers.

150 *Religion, the individual, & individualism*

Concluding remarks

This chapter has explored the ideational and discursive impact of the ethos of individualism on the Western religious field. As part of our first-level reflection, we traced the historical development and constitution of the concept of the "individual" and ethos of individualism as primarily political and social-philosophical ideals. The subsequent development of economic and social individualism, however, brought a considerable expansion in what was referred to as the "vocabulary of the individual." As part of this process, throughout the nineteenth and early twentieth centuries, this expanding vocabulary of the individual also become increasingly integrated into the formal discourses of social domains such as politics, education, and law. These increasingly prevalent and ideationally forceful discourses also become ever more closely entwined with, as well as infused with, the vocabularies of (popular) psychology and therapy (on "self-realization," self-development," "self-enhancement," and so on). By the mid-twentieth century, if not earlier, individualized discourse had become established to such an extent that it had become increasingly difficult to construe social and cultural life, including religious life, in any other terms.

As part of our second-level reflection, we first considered some influential social-theoretical accounts of the impact of individualism on late-modern, "post-traditional" society and culture. We then moved to consider its impact on the post-1950s Western religious field in light of previous scholarship in the area. Here, special attention was devoted to the proliferation of various forms of non-institutional "alternative spirituality" and their associated vocabularies. As noted, not only has the vocabulary of "spirituality" expanded considerably during roughly the past six to seven decades. A corresponding expansion has also occurred in the terminologies through which scholars have tried to make sense of "spirituality" and people's "spiritual, but not religious" outlooks and practices. But while previous scholarship has not failed to note the proliferation of "holistic language," it has rarely devoted any serious attention to the ways in which the category of "spirituality" is itself constituted, reproduced, and made meaningful through discourse and discursive practice. As discussed in detail in Chapter 3, there now exists a diverse body of scholarship that approaches the category of "religion" through the prism of discourse. Considering that the category of "spirituality" has long since become widely established as part of everyday parlance and popular discourse, future scholarship in the area could usefully devote more attention to its ideational and discursive components. To the extent that discourses on "spirituality" (with their typically strong focus on the intuitions and feelings of the individual) become increasingly engrained and naturalized throughout social and cultural life more generally, people are also increasingly likely to perceive "spirituality" as something "real," as something that exists in the world independently of their own experiences or views of it. "Spirituality" has, in other words, developed into an increasingly normalized, "commonsensical" concept. This is why it would be well worthwhile to explore the particular ways in which the increasing naturalization of discursive maxims like "spiritual, but not religious" are affecting people's views and understandings of the category of "religion" more generally. Future research on individualized "spirituality" could therefore usefully also explore the ideational impact of its key vocabulary on scholarly theorizing itself. Our focus, again, should therefore lie on the particular ways in which the category of "spirituality" becomes varyingly construed, constructed, and *used* by people and actors in and across different types of social and cultural contexts and situations. In addition to the above, it would certainly also be worthwhile to explore the extent to which the category of "spirituality" has made its way into the formal discourses of social institutions, such as healthcare (as is already the case with so-called Complementary and Alternative Medicine), education, and perhaps even politics and law.

In the final part of the chapter, we focused on explaining the value of Q methodology for the study of people's religious and "spiritual" outlooks and views. Although the methodology, with the exception of the extensive YARG research project, has so far only rarely been employed in studies of religion, it provides us with a unique way to explore the wider range of different ways in which people position themselves *vis-à-vis* a whole host of "religion"-related issues and discourses. The utility of the method was briefly illustrated in light of some of the findings that it generated for the YARG project in the form of the FQS. Here, we focused on one notable finding in particular; namely, the fact that participants from several different countries who otherwise positioned themselves very differently *vis-à-vis* a range of "religion"-related issues nevertheless expressed strong agreement with the statement "Supports individual freedom of choice in matters of faith and morality." The main aim of our discussion was nevertheless to more generally illustrate the utility of Q methodology for future discourse analytic research in the sociology of religion. This is, not least, because it would provide us with a highly efficacious way of testing our scholarly assumptions. In particular, the method can be used to generate firmly empirically grounded "maps" of how prevalent discourses and discursive formations on "religion," the "religious," "spirituality," and the like actually resonate among different categories of people across different social and cultural settings. These maps, in turn, provide us with highly valuable data to guide further empirical research.

Notes

1 Walls, *Individualism*, 3.
2 Adams, *Self and Social*, 7.
3 Ibid., 4.
4 Ibid., 1.

152 *Religion, the individual, & individualism*

5 Sean McCloud, "Religions are Belief Systems," in *Stereotyping Religion: Critiquing Clichés*, eds. Brad Stoddard and Craig Martin (London: Bloomsbury Academic, 2017), 12.

6 Bruce, *God Is Dead*, 12.

7 Turner, *Religion*, 237.

8 Bruce, *God Is Dead*, 11.

9 For example, Peter L. Berger, *Heretical Imperative: Contemporary Possibilities of Religious Affirmation* (New York: Doubleday, 1980); Ulrich Beck, *A God of Ones' Own: Religion's Capacity for Peace and Potential for Violence* (Cambridge: Polity Press, 2010).

10 Beck, *A God*, 85.

11 Slater, *Consumer Culture*, 40; for an extended discussion see Walls, *Individualism*, 22–34.

12 Slater and Tonkiss, *Market Society*, 29.

13 Walls, *Individualism*, 33.

14 Slater, *Consumer Culture*, 39.

15 François Gauthier, "From Nation-State," 383.

16 Slater, *Consumer Culture*, 39.

17 Ibid., 65.

18 Walls, *Individualism*, 3; 9.

19 Ibid., 13–15.

20 Ibid., 67.

21 Ibid., 74.

22 Bellah *et al.*, *Habits of the Heart*, 27–51; 142–63.

23 Walls, *Individualism*, 64.

24 Ibid., 88.

25 Ibid., 89.

26 Ibid., 90.

27 Ibid., 119.

28 Ibid., 115.

29 Gordon Lynch, *On the Sacred* (Durham: Acumen, 2012), 21.

30 Ibid., 11.

31 For an extended discussion, see for example, W.S.F Pickering, *Durkheim's Sociology of Religion: Themes and Theories* (Cambridge: James Clarke & Co, 2009), 132.

32 For example, Kim Knott, "The Secular Sacred: In Between or Both/And?," in *Social Identities between the Sacred and the Secular*, eds. Abby Day, Giselle Vincent, and Christopher R. Cotter, AHRC/ESRC Religion and Society Series (Farnham: Ashgate, 2013), 148.

33 Émile Durkheim, *The Division of Labour in Society*, Reprinted (London: Macmillan, 1984).

34 Émile Durkheim, *The Elementary Forms of Religious Life* (New York: The Free Press, 1995 [1912]), 425.

35 Émile Durkheim, "Individualism and the Intellectuals," in *Emile Durkheim on Morality and Society*, ed. Robert N. Bellah (Chicago, IL: University of Chicago Press, 1973), 49.

36 Michael Stausberg, "The Sacred, the Holy, the Numinous – And Religion: On the Emergence and Early History of a Terminological Constellation," *Religion* 47, no. 4 (2017): 560.

37 William E. Paden, "Sacred Order," *Method & Theory in the Study of Religion*, 12, no. 1 (2000): 119–20.

38 Mark S. Cladis, "Beyond Solidarity? Durkheim and Twenty-First Century Democracy in a Global Age," in *The Cambridge Companion to Durkheim*, eds. Jeffrey Alexander and Phillip Smith (Cambridge: Cambridge University Press, 2005), 385.

Religion, the individual, & individualism 153

39 Durkheim, *The Elementary Forms*, 434–5.
40 David B. Grusky and Gabriela Galescu, "Is Durkheim a Class Analyst?" in *The Cambridge Companion to Durkheim*, eds. Jeffrey Alexander and Philip Smith (Cambridge: Cambridge University Press, 2005), 328; cf. Hans Joas, *The Sacredness of the Person: A New Genealogy of Human Rights* (Washington, DC: Georgetown University Press, 2013).
41 For a particular take and extended discussion on the "expressivist turn," see for example, Charles Taylor, *Sources of the Self: The Making of the Modern Identity* (Cambridge: Cambridge University Press, 1989).
42 Walls, *Individualism*, 116.
43 Ibid., emphasis added.
44 Ibid., 144.
45 Ibid., 117.
46 Ibid.
47 Bellah *et al.*, *Habits of the Heart*, 46.
48 Jeremy Carrette and Richard King, *Selling Spirituality: The Silent Takeover of Religion* (London: Routledge, 2005), 59.
49 Gergen *An Invitation*, 88.
50 David Riesman, Nathan Glazer, and Reuel Denney, *The Lonely Crowd: A Study of the Changing American Character* (New Haven, CT: Yale University Press, 1950).
51 Richard Sennett, *The Fall of Public Man* (New York: W.W. Norton & Company, 1977).
52 Christopher Lasch, *Culture of Narcissism: American Life in an Age of Diminishing Expectations* (New York: W.W. Norton & Company, 1979).
53 Bellah *et al.*, *Habits of the Heart*.
54 Ibid., 5.
55 Ibid., 20.
56 Ibid., 23.
57 Ibid., 63.
58 Anthony Giddens, *Modernity and Self-Identity: Self and Society in the Late Modern Age* (Cambridge: Polity Press, 1991).
59 Scott Lash, *Reflexive Modernization: Politics, Tradition and Aesthetics in the Modern Social Order* (Chicago, IL: University of Chicago Press, 1995).
60 Robert D. Putman, *Bowling Alone: The Collapse and Revival of American Community* (New York: Simon & Shuster, 2000).
61 Zygmunt Bauman, *The Individualized Society* (Cambridge: Polity Press, 2001).
62 Ulrich Beck and Elisabeth Beck-Gernsheim, *Individualization: Institutionalized Individualism and Its Social and Political Consequences* (London: Sage, 2002).
63 Kath Woodward, *Understanding Identity* (London: Arnold, 2002), 2–4.
64 Chris Weedon, *Identity and Culture: Narratives of Difference and Belonging* (New York. Open University Press, 2004), 8).
65 Ibid., 8–9.
66 Ibid., 19.
67 Ibid., 7.
68 Woodward, *Understanding Identity*, 24–5; Burr, *Social Constructionism*, 143.
69 Giddens, *Modernity and Self-Identity*, 54.
70 Ibid., 81.
71 Zygmunt Bauman, "Foreword: Individually, Together," in Beck and Beck-Gernsheim, *Individualization*, xv.
72 Ibid.
73 Beck and Beck-Gernsheim, *Individualization*, xxii.

154 *Religion, the individual, & individualism*

74 Ibid., 2.
75 Ibid.
76 Ibid., 3.
77 Ibid., 23.
78 Ibid., 4.
79 Craig Martin, *Capitalizing Religion*, 5; for a particular take on the "individualization of religion" in the West, see Beck, *A God*, 79–92.
80 Luckmann, *The Invisible Religion*.
81 Martin, *Capitalizing Religion*, 43.
82 Wade Clark Roof, *A Generation of Seekers: The Spiritual Journeys of the Baby Boom Generation* (San Francisco, CA: Harper Collins, 1993).
83 Robert Wuthnow, *After Heaven: Spirituality in America since the 1950s* (Berkeley: University of California Press, 1998).
84 Bellah *et al.*, *Habits of the Heart*, 228.
85 Beckford, *Social Theory*, 209.
86 Ibid.
87 Colin Campbell, "The Cult, the Cultic Milieu and Secularization," *A Sociological Yearbook of Religion in Britain 5* (London: SCM Press, 1972).
88 For example, Daren Kemp and James R. Lewis, eds., *Handbook of New Age* (Leiden: Brill, 2007).
89 For example, Steven Sutcliffe and Marion Bowman, eds., *Beyond New Age: Exploring Alternative Spirituality* (Edinburgh: Edinburgh University Press, 2000).
90 Paul Heelas, *The New Age Movement: Religion, Culture and Society in the Age of Postmodernity* (London: Wiley, 1996).
91 Paul Heelas, Linda Woodhead *et al.*, *The Spiritual Revolution: Why Religion Is Giving Way to Spirituality* (Oxford: Blackwell, 2005).
92 James R. Lewis, "Legitimating Suicide: Heaven's Gate and New Age Ideology," in *UFO-Religions*, ed. Christopher Partridge (London: Routledge, 2003), 118.
93 Michael Barkun, *A Culture of Conspiracy: Apocalyptic Vision in Contemporary America* (Berkeley: University of California Press, 2003).
94 Meredith B. McGuire, quoted in Heelas and Woodhead, *et al.*, *Spiritual Revolution*, 1–2.
95 Ibid., 6.
96 Carrette and King, *Selling Spirituality*, 32–53.
97 William James, *The Varieties of Religious Experience*, Centenary Edition (Oxon: Routledge, [1902] 2002).
98 Carrette and King, *Selling Spirituality*, 69–70.
99 Ibid., 74–5.
100 Ibid., 43.
101 Beckford, "The Return," 123.
102 Heelas and Woodhead, *et al.*, *The Spiritual Revolution*, 26.
103 Ibid.
104 Ibid., 28.
105 Ibid., 19–20.
106 Ibid., 1; 71.
107 Bellah *et al.*, *Habits of the Heart*, 237.
108 Ibid., 237; cf. Warner, *Secularization*, 154.
109 Ibid., 232.
110 Philip E. Hammond, *Religion and Personal Autonomy: The Third Disestablishment in America* (Columbia: University of South Carolina Press, 1992).
111 Robert Fuller, *Spiritual, but not Religious: Understanding Unchurched America* (Oxford: Oxford University Press, 2001).

Religion, the individual, & individualism   155

112 For example, Olufunke Adeboye, "Pentecostal Challenges in Africa and Latin America: A Comparative Focus on Nigeria and Brazil, *Afrika Zamani*, 11–12 (2003): 136–59; Moberg, "Christian Churches' Responses."

113 Andie R. Alexander and Russell T. McCutcheon, "I'm Spiritual but not Religious," in *Stereotyping Religion: Critiquing Clichés*, eds. Brad Stoddard and Craig Martin (London: Bloomsbury Academic, 2017), 99.

114 Ibid.

115 Seyla Benhabib, *Situating the Self: Gender, Community and Postmodernism in Contemporary Ethics* (Cambridge: Polity Press, 1992), 214.

116 Gauthier, "From Nation-State," 401.

117 Beyer, *Religions in Global Society*, 8.

118 Carrette and King, *Selling Spirituality*, 30.

119 Ibid., 31.

120 Martin, *Capitalizing Religion*, 33.

121 Ibid., 3–4.

122 Ibid., 6.

123 Ibid., 23.

124 Eleanor Maccoby, "Historical Overview of Socialization Research and Theory," in *Handbook of Socialization: Theory and Research*, eds. Joan E. Crusec and Paul D. Hastings (New York: The Guilford Press, 2014), 13.

125 Ibid., 14.

126 Jeffrey Jensen Arnett and Susan Taber, "Adolescence Terminable and Interminable: When Does Adolescence End?" *Journal of Youth and Adolescence* 23/5 (1993): 519.

127 Maccoby, "Historical Overview," 13.

128 Walls, *Individualism*, 5.

129 Paul Vermeer, "Religious Education and Socialization," *Religious Education* 105, no. 1 (2010): 107.

130 Ibid.

131 Philip R. Newman and Barbara M. Newman, "Self-Socialization: A Case of a Parachute Child," *Adolescence* 44, no. 175 (Autumn 2009): 524.

132 Jeffrey Jensen Arnett, "Adolescents' Uses of Media for Self-Socialization," *Journal of Youth and Adolescence* 24, no. 5 (1995): 521.

133 For example, Marcus Moberg and Sofia Sjö, "Mass-Mediated Popular Culture and Religious Socialisation," in *Religion, Media, and Social Change*, eds. Kennet Granholm, Marcus Moberg, and Sofia Sjö (New York: Routledge, 2015), 92.

134 Vern Bengtson *et al.*, "Longitudinal Study of the Intergenerational Transmission of Religion," *International Sociology* 24, no. 3 (2009): 327.

135 For example, Jennifer Glass, Vern L. Bengtson, and Charlotte Chorn Dunham, "Attitude Similarity in Three-Generation Families: Socialization, Status Inheritance, or Reciprocal Influence?" *American Sociological Review* 51, no. 5 (1986): 685–98; Christian Smith, *Soul Searching: The Religious and Spiritual Lives of American Teenagers* (New York: Oxford University Press, 2005).

136 For example, David Voas and Alasdair Crockett, "Religion in Britain: Neither Believing Nor Belonging." *Sociology* 39, no. 1 (2005): 11–28.

137 Christian Smith, with Patricia Snell, *Souls in Transition: The Religious and Spiritual Lives of Emerging Adults* (Oxford: Oxford University Press, 2009).

138 Rafael Fernández, Sidney Castillo Carnedas, and Marcus Moberg, "The Internet, Social Media, and the Critical Interrogation of Traditional Religion among Young Adults in Peru," in *Digital Media, Young Adults and Religion: An International Perspective*, eds. Marcus Moberg and Sofia Sjö (Oxon: Routledge, 2020), 58.

156 Religion, the individual, & individualism

139 McCutcheon, *Manufacturing*, 129.
140 Marvin Washington, Harry J. Van Buren III, and Karen Patterson, "Pastor Practices in the Era of Megachurches: New Organizational Practices and Forms for a Changing Institutional Environment", in *Religion and Organization Theory, Research in the Sociology of Organizations* vol. 41, eds. Paul Tracey, Nelson Phillips, and Michael Lounsbury (Emerald Publishing Group, 2014), 201.
141 For details about YARG project research design and execution, see Peter Nynäs, *et al.*, eds., *The Diversity of Worldviews among Young Adults: Contemporary (Non)Religiosity and Spirituality through the Lens of an International Mixed Method Study* (New York: Springer, 2021); Marcus Moberg and Sofia Sjö, eds., *Digital Media, Young Adults and Religion: An International Perspective* (Oxon: Routledge, 2020).
142 For example, Simon Watts and Paul Stenner, *Doing Q Methodological Research: Theory, Method and Interpretation* (London: Sage, 2012).
143 For example, Job van Exel and Gjalt de Graaf, "Q Methodology: A Sneak Preview." 2005 [available from www.jobvanexel.nl].
144 Ibid., 4.
145 Steven R. Brown, "A Primer on Q methodology." *Operant Subjectivity* 16, no. 3–4 (1993): 94.
146 van Exel and de Graaf, "Q methodology," 5.
147 Ibid.
148 Janne Kontala, *Emerging Non-religious Worldview Prototypes: A Faith Q-sort Study on Finnish Group-Affiliates* (Åbo: Åbo Akademi University Press, 2016), 69–70
149 David Wulff, "Prototypes of Faith: Findings with the Faith Q-Sort," *Journal for the Scientific Study of Religion* 58, no. 3 (2020): 648–9.
150 Ibid., 649.
151 Ibid.
152 For the complete list of statements included in the FQS, see Nynäs *et al.*, *The Diversity*.
153 van Exel and de Graaf, "Q Methodology," 9.

6 Religion in market society

This chapter focuses on the historical constitution and establishment of market society and its ideational and discursive impact on the contemporary Western religious field. During the past couple of decades, the relationship between religion, markets, and consumer culture has become the subject of a diverse and fast-growing multidisciplinary area of study. Given that this relationship pertains directly to the dialectical interplay between broader processes of socio-economic and religious change, the changing character of contemporary religious organizations, and the changing religious and cultural sensibilities of modern populations, it will also likely remain an area of great relevance for the sociological study of religion for the foreseeable future.

The chapter is divided into three main parts. In terms of first-level reflection, the first part starts out by providing a general account of the liberal concept of the "market," its ideational influence on the constitution of Western market economics, and the central role it continues to play in providing the philosophical underpinnings for contemporary neoliberal political economy and consumer culture. As our discussion will illustrate, a critical first-level assessment of previous, both earlier and more recent, theorizations of the relationship between religion and the "market" is contingent upon an adequate understanding of the historical constitution and development of the liberal "Market Idea."[1] The second part of the chapter is devoted to second-level reflection on some of the principal and most influential ways in which religion and religious life in contemporary market society has been approached and theorized in the sociological study of religion over roughly the past three to four decades. Here, our task is therefore to engage in critical reflection on some of the principal ways in which sociologists of religion have theorized – and continue to theorize – the religion–market relationship, as well as the particular ways in which they have employed the concept of the "market," along with other closely related concepts such as "product" and the "consumer." The intention is not to simply revisit and reiterate previous debates, but to highlight how a more sustained focus on the constitutive and constructive function of discourse and discursive practice can help us shed new light on some of the most pressing issues involved.

DOI: 10.4324/9780367435837-6

158 *Religion in market society*

The third part of the chapter focuses on the ideational and discursive impact of market society within the context of religious organizations. In order to provide a crucial complement to previous research in the area, this part of chapter explores some of the most notable ways in which traditional and long-established religious organizations have more recently begun to internalize managerial and market-associated discourses and imperatives and varyingly striven to implement these in actual practice. Focusing on the particular context of the "mainline" Protestant churches in the United States, our discussion aims to further highlight the discourse-driven nature of contemporary processes of social and socio-economic change and the ways in which actual tangible changes in the practices of all types of organizations tend to be both preceded and driven by changes in their discursive practices. The task is therefore to engage in concrete third-level analysis of the discursive practices of traditional religious organizations themselves by applying a set of discourse analytical concepts and tools especially suited for the task.

First-level reflection: the liberal conception of the "market"

Ever since the early-modern period, the various meanings attached to the concept of the "market" have undergone a range of notable shifts and transformations, all of which have been intimately related to the emergence and gradual establishment of new discursive formations on governance and the social organization of modern societies. In pre-modern times, the term "market" primarily denoted a more specific mode, physical space, and event for the actual exchange of tangible goods. Since the advent of the early-modern era, however, the "market" started taking on entirely different meanings and increasingly came to be understood as an organizing principle for social life on the whole. This particular understanding of the market rose to prominence as part of developments in the early liberal thought of the seventeenth and eighteenth centuries, as already discussed in Chapter 5.

As noted in our previous discussion of the liberal view of society and the individual, in their efforts to forge a new type of social order to replace the *ancien régime*, the liberal thinkers of the seventeenth and eighteenth centuries came to establish the foundations of all social and political life in the supreme autonomy of the individual. Hence, in their efforts to provide as solid as possible a foundation for the establishment of a new mode of organization of social life that would amount to a "political zero-sum game between citizens and states,"[2] liberal thinkers turned to the "market" as the principal, independent, and self-regulating ordering mechanism that would be able to facilitate individuals' rational pursuit of their self-interest "without compromising the autonomy of their choices."[3] These ideas found their most enduringly influential expression through the work of Adam Smith. In *The Wealth of Nations*[4] – a work often considered foundational for the development of classical economics – Smith presented a political

Religion in market society 159

economic model that principally rooted a harmonious relationship between the public good and conflicting individual interests in the civil sphere of economic interaction and exchange.[5] In Smith's famous phrase, the "invisible hand" of the market mechanism "allows social order to emerge from the anarchy of diverse individual desires" while simultaneously also enhancing the general level of welfare "as the unintended outcome of intentional individual acts."[6] As Slater comments, these ideas were thus based on a set of quite "peculiar assumptions about how individuals relate to their needs and desires," as well as about what it actually meant to "pursue self-interest *rationally*," ideas that would later come to be "embodied in the dreaded figure of *homo oeconomicus*."[7] It is therefore through the gradual development and crystallization of liberal thought that "the holy trinity of reason, freedom and social progress comes to be seen as manifesting itself pre-eminently in the *economic* pursuit of self-interest by economic man."[8] Although liberal thought partly reflected the increasing "centrality of market behavior" across early-modern Western societies more generally, it would also come to play a pivotal role in establishing market behavior as the principal "model and mechanism for achieving order and ethical life throughout society" as a whole, thereby also providing the philosophical foundations for the notion of "market society." Liberal thought thereby also developed into a central pillar of the classical economics of the late eighteenth century,[9] the development of which also coincided with the initial establishment of economics as an independent academic discipline. The new discipline largely came to understand the "market" in liberalist terms as constituting an autonomous, purely economic, and self-regulating mechanism that could be studied, understood, and analyzed separately from its social, cultural, and institutional dimensions.[10]

The liberal conception of the market, which also remained foundational for the subsequent development of neoclassical economics from the late nineteenth century onwards, did, however, contrast sharply with several other contemporaneous strands of social thought. For example, and perhaps most famously, in Karl Marx's *Capital*[11] the "market" appeared not as an impartial mechanism of social ordering but rather as a key component of a repressive and fundamentally exploitative regime of class domination and alienated labor.[12] Another sharply contrasting view on the function of market exchange as a foundation for moral and social order was set out by Durkheim in *The Division of Labour in Society*.[13] In Durkheim's view, rather than functioning as the mechanism through which social order emerged, all forms of market exchange were to be understood as arising from a pre-existing moral and social order.[14] In a similar vein, the liberalist view of exchange and social order was later also further challenged in the work of anthropologists such as Marcel Mauss,[15] Claude Lévi-Strauss,[16] Marshall Sahlins,[17] and Mary Douglas and Baron Isherwood,[18] all of whom advanced arguments in favor of an "expanded notion of *generalized exchange*,"[19] emphasizing the many ways in which *non-economic* factors, such as cultural

160   *Religion in market society*

mores, religious principles, or kinship ties played a central role in providing the practical conditions for the allocation of material recourses and thus also in determining the possibilities for certain types of exchange to occur in certain social contexts as opposed to others.[20] In addition, the liberal and neoclassical understanding of the market was also forcefully challenged by economic sociologists such as Karl Polanyi,[21] who emphasized the historical and cultural specificity of the modern (Western) institutionalized market economy. In spite of such intellectual resistance, however, the liberal understanding of the market as an independent, impartial, self-regulating, and non-ideological mechanism managed to persist, partly because actual Western economic institutions and structures had already increasingly started to be modeled on the basis of that understanding.[22]

As highlighted above, it is important to recognize that the liberal conception of the "market" was "an idea before it ever was a massive social reality."[23] Hence, as is underscored by Slater and Fran Tonkiss, there are always important distinctions to be made "between the complex range of transactions that take place in actual market settings and the *market ideal*" that constitutes a central component of liberal market society thinking.[24] Market ideologies (whether liberal or other) are therefore not adequately understood as pertaining merely to the economic sphere proper; typically, they also comprise broader visions about the "good" society, its principal (as well as preferred) modes of organization and regulation, the proper role of its citizens, and so on. Liberal thought thus laid the foundations for a new, powerful discursive formation that continues to exert an enormous influence on "the modern West's conceptual and normative universe."[25]

Although the above brief discussion of the liberal understanding of the "market" remains both simplified and incomplete in several important respects, it nevertheless serves to illustrate how different approaches to the "market" have historically been "bound up with competing modern projects – both intellectual and political – aiming to explain and govern the social."[26] It also serves to locate historically and more firmly pinpoint the emergence and development of a new discursive formation through which the liberal understanding of the "market" developed into an integral component of a broader assemblage of economic, social-theoretical, and political thought and discourse. An adequate understanding of the historical foundations, main philosophical underpinnings, development, and diffusion of the liberal concept of the "market" is therefore crucial to an understanding of its later-twentieth- and early-twenty-first-century articulations and manifestations.

Socio-economic change in the post-World War II era: neoliberalism and consumer culture

The "macro-economic orthodoxy" of liberal classical and neoclassical economics, which had dominated Western economic thought and economic

Religion in market society 161

organization since at least the late nineteenth century, crumbled fast in the wake of the economic turmoil of the Great Depression of the 1930s. During the post-World War II period, Western capitalist societies also gradually started transitioning from a "Fordist" economy based on the industrialized mass production of standardized goods towards a "post-Fordist" economy based on more flexible and specialized modes of production. By the early 1970s, however, corporatist structures were facing new and mounting challenges owing to a range of interrelated factors, including the reconfiguring of previous structures of competition and global trade following the rise of new economic powers (particularly in South-East Asia), soaring costs for the maintenance of comprehensive welfare systems, and the re-emergence of unemployment as a social and economic problem.[27] These developments paved the way for the emergence and subsequent establishment of neoliberalism as the new dominant political economic ideology, and especially following its enthusiastic adoption by the newly elected Thatcher and Reagan administrations in the United Kingdom and the United States in the early 1980s.

Neoliberalism

The political-economic doctrine of neoliberalism is rooted in a very particular type of "Market Idea": an unwavering belief in the power, efficiency, and rationality of the free, non-regulated market and its extension across all societal domains. A direct continuation of older liberal ideas as discussed above, neoliberalism is based on the conviction that social well-being and individual prosperity alike are best achieved when as many social functions and spheres as possible are subjected to market conditions and become subsumed under a single, all-encompassing market logic. In order for this to be achieved, state-controlled social functions and sectors are to be "deregulated," subjected to conditions of enterprise and competition, and, wherever possible, be either outsourced or privatized. Once sectors previously controlled and regulated by the state have been deregulated and privatized, and once new spheres have thus been brought into the domain of the market, state intervention should be kept to a minimum.[28]

When it comes to the neoliberal view of the relationship between the individual and wider society, neoliberalism also constitutes a direct continuation of earlier liberal thought in that it "proposes that human well-being can best be advanced by liberating individual entrepreneurial freedoms and skills within an institutional framework characterized by strong private property rights, free markets, and free trade."[29] Understood as an "enactment of individual self-determination" *consumption* consequently becomes a central social mandate in a society composed of radically individualist, rational, and "enterprising" actors.[30] As Slater expresses it, neoliberalism's ideational and discursive force – its "ideological miracle" – thus largely consisted in how it successfully managed to link the "image of unhinged

162   *Religion in market society*

[consumer-culture] superficiality" to "the most profound, deep structural values and promises of modernity: personal freedom, economic progress, civic dynamism and political democracy."[31]

Neoliberalism was not, of course, established overnight. As has been explored in detail by Mark Blyth[32] and David Harvey,[33] beginning already in the 1960s, efforts to construct wider consent for a "neoliberal imaginary" were made on a wide range of fronts and included, most notably, the establishment of neoliberal think-tanks, the forming of alliances with influential segments of the business media, and the increasing penetration of neoliberal theory into the curricula of business schools and university economics departments.[34] But following its wholesale adoption by the Thatcher and Reagan administrations (and further supported by the wide-ranging liberalization of the Chinese economy under Deng Xiaoping) in the early 1980s, it did not take long before neoliberalism became established as the new core ideology of international financial regulatory institutions such as the World Bank and the International Monetary Fund (IMF).[35] Apart from the United States and Western Europe, by the early 1990s, neoliberal precepts had spread and become varyingly implemented on a worldwide scale, including, not least, throughout Latin America and the countries of the former Soviet Union and Eastern Bloc.[36]

The hold of neoliberalism on the global economy was further strengthened in the late 1990s through the emergence of the so-called "new economy," which marked a general transition from a manufacturing-based to a service-based economy, followed by the so-called "knowledge" or "information" economy driven by information and communication technology in the first years of the new millennium. During the past four or so decades, the neoliberal precept of unfettered *laissez-faire* capitalism and the incessant drive towards public-sector deregulation and privatization has thus served to bring about a sweeping and "extensive deconstruction and reconstruction of institutions, often in the name of or in the image of 'markets'"[37] as "Big government and civic institutions have tried to dismantle their institutional past following this model."[38] Neoliberal restructurings have thus typically been (and continue to be) experienced as a "rollback" or "dismantling" of the welfare state as corporatist structures have increasingly been replaced by new types of "public–private partnerships" as part of a more general shift from "government" (in terms of state power on its own) to "governance" (a broader configuration of state and other key actors, organizations, and elements in wider civil society).[39] The extension of neoliberal imperatives and precepts have also been further aided by the development of auxiliary phenomena such as so-called "New Public Management" (NPM) since the 1980s. While appearing in many different guises and more specific articulations, the main objective of NPM is to "reform" and enhance the "effectivity" of public-agency bureaucracies by subjecting them to a range of private-sector measures such as the introduction of new

Religion in market society   163

performance standards, different types of auditing regimes, and new forms of "internal competition" between departments.[40]

Although neoliberalism (as of this writing) represents but the latest instantiation of a particular liberal capitalist market ideology that has been gradually developing over a period of more than three centuries, it has played an instrumental role in further cementing the hegemony of the liberalist "Market Idea," facilitated the emergence of transnational corporations, accelerated the financialization of the global economy, and greatly aided the definitive establishment of consumerism as the principal cultural ethos of late modernity.[41] As such, neoliberalism has served to propel a set of interrelated and highly consequential social and cultural processes "through which economics has dislodged politics as a structuring and embedding force."[42] As a crucial part of all this, market-associated discourse, language, and terminology has spread and become increasingly naturalized across virtually all domains of contemporary society and culture.

Consumer culture and the ethos of consumerism

In close connection with the types of macro-level developments discussed above, from the immediate post-World War II years onwards, consumer culture rapidly developed into the defining feature of Western capitalist societies, and indeed beyond. As argued by Slater, already by the 1920s, the assimilation of consumer goods into everyday life had developed into a social *norm* so that "that all of the features which make up consumer culture take on their mature form."[43] These developments accelerated rapidly in the post-war era following continuous innovations in advertising, promotion, and marketing. A particularly notable innovation of the new marketing practices that emerged in the post-war years was the idea that the ultimate value of products and commodities resided not in their utility value (i.e., simply in what they could be used for), but rather in their *symbolic* value. There now emerged a growing realization among marketers that products could communicate *immaterial, cultural meanings* and function as identity markers and indicators of lifestyle.[44] As explored in detail by scholars such as Daniel Bell[45] and Jean-François Lyotard,[46] the development of increasingly sophisticated advertising and marketing techniques in the post-war years therefore served to propel a general process of market "enculturation" and "dematerialization" that chiefly involved a "shift from the production of material to non-material goods" and a "greater non-material composition of even material goods in the form of 'commodity aesthetics' and 'sign values' constructed through design and promotion."[47] The presumed broader social and cultural effects of these developments were perhaps most colorfully (and influentially) expressed in Jean Baudrillard's contention that late-modern consumer culture had produced a "hyper-real" world of cultural "simulacra" where people no longer consumed tangible commodities or

164   *Religion in market society*

things but merely "signs."[48] But importantly, as Chouliaraki and Fairclough observe, in the world of dematerialized cultural commodities, "What is produced, circulated and consumed ... is words and images."[49] The enculturation and dematerialization of commodities therefore also involves a notable shift whereby "language becomes increasingly commodified – it comes to be treated, worked, according to the logic of commodities."[50]

Market enculturation and dematerialization eventually reached its epitome through the proliferation of *branding* in its modern form, described by Martin Kornberger as the conscious effort to turn "faceless commodities into personal and emotional goods" through the successful association of particular products with particular symbolic cultural meanings or a "personality."[51] Following continuous developments in communication technologies and an ever-expanding media sphere, by the early 1980s, brands had developed into an increasingly vital part of the new "attention economy" and taken on the function as the principal "interface" between the rational sphere of production and the emotive sphere of consumption.[52] As will be discussed further in the third main part of the chapter, this also served to spur the proliferation and increasing normalization of branding practices throughout "non-business" domains such as public agencies and non-profit and religious organizations alike.[53]

The social and cultural effects of the wide establishment of consumer culture and consumerism have been the subject of a great deal of scholarly debate.[54] As was already discussed in Chapter 5, throughout sociology and social theory, the proliferation of consumer culture and consumerism has, perhaps above all, been explored in relation to the emergence of the late-modern "reflexive" self.[55] As Slater argues, even though consumer culture is far from the only frame in which consumption and cultural reproduction is carried out in late-modern everyday life, "it is certainly the *dominant* way and possesses a practical scope and ideological depth which allows it to structure and subsume all others to a very great extent."[56] Following Celia Lury, we can therefore say that the ideational force of consumer culture "is felt to the extent that people's aspirations, their hopes and fears, vocabulary of motives and sense of identity are defined in its terms."[57] As an integral component and central pillar of neoliberal market society, the values of consumer culture therefore exert a profound ideational influence on contemporary social and cultural life through their "metaphorical [and sometimes practical] extension to other social domains,"[58] including that of religion. The accelerating dematerialization and enculturation of markets and the growing centrality of brands, commodity aesthetics, and sign values since the mid-1950s has therefore also entailed notable expansions in the "language of the consumer."[59] As Frank Trentmann observes, during the past five to six decades, the "consumer" has gradually ceased to be considered a "passive dupe" and instead increasingly developed into a "master category of collective and individual identity" and "'co-actor' or 'citizen consumer' in a variety of settings in state, civil society and market."[60] This

Religion in market society 165

new consumer identity did not of course simply appear by itself. Rather, beginning in earnest in the early 1980s, it was actively constructed discursively on the basis of a neoliberal socio-political imaginary and the "heroism of consumption" promoted by it.[61]

Market-discourse and the concept of marketization

The ideational and discursive impact of market society as discussed above has been debated among sociologists and social theorists of various strands for quite some time. In the mid-1990s Fairclough observed how a notable feature of contemporary discursive change could be identified in an increasing general shift towards a consumer or "promotional" culture, central aspects of which included a "general reconstruction of social life on a market basis" and a "generalization of promotion as a communicative function... across orders of discourse."[62] Some years later he went on to note that the common conception of late capitalism as a "knowledge-driven" or "knowledge-based" socio-economic order "implies that it is also 'discourse-driven', suggesting that language may have a more significant role in contemporary socio-economic changes than it has had in the past."[63]

The market society with its ideational and discursive dimensions also constitutes a recurring theme in Luc Boltanski's and Eve Chiapello's *magnum opus The New Spirit of Capitalism*, originally published in French in 1999. As they pointed out at that time, the "spirit of capitalism" had acquired such a degree of ideational and discursive dominance that it had gained the "ability to permeate the whole set of mental representations specific to a given era ... to the point where its presence is simultaneously diffuse and general."[64] Echoing these observations, at the turn of the new millennium Pierre Bourdieu and Loic Wacquant, in their turn, highlighted the increasing perpetuation of what they called "NewLiberalSpeak" or a new "planetary vulgate ... endowed with the performative power to bring into being the very realities it claims to describe."[65] A few years later, in 2005, Nigel Thrift, for his part, provided a detailed exploration of the establishment of an increasingly discursively influential "cultural circuit of capital" that represents "the latest phase" in an intensifying "dissemination of what had hitherto been high-flying management theories on a mass scale."[66] Looking at more recent work still, all of the above observations are echoed by Gerlinde Mautner when she argues that "marketised discourse" has by now become naturalized to such a degree that "'market-speak' no longer stands out, but has entered deeper layers of the language system, regarded as simply expressing 'the way things are.'"[67]

All of these observations attest to the widespread proliferation and extension of market-related discourse, language, and terminology across contemporary social institutional domains. As inspired and propelled by neoliberalism in particular, these developments are usefully approached

166 *Religion in market society*

and understood in light of the concept of *marketization*, which is most commonly and generally employed as a "shorthand for the process by which the laws of the marketplace are transferred to lifeworlds that were not originally organised along such lines."[68] Notwithstanding the development of several slightly different understandings, the concept of marketization can, more specifically, be understood as the "permeation of market exchange as a social principle"[69] and the extended processes whereby previously *non-economic* social and cultural domains and sub-systems are gradually but increasingly visibly "subjected to a deliberate policy of economizing."[70] Following the spread and perpetuation of neoliberalism and NPM since the early 1980s, there are now ample empirical grounds for arguing that processes of marketization have been unfolding at an accelerating pace across an ever-wider range of social organizational and institutional domains throughout the advanced capitalist liberal democracies of the West, including education,[71] healthcare,[72] voluntary and charitable organizations,[73] non-profit and ideological organizations,[74] politics,[75] and religion.[76]

Marketization is most adequately understood as a primarily discourse-driven process whereby late-capitalist, managerial, and market-associated discourses make their ways into and become increasingly established and, most importantly, naturalized across previously non-economic (in the sense of not-for-profit, non-business) social and cultural domains.[77] Most clearly observable on the meso-level of societal institutions and organizations, marketization thus principally entails the gradual adoption and internalization of new market-associated values and imperatives through the medium of discourse and the integration of these values and imperatives as central elements of new ways of conceptualizing social organizational goals, imaginaries, and realities (which itself principally happens through the medium of discourse and discursive practice).[78] Marketization also needs to be understood as a self-perpetuating process. For as Mautner points out, the more widespread and engrained processes of marketization become within the institutional and organizational structures of society and culture as a whole, "the stronger the incentive (or indeed pressure) for the individual organisation to follow suit, to allow more marketised practises and discourses to enter its system, and to allow them to penetrate ever deeper into its organisational structure."[79]

"Marketized discourse" comes in many different, yet closely related and identifiable forms. Examples include (but are far from limited to) discourses particularly associated with and promulgated through neoliberal ideology and NPM such as "managerialism," "entrepreneurialism," "flexibility," "excellence," "total quality management," "cost-effectiveness," "performance standards," "strategic planning/thinking," "maximization," "core competency," "re-engineering," and "customer orientation." In addition, they also include broader discourses associated with market society such as "marketing," "branding," and "entertainment value." Through its naturalization of such discourse, processes of marketization have more generally

Religion in market society   167

contributed to an ongoing "metaphorization of reality,"[80] whereby ever more social and cultural activities and practices are now represented through the vocabulary and idiom of the "market."

The above discussion has aimed to account for the principal ideational tenets of neoliberalism, consumer culture, and the ethos of consumerism, in light of the ways in which these have been explored in previous (critical) sociological and social-theoretical scholarship. While the contributions of several more particular strands of scholarship (such as that of the Frankfurt school, for example) have been left largely unaddressed, the main purpose of the above discussion has been to underscore the fundamental role that discourse and discursive practice has played, and continues to play, in the constitution of contemporary market society. The discussion has also introduced and accounted for the concept of marketization, which we return to below.

First-level conclusions

Through engaging in first-level reflection on the construction and ideational underpinnings of the concept of the "market," we come to see how any particular theory of the "economic," whether it emerges out of academic theorizing, government-policy statements, or popular lay discourse, "is not simply a commentary upon 'real' economic processes that are external to it; it is part of the constitution and operation of markets."[81] Following Slater and Tonkiss, we come to see how the liberal conception of the "market" emerges through a particular set of "discourses that construct things like markets, economizing individuals and competitive relations as objects of governmental practices."[82] But in spite of having been the subject of long-standing and extensive treatment by sociologists and social theorists, market society's ideational and discursive dimensions have (with some notable exceptions) largely been overlooked by sociologists of religion. Indeed, it is no exaggeration to say that many of the shortcomings of both previous and current sociological theorizing in the area of religion, markets, and consumer culture are symptoms of this previous lack of attention, and it is to this issue that we now turn.

Second-level reflection: the study of religion in market society

Historical relationships between religion and socio-economic arrangements have constituted a recurring topic in the sociological study of religion since its very inception. This is probably best exemplified by Max Weber's foundational and highly influential work on the historical "elective affinity" between the Protestant work ethic and the "spirit" of early capitalism.[83] But scholarly interest in the relationship between market economics and religion actually harks back all the way to Smith's *Wealth of Nations*. In line with his broader political economic thinking, Smith argued, for example, that

168   *Religion in market society*

as smaller independent congregations grew and strove to attain higher degrees of respectability, they simultaneously tended to succumb to "learning and indolence" and gradually began neglecting the "art of popularity."[84] True to the basic tenets of liberal thought, Smith therefore concluded that liberal society would benefit from a pluralistic situation and "free market of religion" since that would "prevent any one form of religion becoming too powerful an influence upon the state."[85]

More generally, as religious communities have historically often formed integral components of the very fabric of the societies and cultures in which they have been embedded, they have naturally always also been deeply engaged and implicated in various types of economic affairs and practices. In this sense, as Nikos Passas observes, "there is no clear-cut distinction separating religious organizations from commercial ones and the two are best conceived as the ideal-type ends of a continuum."[86] While this is important to keep in mind, the following discussion will, however, focus on the character of more recent theorizing on the relationship between religion and the modern capitalist market economy.

The scholarship on religion, markets, and consumer culture has developed and diversified considerably in the past couple of decades. Several overviews of key approaches and main focuses have also been provided.[87] Although the intention here is not to provide yet another overview, for present purposes it is nevertheless worthwhile to make a more general distinction between main categories of previous scholarship on the basis of the particular ways in which they have approached and understood the concept of the "market" along with closely associated terms such as "product" and "consumer."[88] Seen from this particular angle, it could be argued that the bulk of all previous scholarship in the area has been grounded in either one of three main approaches, which could respectively be labeled the "religion as market" approach, the "commodification of religion" approach, and the "marketization of religion" approach. In what follows we discuss each of these in turn, devoting proportionately most attention to the "religion as market" approach because of its strong and enduring influence on the sociological study of religion as a whole.

"Religion as market" – the Rational Choice Theory of Religion and the "New Paradigm"

Scholarship in the "religion as market" approach has its roots in the broader so-called "economics of religion"[89] tradition that rose to prominence as part of the increasingly wide establishment of the Rational Choice Theory of Religion (RCTR) and the broader so-called "New Paradigm" of sociology of religion in the United States in the early 1990s. Following the lead of previous scholarship in the area,[90] we might begin our discussion by considering a particular and oft-cited passage from Berger's classic and much-cited work *The Sacred Canopy*,[91] originally published in 1967.

Religion in market society 169

As part of his broader discussion of the gradual historical erosion of the plausibility structures of Western institutional religion in a situation of increased religious pluralism, Berger introduced the notion of a modern "religious marketplace," and appears to have been perhaps the first sociologist of religion to have done so.[92] Under conditions of growing religious pluralism and an attendant increasing "subjectivization" of religion, he argued that "the religious tradition has to be marketed" and "'sold' to a clientele that is no longer constrained to 'buy.'"[93] He went on to contend that a "pluralistic situation is, above all, a market situation," which turns religious institutions into "marketing agencies" and religious traditions into "consumer commodities."[94] Whether Berger intended his employment of terms like "religious marketplace" and "religious consumer commodities" to be understood in a literal sense or not remains the subject of debate. Whatever the case, as pointed out by Gauthier, Berger's arguments can be thought of as constituting the "inaugural moment" of a broader shift in scholarly thinking about the relationship between religion and the capitalist market economy, in which the boundaries between the two were becoming increasingly blurred.[95]

From the mid-1980s onwards, the relationship between markets, economy, and religion assumed center stage in a new body of scholarship that gradually crystalized through the collaborative ventures of American scholars of religion such as Rodney Stark, William Sims Bainbridge, Richard Finke, and Laurence Iannaccone.[96] Primarily drawing on two strands of theorizing in the social sciences – Gary Becker's theory of rational choice as developed in *The Economic Approach to Human Behavior*,[97] coupled with the classical liberal economic theories of Smith (including his thoughts on religion and markets, as discussed above)[98] – this scholarship came to approach religion in market-economic terms and to view religious choices as rooted in the self-interested, rational pursuit of individual interests.

As outlined in Stark's and Finke's *Acts of Faith*,[99] this new approach was underpinned by a particular theory of "religious economy," according to which the religious field *as a whole* was literally to be understood *as* an "economy" or "market" that was governed by the dynamics of competition, supply, demand, price, and so on. Starting from the (highly contentious) assumption that humans are "naturally religious" and that the "demand" for religion would therefore always remain constant, the theory of "religious economy" was thus based on *supply* rather than demand. The theory consequently posited that the presence of a wider "supply" of religious choices or "firms" (e.g., in the form of various kinds of religious communities) would serve to bring about a stronger "religious economy" and thereby work to enhance overall religious vitality.[100] As such, the theory of religious economy aligned directly with the (neo)liberal discursive formation on the impartial organizing principle of the "market" and thus ushered in a new approach to the dynamics of religious change that quickly assumed center stage in contemporaneous and subsequent critical debates on

170   *Religion in market society*

the supposed universal validity of the secularization paradigm, which had dominated the sociological study of religion since at least the mid-1960s.

In connection with this, the new approach also developed a market-related theory of individual religious behavior, which became known as the Rational Choice Theory of Religion. In *Acts of Faith*, Stark and Finke thus expressly approached religion, not "as an expression of human irrationality or non-rationality," but instead "as a *product of* rationality."[101] Having first posited the universality of the liberal, rational, and self-interest-driven figure of *homo oeconomicus* (in effect, the rational "sovereign consumer" who constantly weighs costs and benefits) as the "first axiom"[102] of the theory, they then went on to assert that *all* types of religious behaviors were essentially driven by, and hence could also best be explained by, the rational and self-interested pursuits of individuals.[103] RCTR engendered a great deal of enthusiasm among American scholars of religion in particular and quickly rose to great prominence in the study of religion in the United States. But from early on, it also became the subject of a fierce and frequently contentious critical debate that to some extent continues to this day.[104] In particular, RCTR has been repeatedly (and rightly) criticized for its stubborn reliance on a set of demonstrably untenable neoclassical and (neo)liberal economic presumptions about a "marketplace composed of utilitarian-minded 'rational actors.'"[105] A large part of the criticism levelled at RCTR has consequently centered on the viability of its own basic theoretical premises or, more precisely, on the ways in which the theory "tacitly presumes the characteristics that it seeks to explain."[106] While scholars continue to debate the merits of RCTR for making sense of the religious choices and behaviors of individuals, the theory of "religious economy" also developed into a central tenet of the broader so-called "New Paradigm" for the sociology of religion in the United States, as famously heralded in an article by R. Stephen Warner in 1993.[107]

Representing a broader scholarly movement that remained heavily influenced by the theory of "religious economy" while eschewing some of RCTR's most controversial and widely criticized premises,[108] the New Paradigm expressly positioned itself in opposition to the secularization paradigm and instead sought to approach developments in the contemporary religious field using theoretical perspectives derived from (neo)liberal and neoclassical economic theory. The main objective was to challenge the validity of secularization theory as applied to a North American context by demonstrating how free "market competition" in a "deregulated" religious field (as was argued to be largely the case in the United States) was conducive of religious vitality, whereas state regulation and the enduring presence of national religious "monopolies" (as was argued to be largely the case throughout much of Western Europe) instead worked to stifle religious innovation and vitality, thus effecting further religious stagnation and decline.[109] Hence, the explanation for the enduring religious vitality of the United States as compared to the perpetual religious decline of much of

Religion in market society 171

Western Europe was to be sought in the makeup and organization of their respective "religious economies." Although the New Paradigm approach quickly became firmly established in the sociological study of religion in the United States and successfully managed to recast the longstanding debate on European/American exceptionalism,[110] mainly because of its strong anchoring in the US context, it failed to gain a firmer foothold in Europe.[111] Indeed, for several decades, the New Paradigm–secularization debate has been one of the most vexed issues in the sociological study of religion.

Whatever their lasting impact proves to be, for present purposes it is of greatest importance to note that RCTR and New Paradigm scholarship emerged and crystalized during a period that witnessed an accelerating general proliferation and increasing naturalization of neoliberal market discourses and imperatives throughout Western societies as a whole, and not least in the United States. RCTR and New Paradigm scholars' enthusiastic, but largely unreflexive, adoption of the (neo)liberal conception of the market therefore resonated well with broader dominant socio-political discourses of the time.[112] But beyond this, RCTR and New Paradigm scholarship *itself* also undoubtedly played a central role in the further proliferation and naturalization of (neo)liberal market-associated discourse and terminology in the study of religion. For example, as Andrew McKinnon argues with particular reference to RCTR, in their attempts to "transform the metaphor [of the market] into a literal truth," RCTR theorists were not merely ignorant of the metaphor itself, but deliberately sought to "kill" it by altogether denying its status as a metaphor, postulating instead that the "market" was integral to human nature and behavior.[113] In doing so, they entered the "realm of ideology" by construing the "market" as the reified "'natural' way of things, a dead metaphor in which there is a perfect correspondence between our concept (the market) and religion."[114] In this, McKinnon continues, RCTR came to play "an important supporting ideological role" in buttressing the "commonsensicality" of the (neo)liberal conception of the market in the study of religion.[115]

Although New Paradigm scholars' utilization of the (neo)liberal understanding of the "market" certainly left much to desire in terms of self-reflexivity and conceptual hygiene, the increasing naturalization of the market metaphor throughout the sub-field did not, however, go unnoticed among sociologists of religion at the time.[116] It is, moreover, important to note that even though pro-RCTR New Paradigm scholars tended to understand the "market" in literal, non-metaphorical terms, others, like R.S. Warner for example, openly acknowledged that the New Paradigm was organized above all by "economic imagery."[117] Indeed, taken as a whole, New Paradigm scholarship has been far from uniform when it comes to the degrees, particular ways, consistency, and rigor with which individual scholars have theorized and employed the concept of the "market," along with other closely associated concepts such as "product," "customer," "consumer," and the like. While some studies have indeed been expressly

172 *Religion in market society*

based on the assertion that the religious field constitutes and operates as a *de facto* market, others have been much more ambiguous in their understandings and articulations and instead tended to oscillate between viewing the market as a *de facto* empirical entity on the one hand, and as an analogy or metaphor for the ways in which the religious field *might be taken to* operate and develop on the other hand.

An earlier example of a widely read study that postulates the existence of a literal *de facto* "religious market" is found in Wade Clark Roof's *Spiritual Marketplace* from 1999, which is based on the general premise that "An open, competitive religious economy makes possible an expanded spiritual marketplace which, like any marketplace, must be understood in terms both of 'demand' and 'supply.'"[118] Aiming to understand notable transformations in the religious landscape of the United States since the beginning of the post-World War II era, Roof contended that

> Religion in any age exists in a dynamic and interactive relationship with its cultural environment; and, in our time [the mid- to later 1990s] we witness an expansion and elaboration of spiritual themes that amounts to a major restructuring of religious market dynamics.[119]

But these claims, saturated with the metaphor of the market and economics, are presented as if they are simply self-evident and therefore in need of no further explanation. For Roof does not provide any theorization of the "market" whatsoever, nor does he at any point explicate his employment of other related concepts such as "economy," "product," or "supplier." Another more recent example of a frequently referenced study that constantly vacillates between a *de facto* market and market analogy approach can be found in Mara Einstein's *Brands of Faith* from 2008, which provides a detailed analysis of the multitude of ways in which the capitalist market economy has affected the character of the religious landscape of the United States and served to propel a rapid increase in marketing and branding practices among religious communities and organizations themselves. Expressly situating her study in the New Paradigm and supply-side approach, Einstein maintains that "Viewing religion as a product, rather than as a social mandate" provides many clues as to why religion has remained vital in the United States while it has declined throughout much of Europe.[120] But with the exception of the concept of "brands" (and to some extent the concept of "marketing"), Einstein provides no theorization of the concept of the "market," nor of other concepts central to the study such as "product" and "consumer" – both of which derive their analytic and heuristic value – or lack thereof – from the particular ways in which they are situated and positioned within particular theorizations and understandings of the "market." While there is certainly merit to many of the observations made in *Spiritual Marketplace* and *Brands of Faith*, they both provide examples of studies that take the (neo)liberal conception of the market for

Religion in market society 173

granted and willfully ignore the insights generated by a sociological and social-theoretical debate that has proceeded now for over a century on the constitution and construction of "markets." As such, their studies both contribute to a further naturalization of the "commonsensicality" of the supposed empirical reality of the neoliberal Market Idea, along with its supposedly unproblematic application in the study of religion.

As chiefly advanced through RCTR and New Paradigm scholarship, the notion of "religion as market" has therefore been established as a core premise of a particular type of influential discursive formation on the organization of the religious field in modern late capitalist societies. One notable effect of this has been the gradual naturalization of market-associated vocabularies as *etic* categories throughout the sociological study of religion more broadly. This can clearly be seen in the ways in which the concept of the "market" has become increasingly widely employed among sociologists of religion who are not proponents of either RCTR or the New Paradigm. Here too, however, the concept typically continues to be employed in highly arbitrary and vague ways.[121] In what attests to the ideational influence of the theory of "religious economy" well beyond RCTR and New Paradigm scholarship, the "market" appears to be increasingly employed as a convenient shorthand for ascribing some kind of overarching, although typically unspecified, "logic" to the presumed basic dynamics of the religious field, although mainly in the form of *explanandum* rather than *explanans*. The issue here is not that the religious field *cannot* (or should not) be examined in market terms as long as we openly both recognize and acknowledge the difference between metaphor and empirical reality and the power of language and discourse to shape our conceptions of the "real" (including the "reality" of the "market"). For as McKinnon points out, if we fail to approach religion "'as if' it were an economy" (which remains a perfectly viable option provided that this is made clear) and instead "start assuming that religion *is* an economy, we begin to be used by the metaphor; the metaphor begins to think for us."[122] Avoiding falling into this trap requires a deeper appreciation of the constitution and historical development of the liberal conception of the "market" as discussed above. Following Jean-Claude Usunier, we therefore need to recognize that the more recent (re-) conceptualization of religion and religious life in market-related terms has emerged as a result of a particular type of discursive legitimation process:

> In the legitimation undertaking, every human institution, especially non-economic, is presented as a market-based process by using the basic market vocabulary (e.g. supply, demand, consumption, competition, etc.) combined with terms related to the non-economic institution. This is how people progressively accept such oxymorons as "religious markets" ... "supply of religion," "competition in the global religious market," "consumption of spirituality," "brand loyalty and brand switching" for religious conversion, etc. as meaningful

174 *Religion in market society*

> expressions. Over time, people progressively become acquainted with
> MoR [Markets of Religion] oxymorons and develop ownership of such
> expressions.[123]

Among many other things, Usunier's observations raise the question as to
exactly how, as well as on what exact basis (if any), we are to make meaningful qualitative distinctions between the notion of "religion as market"
and other closely associated notions such as those of "market(s) *of* religion," "market(s) *for* religion," and *"religious* markets?" In addition, and
just as important, to what extent, and in what particular respects, should
these be regarded as mutually constitutive, interrelated, or perhaps even
interchangeable notions? From a discursive perspective, the notion of "religion as market" might at first appear pretty straightforward. As discussed
above, this is the idea that the religious field as a whole constitutes a "market" or "economy" that is governed by the dynamics of supply, demand,
market share, competition, and so on. Understood as a general ordering
mechanism of the religious field as a whole, individual religious communities would therefore presumably be *automatically* situated as participants
in such a market/s. The "religion as market" approach therefore also hinges
on the assumption that individual religious communities, at least in some
sense, need to *recognize* that they are positioned within a market and act
accordingly, lest they wither away and disappear. But even though Billy
Graham wittily proclaimed that he was in the business of "selling the Gospel" already in the 1960s, it is far from self-evident that religious communities would view their activities in such terms. The main point to note here
is that viewing the religious field through this particular theoretical lens
will have a range of particular bearings on how it is researched empirically.

   This question is also brought to the fore by Jörg Stolz and Usunier when
they explicitly describe what they refer to as "religious consumer society"
as a "society in which religious organizations *see themselves* as offering
'products' and 'services' on a 'market,' while individuals *see themselves* as
'consumers' choosing these 'products' and 'services'."[124] Indeed, following
the accelerating spread and establishment of market-associated discourses
and imperatives across ever more social institutional and organizational
domains, some religious communities and organizations might certainly
have come to view themselves and their activities in such terms. But if we
adopt Stolz's and Usunier's perspective, then we are no longer concerned
with whether or not the religious field could or should be viewed *as* a market. At this point we are in fact entering an entirely different conversation
on the empirically observable character and organization of religion and
religious life and practice *in* a particular type of society that *is* undoubtedly saturated by market-associated discourses and values. This observation does not, however, automatically translate into an argument that the
religious field as a whole should be viewed as being governed by market
dynamics. But following decades of contentious debate on this issue, it has

Religion in market society 175

become exceedingly difficult to disentangle the notion of "religion as market" from closely related (and varyingly interchangeable) notions such as "market(s) of religion," "market(s) for religion," "religious markets," or the like. As long as the notion of "religion as market" remains based on the liberal concept of the "market" it will form a complex discursive knot with other closely related notions of this type.

The "commodification of religion"

Apart from "religious economy" scholarship, past decades have also witnessed an explosive growth in scholarship on the *commodification* (or, alternatively, *commoditization*) of religion. This diverse body of scholarship has mainly focused on the wide variety of different ways in which "religion" has been transformed into a commodity for sale and consumption in a broader marketplace of ideas and lifestyle choices. This category of scholarship therefore also includes work primarily focusing on the creation of various types of actual, tangible religious/spiritual "products" or "services" (e.g., religious "kitsch," Christian workout programs, *halal* holiday resorts, various forms of healing, and much more).[125] As reflected in titles such as Kimberly Lau's *New Age Capitalism: Making Money East of Eden*,[126] Carrette's and King's *Selling Spirituality: The Silent Takeover of Religion*,[127] and Heelas's *Spiritualities of Life: New Age Romanticism and Consumptive Capitalism*,[128] a significant portion of previous scholarship in this area has centered on the ways in which different types of "spirituality" have become *co-opted* by the corporate lifestyle industries (e.g., in the form of books, magazines, courses, workshops) and become transformed into conduits for the further perpetuation of capitalist ideology and values. Indeed, as Heelas reflects:

> Of all the controversies surrounding contemporary inner-life spiritualities, by far and away the most significant within the academy and beyond revolves around the criticism that the great majority (or virtually all) of provisions and activities serve as consumer products.[129]

In much of this scholarship, the capitalist economy therefore takes on the role of a powerful and insidious force that impinges on the sphere of religion and spirituality from the "outside." For example, Carrette's and King's *Selling Spirituality* is expressly motivated by the desire "to raise awareness of the ways in which popular discourses about 'spirituality' tend to displace questions of social justice, being increasingly framed by the individualist and corporatist values of a consumer society."[130] Their main objective is to uncover the ways in which "spirituality" has developed into an increasingly prevalent, although highly fuzzy and often quite hollow, "cultural trope" that has since long been "taken over" by "corporate bodies and management consultants to promote efficiency, extend markets and maintain a

176 *Religion in market society*

leading edge in a fast-moving information economy."[131] Extensive in scope and rich in its range of examples, Carrette's and King's study therefore primarily advances an argument about the corporate business sector's active involvement in the perpetuation, and indeed manufacturing, of an increasingly vaguely defined (discourse of) "spirituality." In what connects directly to a longstanding debate in the broader sociological study of religion, Carrette and King go on to contend that the proliferation of what they refer to as "capitalist spiritualities," underpinned by the spread of popular psychology and therapeutic culture, has also served to greatly propel and intensify already ongoing processes of religious privatization and individualization.[132] In spite of the authors' claims to the contrary, however, their account undoubtedly signals a celebratory view of "older," time-honored, and more tradition-bound forms of communal religion and spirituality as opposed to a contemporary "capitalist spirituality" of self-enhancement and absorption.[133] In *Selling Spirituality* it is therefore not the "market," but rather *capitalism* that assumes the position of primary concept, although mainly in the form of an elusive "background force" that turns everything it touches into a conduit for its own further perpetuation.[134]

The scholarship on the "commodification of religion" does, however, extend well beyond these types of expressly critical explorations. Perhaps partly as a reflection of its multidisciplinary character, this broader scholarship has remained highly fragmented and come to encompass a large variety of both varyingly related and contrasting theoretical perspectives and viewpoints. Also, in what further attests to its enduring ideational and discursive influence on scholarship in the area more broadly, the notion of "religion as market" also continues to loom over much of this work. For example, as part of his effort to outline of a "sociology of religious commodification," Pattana Kitiarsa suggested that religious commodification should be viewed as

> [an] emerging multifaceted and multidimensional marketized process which turns a religious faith or tradition into consumable and marketable goods. It is an interactive and iterative relationship between religion and market, simultaneously involving both market force commodifying religion and religious institution taking part in marketplace and consuming culture.[135]

Overall, however, Kitiarsa's account can be described as a quite curious mixture of several, and not always particularly compatible, theoretical perspectives on the religion–market relationship. For example, he never provides any concrete explanation of what the "interactive and iterative relationship between religion and market" actually consists of, nor any explanation whatsoever of the recurring term "marketized." As his argument progresses, it also becomes clear that it is, in fact, firmly based on a "religion as market" view, although this is never stated explicitly. He asserts, for example, that "the rise and fall of a faith is inseparable from its marketable

Religion in market society   177

qualities and entrepreneur leadership"[136] and further that "In reality, most religions are unfortunately unable to resist the market force and culture. They are treated as consumer goods in the marketplace."[137] In this account, "religious commodification" (the precise meaning of which remains unclear) therefore occurs because a. the fortune of "faiths" and "religions" is dependent on their entrepreneurial aptitudes and "marketable qualities," and b. because they are treated (presumably by people in general) as "consumer goods" in a "marketplace." The broader explanation for this state of affairs is to be found in the "specific characters of postmodern life and society,"[138] in which "religion" is "redesigned to fit the moral and spiritual needs of the postmodern social life, where people's religious piety and religiosity are drastically different from previous generations."[139]

It makes little sense to speak of the "commodification" of "religion" and "faiths" in and of themselves, just as it makes little sense to speak about the public visibility of "religion" as such, as discussed in Chapter 4. Indeed, considering our previous discussion of the category of "religion" in Chapter 3, any suggestion to that effect should be regarded as highly dubious to begin with. Usunier provides a useful corrective. Using the term commoditization instead of commodification, he argues that "Commoditization occurs when a previously non-market object (e.g., religion, blood, adoption) enters the market."[140] This, however, involves a deliberate and complex "communication task" characterized by "the systematic use of vocabulary and discourse to acquaint people with a newly commoditized (or a to-be-commoditized-in-the-near-future) object."[141] Before specific products and services can take on meanings as specifically "religious" or "spiritual" products or services, they first need to be rendered and "made" so through active and conscious efforts of discursive construction and legitimation on the part of "religious entrepreneurs," agents of industry and advertising, academics, etc.[142] Recall the qualitative distinction between discursive construal and construction as previously discussed in Chapter 2.[143] Different types of products, services, and provisions can indeed be construed as "religious" or "spiritual" in a wide variety of different ways and contexts. But whether or not such construals ultimately end up having wider constructive effects will depend on the extent to which they are able to correspond and align with already established discursive formations and ways of seeing the world. In other words, the successful construction of "religious products" (or commodities) requires the simultaneous construction of "religious consumers," or, more precisely, the consumer of products and services that have been expressly constructed *as* "religious" or "spiritual." But as Trentmann reminds us, consumers of whatever kinds or categories of products, services, or provisions do not simply come into being by and of themselves either. Rather, they emerge "when information is processed and systematized in such a way that it creates *a sense of being a consumer.*"[144]

Although sweeping claims about the (supposed) consumerist attitudes of contemporary populations abound in scholarship on the "commodification

178   *Religion in market society*

of religion," only rarely are these claims substantiated by any kind of empirical research. Considering the ubiquity of consumer culture and the salience of the ethos of consumerism, there are certainly ample grounds for assuming that growing numbers of people may indeed approach religion and religious life through a consumerist lens. Even so, the particular ways and extent to which people actually do so (if indeed they do) cannot simply be assumed but have to be explored on a firm empirical basis. We should therefore remain wary of scholarly discourses that simply take the consumerist sensibilities of contemporary populations for granted.

The "marketization of religion"

Following continued debates on the merits of RCTR and the New Paradigm, coupled with accelerating processes of marketization across ever more domains of contemporary society and culture, Gauthier, Tuomas Martikainen, and Linda Woodhead have more recently argued for the need to develop a sociological study of religion that openly acknowledges "the growing importance of economics in structuring all spheres of social life since at least the 1980s, under the guise, namely, of consumerism and neoliberalism."[145] Therefore, as Gauthier *et al.* duly point out (and as also noted above), considering that the variegated social and cultural transformations that have followed in the wake of the establishment and accelerating perpetuation of neoliberal political economy have long since developed into central topics of inquiry throughout several disciplines in the humanities and social sciences, it has become ever more "pressing to continue this work in relation to religion, asking fresh questions about how contemporary religious phenomena may be implicated in changing consumer and market logics."[146] The need for such a reorientation in focus is further motivated by the variety of ways in which socio-economic changes driven by market culture since the latter part of the twentieth century have coincided with a set of highly notable transformations in the global religious field.[147] What is argued for, therefore, is the forming of a new heuristic framework that would insist "on the coherence and the systematic character of certain global reconfigurations affecting religion by recasting these against the backdrop of the globalization of economic ideologies and consumer practices."[148] In contrast to RCTR and New Paradigm perspectives, such a framework would not argue for the reduction of social realities to economic determinants, but would instead strive to draw our attention to "the *noneconomic* dimensions and effects of market economics and their correlates in globalizing societies."[149] Such an approach would therefore strive to highlight the role of "Market Ideas"[150] – in the sense of ideologies, discourses, and imperatives inspired by market economics – as prime vectors of contemporary social and cultural change on the whole, religious change included. The marketization approach therefore provides a particularly fruitful framework for discourse-centered explorations of the

Religion in market society 179

changing character of religious organization, life, and practice in contemporary market society.

The past decade has witnessed the emergence of a steadily growing scholarship centered on this type of inquiry and given rise to what has become known as the "marketization of religion" approach. Echoing our previous discussion of the concept of marketization above, as explicated by Gauthier:

> Approaching the study of religion through the marketisation approach signifies that "the market" is identified as the most salient and defining feature of contemporary societies: both the market as a social and societal institution (the actual market), and the market as idea and ideal (Durkheim: a moral ideal) of optimal social regulation and production of meaning.[151]

"Marketization of religion" scholarship consequently focuses on the ideational effects of the spread and perpetuation of neoliberal political economy and post-1980s neoliberal social restructurings on the contemporary religious field. As already noted in our discussion of religious commodification above, it is worth noting that the label "marketization of religion" should by no means be taken to suggest that it would be possible to examine the marketization of "religion" in and of itself. Rather, marketization is understood in terms of an empirically identifiable and largely ideational and discursive process that primarily unfolds, and consequently has to be examined, on the macro-level of national and transnational socio-economic reconfigurations and especially on the meso-level of societal institutions and organizations. The still comparatively few studies in the "marketization of religion" approach that exist at the time of writing (2021) have consequently mainly concentrated on the ways in which neoliberal restructurings have had a range of notable "spill-over effects" on the contemporary religious-organizational field. Some of the most notable of these include changing relations between religious communities and states through the establishment of new modes of "pluricentric" network governance of religion;[152] the emergence of new types of religious–state partnerships in the form, for example, of "faith-based initiatives";[153] and the ideational impact of ongoing processes of marketization on the organizational structures and *modus operandi* of different types of religious organizations.[154]

The marketization approach differs from both previously discussed main approaches in its insistence that scholarly explorations of the impact of the neoliberal market economy on the present-day religious field should remain grounded in adequate and sufficiently historicized theorizations of the "market." As already noted, in its rejection of RCTR and the supply-side arguments of the New Paradigm, the marketization approach is incompatible with the "religion as market" view. But it also takes issue with scholarship in the "commodification of religion" approach in so far as it fails to properly theorize and explain central concepts such as "market,"

180 *Religion in market society*

along with closely related concepts such as "product" or "consumer" (in relation to which "commodification" is supposed to occur). Although the two approaches are otherwise compatible, it is nevertheless important to recognize that they represent "paradigmatically co-extensive yet theoretically distinct processes."[155] To simplify, whereas commodification primarily pertains to the perpetuation of the ethos of consumerism on the micro-level of culture and social practices, marketization primarily pertains to the macro- and meso-level societal effects of the increasingly wide establishment and perpetuation of the (neo)liberal "Market Idea." While still in need of much further conceptual clarification and consolidation, as noted, the marketization-approach provides particularly fruitful avenues for the development of discourse-sensitive approaches to the character of religion and religious life in market society. As will be highlighted in our upcoming discussion in the third main part of this chapter, this is not least because discourse analysis offers a range of analytical tools and methods uniquely equipped for investigating how processes of marketization actually unfold in particular religious-organizational settings.

Second-level conclusions

The respective virtues and weaknesses of the approaches discussed above to the religion–market relationship will surely continue to be debated for the foreseeable future. The goal of engaging in critical second-level deliberation of the type provided here is not to arrive at any final solutions to the main issues involved. Rather, the goal is to arrive at a deeper understanding of both why and how certain types of sub-field-specific theorizing become established during particular points in time as a result of their alignment with wider prevalent contemporaneous social and cultural discourses and discursive formations. The goal is thus also, not least, to gain a deeper understanding of how such theorizing, once established, plays a powerful role in conditioning scholarly thought, in priming scholars to adopt particular suppositions and views of the "realities on the ground," and thereby also to affect the ways in which research projects are set up, how data are viewed, collected, analyzed, interpreted, and so on. The goal, in other words, is to enhance our awareness of the ways and extent to which particular discursive constructions of the religion–market relationship serve to shape and govern our approaches to the field.

Third-level analysis: the proliferation of marketized discourse in traditional religious-organizational settings

Previous scholarship on the character, cultures, and *modus operandi* of modern religious organizations has in large part centered on the extent to which they are subject to the same kinds of broader societal, cultural, and institutional pressures as other types of public, private, and third-sector

Religion in market society   181

organizations.[156] Beginning already with the foundational work of Weber and continuing up until the 1980s, the bulk of scholarship in the area was particularly focused on the effects of accelerating processes of *bureaucratization* (along with its corollary process of *professionalization*) on the Western religious-organizational field.[157] Since the early 1990s, scholarly focus has increasingly shifted towards the proliferation of non-denominational "seeker-sensitive" and "growth-oriented" megachurches which represent a novel, but increasingly prevalent, form of religious organization. But during the past four or so decades, comparatively much less attention has been devoted to the continuous impact of contemporary market society on the present-day self-understandings and practices of *traditional* religious organizations with longstanding historical and structural ties to states and/or national social establishments, which typically retain extensive nationwide bureaucratic organizational structures, and often remain deeply enmeshed in various networks of inter-organizational partnerships (i.e., mostly Christian churches).

In what follows we will be focusing on the notable extent to which traditional religious organizations gradually have reconfigured their own discursive practices, organizational cultures, and *modus operandi* in accordance with currently prevailing market-associated discourses on organizational "effectivity" and "performance." As I have argued elsewhere, these developments are most adequately understood as the result of a combination of mounting (both actual and perceived) external pressures and a series of active and conscious efforts on the part of traditional religious organizations themselves.[158] In order to provide an illustration of these developments that remains sufficiently sensitive to denominational and broader socioeconomic context, the following discussion and analysis will focus solely on examples from the traditional so-called "Seven Sisters" of mainline Protestantism in the United States: the United Methodist Church (UMC), the American Baptist Churches USA (ABCUSA), the Presbyterian Church USA (PCUSA), the Evangelical Lutheran Church in America (ELCA), the Episcopal Church (TEC), the United Church of Christ (UCC), and the Disciples of Christ (DOC).

The discourse of religious organizations

From the perspective of discourse theory and organizational-discourse studies, an organization can be approached as partly constituting "an apparatus of verbal interaction, or an 'order of discourse.'"[159] Organizational discourse can, in turn, be understood as

> the structured collections of texts embodied in the practices of talking and writing (as well as a wide variety of visual representations and cultural artefacts) that bring organizationally related objects into being as these texts are produced, disseminated, and consumed.[160]

182 *Religion in market society*

It is important to point out, however, that even though discourse constitutes a "powerful ordering force" within organizations, the agency and maneuvering space of organizational actors and subjects will always be varyingly constrained by organizational *structures*, which cannot be reduced to discourse.[161] But it is nevertheless primarily through discourse that organizations write themselves into being."[162]

Ideological-discursive formations (IDFs)

Social organizations' orders of discourse tend to be "pluralistic," often containing clearly identifiable assemblages of what Fairclough refers to as "ideological-discursive formations" (IDFs), each of which tends to be particularly associated with certain entities and subjects within a particular organizational setting. An IDF can thus be thought of as an intra-organizational "speech community" that is characterized by its own "discourse norms," "ideological norms,"[163] and particular type of *lexicalization*, or repertoire of vocabulary and terminology.[164] IDFs essentially work to direct the agency of organizational subjects, providing them with certain "frame[s] for action."[165] In spite of the common co-existence of multiple IDFs, most organizations nevertheless tend to be dominated by either one or a smaller set of particular IDFs that have accrued hegemonic status and gained the power to marginalize and subvert other alternative IDFs within the organization in question. The domination of a particular IDF over the order of discourse of an organization serves to naturalize its "(ideological) meanings and practices,"[166] and thus also to render them opaque, i.e., as no longer recognizable as ideologies but rather as taken-for-granted "common sense." Moreover, since discourse always comprises a certain "knowledge base," and since knowledge always includes an ideological component, adopting certain normative ways of "talking" simultaneously also involves adopting certain ideologically infused normative "ways of seeing."[167] For these reasons, IDFs exercise a powerful ideological influence on the perceptions and identifications of organizational subjects.

IDFs come in many different forms. Typically, they argue either for or against certain types of organizational renewal and reform; strive to either establish, maintain, or resist particular types of organizational cultures; or promote or resist particular types of broader social engagements. Which types of IDFs end up achieving dominant positions in certain organizational contexts at certain points in time is dependent on the outcome of intra-organizational hegemonic struggles.[168] Dominant IDFs have a stabilizing effect on organizations as they offer effective means of managing internal disruptions and tensions.[169] But as noted in Chapter 2, dominance and hegemony are, however, never absolute but rather unstable by their nature and always only temporarily achieved.[170] There is always the possibility that unexpected broader extra-organizational developments (for example, of a social, cultural, economic, or political character) might come

Religion in market society 183

to pose such serious challenges to the dominant IDFs of an organization that they end up throwing the organization into crisis. Situations of crisis are particularly conducive to organizational change since they are likely to spark hegemonic struggle between competing organizational actors who devise their own opposing ways of dealing with and resolving the crisis.[171] Such struggles may result in a realignment of power relations within an organization and the establishment of new dominant IDFs.[172] A focus on discourse and discursive practice is therefore crucial to an adequate and more precise understanding of how and why organizations undergo certain types of changes rather than others at certain points in time.

To provide a general illustration from the not-so-distant past, the 1960s set in motion a series of highly consequential social and cultural trans-formations throughout the West that profoundly affected the established traditional Christian churches. The churches found themselves perplexed and taken aback by the social and cultural upheavals of the decade, epito-mized in a range of strongly discourse-driven phenomena such as the civil-rights movement, changing perceptions of family structures, new views on sexuality and sexual mores, calls for gender equality and the civil rights of sexual minorities, increasingly widespread religious indifference, and a general new emphasis on individual self-determination.[173] As the confu-sion in the churches eventually settled, their responses were decidedly ac-commodating in spirit.[174] Among many other things, the churches adopted increasingly liberal and inclusivist positions on core theological issues, be-came increasingly supportive of progressive social causes, opened up for the ordination of women, and took increasingly positive stances towards sexual minorities.[175] From the perspective advanced here, it is important to acknowledge the significant degree to which all of these various responses were inspired by changes that were strongly ideational and discursive in character. Consequently, the responses of the churches, which were them-selves strongly ideational and discursive in character, served to bring about notable and long-lasting changes in their orders of discourse, including the ways in which they talked about and understood themselves and their places and roles in society. The social and cultural upheavals of the 1960s therefore posed such serious challenges to the dominant IDFs of the es-tablished Christian churches that they were cast into crisis. The churches' wide-ranging responses and efforts at reform should, in turn, be viewed as the outcome of hegemonic struggles between opposing conservative and reformist IDFs.

The main point to note about organizational discursive practices and IDFs is that the general understanding that a religious organization has of itself and its place in society at a certain point in time typically becomes en-capsulated in its official discourse. When a particular IDF gains hegemonic status within a given religious organization, the realities and imaginaries it constructs gradually take on the heuristic weight and rhetorical force of "common sense." Exploring changes in the IDFs and orders of discourse of

184 *Religion in market society*

religious organizations therefore also involves exploring the broader flows of inter-organizational discursive influence that they can be shown to be most strongly subjected to at certain points in time.

Inter-organizational discursive influence

Given the weakening societal positions of long-established and bureaucratically structured traditional Christian churches more generally, any exploration of their current orders of discourse and dominant IDFs needs to be based on an adequate understanding of their degree of integration, dependence, or autonomy within the broader social formation in which they are embedded. In other words, an examination of the current orders of discourse of traditional Christian churches needs to unfold on the basis of adequate consideration and understanding of their respective positions *vis-à-vis* other central social domains such as the political, economic, and educational. In the words of Fairclough, one needs to consider where it would be most appropriate to situate a particular church "on a hierarchy of relative importance to the function of the *social formation*, and how this relates to influences from one institution to another on various levels, including the ideological and discoursal."[176] As explained by Burton Mack,

> The term *social formation* refers to a concept of society as a collective, human construct. It differs from the less specific term, *society*, by emphasizing the complex interplay of many human interests that develop systems of signs and patterns of practices, as well as institutions for their communication, maintenance, and reproduction. Social formation indicates the process by which various configurations of these systems of practices are created and relate to one another in the formation of a given society.[177]

A social formation can thus be thought of as an aggregate of dialectically related and mutually supporting societal subsystems. These subsystems are, in turn, made up of the aggregation of various types of organizations. Following Paul Tracey *et al.*, the key point to note is that organizations involved in the production of similar services not only "develop mutual awareness, and see themselves as part of the same community and involved in a common enterprise," but that they also tend to share "organizational forms" and institutional logics.[178] These institutional logics, moreover, provide "social actors with formal and informal rules of action and interaction, cultural norms and beliefs for interpretation, and implicit principles about what constitute legitimate goals and how they may be achieved."[179] Considering the ways in which religious organizations often have to balance between the "more explicitly religious" and "practical" aspects of their organizational life, they are often faced with the challenge of managing "divergent interests, goals and practices rooted in multiple institutional

Religion in market society 185

logics."[180] It is equally important to recognize the large extent to which social formations are structured by language and discourse.[181] Exploring the position of a particular religious organization within a broader social formation therefore also entails considering its position within wider webs of inter- institutional/organizational flows of discursive and ideational influence.[182]

These types of considerations become particularly important when the object of inquiry is a religious organization such as a long-established Christian church that has developed concomitantly with developments in a particular society over a longer period of time and developed complex bureaucratic structures. This is because traditional Christian churches have historically occupied positions of high relative, and indeed central, importance to the functioning of the social formations in which they have been embedded and also exerted considerable inter-institutional and inter-organizational discursive and ideological influence. Their positions in this regard have, however, weakened considerably following modern social and cultural developments such as the increasing rationalization, urbanization, functional differentiation, and religious diversification of modern societies. In spite of their decline, however, these types of churches nevertheless often retain an "establishmentarian" mindset and typically continue to view themselves as integral parts of the very fabric of their respective societies. As will be more concretely illustrated in light of recent developments within the US mainline churches below, since the civic engagements of traditional churches are increasingly carried out on contractual bases within broader cooperative networks that encompass a multitude of different types of social organizations, including states, local governments, and a variety of nonprofit organizations the pressure towards the consolidation of discourses around shared marketized "nodal discourses" is ever present.[183] It is primarily through such discursive alignments that new marketized languages make their ways into official church discourse and develop into integral components of new church imaginaries and IDFs.

"Official" discourse

The dominant IDFs of an organization normally permeate its "official" discourse in a range of different areas. Bureaucratically structured religious organizations like traditional Christian churches constantly produce a wealth of official discourse of various kinds. "Official" discourse in this context denotes different types of discourse produced by churches themselves to direct their own activities, to communicate with external partners or stakeholders, or to articulate their official strategy, stance, position, etc. on any given topic or field of activity. Examples include documents dealing with various aspects of church organization, policies, communication, positions on social issues, or the organization of social activities. In addition to this, traditional churches also produce a great deal of discourse that

186 *Religion in market society*

pertains more strictly to "religious" matters such as church teachings, ethics, or ecclesiology, for example. Official discourse of this kind is primarily found in various types of strategy and steering-group documents, statues, protocols, guidelines, statements, publications, website content, etc. Generally, the larger and more complex the organization of a particular church is, the more extensive and varied its official discourse also tends to be.

Because the official discourse of traditional churches is typically addressed to both internal audiences (such as church employees) and external ones (such as other social organizations or the general public), they are nowadays in large part made publicly available online. Access to parts of such discourse may, however, remain more or less strongly restricted to particular internal audiences. It is also worth noting that the ease, extent, and speed by which traditional churches produce various types of new official discourse has increased exponentially following the proliferation of digital communications and the construction of extensive organizational intranets. Indeed, mirroring similar developments across virtually all social organizational domains, up until approximately the first years of the new millennium, traditional churches did not produce new official strategies, guidelines, whitepapers, etc. at a pace that even closely resembled the frequency with which they typically do so today.

Official organizational discourse aims (and/or purports) to articulate the shared perceptions, concerns, and aspirations of organizations as a whole (including those who work in them). For this reason, it plays a particularly important role in guiding actual organizational activities as well as in the positioning of organizational subjects charged with carrying out these activities. As such, official organizational discourse constitutes a highly valuable category of data for any firmly empirically grounded exploration of religious-organizational change.[184] This is not least because actual tangible changes in the practices of all types of organizations tend to be both *preceded by* and *driven by* changes in their official discourse and discursive practices.[185]

As will be discussed further below, *strategies* make up a particularly significant category of the official discourse of organizations. This is because strategies provide a primary vehicle for "organizational storytelling" and the construction of organizational imaginaries.[186] As such, strategies also provide a principal means by which new discourses and IDFs are (re)produced and disseminated for "consumption" among organizational subjects. Strategy discourse also tends to display a particular set of distinctive features. For example, given their predominant focus on the future, strategies have a marked tendency to be "engulfed by their own 'truth' effects that make the socially constructed realities seem inevitable and taken for granted."[187] This is typically achieved by means of discursive *nominalization*, as outlined in Chapter 2: a "shift from verbs [...] to a particular class of nouns in the representation of actions and processes."[188] Strategies thus play an instrumental role in the establishment

Religion in market society 187

of discursive hegemonies since any attempt to institute a new dominant IDF within an organization will be dependent on its successful integration as part of new strategies.

Lastly, it is also worth noting that, while all religious organizations produce an official discourse, they do not necessarily do so in the form of strategies or other types of "formal" document genres. In such cases, the official discourse of a particular religious organization has to be gleaned from other sources, such as various types of publications and content disseminated by the organization online. Moreover, while some religious organizations have a broader "public" to whom they address (at least parts of) their official discourse,[189] others are primarily, and sometimes exclusively, focused on their own members and/or potential members. The distribution of official discourse and access to it will therefore always depend on the degree of openness of a given religious organization towards non-members as well as its authority and hierarchy structures. For example, the character of the official discourse of religious organizations in the megachurch mold differs notably from that of bureaucratically structured religious organizations of the traditional church type. The official discourse of megachurches is rarely articulated or disseminated in the form of steering-group documents, formal strategies, or the like. Instead, their official discourse mainly tends to derive from books authored by their "visionary" leading and/or founding pastors.[190]

Marketized discourse in the US mainline churches

With the above discussion in mind, we now move to consider the proliferation of marketized discourse within the US mainline churches. The historical roots of the mainline churches can be traced all the way back to the establishment of the Church of England in the original thirteen colonies that were created as part of the British colonization of North America that began in earnest in the early seventeenth century.[191] As the historical development of the mainline churches has already been charted in several previous studies,[192] there is no need for us to repeat it here. Instead, our account will only consider a more limited set of developments over roughly the past century which are of particular importance for understanding the increasing prevalence of marketized discourse in mainline settings.

The early twentieth century marked a time of great socio-economic change and transformation in the United States. Accelerating further industrialization and urbanization gave rise to a range of new social problems such as increasing economic inequality and poverty, poor labor conditions, and racial and immigration-related tensions. The firmly established mainline churches responded to these challenges through a concentrated effort to "craft the Kingdom of God on Earth" that became known as the Social Gospel.[193] While encompassing a wide range of social engagements and causes, as Peter J. Thuesen points out, the Social Gospel was above all a

188   *Religion in market society*

"bureaucratic phenomenon" that "partook deeply of the bureaucratic ethos of big business and the scientific ethos of the university."[194] Although the Great Depression of the 1930s triggered a thorough reassessment of the optimistic aims of the Social Gospel,[195] as the movement continued to expand, the mainline churches increasingly came to adopt an "institutional model" of social activism and advocacy based on an "all-embracing conception of the church's public role."[196]

The policies of Franklin D. Roosevelt's New Deal in the aftermath of the Great Depression of the 1930s, followed by Lyndon B. Johnson's Great Society in the mid-1960s, both resulted in considerable expansions in nearly all government bureaucracies charged with the distribution of various types of social services.[197] US government social-welfare spending throughout the 1960s and 1970s also largely followed the longstanding liberal-regime principle of "third-party government," whereby federal state authorities typically enlisted non-profit organizations (as well as private firms) to carry out social welfare operations in actual practice. These developments therefore also resulted in a considerable expansion in the operations and general economic significance of the non-profit organizational sector, including the mainline churches, during these decades.[198] By the 1960s, however, the intensifying civic engagements of the mainline churches had helped produce "denominational bureaucracies that were more interested in maintaining the status quo" than they were in trying to attract new members.[199] This particular development, in turn, provides an important part of the explanation for the perpetual state of decline that the mainline churches have found themselves in ever since. The membership of most mainline denominations peaked around 1965, after which it entered a spiral of rapid and dramatic decline.[200] By the early 1990s, the mainline churches had lost their "mainline" status as far as membership figures were concerned and had been surpassed by neo-evangelical and non-denominational congregations and "seeker-sensitive" megachurches.[201]

The onset of neoliberalism and the new "Reaganomics" of the early 1980s brought about a range of sweeping changes to the non-profit organizational field of the United States. As Lester M. Salamon puts it, the 1980s witnessed a "decisive turn toward the market, a fundamental 'marketization' of the nonprofit sector."[202] Viewed through the lens of discourse and discursive change, it is crucial to recognize that these developments also entailed the entry of a whole host of new market-associated discourses and imperatives into the domain of non-profit organizations, for example in the form of "marketing," "branding," "promotion," "customer orientation," "total quality management," "management by objectives," "cost-effectiveness," "flexibility," and more recently "social entrepreneurship."[203] The mid-1990s also witnessed the further introduction of so-called "faith-based initiatives" in the area of welfare provision though the "charitable choice" option of the "Personal Responsibility and Work Opportunity Reconciliation Act" of 1996, followed by the George W. Bush administration's

Religion in market society 189

establishment of the White House Office of Community and Faith-based Organizations in 2001.[204] Following these developments and decades of continued perpetual decline, the mainline churches have increasingly geared their bureaucracies towards "institutional survival."[205] But in spite of their numerical decline and gradual loss of social influence, they still retain central positions throughout both national and local non-profit co-operative networks.[206] This has, however, also no doubt made them more susceptible to various types of inter-organizational discursive influence as they have, often rather unreservedly, adopted the types of managerial and market-associated discourses and imperatives that have increasingly come to permeate and govern the broader public and non-profit organizational spheres.

Even though the pressure on various types of non-business social organizations (religious organizations included) to align with currently prevailing market-associated imperatives of organizational "effectivity" and "performance" has been steadily intensifying during the past three to four decades, this does not, by and of itself, result in an increasing adoption of marketized discourse on the part of traditional churches. As I have argued elsewhere, that, crucially, also requires the *active participation* of organizational subjects.[207] In the case of the US mainline churches, the adoption of such new discourses and organizational values have primarily been seen to provide new means and imaginaries for tackling a whole host of issues associated with continued denominational decline. The adoption of marketized discourse within traditional church settings also initially tend to become empirically observable through a general process of religious-organizational *accommodation* to market-associated discourse in the form of a gradual introduction of such discourse into new official strategies, steering documents, whitepapers, guidelines, etc. More concretely, this tends to occur through a typically self-perpetuating *technologization of discourse*, and it is to this issue that we now turn.

The technologization of discourse

Originally coined by Fairclough,[208] the concept of the technologization of discourse draws our attention to the discursive and ideational elements of marketization and aims to outline the more concrete ways and trajectories whereby new types of managerial and market-associated discourses make their ways into non-economic social-organizational domains. Theoretically, the notion of the technologization of discourse is inspired by the work of Foucault[209] and the "technologies of government" that he identified as constituting prime mechanisms for the perpetuation of power and dominance in modern societies.[210]

The technologization of discourse is closely connected to the emergence and increasingly wide establishment of what Fairclough refers to as late-capitalist "discourse technologies" such as "promotion," "auditing,"

190 *Religion in market society*

and "customer orientation," which have become "designed and projected as 'context-free'" and applicable across all and any organizational contexts.[211] This has brought about a situation in which "the projection of such context free techniques into a variety of institutional contexts contributes to a widespread effect of 'colonization' of local institutional orders of discourse by a few culturally salient discourse types."[212] While it is often difficult to locate their exact origins, the emergence and dissemination of these types of discourse technologies have gone hand in hand with the emergence of what Fairclough refers to as "specialist technologists," such as "researchers who look into their efficiency, designers who work out refinements in the light of research and changing institutional requirements, and trainers who pass on the techniques."[213] Examples of discourse technologists include, most notably, management gurus, consultants, and media and communication specialists, but also social scientists involved in various types of consulting.

The central objective of the technologization of discourse is to improve the "efficiency" of an organization with regard to such things as its organizational culture, routines and operations, communication practices, interaction with clients, customers, or "publics," or "the successful projection of 'image.'"[214] More concretely, the technologization of discourse involves "research into [the] existing discursive practices" of social institutions and organizations, "redesign of those practices in accordance with particular strategies and objectives"[215] and expectations of organizational effectivity, as well as "training of institutional personnel in these redesigned practices."[216] As such, the technologization of discourse is, to a significant degree, about the perpetuation and ingraining of a certain type of *"knowledge about discourse itself."*[217] A technologization of discourse therefore occurs when an organization, as a result of either perceived or actual external pressures (or a combination of the two), becomes increasingly susceptible to discourse technologies, adopts new discursive practices and context-free discourse techniques, and deliberately strives to transform its existing discursive practices so as to conform (and be seen to conform) to new criteria of organizational effectivity with regard to, for example, organizational and managerial culture. The technologization of discourse can therefore be thought of as the rationalized and systematic effort whereby discourse technologies are introduced, disseminated, established, and eventually naturalized in particular organizational settings with the ultimate objective of "constructing a new hegemony in the order of discourse of the institution or organization concerned, as part of a more general struggle to impose restructured hegemonies in institutional practices and culture."[218]

Investigating the technologization of discourse consequently involves tracking the entry and spread of new managerial and market-associated discourses within particular organizational settings. However, as with processes of marketization within organizational contexts generally, no technologization of discourse happens by itself; it always needs to be both initiated and perpetuated by organizational subjects themselves (usually by people or units in the upper echelons of organizational leaderships and administrations).[219] It is also worth noting that extensive efforts at technologization of discourse require considerable resources. Such efforts thus by and of themselves signal a greater deal of commitment on the part of organizations to alter their existing discursive practices and establish new market-values-emphasizing IDFs. On a more concrete level, the technologization of discourse therefore also tends to result in three principal and empirically identifiable types of lexical and grammatical changes in the discursive practices of organizations coupled with the introduction and increasing salience of particular discourse types and genres.

In terms of changes in lexis and grammar, as a first stage, we see an increasing *recontextualization* of discourses (e.g., on marketing, advertising, branding) that originate from "outside" the organization coupled with deliberate efforts to integrate these into the dominant IDFs and order of discourse of the organization in question. As explained in Chapter 2, recontextualization involves the transfer of arguments and vocabularies from one type of text into another. It thus also involves a deliberate *abstraction of meaning* away from the situated original contexts of the discourses that are recontextualized.[220] As Fairclough points out, a

> discourse decontextualised from its dialectical relationship with other elements of a field or network of social practices becomes an *imaginary*, very often working in a *metaphorical* way in the reimagining of aspects of the field or practices it is recontextualised within.[221]

We therefore see a deliberate *intermingling* of new market-associated discourses and vocabularies with already established organizational discourses and idioms. This results in the formation of new types of *hybrid* discourses that constitute (sometimes highly creative) mixtures between, for example, for-profit, non-profit, and religious discourse genres. It is therefore principally through such practices of recontextualization and creation of new types of hybrid discourses that the ethos and self-understandings of the mainline churches become articulated through the idiom of the market. It is therefore also through these practices that the dominant IDFs of the mainline churches increasingly come to display an increasing preoccupation with market-centered values and imperatives.

The official "marketing plans" of the UMC and TEC provide US illustrative examples of this. In their respective ways, both construct understandings of "marketing" that reduce it to, as well as effectively equate it with, effective communication as part of conscious efforts to *dissociate* "marketing" (i.e., to *recontextualize* it) from its foundations in the for-profit domain of business and commerce. In both of these cases, we are therefore dealing with a new type of hybrid discourse where the concept of "marketing" not only figures in a largely metaphorical sense but also

192 *Religion in market society*

functions to provide a new imaginary for church practice. For example, the UMCs "Marketing Plan Tool" is introduced thus:

> MARKETING ISN'T A DIRTY WORD. Marketing isn't about sales. Marketing is about understanding your community and using the tools available to speak most effectively to them.[222]

This short excerpt is generally illustrative of the ways in which the recontextualization of marketing discourse into official church discourse typically functions as a way to "reimagine" already established church practice through a new marketing idiom. This type of discourse aims to distance the practices of the church from the world of marketing as that is commonly understood by explicitly redefining marketing as something that "isn't about sales", but rather about "understanding your community." Hence, it must not be considered a "dirty word" in church setting.

Similarly, a particularly clear example of the intermingling of market and religious discourse genres is the TEC's 2013 official eight-page-long guideline document *Marketing your Parish: Advertising Best Practices for Effective Evangelism*, produced and published by the TECs Office of Communication. The document starts out with an "Executive Summary" that, among other things, states the following:

> Despite a legacy of 2,000 years as the greatest marketing organization the world has ever seen, the church has been sitting on the sidelines during the ad revolutions of the past 50 years. Mention "advertising" around Christians and you're sure to provoke a reaction. Suggest churches should market to targeted segments of the population, and you're starting to tread on forbidden turf. However – be it a congregation, diocese, denomination, or the universal Body – the church cannot afford to consider "advertising" a dirty word.
>
> Fundamentally, commercial and church marketing are more similar than you might think. Both require a coordinated strategy of sending messages to a targeted group of people, and both chart their efficacy with one measure: conversions.
>
> Effective commercial advertising sells products, whereas effective church advertising gets confirmed communicants in the pews. In this sense we are all advertisers; the church simply deals in spiritual rather than tangible goods.[223]

A few lines later, under the heading "Advertising as Evangelism: It's Nothing New," the text then goes on to proclaim that

> The church has utilized effective marketing and advertising for a long time now. The Introduction to the Gospel of Luke (1, 1–4) has all the hallmarks of an effective product pitch: It casts doubt on the

Religion in market society 193

competition, appeals to eyewitness testimony, and offers a "satisfaction guarantee."[224]

Apart from being highly illustrative of the practice of recontextualization, these excerpts also provide apt examples of the creation of new hybrid discourses that constitute creative mixtures of the genres of religious and marketing discourse. As in the previous example, the text explicitly strives to dissociate the practices of advertising and marketing from their roots in the world of business by redefining them as practices that have always been fully compatible with the practices of the church.[225] Significant parts of the text are hence devoted to justifying the employment of the practice of marketing in church settings. In terms of vocabulary, the text employs a whole host of market-associated words and terms such as "targeted segment," "product pitch," "competition," "goods," "satisfaction guarantee" (itself put inside quotation marks), and of course "marketing" and "advertising." As to the collocation of the text, in what provides a prime example of a hybrid discourse, market-associated terms are included in every single sentence and are made to figure rather effortlessly alongside words and terms such as "church," "the universal Body," "communicants in the pews," and "the Gospel of Luke." In terms of modality, the text communicates a very high degree of commitment and certainly about what is being said (e.g., "cannot afford to consider," "more similar than you might think," "we are all advertisers"). With regards to genre and style, the text employs a primarily colloquial rather than technical type of language. And so, while the document on the whole is mainly designed to persuade its intended primary audience (church employees), it is simultaneously also geared towards "desensitizing" them to the explicit employment of language and terminology related to marketing and advertising in church settings.

In addition to the theme of "marketing," largely similar developments can also be discerned with regard to US mainline churches' the adoption of the concept and practice of "branding." For example, the DOC, ELCA, TEC, and UMC have all created official "branding guidelines," all of which make manifest inter-discursive connections to broader discourses on branding. But much like the case of "marketing," these official guidelines all employ the term "branding" in ways that reduce it to little more than the creation of an attractive visual profile and logo. Even though the understandings of branding that emerge through such recontextualizing hybrid discourse end up being quite far removed from the standard definition of branding, they nevertheless construct understandings of "branding" that provide new imaginaries for church practice while simultaneously not conflicting too much with established church discourse. It worth noting that recontextualizing discourse of this type tends to be primarily directed towards internal audiences, and particularly church employees. Hence, it also works to position church employees as the ones who are supposed to realize and advance the new church imaginaries thus constructed.

194   *Religion in market society*

Closely related to the practice of recontextualization, the technologization of discourse also typically works to spur a further *homogenization* and *standardization* of discursive practices.[226] This can most clearly be seen in an extension of instrumental-rationalist strategic discourse, a notable new emphasis on strategic planning, and an increasing preoccupation with the constant generation of new strategic initiatives of various kinds. Such activities also tend to be self-perpetuating. Typically, the generation of new strategies serves to spur the further generation of yet more strategies so that more and more areas of a church's organizational thinking and practice become gradually subjected to and governed by strategic thinking and articulated through strategic discourse types and genres. Indeed, as a result, the pace and frequency at which the US mainline churches generate new strategic initiatives has increased significantly within a relatively short period of time. And, as noted, it is mainly through the medium of strategies and their associated lexical and grammatical features that market-associated terms and concepts make their ways into the churches' orders of discourse and come to constitute central elements of new church imaginaries and IDFs.

In an initial example, in 2012 the PCUSA's Presbyterian Mission Agency developed a "Mission Work Plan for 2013 to 2016" that emphasized the need for the church to maintain its "Organizational Integrity." For this purpose, the plan outlined the following main "directional goals":

> Build confidence, trust and engagement in all that we do by being Collaborative, Accountable, Responsive and Excellent (C.A.R.E.).
>
> *If anything is excellent and if anything is admirable, focus your thoughts on these things.*
>
> Philippians 4:8a (CEB)[227]

The main thing to note about the discourse in this short excerpt is the way in which it represents the principal values of PCUSA organizational practice in the form of an acronym, which conveniently reads as "care." This is revealing of the influence of marketized discourse, as is also the use of the word "Excellence." Providing an example of both inter-textuality and inter-discursivity and the hybridization of discourse, the excerpt also includes a Bible reference. Indeed, all of the "directional goals" set out in the document from which the excerpt is taken are accompanied by Bible references, the primary purpose of which is to provide Scriptural justification for the types of actions encouraged by the text.

An earlier white-paper version of the same document from 2012 manifested significantly stronger inter-discursive connections to marketized discourse and NPM-associated values and ideals. The last paragraph of the General Assembly Mission Council's "2013–2016 Mission Work Plan Strategy White Paper" read as follows:

> Preliminary Objectives were developed by staff based upon the directional goals to describe tangible outcome targets that can be measured,

Religion in market society 195

monitored and evaluated for progress. These objectives served as the basis for development of the budgets. In the fall of 2012, these will be completed, then work plans and individual goals will be set, all in alignment with the Vision, Mission and Directional Goals. Each GAMC program will be evaluated for effectiveness, impact and alignment on a four year cycle of evaluations.[228]

This excerpt constitutes a particularly notable example of a wholesale adoption of marketized discourse on the part of the PCUSA. When it comes to the vocabulary employed in this excerpt, we encounter several words, terms, and phrases with conspicuous links to organizational values related to marketing and NPM, such as "directional goals," "tangible outcome targets," and the "measurement," "monitoring," and "evaluation of "effectiveness," "impact," and "progress." Indeed, these types of words and terms dominate the entire text. In terms of modality, the text expresses a high degree of commitment to what is being said (e.g., the repeated use of "will be"). In terms of style, the discourse in this except is highly formal and proclamatory in tone, employing a highly technical and heavily jargon-laden type of language. It also makes clear inter-textual connections to previous texts such as the "Vision, Mission and Directional Goals" and other GAMC programs. The primary purpose of this text is to work up a picture of the PCUSA as a modern and "effective" organization that, like any effective and well-functioning modern organization, systematically plans, executes, and evaluates its activities.

Indeed, in 2016 the PCUSA "Mission Agency Board" published another document outlining its new "2017–2018 Mission Work Plan." The core purpose of the plan is described as follows:

At the heart of the Mission Work Plan are directional goals, which serve as strategic beacons for the work of the agency. In the 2013–2016 plan, effort was given to ensure that all areas of Mission Agency work were reflected somewhere in the strategic plan. Thus, General Assembly Engagement was a directional goal in the former plan, along with Organizational Integrity (incorporating the infrastructure provided by many of our support areas).[229]

The most conspicuous feature of this excerpt is its strong and repeated emphasis on strategic thinking and its permeation throughout the organization as a whole. Indeed, in terms of inter-textual connections, the text is also self-referential in this regard, pointing out important connections between both past and future strategic endeavors. Overall, the text thus serves to work up a picture of strategic thinking as completely central to the aspirations of the PCUSA as a whole. As such, it also provides an illustration of a broader development within the US mainline churches, whereby the focus of official strategic discourse has increasingly shifted towards strategy *itself* in the form of what could be called "strategizing about strategy."

196 *Religion in market society*

Another type of example can be found in a 2012 document outlining the new "Governance Tasks" of the ABCUSA (directly derived from the "technologist" popular management book *Governance as Leadership: Reframing the Work of Nonprofit Boards*[230]). The purpose of the document is to argue for the adoption and implementation of three main "governance tasks" within the church. With regard to the second task the document states the following:

Type II Governance – Strategic

- Views the organization as an open system susceptible to both internal and external forces
- An emphasis upon performance
- Develops the pathway from Point A to Point B
- Type II Governance should involve strategic thinking rather than merely strategic planning.[231]

The perhaps most notable thing about this excerpt is that it lifts a piece of management discourse as articulated in a popular management book almost *verbatim* into official church discourse. In terms of vocabulary, the excerpt is, consequentially, strongly marked by managerial terminology such as "performance," "pathways," "strategic thinking," and "open system." The emphasis put on the importance of nurturing a culture of "strategic thinking" rather than just "strategic planning" is particularly notable since it highlights the need for the ABCUSA to adopt an entirely new approach to its organizational culture. In terms of modality, the text articulates a high degree of certainty about what is being said (e.g., the use of bullet points and phrases like "should involve"). As to its style, the text is highly formal in tone.

A final example of strategic discourse is provided by a 2017 report by the UCCs "Strategic Visioning Task Force" and "Vision Implementation Task Force of the UCC Board of Directors" titled *A Vision: The Transformative United Church of Christ in Ten Years*. The seven-page document announces the introduction of a new overarching organizational guiding principle called "Inclusive Excellence," which is described as follows:

Inclusive Excellence (IE) is the recognition that a community or institution's success is dependent on how well it values, engages and includes the rich diversity of its constituents. More than a short-term project or single office initiative, this comprehensive approach requires a fundamental transformation of the institution by embedding and practicing IE in every effort, aspect, and level of functioning. The goal is to make IE a habit that is implemented and practiced consistently throughout an organization.[232]

Religion in market society 197

This text explicitly encourages the wholesale adoption and integration of "Inclusive Excellence" into all UCC activities and practices. Indeed, as is stated in the text, its adoption will require a "fundamental transformation" of the entire UCC organization. The language of the text is formal, but not overtly technical. In terms of modality, it expresses a high degree of commitment to what is being proposed (e.g., "requires a fundamental transformation"). Manifest inter-discursive connections to external discursive-organizational settings are also made in that "Inclusive Excellence" is an organizational leadership strategy mainly associated with higher education institutions. This, then, provides another clear example of an increasing emphasis on strategic thinking as a key component in the construction of new church imaginaries and IDFs.

The above examples may suffice to illustrate the increasing penetration of managerial and market-associated discourse and discourse genres into the official strategic discourse and dominant IDFs of the US mainline churches. As seen in the above examples, typical lexical and grammatical features of such discourse include the increasing prevalence and repetition of terms such as "strategic" itself, along with terms such as "challenges," "leadership development," "assessment," and "directional goals." This, then, is how strategy discourse contributes to a standardization and homogenization of official mainline discourse by introducing and normalizing certain types of idioms and ways of talking that develop into recurring – and mutually reinforcing – discursive tropes across mainline IDFs and orders of discourse on the whole.

This type of strategic and recontextualizing discourse is most typically produced by various types of church administrative units, some of which may be specifically tasked with improving organizational "effectivity" and "performance" (e.g., the TECs Office of Communication and the PCUSA's Presbyterian Mission Agency, General Assembly Mission Council, and Mission Agency Board in the examples above). These types of units (as opposed to certain identifiable individuals) also tend to function as the "authors" of such discourse. The discourse they produce is primarily addressed to church employees, and is mostly circulated through internal organizational channels (although frequently also made available online). As such, this type of strategic and recontextualizing discourse also works to position church employees in particular ways. Above all, such discourse aims to outline and generate acceptance for what "has to" or "needs to" be done. The technologization of discourse therefore provides the broader context for understanding how and why these types of discourses become produced, distributed, and consumed within US mainline-church contexts, and subsequently develop into central elements of dominant church IDFs. The key point to note is that the repeated employment, circulation, and most importantly, naturalization of this type of discourse not only serves to further the spread of particular discursive tropes but also to foster a more general sense of constant "strategic awareness" among organizational actors and subjects themselves.

198   *Religion in market society*

As an additional effect of the homogenization and standardization of discourse, the technologization of discourse frequently also works to bring about changes in the "policing" of organizational discursive practices. While there are often considerable variations to be observed between different types of organizations in this regard, their respective discursive practices nevertheless tend to be continuously "subjected to checks, corrections and sanctions."[233] Traditional Christian churches provide apt examples of this in that their discursive practices tend to be governed by very particular sets of sometimes time-honored discursive "rules" and conventions which play a central role in determining not only *what* can and cannot be said within their respective organizations, but also *how* they can be said and *by whom*.[234] But the technologization of discourse can work to bring about a shift "in the location of policing agents," including a "shift in their legitimacy."[235] One example of this is when people who occupy leading positions within particular mainline-organizational contexts, and who previously held the authority to oversee and police their discursive practices, increasingly have to adhere to new discursive repertoires and standards, some of which may have been introduced by outside "technologists," or been directly encouraged by new strategic initiatives such as those discussed above.[236] New discursive practices and standards may also be introduced and perpetuated through the hiring of new categories of staff with backgrounds in management, marketing, branding, etc., to oversee religious organizations' public relations or communication offices. This particular effect of the technologization of discourse should not, however, be overstated. While it is beyond question that US mainline churches have engaged in the technologization of discourse to a notable extent and that market imperatives have increasingly come to govern their dominant IDFs, these types of efforts might not always be equally well received among all categories of church personnel. This, however, does not change the fact that market-associated discourse has for some time already started to become concretely *materialized* in organizational structures, and it is to this issue that we now turn.

The operationalization and materialization of discourse

Apart from its mainly discursive effects as outlined above, the technologization of discourse typically also works to inspire changes in the actual structure, practices, and activities of organizations. This is because changes in the discursive practices of organizations sooner or later will result in the actual operationalization and concrete materialization of these new discursive practices. This may occur in a large variety of different ways, some of the most notable being the creation of actual new (either temporal or permanent) administrative units, offices, or working groups, the introduction of new auditing and performance standards and monitoring mechanisms, the establishment of new educational or training programs, or the refashioning of tangible services or provisions. In this, we also see the increasing influence of ideas and practices derived from different types of management literature in particular. Management literature typically argues for the benefits of *network types* of organization, with smaller *teams* working on particular *projects* (reflecting a more general shift towards a "project society" or "society in project form"[237]), directed by the "vision" of the manager or *leader*.[238] The "putting into practice" of new discourses and discursive practices thus marks the stage at which the constitutive power of discourse truly reveals itself. In what is essentially a Foucauldian observation, once new discourses (e.g., on marketing or branding) become materialized in actual, tangible form in the creation of new administrative offices, units, or working groups charged with the operationalization of these discourses in actual practice, the mere existence of these will, in turn, work to significantly further legitimize and naturalize the discourses that brought them into being in the first place. Put another way, the more firmly materialized and tangibly cemented new market-associated discourses and discursive practices become as part of the "hardware"[239] of organizations, the more difficult it consequentially also becomes to "undo" or reverse their actual effects.

Examples of (relatively recently) established US mainline-church offices and units directly charged with improving organizational "effectivity" and/ or overseeing organizational marketing, advertising, and branding include the ELCA's "Mission Advancement Unit,"[240] the UCCs "Vision Implementation Task Force of the UCC Board of Directors,"[241] the UMCs "Marketing and Public Relations,"[242] division, the TECs office of "Communication, Advertising, and Marketing,"[243] and the DOC's office of "Marketing and Communications."[244] Further examples include the execution of actual advertising and marketing campaigns such as, most notably, the UMCs major 2001 *Igniting Ministry*, 2009 *Rethink Church*, and 2020 *Finding Hope Together* campaigns. As these examples illustrate, marketing, advertising, and branding have clearly developed into integral parts of the "hardware" of the US mainline churches, as is further evidenced by an increasing recruitment of new categories of personnel with professional backgrounds in these and related fields.[245] Whether these new units, offices, and categories of personnel actually engage in marketing, advertising, or branding as these practices are commonly understood in the for-profit sector is, however, an altogether different matter. Once established, however, they tend to assume particularly central roles in the further promulgation and dissemination of new market-centered IDFs and imaginaries for church practice.

In order to adequately explore these types of materializations of market-associated discourses, our analyses have to move beyond the level of official discourse alone. Further data may, for example, be gathered by means of interviews with different categories of organizational personnel, and especially among those categories of personnel who are charged with the actual operationalization of new discursive practices and hybrid discourses. But, importantly, most is learned when the views expressed by individual employees are

200 *Religion in market society*

explored in direct relation to the official discourse of the organization as a whole. The two are intimately connected since official discourse, while typically lacking an identifiable author, nevertheless has to be produced by *some-one*. Interviews can therefore provide a crucial means for reaching "behind the veil" of official discourse and finding out what actually goes on within the walls of various organizational units, offices, and working groups.[246] Such methods can therefore also be of great help in gaining a more precise understanding of exactly why and how technologization of discourse efforts are initiated and perpetuated within particular organizational settings at certain points in time. In addition, interviews also open up the possibility of further inquiries into the degrees to which new discursive practices may also influence the perceptions and professional ethos and identities of organizational employees, and with what degrees of acceptance or resistance.

The actual operationalization and materialization of new market-associated discourses in religious-organizational settings may also work to spur a final process of amalgamation, whereby market-associated strategic and effectivity-related concerns increasingly start to become *fused* with organizational activities and tasks that were not previously governed by such concerns.[247] In these cases, new hybrid discourses thus serve to bring about a "hybridization" of discourse and actual organizational *practice*. Amalgamation is therefore closely associated with the growing discursive influence of new strategic and/or "marketing" offices or units across organizational structures and hierarchies as a whole. As such, it tends to further contribute to fostering an organizational culture of constant "strategic awareness" and thus work to further reinforce the dominance of market-emphasizing IDFs. As an example, the increasingly strategically central notion of "church growth," along with the market-associated discourses that underpin it and the organizational offices that work to realize it, may increasingly take on the function of a *practical imperative* so that ever more aspects and areas of church activities are fashioned and carried out with this imperative in mind. Indeed, the fusion of discourse and practice is sometimes directly encouraged by official mainline-church discourse itself. One example is provided by the description of "Section 4: Planning for Success" in the UMC's previously mentioned "Marketing Plan Tool." Commenting on how to assess the results of extensive demographic and community research carried out previously, the text provides the following recommendation:

> Your measurements for success will come directly from the results of work toward your goals. That's the simplest way to rate your progress. Perhaps those measurements will include growth in attendance or giving, a new focus on ministries or small groups ... progress toward attendance goals may be simple to assess. Numbers will tell the tale. New and returning attenders will provide that metric ... Rating improvements in spiritual growth may be the most difficult. How does one put numbers to faith? Thus, choosing your metrics and how to compile them

Religion in market society 201

is key. Perhaps this work requires more than one way to find answers. Are your small groups maintaining and/or growing their attendance? Do your members feel that their prayer habits have led them to a closer relationship with God? A mixture of numbers-based and opinion-based questions may yield your best data regarding spiritual growth.[248]

While much could be said about the text in this excerpt, its strongly instrumental-rational approach to "church marketing" and its desired results is particularly noteworthy. In terms of vocabulary and collocation, the text continually employs words and terms such as "measurements," "attendance goals," and "metric" alongside terms such as "ministries," "spiritual growth," "faith," and "relationship with God." Although the administrative units of various types of churches have long been utilizing demographic data and the like for purposes of church expansion, this excerpt is taken from a package of educational materials that is intended to foster the establishment of effective "church marketing teams" at every local congregational level. Church marketing, in short, is presented as something that everyone should learn about and get involved with. In terms of style, the language of the text tries to strike a balance between the formal/technical and the colloquial. In terms of modality, however, the text is more ambiguous, highlighting both potential challenges and difficulties (e.g., the use of "perhaps" and the repeated use of questions).

Another similar example is provided by the DOC's "New Church Ministry" coaching program which offers training in a demographic analytical software called MissionInsite. This software is described as providing new "church planters" with essential tools to

explore solutions to complex strategic missional challenges in your choice geographical location for ministry. Connect socio-economic, behavioral, life-style and psychographic intelligence about your members, visitors and local community at large.[249]

The language in this except generally reflects the fact that it advertises a particular type of technical tool. More generally, it provides a further illustration of how proselytizing and outreach activities have become increasingly cloaked in managerial and technical vocabulary such as "complex strategic missional challenges." Through making inter-discursive connections to broader managerial discourses on work based on projects and research, evangelism is transformed into a rationalized and calculable activity carried out by new teams of tech-savvy "church planters."

As the above examples illustrate, processes of amalgamation tend to contribute further to fostering an organizational culture of constant "strategic awareness." Underpinned by an intensifying technologization of discourse and an increasing operationalization and materialization of new market-associated discourses and imperatives in actual practice, processes

202 *Religion in market society*

of amalgamation may then ultimately also serve to bring about situations where market-associated values and imperatives are allowed to *subjugate* previously established organizational logics, routines, and practices.[250] When this point has been reached, new imaginaries as constructed through market-emphasizing IDFs have transformed into palpable realities which are likely to have a long-lasting impact on the future practices and *modus operandi* of the organization concerned.

Third-level conclusions

The above discussion and analysis has illustrated some principal ways in which marketized discourse has proliferated within US mainline-church contexts largely as a result of an intensifying technologization of discourse on the part of these churches themselves. Clear empirical evidence for this is to be found in the ways in which (1) mainline churches have consciously striven to align their discursive practices with the types of managerial and market-associated discourses that have increasingly come to govern the broader public and non-profit organizational spheres as part of (2) their own efforts to construct new church imaginaries and IDFs in the face of continuing denominational decline.

The main sociological explanation for *why* US mainline churches have become increasingly susceptible to processes of marketization is to be found in a combination of the following three main factors: (1) their dense bureaucratic structures and longstanding ethos of civic engagement; (2) the larger degrees of inter-organizational discursive influence they are subjected to due to their deep involvements in various types of non-profit cooperative networks; and (3) their continued numerical decline. It is also because of these factors that the dominant IDFs of the mainline churches have become increasingly focused on strategic thinking and the improvement of organizational "effectivity" as part of broader efforts towards thoroughgoing "reform." Lastly, it is also worth noting that long-established, traditional churches in several parts of the Western world have been experiencing some very similar developments in the past couple of decades.[251]

Concluding remarks

This chapter has provided a critical discussion of the religion-market relationship in light of previous scholarship in the area. Our discussion has foregrounded the strongly discourse-driven character of the constitution and establishment of modern market society thinking and how various understandings of the "market" always emerge as the result of deliberate efforts of discursive construction and legitimation. As such, following Slater and Tonkiss, the principal aim of our first-level reflection was to highlight how "the very ideas of 'an economy' or 'the market' are part of a language through which the social world is represented and acted upon."[252]

Our second-level reflection illustrated the strong and enduring ideational influence of the (neo)liberal conception of the "market" on sociological theorizing on the character and organization of the modern-time Western religious field. In particular, our discussion highlighted some of the main, albeit typically ambiguous and unspecific, ways in which the metaphor of the "market" continues to be employed as an analytical and explanatory concept in the sociological study of religion more broadly. As noted, to speak of various types of hypothetical relationships or associations (e.g., in terms of "similarities," "shared elements," "affinities") between religion and the "market/markets" is one thing. But to speak of, and thereby at least implicitly assume, that the religious field *as a whole* will always be governed by market-dynamics such as competition, supply, and demand is an entirely different thing. It is important not to confuse or conflate the two. A sustained focus on the constitutive function of discourse (including, not least, in the context of academic theorizing) sensitizes us to the ways in which particular constructions of the religion-market relationship become established and acquire the status of analytical and descriptive categories.

In terms of third-level analysis, this chapter has outlined a general analytical framework in relation to which future research on the proliferation of marketized discourse within traditional religious-organizational settings could usefully be pursued, including the analytical tools most conducive to the empirical investigation and analysis of such processes in actual practice. But, as noted, in order to explore the tangible materialization of marketized discourse in traditional religious-organizational settings, our analyses will need to move beyond official discourse per se. This constitutes a pertinent area for future research. For in so far as marketized discourse will become ever more deeply engrained in the structures of traditional religious organizations, this might serve to bring about more fundamental and long-lasting changes in the ways in which they perceive themselves and their roles in society.

Notes

1 James G. Carrier, "Preface," in *Meanings of the Market: The Free Market in Western Culture*, ed. James G. Carrier (Oxford: Berg, 1997), vii–xv.
2 Slater and Tonkiss, *Market Society*, 29.
3 Slater, *Consumer Culture*, 42.
4 Adam Smith, *The Wealth of Nations: An Inquiry into the Nature and Causes of the Wealth of Nations* (Overland Park, KS: Digireads.com Publishing, 2009 [1776]).
5 Slater and Tonkiss, *Market Society*, 41.
6 Ibid., 41.
7 Slater, *Consumer Culture*, 43.
8 Ibid., 41.
9 Slater and Tonkiss, *Market Society*, 121.
10 Ibid., 93.

204 *Religion in market society*

11 Karl Marx, *Capital: A Critique of Political Economy*, Reprinted (New York: Dover Publications, 2011 [1867]).
12 Cf. Slater and Tonkiss, *Market Society*, 33.
13 Durkheim, *The Division of Labour*.
14 Slater and Tonkiss, *Market Society*, 83; François Gauthier, "From Nation-State," 385.
15 Marcel Mauss, *The Gift: The Form and Reason for Exchange in Archaic Societies*, 1925, Reprinted (New York: Norton, 1990).
16 Claude Lévi-Strauss, *The Elementary Structures of Kinship*, 1949, Reprinted (Boston, MA: Beacon Press, 1969).
17 Marshall Sahlins, *Stone Age Economics* (London: Tavistock, 1974).
18 Mary Douglas and Baron Isherwood, *The World of Goods: Towards and Anthropology of Consumption* (New York: Basic Books, 1978).
19 Slater and Tonkiss, *Market Society*, 99.
20 Ibid. 100.
21 Karl Polanyi, *The Great Transformation: The Political and Economic Origins of Our Time*, 1944, Reprinted (Boston, MA: Beacon Press, 1957).
22 For an extended discussion of the "non-ideological" representation of the market, see Luc Boltanski and Eve Chiapello, *The New Spirit of Capitalism* (London: Verso, 2005).
23 Ibid.
24 Slater and Tonkiss, *Market Society*, 3.
25 Ibid., 9; cf. Gerlinde Mautner, *Language and the Market Society: Critical Reflections on Discourse and Dominance* (New York: Routledge 2010), 1.
26 Slater and Tonkiss, *Market Society*, 2.
27 Ibid., 135.
28 Ibid., 65.
29 David Harvey, *A Brief History of Neoliberalism* (Oxford: Oxford University Press, 2007), 2.
30 Slater, *Consumer Culture*, 35.
31 Ibid., 11; cf. Celia Lury, *Consumer Culture* (Oxford: Polity Press, 2011), 6.
32 Mark Blyth, *Great Transformations: Economic Ideas and Institutional Change in the Twentieth Century* (Cambridge: Cambridge University Press, 2002).
33 Harvey, *A Brief History*; cf. James Dennis LoRusso, *Spirituality, Corporate Culture, and American Business: The Neoliberal Ethic and the Spirit of Global Capital* (London: Bloomsbury Academic, 2017), 46.
34 Ibid., 40; 54; cf. Fairclough, *Critical Discourse*, 13.
35 Ibid.
36 Ibid., 3.
37 Adam Tickell and Jaime Peck, "Making Global Rules: Globalization or Neoliberalism?" in *Remaking the Global Economy: Economic-Geographical Perspectives*, eds. Jaime Peck and Henry Wai-Chung Yeung (London: SAGE, 2003), 167–8.
38 Richard Sennett, *The Culture of the New Capitalism* (New Haven, CT: Yale University Press, 2006), 45–6.
39 Slater and Tonkiss, *Market Society*, 143.
40 For example, Christopher Pollitt, Sandra van Thiel, and Vincent Homburg, eds., *New Public Management in Europe: Adaptations and Alternatives* (Basingstoke: Palgrave Macmillan, 2007); Kathleen McLaughlin, Stephen P. Osborne, and Ewan Ferlie, eds. *New Public Management: Current Trends and Future Prospects* (London: Routledge, 2002).
41 For example, Slater, *Consumer Culture*, 24–5.
42 François Gauthier, "Religion, Media and the Dynamics of Consumerism in Globalising Societies," in *Religion, Media, and Social Change*, eds. Kennet Granholm, Marcus Moberg, and Sofia Sjö (New York: Routledge, 2015), 71;

cf. Jason Hackworth, "Faith, Welfare and the Formation of the Modern American Right," in *Religion in the Neoliberal Age: Political Economy and Modes of Governance*, eds. Tuomas Martikainen and François Gauthier (Farnham: Ashgate, 2013), 94.
43 Slater, *Consumer Culture*, 13.
44 See for example Adam Arvidsson, *Brands: Meaning and Value in Media Culture* (Oxon: Routledge, 2006), 15.
45 Daniel Bell, *The Coming of Post-Industrial Society: A Venture in Social Forecasting* (New York: Basic Books, 1976).
46 Jean-François Lyotard, *The Postmodern Condition: A Report on Knowledge* (Manchester: Manchester University Press, 1986).
47 Slater and Tonkiss, *Market Society*, 179–80.
48 Jean Baudrillard, *Simulacra and Simulation* (Ann Arbor: The University of Michigan Press, 1981).
49 Chouliaraki and Fairclough, *Discourse in Late Modernity*, 10.
50 Ibid.
51 Martin Kornberger, *Brand Society: How Brands Transform Management and Lifestyle* (Cambridge: Cambridge University Press, 2010), 13.
52 Ibid., 10; Arvidsson, *Brands*, 2–5.
53 Lury, *Consumer Culture*, 143–6.
54 Ibid., 11.
55 Ibid., 28; See for example Giddens, *Modernity and Self-Identity*; Lash, *Reflexive Modernization*; Bauman, *The Individualized Society*.
56 Slater, *Consumer Culture*, 9.
57 Lury, *Consumer Culture*, 13.
58 Ibid., 25.
59 Frank Trentmann, "Knowing Consumers: Consumers in Economics, Law and Civil Society," in *The Making of the Consumer: Knowledge, Power and Identity in the Modern World*, ed. Frank Trentmann (Oxford: Berg, 2006), 11.
60 Ibid., 3.
61 Slater, *Consumer Culture*, 35.
62 Fairclough, *Critical Discourse*, 141.
63 Ibid., 282.
64 Boltanski and Chiapello, *The New Spirit*, 57.
65 Pierre Bourdieu and Loic Wacquant, cited in Fairclough, *Critical Discourse*, 282.
66 Nigel Thrift, *Knowing Capitalism* (London: Sage, 2005), 6.
67 Mautner, *Language and the Market*, 10.
68 Ibid., 16.
69 Slater and Tonkiss, *Market Society*, 25.
70 Uwe Schimank and Ute Volkmann, "Economizing and Marketization in a Functionally Differentiated Capitalist Society – A Theoretical Conceptualization," in *The Marketization of Society: Economizing the Non-Economic*, eds. Uwe Schimank and Ute Volkmann. Research Network "Welfare Societies" conference papers (University of Bremen, 37. http://welfare-societies.com/uploads/file/WelfareSocietiesConferencePaper-No1_Schimank_Volkmann.pdf, accessed 9 October 2016.
71 For example, Fairclough, *Critical Discourse*.
72 For example, Morten Balle Hansen, "Marketization and Economic Performance," *Public Management Review* 12, no. 2 (2010): 255–74
73 For example, Ian Bruce and Celine Chew, "Debate: The Marketization of the Voluntary Sector," *Public Money & Management*, May (2011).
74 For example, Marie-Laure Djelic, "Marketization: From Intellectual Agenda to Global Policy Making," in *Transnational Governance: Institutional Dynamics of Regulation*, eds. Marie-Laure Djelic and Kerstin Sahlin-Andersson (Cambridge: Cambridge University Press, 2006).

206 *Religion in market society*

75 For example, Fairclough, *Critical Discourse.*
76 For example, Mautner, *Language and the Market.*
77 Slater and Tonkiss, *Market Society*, 1.
78 See for example, Matthew L. Sanders, "Theorizing Nonprofit Organizations as Contradictory Enterprises: Understanding the Inherent Tensions of Nonprofit Marketization," *Management Communication Quarterly* 26, no. 1 (2012): 180.
79 Mautner, *Language and the Market*, 18.
80 Fairclough, *Discourse and Social*, 195.
81 Slater and Tonkiss, *Market Society*, 191.
82 Ibid., 194.
83 Max Weber, *The Protestant Ethic and the "Spirit" of Capitalism* (Chicago, IL: Fitzroy Dearborn Publishers, 2001 [1905]).
84 Smith, cited in Warner, *Secularization*, 70.
85 Ibid., 70–1.
86 Nikos Passas, "The Market for Gods and Services: Religion, Commerce, and Deviance," in *Between Sacred and Secular: Research and Theory on Quasi-Religion*. Religion and the Social Order, vol. 4, eds. Arthur L. Greil and Thomas Robbins (London: Jai Press, 1994), 225.
87 See for example, Tuomas Martikainen, François Gauthier, and Linda Woodhead, "Introduction: Religion in Market Society," in *Religion in the Neoliberal Age: Political Economy and Modes of Governance*, eds. Tuomas Martikainen and François Gauthier (Farnham: Ashgate, 2013); Marcus Moberg and Tuomas Martikainen, "Religious Change in Market and Consumer Society: The Current State of the Field and New Ways Forward," *Religion* 48, no. 3 (2018): 418–35.
88 For a related and purportedly "discursive" account that basically simply reiterates the main positions of the "religion-market"-debate and fails to theorize the concept of the "market," see Guy Redden, "Religion, Discourse, and the Economy Question: Fraught Issues in Market Societies," in *Discourse Research and Religion: Disciplinary Use and Interdisciplinary Dialogues*, eds. Jay Johnston and Kocku von Stuckrad (Berlin: De Gruyter, 2021).
89 e.g. Rachel M. McCleary, ed., *The Oxford Handbook of the Economics of Religion* (Oxford: Oxford University Press, 2011).
90 For example, Gauthier, "From Nation-State."
91 Berger, *The Sacred Canopy.*
92 Gauthier, "From Nation-State," 383.
93 Ibid.
94 Ibid.
95 Ibid., 383. Largely analogous arguments were also advanced by Luckmann in *The Invisible Religion.*
96 For example, Rodney Stark and William Sims Bainbridge, *The Future of Religion: Secularization, Revival and Cult Formation* (Berkeley: University of California Press, 1985); Rodney Stark and William Sims Bainbridge, *A Theory of Religion* (New York: Peter Lang, 1987).
97 Gary Becker, *The Economic Approach to Human Behavior* (Chicago, IL: Chicago University Press, 1976).
98 For a more detailed discussion, see e.g. Davie, *The Sociology of Religion* (London: Sage, 2007), 67–87.
99 Rodney Stark and Richard Finke, *Acts of Faith: Exploring the Human Side of Religion* (Berkeley: University of California Press, 2000).
100 Berger, Davie, and Fokas, *Religious America*, 35.
101 For example, Gregory D. Alles, "Religious Economies and Rational Choice: On Rodney Stark and Roger Finke, *Acts of Faith* (2000)," in *Contemporary*

Religion in market society 207

Theories of Religion: A Critical Companion, ed. Michael Stausberg (Oxon: Routledge, 2009), 85, emphasis added.

102 Andrew M. McKinnon, "Ideology and the Market Metaphor in Rational Choice Theory of Religion: A Rhetorical Critique of 'Religious Economies'," *Critical Sociology* 39, no. 4 (2013): 7.

103 Berger, Davie, and Fokas, *Religious America*, 34.

104 For example, Alles, "Religious Economies;" Steve Bruce, "Authority and Freedom: Economics and Secularization," in *Religions as Brands: New Perspectives on the Marketization of Religion and Spirituality*, eds. Jörg Stolz and Jean-Claude Usunier (Farnham: Ashgate, 2014); Doyle Paul Johnson, "The Theoretical Trajectory," in *American Sociology of Religion*, ed. Anthony J. Blasi (Leiden: Brill, 2007), 75.

105 François Gauthier, Tuomas Martikainen and Linda Woodhead, "Acknowledging a Global Shift: A Primer for Thinking about Religion in Consumer Societies," *Implicit Religion* 16, no. 3 (2013): 268.

106 Bruce, "Authority and Freedom," 189–204; Jean-Claude Usunier, "'9591': The Global Commoditization of Religions through GATS, WTO, and Marketing Practices," in *Religions as Brands: New Perspectives on the Marketization of Religion and Spirituality*, eds. Jörg Stolz and Jean-Claude Usunier (Farnham: Ashgate, 2014), 42.

107 Stephen R. Warner, "Work in Progress toward a New Paradigm for the Sociological Study of Religion in the United States," *American Journal of Sociology* 98, no. 5 (1993); for an expanded version of the argument, see Stephen R. Warner, "A Paradigm Is Not a Theory: Reply to Lechner," *American Journal of Sociology* 103, no. 1 (1997).

108 Warner, *Secularization*, 81.

109 For example, Bruce, "Authority and Freedom."

110 For example, Berger, Davie, and Fokas, *Religious America*.

111 Berger, Davie, and Fokas, *Religious America*, 36.

112 McKinnon, "Ideology and the Market," 2.

113 Ibid.

114 Ibid.

115 Ibid., 3; cf. Gauthier, "From Nation-State," 386.

116 See for example, Roland Robertson, "The Economization of Religion: Reflections on the Promise and Limitations of the Economic Approach," *Social Compass* 39, no. 1 (1992).

117 Warner, "Work in Progress;" cf. McKinnon, "Ideology and the Market."

118 Wade Clarke Roof, *Spiritual Marketplace: Baby Boomers and the Remaking of American Religion* (Princeton, NJ: Princeton University Press, 1999), 78.

119 Ibid.

120 Mara Einstein, *Brands of Faith: Marketing Religion in a Commercial Age* (New York: Routledge, 2008), 19.

121 For example, Davie, *Religion in Britain*, 135.

122 McKinnon, "Ideology and the Market," 3.

123 Ibid.

124 Jörg Stolz and Jean-Claude Usunier, "Religions as Brands: New Perspectives on the Marketization of Religion and Spirituality," in *Religions as Brands: New Perspectives on the Marketization of Religion and Spirituality*, eds. Jörg Stolz and Jean-Claude Usunier (Farnham: Ashgate, 2014), 4; 6.

125 For example, Michael York, "New Age Commodification and Appropriation of Spirituality." *Journal of Contemporary Religion* 16, no. 3 (2001); Twitchell, *Shopping for God*; Vincent J. Miller, *Consuming Religion: Christian Faith and Practice in a Consumer Culture* (New York: Continuum, 2008); Heelas,

208 *Religion in market society*

Spiritualities of Life: New Age Romanticism and Consumptive Capitalism (Oxford: Blackwell, 2008); Özlem Sandıkcı, and Gillar Rice, eds. *Handbook of Islamic Marketing* (Northampton, MA: Edward Elgar, 2011); Faegheh Shirazi, *Brand Islam: The Marketing and Commodification of Piety* (Austin: University of Texas Press, 2016).

126 Kimberly Lau, *New Age Capitalism: Making Money East of Eden* (Philadelphia: University of Pennsylvania Press, 2000).

127 Carrette and King, *Selling Spirituality*.

128 Paul Heelas, *Spiritualities of Life*.

129 Ibid., 6.

130 Carrette and King, *Selling Spirituality*, x.

131 Ibid., 1.

132 Ibid., 20.

133 Ibid., 53.

134 For a more detailed discussion, see Teemu Taira, "The Problem of Capitalism in the Scholarship on Contemporary Spirituality," in *Postmodern Spirituality*, ed. Tore Ahlbäck (Åbo: The Donner Institute for Research in Religious and Cultural History, 2008), 231.

135 Pattana Kitiarsa, "Towards a Sociology of Religious Commodification," in *The New Blackwell Companion to the Sociology of Religion*, ed. Bryan S. Turner (Chichester: Blackwell, 2010), 565.

136 Ibid., 563.

137 Ibid., 565.

138 Ibid., 572.

139 Ibid., 573.

140 Usunier, "9591," 30.

141 Ibid., 33.

142 Ibid.

143 Fairclough, *Critical Discourse*, 4.

144 Trentmann, "Knowing Consumers," 6, emphasis added.

145 Gauthier, Martikainen, and Woodhead, "Acknowledging a Global," 263.

146 Ibid., 263–4.

147 François Gauthier, Linda Woodhead and Tuomas Martikainen, "Introduction: Consumerism as the Ethos of Consumer Society," in *Religion in Consumer Society: Brands, Consumers, Markets*, eds. François Gauthier and Tuomas Martikainen (Farnham: Ashgate, 2013), 4.

148 Gauthier, "Religion, Media," 72.

149 Ibid., emphasis added.

150 Carrier, "Preface."

151 Gauthier, "From Nation State," 390.

152 Martikainen, "Multilevel and Pluricentric."

153 Hackworth, "Faith, Welfare." David Ashley and Ryan Sandefer, "Neoliberalism and the Privatization of Welfare and Religious Organizations in the United States of America," in *Religion in the Neoliberal Age: Political Economy and Modes of Governance*, eds. Tuomas Martikainen and François Gauthier (Farnham: Ashgate, 2013).

154 Tuomas Martikainen, "Towards a New Political Economy of Religion: Reflections on Marion Maddox and Nicolas de Bremond d'Ars," *Social Compass* 59, no. 2 (2012): 178; Jens Schlamelcher, "The Decline of the Parishes and the Rise of City Churches: The German Evangelical Church in the Age of Neoliberalism," in *Religion in the Neoliberal Age: Political Economy and Modes of Governance*, eds. Tuomas Martikainen and François Gauthier (Farnham: Ashgate, 2013); Moberg, *Church, Market*; Marcus Moberg, "Studying Change

in Religious Organizations: A Discourse-Centered Framework," *Method & Theory in the Study of Religion* 32, no. 2 (2020): 89–114.

155 François Gauthier, *Religion, Modernity, Globalisation: Nation-State to Market* (Oxon: Routledge, 2020), 202; cf. Russell W. Belk, "Commodification as Part of Marketization," in *Marketization: Theory and Evidence from Emerging Economies*, eds. Himadri Roy Chaudhuri and Russell W. Belk (Singapore: Springer Nature Singapore Pte Ltd., 2020).

156 For example, C.R. Hinings and Mia Raynard. "Organizational Form, Structure, and Religious Organizations," in *Religion and Organization Theory, Research in the Sociology of Organizations* vol. 41, eds. Paul Tracey, Nelson Phillips, and Michael Lounsbury (Emerald Publishing Group, 2014).

157 For an early overview, see e.g. James A. Beckford, "Religious Organizations," in *The Sacred in a Secular Age*, ed. P. E. Hammond (The Hague: Mouton, 1985).

158 Marcus Moberg, "Understanding Religious-Organizational Marketization: The Case of the United States Mainline," *Journal of the American Academy of Religion*, forthcoming 2021.

159 Fairclough, *Critical Discourse*, 40; cf. Cooren, *Organizational Discourse*.

160 David Grant and Cynthia Hardy, "Introduction: Struggles with Organizational Discourse," *Organization Studies* 25, no. 1 (2003): 6.

161 Ibid.

162 See for example, Paul Tracey, Nelson Phillips, and Michael Lounsbury, "Taking Religion Seriously in the Study of Organizations," in *Religion and Organization Theory*, eds. Paul Tracey, Nelson Phillips, and Michael Lounsbury (Bingley: Emerald Publishing Limited, 2014), 9–10.

163 Fairclough, *Critical Discourse*, 41.

164 Ibid., 37.

165 Ibid.

166 Ibid., 27.

167 Ibid., 44.

168 For an earlier related broader argument, see Mark Chaves, "Denominations as Dual Structures: An Organizational Analysis," *Sociology of Religion* 54, no. 2 (1993): 147–69.

169 Norman Fairclough, "Discourse Analysis in Organization Studies: The Case for Critical Realism," *Organization Studies* 26, no. 6 (2005): 931.

170 Fairclough, *Critical Discourse*, 61–2.

171 Fairclough, "Discourse Analysis," 930–1.

172 For a detailed account of how to analyze changing discursive practices in times of organizational crises, see Fairclough, *Critical Discourse*, 19–20.

173 For example, Jeff Manza and Clem Brooks, "The Changing Political Fortunes of Mainline Protestants," in *The Quiet Hand of God: Faith-Based Activism and the Public Role of Mainline Protestantism*, eds. Robert Wuthnow and John H. Evans (Berkeley: University of California Press, 2002), 162; Hugh McLeod, *The Religious Crisis*.

174 For example, Davie, *Religion in Modern Britain*, 31.

175 For example, Lantzer, *Mainline Christianity*; Linda Woodhead, "Introduction," in *Religion and Change in Modern Britain*, eds. Linda Woodhead and Rebecca Catto (London: Routledge, 2012).

176 Fairclough, *Critical Discourse*, 51, emphasis added.

177 Burton L. Mack, *Myth and the Christian Nation: A Social Theory of Religion* (Oxon: Routledge, 2014), 49; 50–2.

178 Tracey, Phillips, and Lounsbury, "Taking Religion Seriously," 12.

179 Ibid.

210 Religion in market society

180 Ibid.
181 Mack, *Myth and the Christian*, 74.
182 Moberg, *Church, Market*, 50–1.
183 Fairclough, "Discourse Analysis," 933.
184 Cf. Schlamelcher, "The Decline of the Parishes," 55.
185 For example, Fairclough, "Discourse Analysis."
186 Ibid., 932.
187 Thomas Greckhamer, "The Stretch of Strategic Management Discourse: A Critical Analysis," *Organization Studies* 31, no. 7 (2010): 844; cf. Iedema, *Discourses*, 73.
188 Fairclough, "Discourse Analysis," 926.
189 Fairclough, *Critical Discourse*, 41.
190 Ibid., 199–200.
191 Ibid., 15; cf. Peter J. Thuesen, "The Logic of Mainline Churchliness: Historical Background since the Reformation," in *The Quiet Hand of God: Faith-Based Activism and the Public Role of Mainline Protestantism*, eds. Robert Wuthnow and John H. Evans (Berkeley: University of California Press, 2002), 31–2.
192 For example, Jason S. Lantzer, *Mainline Christianity*.
193 Thuesen, "The Logic of Mainline," 37.
194 Ibid.
195 Ibid.
196 Ibid., 27.
197 Lester M. Salamon, "The Marketization of Welfare: Changing Nonprofit and For-Profit Roles in the American Welfare State," *Social Service Review* 67, no. 1 (1993): 16–39.
198 Ibid., 18–20.
199 Lantzer, *Mainline Christianity*, 89.
200 Pew Research Center. *2014 Religious Landscape Study*, http://www.pew-forum.org/2015/05/12/americas-changing-religious-landscape/. Accessed 17 October 2016.
201 For example, Miller, *Reinventing American* Protestantism; Pew, *2014 Religious Landscape Study*; Stephen Ellingson, *The Megachurch and the Mainline: Remaking Religious Tradition in the Twenty-First Century* (Chicago, IL: The University of Chicago Press, 2007).
202 Salomon, "The Marketization," 26.
203 For example, Sarah E. Dempsey and Matthew L. Sanders, "Meaningful Work? Nonprofit Marketization and Work/life Imbalance in Popular Autobiographies of Social Entrepreneurship," *Organization* 17, no. 4 (2010): 437–59; Sanders, "Theorizing Nonprofit Organizations."
204 Ashley and Sandefer, "Neoliberalism and the Privatization," 109; for a more detailed discussion, see Robert Wuthnow, *Saving America? Faith-based Services and the Future of Civil Society* (Princeton, NJ: Princeton University Press, 2006).
205 Lantzer, *Mainline Christianity*, 89.
206 For example, Nancy T. Ammerman, "Connecting Mainline Protestant Churches with Public Life," in *The Quiet Hand of God: Faith-Based Activism and the Public Role of Mainline Protestantism*, eds. Robert Wuthnow and John H. Evans (Berkeley: University of California Press, 2002), 132–6.
207 Moberg, "Understanding Religious-Organizational;" for similar observations in the German context, see Schlamelcher, "The Decline of the Parishes."
208 Fairclough, *Discourse and Social*.

209 Michel Foucault, *Discipline and Punish: The Birth of the Prison* (Harmondsworth: Penguin, 1979).
210 Fairclough, *Critical Discourse*, 88.
211 Ibid.
212 Ibid., 139.
213 Fairclough, *Discourse and Social*, 215.
214 Fairclough, *Critical Discourse*, 138.
215 Fairclough, *Discourse and Social*, 126.
216 Fairclough, *Critical Discourse*, 126.
217 Fairclough, *Language and Power*, 212.
218 Fairclough, *Discourse and Social*, 137.
219 Ibid., 215–16; Fairclough, *Critical Discourse*, 138.
220 Grant and Hardy, "Introduction," 8; Rick Iedema and Ruth Wodak, "Introduction: Organizational Discourses and Practices," *Discourse and Society* 10, no. 1 (1999): 11.
221 Fairclough, *Critical Discourse*, 79, emphases added.
222 UMCa, "Church Marketing Plan Tool." https://www.resourceumc.org/en/content/church-marketing-plan-tool. Accessed 20 February 2021.
223 TEC, *Marketing Your Parish: Advertising Best Practices for Effective Evangelism* (New York: Office of Communication of the Episcopal Church, 2013), 1. http://episcopaldigitalnetwork.com/wp-content/uploads/2013/03/marketing-your-parish.pdf. Accessed 20 March 2020.
224 Ibid., 2.
225 For similar observations in a German context, see Schlamelcher, "The Decline of the Parishes," 55.
226 Fairclough, *Critical Discourse*, 552.
227 PCUSAc, "Mission Work Plan for 2013 to 2016" (Presbyterian Mission Agency, 2012), 1. https://www.pcusa.org/site_media/media/uploads/gamc/pdf/mwpwhomdoweserve.pdf. Accessed 24 October 2016.
228 PCUSAa, "'2013–2016 Mission Work Plan Strategy White Paper" (General Assembly Mission Council, 2012), 5. https://www.pcusa.org/site_media/media/uploads/gamc/pdf/strategy_white_paper_2013_2016_strategy_5_15_12.pdf. Accessed 24 October 2016.
229 PCUSAb, "General Assembly Mission Council Mission Work Plan 2013–2016" (Mission Agency Board, 2016), 3. https://www.pcusa.org/site_media/media/uploads/presbyterian_mission_agency/pdf/business_items_2016/february/action_information_items/h.105_2017-2018_mission_work_plan_revised_02.01.16.pdf. Accessed 23 November 2020.
230 Richard P. Chait, William P. Ryan, and Barbara E. Taylor, *Governance as Leadership: Reframing the Work of Nonprofit Boards* (Hoboken, NJ: John Wiley & Sons, 2004).
231 ABCUSA. "United Baptist Church: Governance tasks" (compiled by Dr. C. Jeff Woods, 2012), 1. www.abc-usa.org/wp-content/uploads/2012/06/Governance-Short.doc. Accessed 1 March 2019.
232 UCC, *A Vision: The Transformative United Church of Christ in Ten Years* (Strategic Visioning Task Force, 2017), 4. https://www.uccfiles.com/pdf/UCC-Strategic-Vision-Report-March-2017.pdf. Accessed 21 March 2020.
233 Fairclough, *Critical Discourse*, 138.
234 For a broader discussion of this aspect of organizations, see for example, Bauman and May, *Thinking Sociologically*, 65.
235 Ibid., 139.
236 Ibid., 138.

212 *Religion in market society*

237 Boltanski and Chiapello, *The New Spirit*, 105.

238 Ibid., 73,

239 Fairclough, *Critical Discourse*, 283.

240 ECLA, Mission Advancement Unit. https://www.elca.org/About/Churchwide/Mission-Advancement. Accessed 21 March 2020.

241 UCC, Task Force Identifies Future Priorities for UCC Focus. https://www.ucc.org/news_task_force_identifies_future_priorities_for_ucc_focus_03142017. Accessed 21 March 2020.

242 UMCb, Marketing and Public Relations. http://www.umcom.org/about/marketing-and-public-relations. Accessed 21 March 2020.

243 TEC, "Jake Dell named Episcopal Church Office of Communication Advertising and Marketing Senior Manager." https://episcopalchurch.org/posts/publicaffairs/jake-dell-named-episcopal-church-office-communication-advertising-and-marketing. Accessed 21 March 2020.

244 DOC, "Church Extension Selects New Marketing Person." https://disciples.org/uncategorized/church-extension-selects-new-marketing-person/. Accessed 21 March 2020.

245 Cf. Mara Einstein, "From Static to Social. Marketing Religion in the Age of the Internet," *Sociologica* 3 (September–December, 2014), 1–14.

246 Cf. Schillemans, *Mediatization*, 87.

247 Ibid. The concept of "amalgamation is adapted from Schillemans' work on organizational mediatization.

248 UMCc, "Strategy & Implementation." https://www.resourceumc.org/en/content/church-marketing-plan-tool-phase-2-4. Accessed 25 November 2020.

249 hopepmt.org. 2018. "New Church Ministry." https://www.hopepmt.org/plant/. Accessed 21 March 2020.

250 Cf. Schillemans, *Mediatization*, 87.

251 Moberg, *Church, Market*.

252 Slater and Tonkiss, *Market Society*, 194.

Bibliography

ABCUSA. "United Baptist Church: Governance Tasks," compiled by Dr. C. Jeff Woods, 2012. www.abc-usa.org/wp-content/uploads/2012/06/Governance-Short.doc. Accessed 1 March 2019.

Adams, Matthew. *Self and Social Change*. London: Sage, 2007.

Adeboye, Olufunke. "Pentecostal Challenges in Africa and Latin America: A Comparative Focus on Nigeria and Brazil." *Afrika Zamani: Annual Journal of African History*, no. 11–12 (2003): 136–59.

Alexander, Andie R., and Russell T. McCutcheon. "I'm Spiritual but Not Religious." In *Stereotyping Religion: Critiquing Clichés*, edited by Brad Stoddard and Craig Martin, 97–112. London: Bloomsbury Academic, 2017.

Alles, Gregory D.. "Religious Economies and Rational Choice: On Rodney Stark and Roger Finke, *Acts of Faith* (2000)." In *Contemporary Theories of Religion: A Critical Companion*, edited by Michael Stausberg, 83–98. Oxon: Routledge, 2009.

Ammerman, Nancy T. "Connecting Mainline Protestant Churches with Public Life." In *The Quiet Hand of God: Faith-Based Activism and the Public Role of Mainline Protestantism*, edited by Robert Wuthnow and John H. Evans, 129–58. Berkeley: University of California Press, 2002.

Arnal, William E., and Russell T. McCutcheon. *The Sacred Is the Profane: The Political Nature of Religion*. Oxford: Oxford University Press, 2013.

Arnett, Jeffrey Jensen, and Susan Taber. "Adolescence Terminable and Interminable: When Does Adolescence End?" *Journal of Youth and Adolescence* 23, no. 5 (1993): 517–37.

Årsheim, Helge. "Whose Religion, What Freedom? Discursive Constructions of Religion in the Work of UN Special Rapporteurs on the Freedom of Religion or Belief." In *Making Religion: Theory and Practice in the Discursive Study of Religion*, edited by Kocku von Stuckrad and Frans Wijsen, 287–316. Leiden: Brill, 2016.

Arvidsson, Adam. *Brands: Meaning and Value in Media Culture*. Oxon: Routledge, 2006.

Asad, Talal. *Formations of the Secular: Christianity, Islam, Modernity*. Redwood City, CA: Stanford University Press, 2003.

Asad, Talal. *Genealogies of Religion: Discipline and Reasons of Power in Christianity and Islam*. Baltimore, MD: The Johns Hopkins University Press, 1993.

Ashley, David, and Ryan Sandefer. "Neoliberalism and the Privatization of Welfare and Religious Organizations in the United States of America." In *Religion in the Neoliberal Age: Political Economy and Modes of Governance*, edited by Tuomas Martikainen and François Gauthier, 109–28. Farnham: Ashgate, 2013.

214 Bibliography

Barkun, Michael. *A Culture of Conspiracy: Apocalyptic Vision in Contemporary America*. Berkeley: University of California Press, 2003.

Baudrillard, Jean. *Simulacra and Simulation*. Ann Arbor: The University of Michigan Press, 1981.

Bauman, Zygmunt. *The Individualized Society*. Cambridge: Polity Press, 2001.

Bauman, Zygmunt, and Tim May. *Thinking Sociologically*, Second edition. Malden, MA: Blackwell Publishing, 2001.

Beaumont, Justin, and Klaus Eder. "Concepts, Processes, and Antagonisms of Postsecularity." In *The Routledge Handbook to Postsecularity*, edited by Justin Beaumont, 3–24. Oxon: Routledge, 2019.

Beck, Ulrich. *A God of Ones' Own: Religion's Capacity for Peace and Potential for Violence*. Cambridge: Polity Press, 2010.

Beck, Ulrich, and Elisabeth Beck-Gernsheim. *Individualization: Institutionalized Individualism and Its Social and Political Consequences*. London: Sage, 2002.

Becker, Gary. *The Economic Approach to Human Behavior*. Chicago, IL: Chicago University Press, 1976.

Beckford, James A. "Public Religions and the Postsecular: Critical Reflections." *Journal for the Scientific Study of Religion* 5, no. 1 (2012): 1–19.

Beckford, James A. "The Return of Public Religion: A Critical Assessment of a Popular Claim." *Nordic Journal of Religion and Society* 23, no. 2 (2010): 121–36.

Beckford, James A. *Social Theory & Religion*. Cambridge, Cambridge University Press, 2003.

Beckford, James A. "Religious Organizations." In *The Sacred in a Secular Age*, edited by P. E. Hammond, 125–38. The Hague: Mouton, 1985.

Belk, Russell W. "Commodification as Part of Marketization." In *Marketization: Theory and Evidence from Emerging Economies*, edited by Himadri Roy Chaudhuri and Russell W. Belk, 31–72. Singapore: Springer Nature Singapore Pte Ltd., 2020.

Bell, Daniel. *The Coming of Post-Industrial Society: A Venture in Social Forecasting*. New York: Basic Books, 1976.

Bellah, Robert N., Richard Madsen, William S. Sullivan, Ann Swidler, and Steven M. Tipton. *Habits of the Heart: Individualism and Commitment in American Life*. Berkeley: University of California Press, 2008 [1985].

Bender, Courtney, Wendy Cadge, Peggy Levitt, and David Smilde. "Religion on the Edge: De-Centering and Re-Centering." In *Religion on the Edge: De-Centering and Re-Centering the Sociology of Religion*, edited by Courtney Bender, Wendy Cadge, Peggy Levitt, and David Smilde, 1–22. Oxford: Oxford University Press, 2012.

Bengtson, Vern, Cassey E. Copen, Norella M. Putney, and Merril Silverstein. "Longitudinal Study of the Intergenerational Transmission of Religion." *International Sociology* 24, no. 3 (2009): 325–45.

Benhabib, Seyla. *Situating the Self: Gender, Community and Postmodernism in Contemporary Ethics*. Cambridge: Polity Press, 1992.

Berger, Peter L. *Heretical Imperative: Contemporary Possibilities of Religious Affirmation*. New York: Doubleday, 1980.

Berger, Peter L. *The Sacred Canopy: Elements of a Sociological Theory of Religion*. Garden City, NY: Doubleday, 1967.

Berger, Peter L., Grace Davie, and Effie Fokas. *Religious America, Secular Europe?: A Theme and Variations*. Aldershot: Ashgate, 2008.

Berger, Peter L., and Thomas Luckmann. *The Social Construction of Reality: A Treatise in the Sociology of Knowledge*. Harmondsworth: Penguin, 1966.

Beyer, Peter. "Religion in Global Civil Society." In *Religion in Global Civil Society*, edited by Mark Juergensmeyer, 11–22. Oxford: Oxford University Press, 2006.

Beyer, Peter. *Religions in Global Society*. Oxon: Routledge, 2006.

Blyth, Mark. *Great Transformations: Economic Ideas and Institutional Change in the Twentieth Century*. Cambridge: Cambridge University Press, 2002.

Boltanski, Luc, and Eve Chiapello. *The New Spirit of Capitalism*. London: Verso, 2005.

Braun-Poppelaars, Caelesta, and Marcel Hanegraaff. "Conceptualizing Religious Advocacy: Religious Interest Groups and the Process of Public Policy Making." In *Religious Actors in the Public Sphere: Means, Objectives, and Effects*, edited by Jeffrey Haynes and Anja Hennig, 132–48. Oxon: Routledge, 2011.

Brown, Steven R. "A Primer on Q Methodology." *Operant Subjectivity* 16, no. 3–4 (1993): 91–138.

Bruce, Ian, and Celine Chew. "Debate: The Marketization of the Voluntary Sector." *Public Money and Management* 31, no. 3 (2011): 155–7.

Bruce, Steve. "Authority and Freedom: Economics and Secularization." In *Religions as Brands: New Perspectives on the Marketization of Religion and Spirituality*, edited by Jörg Stolz and Jean-Claude Usunier, 189–204. Farnham: Ashgate, 2014.

Bruce, Steve. *God Is Dead: Secularization in the West*. Oxford: Blackwell Publishing, 2002.

Bullimore, Matt. "Redeeming the Secular." In *The Routledge Handbook to Postsecularity*, edited by Justin Beaumont, 137–52. Oxon: Routledge, 2019.

Burr, Vivien. *Social Constructionism*. London: Routledge, 2003.

Cahn, Michael. "The Rhetoric of Rhetoric: Six Tropes of Disciplinary Self-Constitution." In *The Recovery of Rhetoric: Persuasive Discourse and Disciplinarity in the Human Sciences*, edited by R. H. Roberts and J. M. M. Good, 61–84. Charlottesville: University Press of Virginia, 1993.

Calhoun, Craig. "Time, World, and Secularism." In *The Post-Secular in Question: Religion in Contemporary Society*, edited by Philip S. Gorski, David Kyuman Kim, John Torpey, and Jonathan VanAntwerpen, 335–64. New York: New York University Press, 2012.

Calhoun, Craig. "Secularism, Citizenship, and the Public Sphere." In *Rethinking Secularism*, edited by Craig Calhoun, Mark Juergensmeyer, and Jonathan VanAntwerpen, 75–91. Oxford: Oxford University Press, 2011.

Calhoun, Craig, Eduardo Mendieta, and Jonathan VanAntwerpen. "Editor's Introduction." In *Habermas and Religion*, edited by Craig Calhoun, Eduardo Mendieta, and Jonathan VanAntwerpen, 1–26. Cambridge: Polity Press, 2013.

Calhoun, Craig, Eduardo Mendieta, and Jonathan VanAntwerpen, eds. *Habermas and Religion*. Cambridge: Polity Press, 2013.

Calhoun, Craig, Mark Juergensmeyer, and Jonathan VanAntwerpen. "Introduction." In *Rethinking Secularism*, edited by Craig Calhoun, Mark Juergensmeyer, and Jonathan VanAntwerpen, 3–30. Oxford: Oxford University Press, 2011.

Campbell, Colin. "The Cult, the Cultic Milieu and Secularization." In *A Sociological Yearbook of Religion in Britain 5*, edited by Michael Hill, 119–136. London: SCM Press, 1972.

216 Bibliography

Carabine, Jean. "Unmarried Motherhood 1830–1990: A Genealogical Analysis." In *Discourse as Data: A Guide for Analysis*, edited by Margaret Wetherell, Stephanie Taylor, and Simeon J. Yates, 267–310. London: Sage, 2001.

Carrette, Jeremy, and Richard King. *Selling Spirituality: The Silent Takeover of Religion*. London: Routledge, 2005.

Carrier, James G. "Preface." In *Meanings of the Market: The Free Market in Western Culture*, edited by James G. Carrier, vii–xvi. Oxford: Berg, 1997.

Carta, Giuseppe. "Islamophobia, Apophatic Pluralism, and Imagination." In *The Routledge Handbook to Postsecularity*, edited by Justin Beaumont, 325–35. Oxon: Routledge, 2019.

Casanova, José. "Exploring the Postsecular: Three Meanings of 'the Secular' and Their Possible Transcendence." In *Habermas and Religion*, edited by Craig Calhoun, Eduardo Mendieta, and Jonathan VanAntwerpen, 27–48. Cambridge: Polity Press, 2013.

Casanova, José. "The Secular, Secularizations, Secularisms." In *Rethinking Secularism*, edited by Craig Calhoun, Mark Juergensmeyer, and Jonathan VanAntwerpen, 54–74. Oxford: Oxford University Press, 2011.

Casanova, José. "A Secular Age: Dawn or Twilight?" In *Varieties of Secularism in a Secular Age*, edited by Michael Warner, Jonathan VanAntwerpen, and Craig Calhoun, 265–81. Cambridge, MA: Harvard University Press, 2010.

Casanova, José. *Public Religions in the Modern World*. Chicago, IL: University of Chicago Press, 1994.

Chait, Richard P., William P. Ryan, and Barbara E. Taylor. *Governance as Leadership: Reframing the Work of Nonprofit Boards*. Hoboken, NJ: John Wiley & Sons, 2004.

Chao, L. Luke, and Fengang Yang. "Measuring Religiosity in a Religiously Diverse Society: The China Case." *Social Science Research* 74 (August 2018): 187–91.

Chaves, Mark. "Denominations as Dual Structures: An Organizational Analysis." *Sociology of Religion* 54, no. 2 (1993): 147–69.

Chiapello, Eve, and Norman Fairclough. "Understanding the New Management Ideology: A Transdisciplinary Contribution from Critical Discourse Analysis and New Sociology of Capitalism." *Discourse & Society* 13, no. 2 (2002): 185–208.

Chidester, David. *Empire of Religion: Imperialism and Comparative Religion*. Chicago, IL: University of Chicago Press, 2014.

Chidester, David. *Savage Systems: Colonialism and Comparative Religion in Southern Africa*. Charlottesville: University of Virginia Press, 1996.

Chouliaraki, Lilie, and Norman Fairclough. *Discourse in Late Modernity: Rethinking Critical Discourse Analysis*. Edinburgh: Edinburgh University Press, 1999.

Cladis, Mark S. "Beyond Solidarity? Durkheim and Twenty-First Century Democracy in a Global Age." In *The Cambridge Companion to Durkheim*, edited by Jeffrey Alexander and Phillip Smith, 383–409. Cambridge: Cambridge University Press, 2005.

Coleman, Stephen, and Karen Ross. *The Media and the Public: "Them" and "Us" in Media Discourse*. Chichester: John Wiley & Sons Ltd., 2010.

Collins, P. "Performative Utterances." In *Concise Encyclopedia of Language and Religion*, edited by John F. Sawyer and J. M. Y. Simpson, 277–8. Oxford: Elsevier, 2001.

Bibliography 217

Cooren, François. *Organizational Discourse: Communication and Constitution.* Cambridge: Polity Press, 2015.

Cotter, Christopher R. *The Critical Study of Non-Religion: Discourse, Identification and Locality.* London: Bloomsbury Academic, 2020.

Davie, Grace. *Religion in Britain: A Persistent Paradox.* Malden, MA: Blackwell Publishers, 2015.

Davie, Grace. "Resacralization." In *The New Blackwell Companion to the Sociology of Religion*, edited by Bryan S. Turner, 160–78. Chichester: Blackwell, 2010.

Davie, Grace. *The Sociology of Religion.* London: Sage, 2007.

Davie, Grace. *Europe: The Exceptional Case: Parameters of Faith in the Modern World.* London: Darton, Longman and Todd, 2002.

de Vries, Hent. "Global Religion and the Postsecular Challenge." In *Habermas and Religion*, edited by Craig Calhoun, Eduardo Mendieta, and Jonathan VanAntwerpen, 203–29. Cambridge: Polity Press, 2013.

De Vriese, Herbert, and Guido Vansheewijck. "The Performative Force of the Postsecular." In *The Routledge Handbook to Postsecularity*, edited by Justin Beaumont, 87–97. Oxon: Routledge, 2019.

Demerath III, N. J., Peter Dobkin Hall, Terry Schmitt, and Rhys H. Williams, eds. *Sacred Companies: Organizational Aspects of Religion and Religious Aspects of Organizations.* New York: Oxford University Press, 1998.

Dempsey, Sarah E., and Matthew L. Sanders. "Meaningful Work? Nonprofit Marketization and Work/Life Imbalance in Popular Autobiographies of Social Entrepreneurship." *Organization* 17, no. 4 (2010): 437–59.

Dillon, Michele. "Jürgen Habermas and the Post-Secular Appropriation of Religion: A Sociological Critique." In *The Post-Secular in Question: Religion in Contemporary Society*, edited by Philip S. Gorski, David Kyuman Kim, John Torpey, and Jonathan VanAntwerpen, 249–78. New York: New York University Press, 2012.

Dillon, Michele. "Can Post-Secular Society Tolerate Religious Differences?" *Sociology of Religion* 71, no. 2 (2010): 139–56.

Djelic, Marie-Laure. "Marketization: From Intellectual Agenda to Global Policy Making." In *Transnational Governance: Institutional Dynamics of Regulation*, edited by Marie-Laure Djelic and Kerstin Sahlin-Andersson, 53–73. Cambridge: Cambridge University Press, 2006.

DOC. "Church Extension Selects New Marketing Person." https://disciples.org/uncategorized/church-extension-selects-new-marketing-person/. Accessed 21 March 2020.

Douglas, Mary, and Baron Isherwood. *The World of Goods: Towards and Anthropology of Consumption.* New York: Basic Books, 1978.

Durkheim, Émile. *The Elementary Forms of Religious Life.* New York: The Free Press, 1995 [1912].

Durkheim, Émile. *The Division of Labour in Society.* Reprinted. London: Macmillan, 1984.

Durkheim, Émile. "Individualism and the Intellectuals." In *Emile Durkheim on Morality and Society*, edited by Robert N. Bellah, 43–57. Chicago, IL: University of Chicago Press, 1973.

Dyck, Bruno, and Elden Wiebe. "Salvation, Theology and Organization Theory across the Centuries." *Organization* 19, no. 3 (2012): 52–77.

218 Bibliography

ECLA. Mission Advancement Unit. https://www.elca.org/About/Churchwide/Mission-Advancement. Accessed 21 March 2020.

Edge, Peter W. *Religion and Law: An Introduction.* Aldershot: Ashgate, 2006.

Einstein, Mara. "From Static to Social. Marketing Religion in the Age of the Internet." *Sociologica* 3 (September–December, 2014): 1–14.

Einstein, Mara. *Brands of Faith: Marketing Religion in a Commercial Age.* New York: Routledge, 2008.

Eisenstedt, Shmuel N., ed. *Multiple Modernities.* Oxon: Routledge, 2002.

Ellingson, Stephen. *The Megachurch and the Mainline: Remaking Religious Tradition in the Twenty-First Century.* Chicago, IL: The University of Chicago Press, 2007.

Engler, Steven. "Constructionism versus What?" *Religion* 34, no. 4 (2004): 293–313.

Epstein, Mikhail. "Postatheism and the Phenomenon of Minimal Religion in Russia." In *The Routledge Handbook to Postsecularity,* edited by Justin Beaumont, 73–85. Oxon: Routledge, 2019.

Fairclough, Norman. *Language and Power,* Third edition. Oxon: Routledge, 2015.

Fairclough, Norman. *Critical Discourse Analysis: The Critical Study of Language.* Oxon: Routledge, 2010.

Fairclough, Norman. "Discourse Analysis in Organization Studies: The Case for Critical Realism." *Organization Studies* 26, no. 6 (2005): 915–39.

Fairclough, Norman. "Critical Discourse Analysis and the Marketization of Public Discourse: The Universities." *Discourse and Society* 4, no. 2 (1993): 133–68.

Fairclough, Norman. *Discourse and Social Change.* Cambridge: Polity Press, 1992.

Fernández, Rafael, Sidney Castillo Carnedas, and Marcus Moberg. "The Internet, Social Media, and the Critical Interrogation of Traditional Religion among Young Adults in Peru." In *Digital Media, Young Adults and Religion: An International Perspective,* edited by Marcus Moberg and Sofia Sjö, 55–68. Oxon: Routledge, 2020.

Fitzgerald, Timothy. *Religion and Politics in International Relations: The Modern Myth.* London: Continuum, 2011.

Fitzgerald, Timothy. *Discourse on Civility and Barbarity: A Critical Theory of Religion and Related Categories.* Oxford: Oxford University Press, 2007.

Fitzgerald, Timothy. *The Ideology of Religious Studies.* Oxford: Oxford University Press, 2000.

Foucault, Michel. *Discipline and Punish: The Birth of the Prison.* Harmondsworth: Penguin, 1979.

Foucault, Michel. *The Archaeology of Knowledge.* London: Tavistock, 1972.

Fox, Jonathan. *An Introduction to Religion and Politics: Theory and Practice.* Oxon: Routledge, 2013.

Fox, Judith. "Secularization." In *The Routledge Companion to the Study of Religion,* edited by John R. Hinnells, 291–305. Oxon: Routledge, 2005.

Fuller, Robert. *Spiritual, but not Religious: Understanding Unchurched America.* Oxford: Oxford University Press, 2001.

Gauthier, François. *Religion, Modernity, Globalisation: Nation-State to Market.* Oxon: Routledge, 2020.

Gauthier, François. "From Nation-State to Market: The Transformations of Religion in the Global Era, as Illustrated by Islam." *Religion* 48, no. 3 (2018): 382–417.

Bibliography 219

Gauthier, François. "Religion, Media and the Dynamics of Consumerism in Globalising Societies." In *Religion, Media, and Social Change*, edited by Kennet Granholm, Marcus Moberg, and Sofia Sjö, 71–88. New York: Routledge, 2015.

Gauthier, François, Tuomas Martikainen, and Linda Woodhead. "Acknowledging a Global Shift: A Primer for Thinking about Religion in Consumer Societies." *Implicit Religion* 16, no. 3 (2013): 261–75.

Gauthier, François, Linda Woodhead, and Tuomas Martikainen. "Introduction: Consumerism as the Ethos of Consumer Society." In *Religion in Consumer Society: Brands, Consumers, Markets*, edited by François Gauthier and Tuomas Martikainen, 1–26. Farnham: Ashgate, 2013.

Gergen, Kenneth, J. *An Invitation to Social Construction*, Second edition. London: Sage, 2009.

Gergen, Kenneth, J. *An Invitation to Social Construction*. London: Sage, 1999.

Giddens, Anthony. *Modernity and Self-Identity: Self and Society in the Late Modern Age*. Cambridge: Polity Press, 1991.

Glass, Jennifer, Vern L. Bengtson, and Charlotte Chorn Dunham. "Attitude Similarity in Three-Generation Families: Socialization, Status Inheritance, or Reciprocal Influence?" *American Sociological Review* 51, no. 5 (1986): 685–98.

Goldstein, Warren S. "Redemptive Criticism or the Critique of Religion." In *The Routledge Handbook to Postsecularity*, edited by Justin Beaumont, 59–72. Oxon: Routledge, 2019.

Good, James M. M., and Richard H. Roberts. "Introduction: Persuasive Discourse In and Between Disciplines in the Human Sciences." In *The Recovery of Rhetoric: Persuasive Discourse and Disciplinarity in the Human Sciences*, 1–22. Charlottesville: University Press of Virginia, 1993.

Gorski, Philip S. "Historicizing the Secularization Debate: An Agenda for Research." In *Handbook of the Sociology of Religion*, edited by Michele Dillon, 110–22. Cambridge: Cambridge University Press, 2003.

Gorski, Philip S., David Kyuman Kim, John Torpey, and Jonathan VanAntwerpen, eds. *The Post-Secular in Question: Religion in Contemporary Society*. New York: New York University Press, 2012.

Gramsci, Antonio. *Selections from the Prison Notebooks*. London: Lawrence & Wishart, 1971.

Granholm, Kennet. *Dark Enlightenment: The Historical, Sociological, and Discursive Contexts of Contemporary Esoteric Magic*. Leiden: Brill, 2014.

Grant, David, and Cynthia Hardy. "Introduction: Struggles with Organizational Discourse." *Organization Studies* 25, no. 1 (2003): 5–13.

Greckhamer, Thomas. "The Stretch of Strategic Management Discourse: A Critical Analysis." *Organization Studies* 31, no. 7 (2010): 841–71.

Grusky, David B., and Gabriela Galescu, "Is Durkheim a Class Analyst?" In *The Cambridge Companion to Durkheim*, edited by Jeffrey Alexander and Philip Smith, 322–59. Cambridge: Cambridge University Press, 2005.

Habermas, Jürgen. "Reply to My Critics." In *Habermas and Religion*, edited by Craig Calhoun, Eduardo Mendieta, and Jonathan VanAntwerpen, 347–90. Cambridge: Polity Press, 2013.

Habermas, Jürgen. "An Awareness of What Is Missing." In *An Awareness of What Is Missing: Faith and Reason in a Post-Secular Age*, edited by Jürgen Harbermas, 15–23. Cambridge: Polity Press, 2010.

220 *Bibliography*

Habermas, Jürgen. "Notes on Post-Secular Society." *New Perspectives Quarterly* 25, no. 4 (2008): 17–29.

Habermas, Jürgen. "Religion in the Public Sphere." *European Journal of Philosophy* 14, no. 1 (2006): 1–25.

Habermas, Jürgen. *The Structural Transformation of the Public Sphere*. Cambridge: Polity Press, 1992 [1964].

Hackworth, Jason. "Faith, Welfare and the Formation of the Modern American Right." In *Religion in the Neoliberal Age: Political Economy and Modes of Governance*, edited by Tuomas Martikainen and François Gauthier, 91–108. Farnham: Ashgate, 2013.

Hall, Stuart. "Introduction." In *Representation: Cultural Representations and Signifying Practices*, edited by Stuart Hall, 1–12. London: Sage, 1997.

Hammond, Philip E. *Religion and Personal Autonomy: The Third Disestablishment in America*. Columbia: University of South Carolina Press, 1992.

Hansen, Morten Balle. "Marketization and Economic Performance." *Public Management Review* 12, no. 2 (2010): 255–74.

Hanson, Sharon. "The Secularisation Thesis: Talking at Cross Purposes." *Journal of Contemporary Religion* 12, no. 2 (1997): 159–79.

Harrington, Austin. "Habermas and the 'Post-Secular' Society." *European Journal of Social Theory* 10, no. 4 (2007): 543–60.

Harvey, David. *A Brief History of Neoliberalism*. Oxford: Oxford University Press, 2007.

Haynes, Jeffrey, and Anja Hennig, "Introduction." In *Religious Actors in the Public Sphere: Means, Objectives, and Effects*, edited by Jeffrey Haynes and Anja Hennig, 1–13. Oxon: Routledge, 2011.

Heather, Noel. *Religious Language and Critical Discourse Analysis: Ideology and Identity in Christian Discourse Today*. Oxford: Peter Lang, 2000.

Heelas, Paul. *Spiritualities of Life: New Age Romanticism and Consumptive Capitalism*. Oxford: Blackwell, 2008.

Heelas, Paul. *The New Age Movement: Religion, Culture and Society in the Age of Postmodernity*. London: Wiley, 1996.

Heelas, Paul, Linda Woodhead, with Benjamin Seel, Bronislaw Szerszynski, and Karin Tusting. *The Spiritual Revolution: Why Religion Is Giving Way to Spirituality*. Oxford: Blackwell, 2005.

Hermann, Adrian. "Distinctions of Religion: The Search for Equivalents of 'Religion' and the Challenge of Theorizing a 'Global Discourse of Religion'." In *Making Religion: Theory and Practice in the Discursive Study of Religion*, edited by Frans Wijsen and Kocku von Stuckrad, 97–124. Leiden: Brill, 2016.

Hibberd, Fiona J. *Unfolding Social Constructionism*. New York: Springer, 2005.

Hinings, C. R., and Mia Raynard. "Organizational Form, Structure, and Religious Organizations." In *Religion and Organization Theory*, Research in the Sociology of Organizations vol. 41, edited by Paul Tracey, Nelson Phillips, and Michael Lounsbury, 159–86. Bingley: Emerald Publishing Group, 2014.

Hjelm, Titus. "Mapping the Discursive Study of Religion." *Journal of the American Academy of Religion* 88, no. 4 (2020): 1002–25.

Hjelm, Titus. "One Volk, One Church? A Critique of the 'Folk Church' Ideology in Finland." *Journal of Church and State* 62, no. 2 (2019): 294–315.

Hjelm, Titus. "Theory and Method in Critical Discursive Study of Religion: An Outline." In *Making Religion: Theory and Practice in the Discursive Study of Religion*, edited by Kocku von Stuckrad and Frans Wijsen, 15–34. Leiden: Brill, 2016.

Hjelm, Titus. "National Piety: Religious Equality, Freedom of Religion and National Identity in Finnish Political Discourse." *Religion* 44, no. 1 (2014): 28–45.

Hjelm, Titus. "Understanding the New Visibility of Religion." *Journal of Religion in Europe* 7, no. 3–4 (2014): 203–22.

Hjelm, Titus. "Religion, Discourse and Power: A Contribution towards a Critical Sociology of Religion." *Critical Sociology* 40, no. 6 (2013): 855–72.

Hjelm, Titus, "Discourse Analysis." In *The Routledge Handbook of Research Methods in the Study of Religion*, edited by Michael Stausberg and Steven Engler, 134–50. London: Routledge, 2011.

hopepmt.org. 2018. "New Church Ministry." https://www.hopepmt.org/plant/. Accessed 21 March 2020.

Horii, Mitsutoshi. "Critical Reflections on the Category of 'Religion' in Contemporary Sociological Discourse." *Nordic Journal of Religion and Society* 28, no. 1 (2015): 21–36.

Iedema, Rick. *Discourses of Post-Bureaucratic Organization.* Philadelphia, PA: John Benjamins Publishing Company, 2003.

Iedema, Rick, and Ruth Wodak. "Introduction: Organizational Discourses and Practices." *Discourse and Society* 10, no. 1 (1999): 5–19.

James, William. *The Varieties of Religious Experience*, Centenary edition. Oxon: Routledge, [1902] 2002.

Joas, Hans. *The Sacredness of the Person: A New Genealogy of Human Rights.* Washington, DC: Georgetown University Press, 2013.

Johnson, Doyle Paul. "The Theoretical Trajectory." In *American Sociology of Religion*, edited by Anthony J. Blasi, 43–86. Leiden: Brill, 2007.

Jørgensen, Marianne, and Louise Phillips. *Discourse Analysis as Theory and Method.* London: Sage, 2002.

Kemp, Daren, and James R. Lewis, eds. *Handbook of New Age.* Leiden: Brill, 2007.

Kippenberg, Hans G. "Dynamics of the Human Rights Discourse on Freedom of Religion – Observed from the Religious Studies Angle." In *Discourse Research and Religion: Disciplinary Use and Interdisciplinary Dialogues*, edited by Jay Johnston and Kocku von Stuckrad, 169–81. Berlin: De Gruyter, 2021.

Kitiarsa, Pattana. "Towards a Sociology of Religious Commodification." In *The New Blackwell Companion to the Sociology of Religion*, edited by Bryan S. Turner, 563–83. Chichester: Blackwell, 2010.

Knott, Kim. "The Secular Sacred: In between or Both/And?" In *Social Identities between the Sacred and the Secular*, edited by Abby Day, Giselle Vincent, and Christopher R. Cotter, 146–60. Farnham: Ashgate, 2013.

Knott, Kim. "Cutting through the Postsecular City: A Spatial Interrogation." In *Exploring the Postsecular: The Religious, the Political and the Urban*, edited by Arie L. Molendijk, Justin Beaumont, and Christopher Jedan, 19–38. Leiden: Brill, 2010.

Kohnen, Thomas. "Religious Discourse." In *Historical Pragmatics*, edited by Andreas H. Jucker and Irma Taavitsainen, 523–47. Berlin: de Gruyter, 2010.

Köhrsen, Jens. "How Religious Is the Public Sphere? A Critical Stance on the Debate about Public Religion and Post-Secularity." *Acta Sociologica* 55, no. 3 (2012): 273–88.

Kong, Lily, and Junxi Qian. "Dialogue with Religious Life in Asia." In *The Routledge Handbook to Postsecularity*, edited by Justin Beaumont, 258–68. Oxon: Routledge, 2019.

222 Bibliography

Kontala, Janne. *Emerging Non-religious Worldview Prototypes: A Faith Q-Sort Study on Finnish Group-Affiliates.* Åbo: Åbo Akademi University Press, 2016.

Kornberger, Martin. *Brand Society: How Brands Transform Management and Lifestyle.* Cambridge: Cambridge University Press, 2010.

Laclau, Ernesto, and Chantal Mouffe. *Hegemony and Socialist Strategy: Towards a Radical Democratic Politics.* London: Verso, 1985.

Lantzer, Jason S. *Mainline Christianity: The Past and Future of America's Majority Faiths.* New York: New York University Press, 2012.

Lasch, Christopher. *Culture of Narcissism: American Life in an Age of Diminishing Expectations.* New York: W.W. Norton & Company, 1979.

Lash, Scott. *Reflexive Modernization: Politics, Tradition and Aesthetics in the Modern Social Order.* Chicago, IL: University of Chicago Press, 1995.

Lau, Kimberly. *New Age Capitalism: Making Money East of Eden.* Philadelphia: University of Pennsylvania Press, 2000.

Leezenberg, Michiel. "Postsecularism, Reason, and Violence." In *The Routledge Handbook to Postsecularity,* edited by Justin Beaumont, 98–110. Oxon: Routledge, 2019.

Lévi-Strauss, Claude. *The Elementary Structures of Kinship.* 1949. Reprinted. Boston, MA: Beacon Press, 1969.

Lewis, James R. "Legitimating Suicide: Heaven's Gate and New Age Ideology." In *UFO-Religions,* edited by Christopher Partridge, 103–28. London: Routledge, 2003.

Lincoln, Bruce. *Gods and Demons, Priests and Scholars: Critical Explorations in the History of Religions.* Chicago, IL: Chicago University Press, 2012.

Lincoln, Bruce. *Holy Terrors: Thinking about Religion after September 11.* Chicago, IL: University of Chicago Press, 2003.

Liu, Lydia H. *Translingual Practice: Literature, National Culture, and Translated Modernity; China, 1900–1937.* Stanford, CA: Stanford University Press, 1995.

LoRusso, James Dennis. "Everyone Has a Faith." In *Stereotyping Religion: Critiquing Clichés,* edited by Brad Stoddard and Craig Martin, 131–46. London: Bloomsbury Academic, 2017.

LoRusso, James Dennis. *Spirituality, Corporate Culture, and American Business: The Neoliberal Ethic and the Spirit of Global Capital.* London: Bloomsbury Academic, 2017.

Lövheim, Mia. "Religion, Mediatization, and 'Complementary Learning Processes' in Swedish Editorials." *Journal of Religion in Europe* 19, no. 4 (2017): 366–83.

Lövheim, Mia, and Marta Axner. "Mediatised Religion and Public Spheres: Current Approaches and New Questions." In *Religion, Media, and Social Change,* edited by Kennet Granholm, Marcus Moberg, and Sofia Sjö, 38–53. New York: Routledge, 2015.

Luckmann, Thomas. *The Invisible Religion: The Problem of Religion in Modern Society.* Basingstoke: MacMillan, 1967.

Lury, Celia. *Consumer Culture.* Oxford: Polity Press, 2011.

Lynch, Gordon. *On the Sacred.* Durham, NC: Acumen, 2012.

Lyotard, Jean-François. *The Postmodern Condition: A Report on Knowledge.* Manchester: Manchester University Press, 1986.

Maccoby, Eleanor. "Historical Overview of Socialization Research and Theory." In *Handbook of Socialization: Theory and Research,* edited by Joan E. Crusec and Paul D. Hastings, 13–41. New York: The Guilford Press, 2014.

Bibliography 223

Mack, Burton L. *Myth and the Christian Nation: A Social Theory of Religion*. Oxon: Routledge, 2014.

Maddox, Marion. "'In the Goofy Parking Lot': Growth Churches as a Novel Religious Form for Late Capitalism." *Social Compass* 59, no. 2 (2012): 146–58.

Maingueneau, Dominique. "Religious Discourse and Its Modules." In *Discourse Research and Religion: Disciplinary Use and Interdisciplinary Dialogues*, edited by Jay Johnston and Kocku von Stuckrad, 57–75. Berlin: De Gruyter, 2021.

Manza, Jeff, and Clem Brooks. "The Changing Political Fortunes of Mainline Protestants." In *The Quiet Hand of God: Faith-Based Activism and the Public Role of Mainline Protestantism*, edited by Robert Wuthnow and John H. Evans, 159–79. Berkeley: University of California Press, 2002.

Martikainen, Tuomas. "Towards a New Political Economy of Religion: Reflections on Marion Maddox and Nicolas de Bremond d'Ars." *Social Compass* 59, no. 2 (2012): 173–82.

Martikainen, Tuomas, François Gauthier, and Linda Woodhead. "Introduction: Religion in Market Society." In *Religion in the Neoliberal Age: Political Economy and Modes of Governance*, edited by Tuomas Martikainen and François Gauthier, 1–20. Farnham: Ashgate, 2013.

Martin, David. *On Secularization: Towards a Revised General Theory*. Hampshire: Ashgate, 2005.

Martin, David. *The Religious and the Secular*. London: Routledge & Kegan Paul, 1969.

Marx, Karl. *Capital: A Critique of Political Economy*. Reprinted. New York: Dover Publications, 2011 [1867].

Masuzawa, Tomoko. *The Invention of World Religions: On How European Universalism Was Preserved in the Language of Pluralism*. Chicago, IL: Chicago University Press, 2005.

Matheson, Donald. *Media Discourses: Analyzing Media Texts*. Maidenhead: Open University Press, 2005.

Matuštík, Martin Beck. "The Difficulty of Unforgiving." In *The Routledge Handbook to Postsecularity*, edited by Justin Beaumont, 38–50. Oxon: Routledge, 2019.

Mauss, Marcel. *The Gift: The Form and Reason for Exchange in Archaic Societies*. 1925. Reprinted. New York: Norton, 1990.

Mautner, Gerlinde. *Language and the Market Society: Critical Reflections on Discourse and Dominance*. New York: Routledge 2010.

McCarthy, Thomas. "The Burdens of Modernized Faith and Postmetaphysical Reason in Habermas' 'Unfinished Project of Enlightenment'." In *Habermas and Religion*, edited by Craig Calhoun, Eduardo Mendieta, and Jonathan VanAntwerpen, 115–31. Cambridge: Polity Press, 2013.

McCleary, Rachel M., ed. *The Oxford Handbook of the Economics of Religion*. Oxford: Oxford University Press, 2011.

McCloud, Sean. "Religions Are Belief Systems." In *Stereotyping Religion: Critiquing Clichés*, edited by Brad Stoddard and Craig Martin, 11–22. London: Bloomsbury Academic, 2017.

McKinnon, Andrew M. "Ideology and the Market Metaphor in Rational Choice Theory of Religion: A Rhetorical Critique of 'Religious Economies'." *Critical Sociology* 39, no. 4 (2013): 529–43.

McLaughlin, Kathleen, Stephen P. Osborne, and Ewan Ferlie, eds. *New Public Management: Current Trends and Future Prospects*. London: Routledge, 2002.

224 Bibliography

McLeod, Hugh. *The Religious Crisis of the 1960s*. Oxford: Oxford University Press, 2007.

Mendieta, Eduardo. "Appendix: Religion in Habermas' Work." In *Habermas and Religion*, edited by Craig Calhoun, Eduardo Mendieta, and Jonathan VanAntwerpen, 391–407. Cambridge: Polity Press, 2013.

Mendieta, Eduardo. "The Postsecular Condition and Genealogy of Postmetaphysical Thinking." In *The Routledge Handbook to Postsecularity*, edited by Justin Beaumont, 51–8. Oxon: Routledge, 2019.

Miller, Donald E. *Reinventing American Protestantism: Christianity in the New Millennium*. Berkeley: University of California Press, 1997.

Miller, Vincent J. *Consuming Religion: Christian Faith and Practice in a Consumer Culture*. New York: Continuum, 2008.

Moberg, Marcus. "Understanding Religious-Organizational Marketization: The Case of the United States Mainline." *Journal of the American Academy of Religion*, forthcoming 2021.

Moberg, Marcus. "Christian Churches' Responses to Marketization: Comparing Institutional and Non-denominational Discourse." In *Routledge International Handbook of Religion in Global Society*, edited by Jayeel Serrano Cornelio, François Gauthier, Tuomas Martikainen, and Linda Woodhead, 19–30. Oxon: Routledge, 2020.

Moberg, Marcus. "Studying Change in Religious Organizations: A Discourse-Centered Framework." *Method & Theory in the Study of Religion* 32, no. 2 (2020): 89–114.

Moberg, Marcus. *Church, Market, and Media: A Discursive Approach to Institutional Religious Change*. London: Bloomsbury Academic, 2017.

Moberg, Marcus. 'First-, Second-, and Third-Level Discourse Analytic Approaches in the Study of Religion: Moving from Meta-Theoretical Reflection to Implementation in Practice." *Religion* 43, no. 1 (2013): 4–25.

Moberg, Marcus, and Tuomas Martikainen, "Religious Change in Market and Consumer Society: The Current State of the Field and New Ways Forward." *Religion* 48, no. 3 (2018): 418–35.

Moberg, Marcus and Sofia Sjö, eds. *Digital Media, Young Adults and Religion: An International Perspective*. Oxon: Routledge, 2020.

Moberg Marcus, and Sofia Sjö. "Mass-Mediated Popular Culture and Religious Socialisation." In *Religion, Media, and Social Change*, edited by Kennet Granholm, Marcus Moberg, and Sofia Sjö, 91–109. New York: Routledge, 2015.

Molendijk, Arie L., Justin Beaumont, and Christopher Jedan, eds. *Exploring the Postsecular: The Religious, the Political and the Urban*. Leiden: Brill, 2010.

Murphy, Tim. "Discourse." In *Guide to the Study Religion*, edited by Willi Braun and Russell T. McCutcheon, 396–408. London: Cassell, 2000.

Narkowicz, Kasia, and Richard Phillips. "After or Against Secularism: Muslims in Europe." In *The Routledge Handbook to Postsecularity*, edited by Justin Beaumont, 349–59. Oxon: Routledge, 2019.

Nawratek, Krzysztof. "Architecture of Radicalized Postsecularism." In *The Routledge Handbook to Postsecularity*, edited by Justin Beaumont, 315–24. Oxon: Routledge, 2019.

Nynäs, Peter, Ariela Keysar, Janne Kontala, Ben-Willie Kwaku Golo, Mika Lassander, Marat Shterin, Sofia Sj, and Paul Stenner, eds. *The Diversity of Worldviews among Young Adults: Contemporary (Non)Religiosity and Spirituality*

Bibliography 225

through the Lens of an International Mixed Method Study. New York: Springer, 2021.

Nynäs, Peter, Mika Lassander, and Terhi Utriainen, eds. *Post-Secular Society.* Brunswick, NJ: Transaction Publishers, 2012.

Paden, William E. "Sacred Order." *Method & Theory in the Study of Religion* 12, no. 1 (2000): 207–25.

Parmaksız, Umut. "Beyond Salvaging Solidarity." In *The Routledge Handbook to Postsecularity,* edited by Justin Beaumont, 280–91. Oxon: Routledge, 2019.

Partridge, Christopher. *The Re-Enchantment of the West (Vol. 1): Understanding Popular Occulture.* London: Continuum, 2004.

Passas, Nikos. "The Market for Gods and Services: Religion, Commerce, and Deviance." In *Between Sacred and Secular: Research and Theory on Quasi-Religion.* Religion and the Social Order, vol. 4, edited by Arthur L. Greil and Thomas Robbins, 217–40. London: Jai Press, 1994.

PCUSA. "General Assembly Mission Council Mission Work Plan 2017–2018." Mission Agency Board, 2016. https://www.pcusa.org/site_media/media/up-loads/presbyterian_mission_agency/pdf/business_items_2016/february/action_information_items/h.105_2017-2018_mission_work_plan_revised_02.01.16.pdf. Accessed 23 November 2020.

PCUSA. "2013–2016 Mission Work Plan Strategy White Paper." General Assembly Mission Council, 2012, 5. https://www.pcusa.org/site_media/media/uploads/gamc/pdf/strategy_white_paper_2013_2016_strategy_5_15_12.pdf. Accessed 24 October 2016.

PCUSA. "Mission Work Plan for 2013 to 2016." Presbyterian Mission Agency, 2012. https://www.pcusa.org/site_media/media/uploads/gamc/pdf/mwpwhom-doweserve.pdf. Accessed 24 October 2016.

Peters, Ted. "Protestantism and the Sciences." In *The Blackwell Companion to Protestantism,* edited by Alister E. McGrath and Darren C. Marks, 306–21. Oxford: Blackwell, 2004.

Pew Research Center. *Religious Landscape Study.* 2014. http://www.pewforum.org/2015/05/12/americas-changing-religious-landscape/. Accessed 17 October 2016.

Pickering, W. S. F. *Durkheim's Sociology of Religion: Themes and Theories.* Cambridge: James Clarke & Co, 2009.

Polanyi, Karl. *The Great Transformation: The Political and Economic Origins of Our Time.* 1944. Reprinted. Boston, MA: Beacon Press, 1957.

Pollitt, Christopher, Sandra van Thiel, and Vincent Homburg, eds. *New Public Management in Europe: Adaptations and Alternatives.* Basingstoke: Palgrave Macmillan, 2007.

Potter, Jonathan. *Representing Reality: Discourse, Rhetoric and Social Construction.* London: Sage, 1996.

Putman, Robert D. *Bowling Alone: The Collapse and Revival of American Community.* New York: Simon & Shuster, 2000.

Ramey, Steven W. "Religions Are Mutually Exclusive." In *Stereotyping Religion: Critiquing Clichés,* edited by Brad Stoddard and Craig Martin 83–96. London: Bloomsbury Academic, 2017.

Redden, Guy. "Religion, Discourse, and the Economy Question: Fraught Issues in Market Societies." In *Discourse Research and Religion: Disciplinary Use and Interdisciplinary Dialogues,* edited by Jay Johnston and Kocku von Stuckrad, 145–67. Berlin: De Gruyter, 2021.

226 Bibliography

Reisigl, Martin, and Ruth Wodak. 'The Discourse-Historical Approach'. In *Methods of Critical Discourse Analysis*, Second edition, edited by Ruth Wodak and Michael Meyer, 85–121. London: Sage, 2008.

Riesman, David, Nathan Glazer, and Reuel Denney. *The Lonely Crowd: A Study of the Changing American Character.* New Haven, CT: Yale University Press, 1950.

Robertson, Roland. "The Economization of Religion: Reflections on the Promise and Limitations of the Economic Approach." *Social Compass* 39, no. 1 (1992): 147–57.

Roof, Wade Clarke. *Spiritual Marketplace: Baby Boomers and the Remaking of American Religion.* Princeton, NJ: Princeton University Press, 1999.

Roof, Wade Clark. *A Generation of Seekers: The Spiritual Journeys of the Baby Boom Generation.* San Francisco, CA: Harper Collins, 1993.

Sahlins, Marshall. *Stone Age Economics.* London: Tavistock, 1974.

Salamon, Lester M. "The Marketization of Welfare: Changing Nonprofit and For-Profit Roles in the American Welfare State." *Social Service Review* 67, no. 1 (1993): 16–39.

Sanders, Matthew L. "Theorizing Nonprofit Organizations as Contradictory Enterprises: Understanding the Inherent Tensions of Nonprofit Marketization." *Management Communication Quarterly* 26, no. 1 (2012): 179–85.

Sandıkcı, Özlem, and Gillar Rice, eds. *Handbook of Islamic Marketing.* Northampton, MA: Edward Elgar, 2011.

Sawyer, John F. "Beliefs about Language: Introduction." In *Concise Encyclopedia of Language and Religion*, edited by John F. Sawyer and J. M. Y. Simpson, 285–6. Oxford: Elsevier, 2001.

Sawyer, John F. "Language in the Context of Particular Religions: Introduction." In *Concise Encyclopedia of Language and Religion*, edited by John F. Sawyer and J. M. Y. Simpson, 3–4. Oxford: Elsevier, 2001.

Sawyer, John F. "Sacred Texts and Translations: Introduction." In *Concise Encyclopedia of Language and Religion*, edited by John F. Sawyer and J. M. Y. Simpson, 99–100. Oxford: Elsevier, 2001.

Sawyer, John F. "Special Language Uses: Introduction." In *Concise Encyclopedia of Language and Religion*, edited by John F. Sawyer and J. M. Y. Simpson, 237–8. Oxford: Elsevier, 2001.

Schillemans, Thomas. *Mediatization of Public Services: How Organizations Adapt to News Media.* Frankfurt am Main: Peter Lang, 2012.

Schimank, Uwe, and Ute Volkmann. 'Economizing and Marketization in a Functionally Differentiated Capitalist Society – A Theoretical Conceptualization'. In *The Marketization of Society: Economizing the Non-economic*, edited by Uwe Schimank and Ute Volkmann, 37–63. Research Network "Welfare Societies" conference papers. University of Bremen. http://welfare-societies.com/uploads/file/WelfareSocietiesConferencePaper-No1_Schimank_Volkmann.pdf, accessed 9 October 2016.

Schlamelcher, Jens. "The Decline of the Parishes and the Rise of City Churches: The German Evangelical Church in the Age of Neoliberalism." In *Religion in the Neoliberal Age: Political Economy and Modes of Governance*, edited by Tuomas Martikainen and François Gauthier, 53–67. Farnham: Ashgate, 2013.

Sennett, Richard. *The Culture of the New Capitalism.* New Haven, CT: Yale University Press, 2006.

Bibliography 227

Sennett, Richard. *The Fall of Public Man.* New York: W.W. Norton & Company, 1977.

Shirazi, Faegheh. *Brand Islam: The Marketing and Commodification of Piety.* Austin: University of Texas Press, 2016.

Slater, Don. *Consumer Culture and Modernity.* Cambridge: Polity Press, 1993.

Slater, Don, and Fran Tonkiss. *Market Society: Markets and Modern Social Theory.* Cambridge: Polity Press, 2001.

Smith, Adam. *The Wealth of Nations: An Inquiry into the Nature and Causes of the Wealth of Nations.* 1776. Reprinted. Overland Park, KS: Digireads.com Publishing, 2009.

Smith, Christian, with Patricia Snell. *Souls in Transition: The Religious and Spiritual Lives of Emerging Adults.* Oxford: Oxford University Press, 2009.

Smith, Christian. *Soul Searching: The Religious and Spiritual Lives of American Teenagers.* New York: Oxford University Press, 2005.

Smith, Jonathan Z. *Imagining Religion: From Babylon to Jonestown.* Chicago, IL: The University of Chicago Press, 1982.

Smith, Jonathan Z. *Map Is Not Territory: Studies in the History of Religions.* Leiden: Brill, 1978.

Soskice, Martin. "Christian Views on Language." In *Concise Encyclopedia of Language and Religion*, edited by John F. Sawyer and J. M. Y. Simpson, 291–3. Oxford: Elsevier, 2001.

Spickard, James V. "Narrative versus Theory in the Sociology of Religion: Five Stories of Religion's Place in the Late Modern World." In *Therorising Religion: Classical and Contemporary Debates*, edited by James A. Beckford and John Walliss, 169–81. Hampshire: Ashgate, 2006.

Spickard, James V. "What Is Happening to Religion? Six Sociological Narratives." *Nordic Journal of Religion and Society* 19, no. 1 (2006): 13–29.

Stark, Rodney, and Richard Finke. *Acts of Faith: Exploring the Human Side of Religion.* Berkeley: University of California Press, 2000.

Stark, Rodney, and William Sims Bainbridge. *A Theory of Religion.* New York: Peter Lang, 1987.

Stark, Rodney, and William Sims Bainbridge. *The Future of Religion: Secularization, Revival and Cult Formation.* Berkeley: University of California Press, 1985.

Stausberg, Michael, "The Sacred, the Holy, the Numinous – And Religion: On the Emergence and Early History of a Terminological Constellation." *Religion* 47, no. 4 (2017): 557–90.

Stiver, Dan S. *The Philosophy of Religious Language: Sign, Symbol & Story.* Malden, MA: Blackwell Publishing, 1996.

Stoddard, Brad, and Craig Martin, "Introduction." In *Stereotyping Religion: Critiquing Clichés*, edited by Brad Stoddard and Craig Martin, 1–10. London: Bloomsbury Academic, 2017.

Stolz, Jörg, and Jean-Claude Usunier. "Religions as Brands: New Perspectives on the Marketization of Religion and Spirituality." In *Religions as Brands: New Perspectives on the Marketization of Religion and Spirituality*, edited by Jörg Stolz and Jean Claude Usunier, 3–25. Franham: Ashgate, 2014.

Sumiala, Johanna. "Introduction: Mediatization in Post-Secular Society—New Perspectives in the Study of Media, Religion and Politics." *Journal of Religion in Europe* 10, no. 4 (2017): 361–5.

228   *Bibliography*

Sutcliffe, Steven, and Marion Bowman, eds. *Beyond New Age: Exploring Alternative Spirituality*. Edinburgh: Edinburgh University Press, 2000.

Taira, Teemu. "Discourse on 'Religion' in Organizing Social Practices: Theoretical and Practical Considerations." In *Making Religion: Theory and Practice in the Discursive Study of Religion*, edited by Kocku von Stuckrad and Frans Wijsen, 125–46. Leiden: Brill, 2016.

Taira, Teemu. "Making Space for Discursive Study in Religious Studies." *Religion* 43, no. 1 (2013): 27–46.

Taira, Teemu. "Religion as a Discursive Technique: The Politics of Classifying Wicca." *Journal of Contemporary Religion* 25, no. 3 (2010): 379–94.

Taira, Teemu. "The Problem of Capitalism in the Scholarship on Contemporary Spirituality." In *Postmodern Spirituality*, edited by Tore Ahlbäck, 230–44. Åbo: The Donner Institute for Research in Religious and Cultural History, 2008.

Taylor, Charles. "Western Secularity." In *Rethinking Secularism*, edited by Craig Calhoun, Mark Juergensmeyer, and Jonathan VanAntwerpen, 31–53. Oxford: Oxford University Press, 2011.

Taylor, Charles. *A Secular Age*. Cambridge, MA: The Belknap Press of Harvard University Press: 2007.

Taylor, Charles. *Sources of the Self: The Making of the Modern Identity*. Cambridge: Cambridge University Press, 1989.

Taylor, Stephanie. "Locating and Conducting Discourse Analytic Research." In *Discourse as Data: A Guide for Analysis*, edited by Margaret Wetherell, Stephanie Taylor, and Simeon T. Yates, 5–48. London: Sage, 2001.

TEC. "Jake Dell named Episcopal Church Office of Communication Advertising and Marketing Senior Manager." https://episcopalchurch.org/posts/publicaffairs/jake-dell-named-episcopal-church-office-communication-advertising-and-marketing. Accessed 21 March 2020.

TEC. *Marketing Your Parish: Advertising Best Practices for Effective Evangelism*. New York: Office of Communication of the Episcopal Church, 2013. http://episcopaldigitalnetwork.com/wp-content/uploads/2013/03/marketing-your-parish.pdf. Accessed 20 March 2020.

Thanissaro, Phra Nicholas. "Postsecularity in Twenty Questions: A Case Study in Buddhist Teens." In *The Routledge Handbook to Postsecularity*, edited by Justin Beaumont, 360–70. Oxon: Routledge, 2019.

Thomas, Pete. "Ideology and the Discourse of Strategic Management: A Critical Research Framework." *Electronic Journal of Radical Organisation Theory* 4, no. 1 (1998).

Thomas, William Isaac, and Dorothy Swaine Thomas. *The Child in America: Behavior Problems and Programs*. New York: Knopf, 1928.

Thompson, John. *Studies in the Theory of Ideology*. Cambridge: Polity Press, 1984.

Thrift, Nigel. *Knowing Capitalism*. London: Sage, 2005.

Thuesen, Peter J. "The Logic of Mainline Churchliness: Historical Background since the Reformation." In *The Quiet Hand of God: Faith-Based Activism and the Public Role of Mainline Protestantism*, edited by Robert Wuthnow and John H. Evans, 27–53. Berkeley: University of California Press, 2002.

Tickell, Adam, and Jaime Peck. "Making Global Rules: Globalization or Neoliberalism?" In *Remaking the Global Economy: Economic-Geographical Perspectives*, edited by Jaime Peck and Henry Wai-Chung Yeung, 163–81. London: SAGE, 2003.

Bibliography   229

Toft, Monica D., Daniel Philpott, and Timothy S, Shah. *God's Century: Resurgent Religion and Global Politics*. New York: W. W. Norton, 2011.

Tracey, Paul, Nelson Phillips, and Michael Lounsbury. "Taking Religion Seriously in the Study of Organizations." In *Religion and Organization Theory*, Research in the Sociology of Organizations, vol. 41, edited by Paul Tracey, Nelson Phillips, and Michael Lounsbury, 3–21. Bingley: Emerald Publishing Limited, 2014.

Trentmann, Frank. "Knowing Consumers: Consumers in Economics, Law and Civil Society." In *The Making of the Consumer: Knowledge, Power and Identity in the Modern World*, edited by Frank Trentmann, 1–27. Oxford: Berg, 2006.

Turner, Bryan S. *Religion and Modern Society: Citizenship, Secularisation and the State*. Cambridge: Cambridge University Press, 2011.

Turner, Bryan S. "Religion in a Post-Secular Society." In *The New Blackwell Companion to the Sociology of Religion*, edited by Bryan S. Turner, 649–67. Chichester: Blackwell, 2010.

Twitchell, James B. *Shopping for God: How Christianity Went from in Your Heart to in Your Face*. New York: Simon & Schuster, 2007.

UCC. "A Vision: The Transformative United Church of Christ in Ten Years." Strategic Visioning Task Force, 2017. https://www.uccfiles.com/pdf/UCC-Strategic-Vision-Report-March-2017.pdf. Accessed 21 March 2020.

UCC. "Task Force Identifies Future Priorities for UCC Focus." https://www.ucc.org/news_task_force_identifies_future_priorities_for_ucc_focus_03142017. Accessed 21 March 2020.

UMC. "Church Marketing Plan Tool." https://www.resourceumc.org/en/content/church-marketing-plan-tool. Accessed 20 February 2021.

UMC. "Marketing and Public Relations." http://www.umcom.org/about/marketing-and-public-relations. Accessed 21 March 2020.

UMC. "Strategy & Implementation." https://www.resourceumc.org/en/content/church-marketing-plan-tool-phase-2-4. Accessed 25 November 2020.

Usunier, Jean-Claude. "'9591': The Global Commoditization of Religions through GATS, WTO, and Marketing Practices." In *Religions as Brands: New Perspectives on the Marketization of Religion and Spirituality*, edited by Jörg Stolz and Jean-Claude Usunier, 27–43. Farnham: Ashgate, 2014.

van Exel, Job, and Gjalt de Graaf. "Q methodology: A Sneak Preview." 2005. www.jobvanexel.nl.

Vásquez, Manuel A. "Grappling with the Legacy of Modernity: Implications for the Sociology of Religion." In *Religion on the Edge: De-Centering and Re-Centering the Sociology of Religion*, edited by Courtney Bender, Wendy Cadge, Peggy Levitt, and David Smilde, 23–42. Oxford: Oxford University Press, 2012.

Voas, David, and Alasdair Crockett. "Religion in Britain: Neither Believing Nor Belonging." *Sociology* 39, no. 1 (2005): 11–28.

von Stuckrad, Kocku. *The Scientification of Religion: A Historical Study Discursive Change, 1800–2000*. Boston, MA: de Gruyter, 2015.

von Stuckrad, Kocku. "Discursive Study of Religion: Approaches, Definitions, Implications." *Method & Theory in the Study of Religion* 25, no 1 (2013): 5–25.

von Stuckrad, Kocku. "Secular Religion: A Discourse-Historical Approach to Religion in Contemporary Western Europe." *Journal of Contemporary Religion* 28, no. 1 (2013): 1–14.

von Stuckrad, Kocku. *Locations of Knowledge in Medieval and Early Modern Europe: Esoteric Discourse and Western Identities*. Leiden: Brill, 2010.

230 Bibliography

von Stuckrad, Kocku. "Reflections on the Limits of Reflection: An Invitation to the Discursive Study of Religion." *Method & Theory in the Study of Religion* 22, no. 2–3 (2010): 156–69.

von Stuckrad, Kocku. "Discursive Study of Religion: From States of the Mind to Communication and Action." *Method & Theory in the Study of Religion* 15, no. 3 (2003): 255–71.

Walls, Stephanie M. *Individualism in the United States: A Transformation in American Political Thought*. London: Bloomsbury Academic, 2015.

Walsh, Robyn Faith. "Religion Is a Private Matter." In *Stereotyping Religion: Critiquing Clichés*, edited by Brad Stoddard and Craig Martin, 69–82. London: Bloomsbury Academic, 2017.

Warner, Stephen R. "A Paradigm Is Not a Theory: Reply to Lechner." *American Journal of Sociology* 103, no. 1 (1997): 192–8.

Warner, Stephen R. "Work in Progress toward a New Paradigm for the Sociological Study of Religion in the United States." *American Journal of Sociology* 98, no. 5 (1993): 1044–93.

Washington, Marvin, Harry J. Van Buren III, and Karen Patterson. "Pastor Practices in the Era of Megachurches: New Organizational Practices and Forms for a Changing Institutional Environment," in *Religion and Organization Theory*, Research in the Sociology of Organizations, vol. 41, edited by Paul Tracey, Nelson Phillips, Michael Lounsbury, 187–213. Bingley: Emerald Publishing Group, 2014.

Watts, Simon, and Paul Stenner. *Doing Q Methodological Research: Theory, Method and Interpretation*. London: Sage, 2012.

Weaver, Gary R. and Bradley R. Agle. "Religiosity and Ethical Behavior in Organizations: A Symbolic Interactionist Perspective." *Academy of Management Review* 27, no. 1 (2002): 77–97.

Weber, Max. *The Protestant Ethic and the "Spirit" of Capitalism*. Chicago, IL: Fitzroy Dearborn Publishers, 2001 [1905].

Weedon, Chris. *Identity and Culture: Narratives of Difference and Belonging*. New York. Open University Press, 2004.

Wetherell, Margareth. "Debates in Discourse Research." In *Discourse Theory and Practice*, edited by Margaret Wetherell, Stephanie Taylor, and Simeon J. Yates, 380–99. London: Sage, 2001.

Wijsen, Frans. "Indonesian Muslim or World Citizen? Religious Identity in the Dutch Integration Discourse." In *Making Religion: Theory and Practice in the Discursive Study of Religion*, edited by Fans Wijsen and Kocku von Stuckrad, 225–38. Leiden: Brill, 2016.

Wijsen, Frans. "'There Are Radical Muslims and Normal Muslims': An Analysis of the Discourse on Islamic Extremism." *Religion* 43, no. 1 (2013): 70–88.

Wijsen, Frans, and Kocku von Stuckrad, ed. *Making Religion: Theory and Practice in the Discursive Study of Religion*. Leiden: Brill, 2016.

Wilson, Bryan R. *Religion in Secular Society: A Sociological Comment*. Oxford: Oxford University Press, 1966.

Wodak, Ruth. "Introduction: Discourse Studies – Important Concepts and Terms." In *Qualitative Discourse Analysis in the Social Sciences*, edited by Ruth Wodak and Michal Krzyżanowski, 1–29. Hampshire: Palgrave Macmillan, 2008.

Bibliography 231

Wodak, Ruth, "What CDA Is About – A Summary of Its History, Important Concepts and Its Developments." In *Methods of Critical Discourse Analysis*, Second edition, edited by Ruth Wodak and Michael Meyer, 1–13. London: Sage, 2008.

Woodhead, Linda. "Introduction." In *Religion and Change in Modern Britain*, edited by Linda Woodhead and Rebecca Catto, 1–33. London: Routledge, 2012.

Woodhead Linda. "Old, New, and Emerging Paradigms in the Sociological Study of Religion." *Nordic Journal of Religion and Society*, 22, no. 2 (2009): 103–21.

Woodward, Kath. *Understanding Identity*. London: Arnold, 2002.

Wooffitt, Robin. *The Language of Mediums and Psychics: The Social Organization of Everyday Miracles*. Aldershot: Ashgate, 2006.

Wulff, David. "Prototypes of Faith: Findings with the Faith Q-Sort." *Journal for the Scientific Study of Religion* 58, no. 3 (2020): 643–65.

Wuthnow, Robert. *Saving America? Faith-Based Services and the Future of Civil Society*. Princeton, NJ: Princeton University Press, 2006.

Wuthnow, Robert. *After Heaven: Spirituality in America since the 1950s*. Berkeley: University of California Press, 1998.

Wuthnow, Robert, and John H. Evans. "Introduction." In *The Quiet Hand of God: Faith-Based Activism and the Public Role of Mainline Protestantism*, edited by Robert Wuthnow and John H. Evans, 1–25. Berkeley: University of California Press, 2002.

Xiao Dong Sun, Anna. *Confucianism as a World Religion: Contested Histories and Contemporary Realities*. Princeton, NJ and Oxford: Princeton University Press, 2013.

Yang, Fengang. "The Red, Black, and Gray Markets of Religion in China." *The Sociological Quarterly* 47, no. 1 (2006): 93–122.

York, Michael. "New Age Commodification and Appropriation of Spirituality." *Journal of Contemporary Religion* 16, no. 3 (2001): 361–72.

Index

advertising 27, 163, 177, 191–3, 199, 201
Alexander, A. E. 130
Allport, G. 127–8
amalgamation of discourse and practice 200–2
American Baptist Churches USA (ABCUSA) 181, 202
American/European exceptionalism 76, 171
ancien régime 67, 115, 158
Aquinas, T. 24
Arab Charter of Human Rights 44
Arab Spring 78
archaeology (Foucauldian) 9, 11, 13
Arnal, W. 26, 40, 42, 44
Arnett, J. 133
Asad, T. 38, 68–9, 73, 79
ASEAN Declaration of Human Rights 44
Austin, J. 10
Australia 84
Axner, M. 81

Bainbridge, W. S. 169
Baudrillard, J. 163
Bauman, Z. 3, 123–4
Beaumont, J. 96–8
Beck, U. 123–4
Becker, G. 169
Beckford, J. 51, 79–80, 89, 93–5, 97–8, 126
Beck-G. E. 123–4
belief 4, 18, 24, 35, 42–4, 53, 57, 68, 70, 76, 81, 87, 115, 119, 125–6, 134, 139, 142–4, 147
Bell, D. 163
Bellah, R. 59, 117, 121–2, 129
Bentham, J. 67
Berger, P. L. 9, 42, 70, 75, 168–9
Beyer, P. 41, 51, 131

Bible 25, 148, 194
Blyth, M. 162
Boltanski, L. 165
Bourdieu, P. 165
branding/brand 20, 27, 164, 166, 172–3, 188, 191, 193, 198–99
Britain 80
Brown, S. R. 140
Bruce, S. 75, 115
Buddhism 41, 48, 126
bureaucratization/bureaucratic 90–1, 93, 162, 181, 184–5, 187–9, 202
Burr, V. 4, 15, 46
Bush, G. W. 188
Byrne, R. 137

Calhoun, C. 6, 66–7
Canada 84, 138, 144
capitalism/capitalist 27, 56, 122, 128, 161–3, 165–9, 172–3, 175–6, 189
Carrette, J. 121, 127–8, 131, 175–6
Casanova, J. 66, 69, 71, 74, 76–9, 83–5, 92, 100
Catholicism/Catholic Church 23, 48, 73, 115, 135, 147–8
charitable choice option 188
Charlie Hebdo 73
Chidester, D. 38
China/Chinese 48–9, 99, 100, 138, 143–4, 162
Chopra, D. 137
Chouliaraki, L. 2, 15, 20–1, 164
Christianity/Christian 24–5, 27, 41, 44, 57, 66, 68, 74–5, 82, 88, 97–8, 115, 128–9, 135, 143–4, 148–9, 175, 181, 183–5, 192, 198
Church of England 187
civil society 17, 79–80, 162, 165
Cladis, M. 119

234 Index

coherence (discourse) 20
Coleman, S. 80
collocation (discourse) 20, 193, 201
commodification/commoditization 1–2, 168, 175–7, 179–80
common sense 3, 121, 182–3
communication and information technology 1, 162
concourse 140, 142
Confucianism 49
congregation/congregational 76, 168, 188, 192, 201
constitutional democracy 68, 70, 86–8
consumer 125, 157, 164–5, 168, 170–2, 174, 177–8, 180
consumer culture 6, 122, 157, 160, 162–4, 167–8, 178
consumerism 122, 138, 163–4, 167, 178, 180
critical discourse analysis (CDA) 13, 16–18, 52, 54
critical religion 5, 34, 36–44, 56
cult of the individual (*culte de la personne*) 119
cultural dominant 27–8, 113
cultural turn 8

14th Dalai Lama 71
Danish Muhammad cartoon controversy 73
Daoism 49
Davie, Grace 54
de Saussure, F. 9
De Vriese, H. 98
Decalogue 24
Denmark 73
denomination/denominational 76, 181, 188–9, 192, 202
Derrida, J. 9
Descartes, R. 116
description (level of analysis) 19–21, 26, 27
desecularization 54
Dillon, M. 84, 88, 106
Disciples of Christ (DOC) 181, 193
discourse, definition of 13–16, 45–6; enacting of 2, 59; homogenization of 194, 197–8; materialization of 22, 56, 92, 198–201, 203; naturalization of 2, 6, 22, 27, 56, 122, 130, 149, 151, 163, 165–6, 171, 173, 182, 190, 197, 199; official 183, 185–7, 189, 199–200, 203; operationalization

of 2, 27, 47, 59, 72–3, 92, 198–201; standardization of 194, 197–8; strategic 186–7, 189–90, 192, 194–7, 200; technologization of 189–91, 194, 197–8, 200–2
discourse analysis, critical 13, 16–18, 52, 54; Foucauldian 5, 14, 44–7; historical 27, 45–8; three-dimensional 13, 18, 54
discourse-driven 2, 28, 88, 90, 121, 124, 158, 165–6, 183, 202
discursive formation 7, 11, 14, 22–3, 27, 39, 53–5, 65, 82–4, 91–2, 94, 97, 105–6, 114, 120, 122, 131, 151, 158, 160, 169, 173, 177, 180, 182
discursive study of religion (DSR) 5, 34, 44–50
discursive turn 8
Douglas, M. 159
Druze 138
Durkheim, É. 42, 74, 118–20, 159, 179

Eastern Bloc 78, 162
economics 6, 39, 157; classical 158–9; discipline of 159; neoclassical 159
economy 2, 23, 45, 79, 160–5, 168–9, 172–6, 179, 202
Eder, K. 96–8
education 23, 27, 39, 41–2, 70, 76, 120, 124, 150–1, 166, 184, 197–8, 201
Eliade, M. 37
Engler, M. 37
Enlightenment 6, 36, 66–7, 73, 76, 103, 114, 116
Episcopal Church (TEC) 181, 191–3, 197, 199
European Convention of Human Rights 44
European Wars of Religion 66, 73
Evangelical Lutheran Church in America (ELCA) 181, 193, 199
evangelical/evangelicals 75, 129, 137, 188
Exel, van J. 140

factor analysis 141, 144
Fairclough, N. 2, 8, 13, 15–21, 23, 27, 54, 164–5, 182, 184, 189, 190–1
Faith Q-Sort (FQS) 138–9, 142–5, 148–9, 151
faith 24, 42–4, 87, 99–100, 115, 119, 128–9, 143–5, 147–9, 151, 176–9, 188, 200–1

Finke, R. 169–70
Finland 57, 138, 142, 146
First Amendment (United States Constitution) 76
first-level reflection 34–9, 44, 47, 49, 50–3, 56, 58, 60, 65, 113, 150, 157, 167, 202
Fitzgerald, T. 38–40, 68
forced distribution 141
forms of life 10
Foucault, M. 9, 11, 13–14, 16, 22–3, 189
France 72, 170
freedom of speech 73
Fuller, R. C. 129
functional differentiation 75, 78, 80, 83, 185

Garfinkel, H. 9
Gauthier, F. 130, 169, 178–9
Gawain, Shakti 137
genealogy/genealogical 9, 11, 13, 38, 46–7, 65, 98
Genesis 25
genre (discourse) 4, 21–3, 26, 58, 79, 191–4, 197
Gergen, K. 10, 121
Ghana 138, 147
Giddens, A. 122–3
globalization 54, 178
glossolalia 25
Goldstein, W. S. 87
Graaf, de, G. 140
grammar 20–1, 47, 191
Gramsci, A. 17
Granholm, K. 57
Great Depression 161, 188
Great Society 188

Habermas, J. 79, 84–92, 94, 103, 105
Hall, S. 14–15, 46
Hammond, P. E. 129
Hanson, S. 77
Harvey, D. 162
Haynes, J. 81
Heather, N. 57
Heelas, P. 127–8, 136, 175
hegemony 17, 54, 163, 182, 190
Hennig, A. 81
Hermann, A. 47, 51
Hindu mythology 25
Hjelm, T. 14, 46, 49–50, 52, 57
Hobbes, T. 67, 116

homo oeconomicus 56, 159, 170
Horii, M. 56
Huxley, A. 128
Hybels, B. 137
hyper-real 163

Iannaccone, L. 169
identity 45, 68, 121–4, 126, 135, 143, 163–5
ideological discursive formation (IDF) 182–7, 191, 194, 197–200, 202
ideology/ideological 16–18, 27, 38, 42, 48–9, 52, 67, 69–71, 79, 84–6, 97, 100, 113, 118, 144, 160–4, 166, 171, 175, 178, 182, 184–5
India 138, 143–4
individual 2, 41–4, 56, 68, 72, 120–1, 183; concept of 4, 113–16, 121–2, 127, 132–3, 150, 161, 176; and rationality 116, 158, 169–70; and society 68, 114–16, 125, 131, 158–9, 164–5; vocabulary of 6, 21, 122, 129, 150
individualism 5–6, 28, 44, 113–19, 121, 124–5, 132–4, 137, 150; discursive components of 5–6, 121–2, 125, 127, 129, 131, 134, 137, 167; economic 117–18, 120–1; expressive 117, 120–1; moral 119; political 117, 120; social 117–18, 120–1, 126, 150; of uniqueness 120
individualization 2, 28, 54, 114–15, 119, 122, 124–6, 134
individuation 133
Indonesia 57
interdiscursivity 21, 26, 96
International Monetary Fund (IMF) 162
interpretation (level of analysis) 18, 21–7
intertextuality 21, 26, 96
invisible hand of the market 159
Isherwood, B. 159
Islam 24, 41, 48, 57, 72–3, 78, 88
Islamic Revolution in Iran 78
Islamic State in Iraq and Syria (ISIS) 78
Islamic veil 72–3
Israel 138

James, W. 34, 127–8
Japan 48, 138
Joas, H. 86
Johnson, L. B. 188
Judaism 24–5, 88

236 Index

King, R. 121, 127–8, 131, 175–6
Köhrsen, J. 80
Kornberger, M. 164

Laclau, E. 13
language game 10
Larson, S. 59
Lasch, C. 122
Lash, S. 122
late-modern 1, 3, 113, 123–4, 127, 135, 150, 163–4
Latin America 135, 162
Lau, K. 174
law/legislation 18, 38–9, 44, 68. 70, 72–3, 79, 97, 103, 120, 124, 129, 150–1
Lawson, T. 37
Leary, T. 128
Leezenberg, M. 88
Lévi-Strauss, C. 159
lexis 19–21, 47, 97, 191
LGBTQ 97
liberalism/liberal thought 6, 67–8, 73, 79, 114–17, 158–61, 167–70, 172–3, 175
Lincoln, B. 25–6, 39, 42
linguistic turn 8
Liu, L. 48
Locke, J. 67–8, 116–17
Lövheim, M. 81, 91, 93
Luckmann, T. 9, 42, 75, 125
Luhmann, N. 51
Lury, C. 164
Lutheran 70, 115, 146–7, 181
Lynch, G. 118
Lyotard, J-F. 163

Maccoby, E. 133
mainline Protestant churches (United States) 6, 158, 181, 185, 187–9, 191, 194–6
management/managerial 6, 21, 137, 158, 165–6, 175, 188–90, 196–9, 201–2
Market Idea 157, 161, 163, 173, 178, 180
marketing 20, 27, 163, 166, 169, 172, 188, 191–3, 195, 198–201
marketization 27–8, 166–7, 178; discursive components of 57, 166, 180, 185, 187, 189, 194–5, 202–3
Martikainen, T. 178
Martin C. 36, 56, 132
Martin, D. 75

Marx, K. 159
Maslow, A. 128
Masuzawa, T. 38
Matheson, D. 20–2
Mauss, M. 159
Mautner, G. 165–6
May, T. 3
McCauley, R. 37
McCloud, S. 43
McCutcheon, R. 26, 37–8, 40, 42, 130
McGuire, M. B. 127
McKinnon, A. 171, 173
McLeod, H. 77
Mead, G. H. 9
mega-church 181, 187–8
Mendieta, E. 87
meta-narrative 8, 11
metaphor 9–10, 15, 20, 25–6, 164, 167, 171–3, 191, 203
Meyer, J. 137
Milbank, J. 99
modality 20, 193, 195–7, 201
modernity 1, 39, 66, 74, 76–7, 85, 103, 162
modernization 74–8
Moses 24
Mouffe, C. 13
Muhammad 24, 73
Murphy, T. 11, 27
muslim 57, 72, 85, 138

narrative 21, 53, 75, 89, 123–4
nation-state 39, 67, 90
neoliberalism/neoliberal 6, 27, 118, 157, 160–7, 171, 173, 178–9, 188
New Deal 188
Newman, B. M. 133
Newman, P. R. 133
New Paradigm 168, 170–3, 178–9
New Public Management 162, 166, 194–5
New Zealand 84
nominalization 20, 186
non-demoninational 181, 188
non-profit organizations 27, 164, 166, 188–9, 202
non-religion/religious 1, 24, 26, 41, 81, 87, 92, 128, 135, 144–5, 149
Nordic countries 80
North America/North American 68, 125–6, 142, 170, 187
numinous 43
Nynäs, P. 138

Index 237

order of discourse 23, 27, 65, 82–3, 91, 106, 165, 182–4, 190–1, 194, 197
Osteen, J. 137
Otto, R. 43, 103

Paden, W. 119
Passas, N. 168
Pentecostalism 75, 135
personal autonomy 2, 28, 120, 126, 129, 133, 136, 145
personal choice 2, 28, 43, 56, 126, 136, 142
Personal Responsibility and Work Opportunity Reconciliation Act 88
Peru 38, 144, 148
Peters, T. 24
pluralism 38, 75, 79, 87, 92, 104, 168–9
Poland 138, 143
Polanyi, K. 160
politics/political 2–3, 5–6, 17–18, 21, 23, 36, 39, 41–2, 48, 57, 66–8, 70–3, 76, 78–82, 84–8, 91–6, 99, 113, 116–21, 123, 129, 133, 150–1, 158, 160, 162–6, 171, 182
Pope Francis 71
populist politics 72
Portrait Values Questionnaire 138
post-Marxism 13, 52
post-modern critique 8, 11
post-secular 3, 5, 35, 54, 65–6, 73, 79, 83–106; emerging discursive formation of 83–4; empirical basis of 89–1; normative dimension of 65, 86–8
post-secularism 89, 93, 97, 100, 102–3
post-secularity 89, 93, 96–7, 100, 102
post-secularization 89, 100–1
post-structuralism 11
post-World War II era 27, 84, 127, 160–1, 163, 172
Potter, J. 59
power relations 13–14, 16–17, 25, 36, 45, 49, 50, 52, 79, 162, 183, 189
Prajapati 25
Presbyterian Church USA (PCUSA) 181, 194–5
product 157, 168, 171–2, 180, 193
profane 66, 118–19
professionalization 181
Protestant/Protestantism 6, 44, 158, 167
Protestant Reformation 66, 70, 114–15
psychology 121, 127–8, 139, 142; popular 150, 176

public religion 5, 35, 65, 73, 78–85, 89, 92–3
public sphere/s 70, 78–81, 83, 86, 88, 90, 94, 97
Putnam, R. 122

Q methodology 139–41, 148, 151, 156
Q-set 140–2
Qur'an 24

Rational Choice Theory of Religion (RCTR) 168, 170–1, 173, 178–9
rationalization 75, 103, 185
rational/rationality 79, 86, 116, 143, 158, 161, 164, 169–70, 201
Reagan, R. 161
recontextualization 20, 191–4, 197
reflexive project of the self 123
Reformers 24, 115
religion, and market 167–80; category/concept of 4–5, 13, 16, 34–45, 48, 50–2, 56–8, 65–6, 88–9, 95, 97, 102–4, 113, 129, 131–2, 136, 150–1, 177; commodification of 168, 175–7, 179; deprivatization of 3, 54, 79–80, 85, 89, 92; individual/individualized 1, 6, 56, 59, 125, 136–7, 144, 151; individualization of 2, 126, 135, 142; as market 168, 174–6, 179; marketization of 1–2, 168, 178–80; privatization of 75, 78–80, 83, 176; public presence/visibility of 1–2, 72, 80, 86, 92, 117; study of 1, 3–7, 13. 15, 24, 34–40, 42, 44–7, 50, 52–5, 57–8, 65–6, 96, 114, 131, 157, 167–8, 170–1, 173, 176, 178–9, 203; sui generis 37–8, 42, 102–4, 136
Religious Right 78
religious: change 1–3, 77, 82–3, 91, 95, 135, 157, 169, 178; community 17, 20–1, 26–7, 39, 68, 71, 78–9, 84, 86–8, 90–1, 93, 104, 120, 129, 134–5, 147, 168–9, 172, 174, 179; decline 1, 75–6, 78, 83, 105, 135, 170, 185, 188–9, 202; language 24–6, 50, 58, 128, 134–5; pluralism 92, 169; privatization 75, 78–80, 83, 176; subjectivization 28, 45, 54, 169
Ricardo, D. 67
Riesman, D. 122
Roof, W. C. 125, 172
Roosevelt, F. D. 188
Ross, K. 88

238 *Index*

Rousseau, J-J. 67, 116
Rushdie affair 73
Russia 73, 138, 144

sacred 24–5, 43, 66, 104, 118–21
Sahlins, M. 159
Salamon, L. M. 188
Sawyer, J. P. 24
Schleiermacher, F. 43
scholarly theorizing 3–4, 28, 34–5,
  53, 55–6, 60, 65, 74–7, 92, 124–5,
  131–2, 135, 167–8, 180, 203
second-level reflection 35, 53–4, 56–8, 60,
  65, 83, 84, 114, 150, 157, 180, 203
secular (concept) 3–6, 34–6, 38, 52–4,
  58, 65–81, 84–95, 97, 100–3, 105–6,
  113, 119, 130, 145
secularist stadial consciousness 69, 74,
  76–7, 85, 100
secularization 1, 35, 38, 53, 55, 65;
  discursive formation of 54, 74, 82–3
seeker-sensitive 129, 181, 188
semiotic/semiosis 11
Sennett, R. 122
September 11 attacks 78, 83
Sheilaism 59
signifier 10
signified 10
sign value 163–4
Singapore 99
Slater, D. 6, 116, 159, 160–1, 163–4,
  167, 202
Smith, A. 67, 117, 158, 167–9
Smith, C. 135
Smith, J. Z. 36–7
Smith, W. C. 43
social action 10, 12, 15, 51, 116
social construction 9, 12
social constructionism 9, 10–12, 50–1
Social Darwinism 117
social fact 42, 51
social formation 184–5
Social Gospel 187–8
socialization 25, 32; broad 133;
  narrow 133; primary 132; religious
  134–5, 138, 146; secondary 132; self-
  socialization 133–4
social practice 13, 15, 19, 27
sociolinguistics 9
South-East Asia 161
Soviet Union 78, 162
speech-act theory 10
Spencer, H. 117

Spickard, J. 53–4
"spiritual, but not religious" 130–2,
  136, 142, 150–1
spirituality: concept of 6, 56, 126–9,
  137, 142–5, 150, 172, 176–7;
  discourse of 129–32, 135–7, 142,
  150–1, 176
Stark, R. 169–70
state 38–9, 41–4, 48–9, 57, 67–70, 72,
  76, 78–80, 82, 86–8, 90, 93, 99, 100,
  117, 162, 165, 168, 170, 179, 181,
  185, 188; nation-state 39, 67, 90
Stausberg, M. 119
Stiver, D- 10, 24
Stoddard, B. 36
Stolz, J. 174
strategic awareness 197, 200–1
style (discourse) 21–3, 26, 103, 193,
  195–6
subject position 14, 16, 45, 123, 130,
  137, 140–2, 145, 148–9, 151, 186,
  193, 197
Sweden 138, 143
Switzerland 72–3
Syrian Civil War 78
systems theory 51

Taber, S. 133
Taira, T. 57
Tanzania 57
Taylor, C. 66, 69–70, 92
Thatcher, M. 161–2
theory of religious economy 83, 169
therapy 121–2, 129, 150, 176
third-level analysis 34–5, 53, 57–60, 65,
  91, 96, 104, 114, 137, 148, 158, 180,
  202–3
Thomas theorem 42
Thrift, N. 165
Thuesen, P. J. 187
Tocqueville de, A. 116
Toft, M. 81
Tolle, E. 137
Tonkiss, F. 160, 167, 202
Tracey, P. 184
transitivity (discourse) 20
Treaty of Westphalia 67
Trentmann, F. 164, 177
Turkey 138
Turner, B. S. 3, 25, 88, 115

United Church of Christ (UCC) 181,
  196–7, 199

Index 239

United Kingdom 161
United Methodist Church (UMC) 181, 191, 193
United Nations 38, 41
United States 6, 76–8, 85, 116–17, 122, 125, 129, 135, 138, 143–4, 158, 161–2, 168, 170–2, 181, 187–8
United States Constitution 68, 76, 116–17
United States Declaration of Independence 68, 116
UN Special Rapporteur on the Freedom of Religion and Belief 43, 57
Usunier, J-C. 173–4, 177

Van der Leeuw, G. 43
van Dijk, T. 18
Vansheewijk, G. 98
Vedas 24
Vermeer, P. 133
vocabulary 6, 9, 56, 74, 82, 105, 121–2, 125–6, 128, 136, 149–51, 164, 167, 173, 177, 182, 193, 195–6, 201
von Stuckrad, K. 44–7

Wacquant, L. 165
Walls, S. 114, 116–18, 120, 123

Walsh, R. F. 42
Ward, G. 99
Warner, R. S. 170–1
Warren, R. 137
Weber, M. 74, 181
Weedon, C. 123
Western Europe/Western European 71–3, 76–7, 83, 162, 170–1
White House Office of Community and Faith-based Organizations 189
Wijsen, F. 57
Wilson, B. 75
Wittgenstein, L. 9–10, 24
Woodhead, L. 127–8, 136, 178
Wooffitt, R. 57
World Bank 162
World Religions-paradigm 42
World's Parliament of Religions 38
World War II 27, 84, 127, 160–1, 163, 172
Wuthnow, R. 125

Xiaoping, D. 162

Young Adults and Religion in a Global Perspective (YARG) 6, 114–15, 137–9, 142–5, 148–9, 151

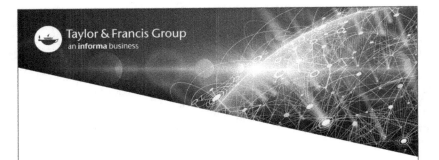

Printed in the USA
CPSIA information can be obtained
at www.ICGtesting.com
LVHW021735041124
795688LV00040B/1244